MOUNT ALLISON UNIVERSITY: A HISTORY, TO 1963
VOLUME I: 1843–1914

JOHN G. REID

Mount Allison University: A History, to 1963

VOLUME I: 1843–1914

Published for Mount Allison University by
University of Toronto Press
Toronto Buffalo London

Toronto Buffalo London
Printed in Canada
Reprinted in 2018
ISBN 0-8020-3396-2
ISBN 978-1-4875-8516-7 (paper)

Canadian Cataloguing in Publication Data

Reid, John G. (John Graham), 1948–
Mount Allison University: a history, to 1963

ISBN 0-8020-3396-2 (v. 1). – 0-8020-3397-0 (v. 2).
1. Mount Allison University – History. I. Title.

LE3.M92R54 1984 378.715'23 C83-098822-X

All photographs are from the collections of
the Mount Allison Archives.

FRONTISPIECE: The Wesleyan Academy, opened 1843. From an oil painting in Mount Allison University Archives, attributed to Rev. Charles Churchill

Contents

PREFACE vii

1 Introduction: A 'Liberal Offer' 3

PART ONE

2 The Wesleyan Academy: 1843–1855 29
3 Sackville Institutions: 1855–1869 67
4 Questions of Identity: 1869–1881 108

PART TWO

5 Restoring Foundations: 1881–1891 155
6 An Age of Improvement: 1891–1904 200
7 Strains of the Twentieth Century: 1904–1914 244

ABBREVIATIONS 290
NOTES 291
TABLES 1–17 353
INDEX TO VOLUME I 377

Preface

This study is concerned with the development of the three Mount Allison institutions – the original academy, the ladies' college, and the university – from their nineteenth-century origins up until 1963. By that time the academy and the ladies' college had ceased to exist as such, although certain of their teaching programmes had been incorporated into the curricula of the university. The adaptations that took place during that eventful period of well over a century, the internal dynamics of institutional change, comprise one important part of this history. Yet a university history cannot be focused narrowly if it is to be successful in explaining institutional developments rather than simply chronicling them. No institution exists in isolation from the society that gives it birth and nurtures it. No university exists in isolation from the wider world of human knowledge and thought. A university history must be, among other things, an endeavour in social and intellectual history.

The Mount Allison Wesleyan Academy opened in 1843 in the small town of Sackville, located in the province of New Brunswick but within a few miles of the Nova Scotian border and conveniently close also to the crossings to Prince Edward Island. Founded by Charles Frederick Allison, a Nova Scotian whose merchant career had prospered in New Brunswick, Mount Allison functioned from the start as a New Brunswick institution that accepted a responsibility to serve all three Maritime provinces. The Maritimes in 1843 had a combined population that perhaps approached half a million. It was not an outstandingly large figure, especially when compared to the million or more of the newly created neighbouring province of Canada, but was rapidly growing. Still overwhelmingly rural, the populations of the Maritime provinces were already profoundly affected by the commercial shipping ventures that were increasingly being stimulated by the export of commodities ranging from timber and coal to grains, meat, and fish. In New Brunswick, the timber trade occupied a dominant position, and its influence was felt directly even in Sackville, which was situated in the predominantly agricultural county of Westmorland: not only in that surplus local produce was supplied by merchants such as Charles Allison to lumbermen elsewhere in the province, but also in the establishment by the 1840s of a thriving wooden shipbuilding industry. The capital which Allison used for his educational plans was derived from his participation in the regional economy of the time, and his insistence that the Wesleyan Academy must serve all three Maritime provinces ensured that the fortunes of Mount Allison would continue to be joined inseparably with those of the region as a whole.

The fortunes of Mount Allison were also bound to be influenced by the cross-currents of nineteenth- and twentieth-century thought, especially in that the intellectual assumptions that prevailed at a Methodist institution in 1843 would soon come under severe pressure as the discoveries of science and social science increasingly cast doubt on traditional forms of religious belief. The denominational character of Mount Allison was not unusual in the Maritime provinces in 1843, any more than elsewhere in British North America or in North America as a whole. Nor did it present any evident intellectual difficulties at that time, for truth known by divine revelation and truth known by empirical discovery were held to be incapable of conflicting. Yet by the end of the century Mount Allison, along with other denominational institutions, was struggling to find ways of maintaining its dual commitment to Christianity and to intellectual rigour in teaching and scholarship. Increasingly too, during the early decades of the twentieth century, Mount Allison's particular location and its commitment to the service of the Maritime provinces led to a further dilemma. The Maritime region, having experienced economic fluctuations following the decline of its seaborne trades in the late nineteenth century, emerged after the First World War as an area of persistent economic depression and social dislocation. Mount Allison, never a rich institution, was faced once again with potentially conflicting demands: to maintain intellectual quality, through such means as attracting and retaining faculty members of high competence, while at the same time obeying the Christian obligation (profoundly influenced by the social gospel movement within the Methodist denomination and its successor, the United Church of Canada) to make education widely available at low cost. If there is a central dynamic of Mount Allison's history, and thus an overall context within which the experiences of students, faculty, and other participants must be interpreted, it is one of struggle to reconcile responsibilities – intellectual, moral, social – which could not easily be reconciled.

The history of Mount Allison, however, is not solely a history of social and intellectual forces. It is also a history of individual people: their experiences of the institution and their influence on it. Many who have experienced Mount Allison, at various times and in various capacities, are cited in this study. Many are portrayed who have left their imprint upon the institution. Yet because this is a history and not a chronicle, there has been no attempt to compile exhaustive lists of names. The names of each year's graduates, faculty members, and regents are on record in official Mount Allison publications; they are not necessarily repeated here. Nor, it should be said, can a university history take the form of a mere tribute to progress, or to the great men and women of years gone by. The university and all its members may legitimately take pride in past achievements, and achievements there have been at Mount Allison. The essential task of the historian, however, is not to glorify the past but to interpret it, and such has been the guiding principle of this study.

This point would seem to be a suitable one from which to embark on the pleasant duty of offering acknowledgments, for it has been my good fortune at Mount Allison that this commissioned history has been understood from the beginning to be a scholarly endeavour and not one aimed at the production of an 'authorized' or 'official' account. This was made clear when the project was first suggested to me in 1978 by Alexander Fancy, then dean of arts and science, and during the intervening years I have received and appreciated encouragement in the same vein from successive presidents of the university, W.S.H. Crawford and Guy R. MacLean. Other administrative officers also gave valuable assistance as research proceeded, notably the registrar, Donald Cameron, successive alumni directors Vaughan Tower and Peter MacRae, and the comptroller and assistant comptroller, Ian Hess and Lorne Booth. My colleagues in the history department and at the centre for Canadian studies were also supportive: I thank especially Bill Godfrey, who read the entire manuscript and contributed many valuable suggestions, Douglas Lochhead, and John Schultz. Among scholars elsewhere who gave their assistance, I am especially grateful to Ernie Forbes and Bill Hamilton, both of whom read the manuscript and commented on it to my great benefit, as well as to Robin S. Harris and Peter Waite. Mount Allison faculty members in other disciplines were also generous with their time and expertise, including Robin Armstrong, Bill Cunningham, Gwen Davies, Willie Eliot, Peter Ennals, David Fensom, Tom Goff, Thaddeus Holownia, Larry McCann, Gerald Rimmington, Eric Ross, and Nancy Vogan. The entire staff of the Ralph Pickard Bell Library deserves my thanks, and none more so than the staff of the university archives: Lynne Owen, her successor Cheryl Ennals, and assistant archivist

Donna Beal were congenial as well as efficient co-workers in the task of ensuring that all available source materials were consulted for this study. So too were special collections librarians Ruth Cunningham and Margaret Fancy, and university librarians Eleanor Magee and Ted Phillips.

Outside of the confines of the university, the archival repository at which I necessarily spent the most time was that of the Maritime Conference of the United Church, in Halifax, where my helpful and genial hosts were E. Arthur Betts and Neil MacLeod. Glenn Lucas and the staff members of the central United Church Archives in Toronto contributed in a like manner, and I extend my warm thanks also to the staffs of the Provincial Archives of New Brunswick, the Public Archives of Nova Scotia, the Public Archives of Canada, the New Brunswick Museum, and the university archives of Acadia University, Dalhousie University, and the University of New Brunswick. Among those organizations which generously allowed me access to archival resources at their private disposal were the Canadian Association of University Teachers, the Carnegie Corporation of New York, the Mount Allison Faculty Association, the Overseas Division of the Methodist Church (Methodist Missionary Society), and the Town of Sackville.

One of the great pleasures of researching the history of Mount Allison was the opportunity to meet many alumni, and others who were or had been associated with the university, who were willing to contribute to the project through personal interviews, correspondence, or by donating documentary material. Because these contributors are too numerous to be named here, they are acknowledged in a list appended to this study: in very many cases, their assistance was accompanied by personal kindnesses and warm hospitality. As well as the insights gained from these generous helpers, I also benefited from the work of several former Mount Allison administrators and faculty members who had previously begun research on the history of the university and whose notes or draft manuscripts were available to me in the university archives: R.C. Archibald, F.W.W. DesBarres, W.T. Ross Flemington, D.G.G. Kerr, G.J. Trueman, and W.M. Tweedie. More recent researchers who generously shared with me the products of their work on specific aspects of Mount Allison's history were Mary Godfrey Evans and W. Alex Morrison. Also, I benefited from frequent contacts with two retired faculty members who were always willing to share their recollections and answer my questions: Donald W. MacLauchlan and the late Allison G. Patterson.

It remains only to make the conventional but necessary affirmation that none of those mentioned in these acknowledgments is in any way responsible for whatever faults this study contains, and then to add some further special words of thanks. Without Jean Jones, who contributed not only her excellent secretarial skills but also her long experience at Mount Allison, the entire project inevitably would have been more arduous and less enjoyable. Darlene Warren was a hard-working, cheerful, and efficient student assistant over a two-year period. Other student assistants who deserve special mention are Pamela Swainson, who began the university archives' programme of interviews in 1976, and Erik Sande.

The research for the history of Mount Allison project was funded entirely by a grant from the Marjorie Young Bell Endowment Fund, while publication was assisted by grants from that fund, from the Ross Flemington Memorial Fund, and from the governments of New Brunswick and Canada through the New Brunswick Bicentennial Commission. I gratefully acknowledge this generous support. I thank also all those who have assisted in various other ways in the publication process, including the journal *Acadiensis*, which published two previous articles of mine on the history of Mount Allison, on which I have drawn in some portions of this study; the University of Toronto Press, and especially Judy Williams as editor; and Mark and Lorna Davis, for their work on the index.

Finally, my debt to Jacquelyn Hicks is too great to be fully stated here. Had it not been for her support, and at times her remarkable forbearance, this study could not have been completed.

Charles Frederick Allison

Humphrey Pickard

Enoch Wood

Mary Electa Adams

John and Martha Allison

Sackville in 1862. Mount Allison buildings at back. The large building on the left is the ladies' academy, flanked by the small gymnasium further left and Lingley Hall to the right. Partly visible to the right of Lingley Hall is the president's cottage. Further right is the newly completed college building, and across the road the first academy.

The first graduating class, 1863: Josiah Wood (left) and Howard Sprague

The second academy building, opened 1867

The campus in 1872, from a drawing by John Warren Gray.

Grace Annie Lockhart

Harriet Starr Stewart

The college faculty, 1878–9. Left to right: John Burwash, A.D. Smith, J.R. Inch (president), Charles Stewart, R.C. Weldon

Centennial Hall (left), and the old college building, probably late 1880s

The third academy, opened 1883, with the commercial college building on the left, opened 1875

The William Black Chapel, in Centennial Hall, late nineteenth century

The campus, 1880s

Ladies' college, 1887

David Allison

J.R. Inch

W.M. Tweedie

Ladies' college art class, 1886–7

The view from the ladies' college, about 1885
The view from the ladies' college, about 1885

Academy students and bicycle, 1888–9. Principal T.T. Davis stands fifth from left in third row.

First university football team, 1890

Conservatory of music, opened 1890

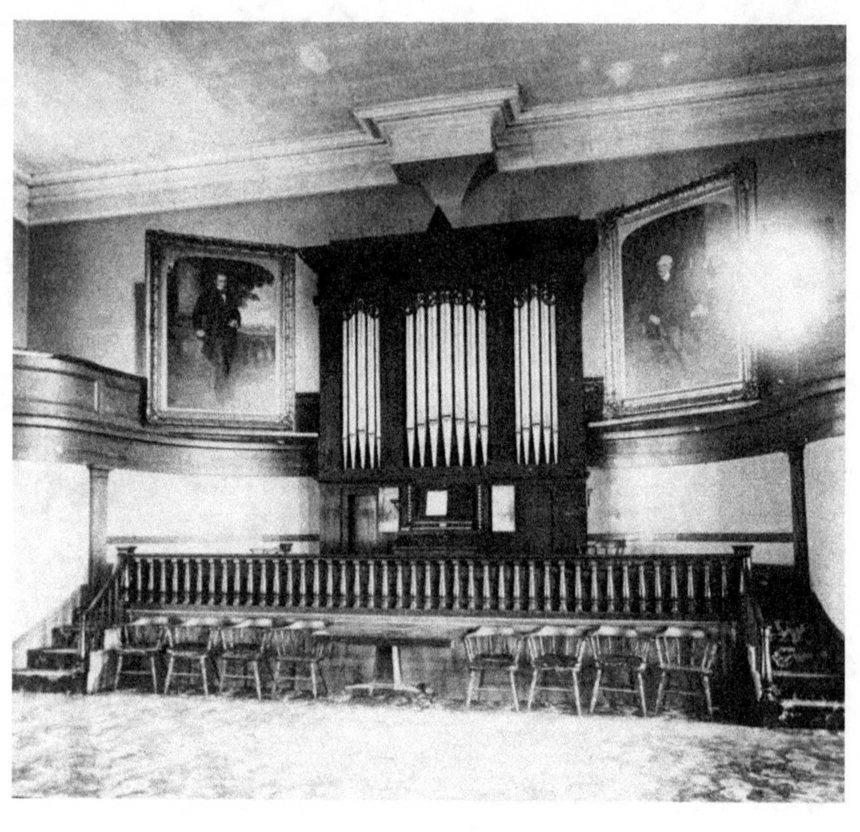

Platform of Lingley Hall, about 1891

Ladies' college reception room, about 1891

Latin class, 1891. 'Worst class ever known'

Ladies' college tennis, 1892–3

Midnight supper at the ladies' college, 1894

The Owens gallery, opened 1895

Interior of the Owens gallery, 1890s

Fine arts class in the Owens gallery, 1890s

B.C. Borden

Mary Mellish Archibald

The campus, from the spire of Sackville United Church, 1898. The former residence of Charles Frederick Allison is in the left foreground.

Argosy editors, 1897–8. The lone woman is Annie Sprague, later vice-principal of the ladies' college.

University men's residence, opened 1900

Student's room in the ladies' college, early twentieth century

Skating on the ladies' college pond, early twentieth century

Sketching class, under the instruction of John Hammond, early twentieth century

Reading room, university residence, probably early twentieth century

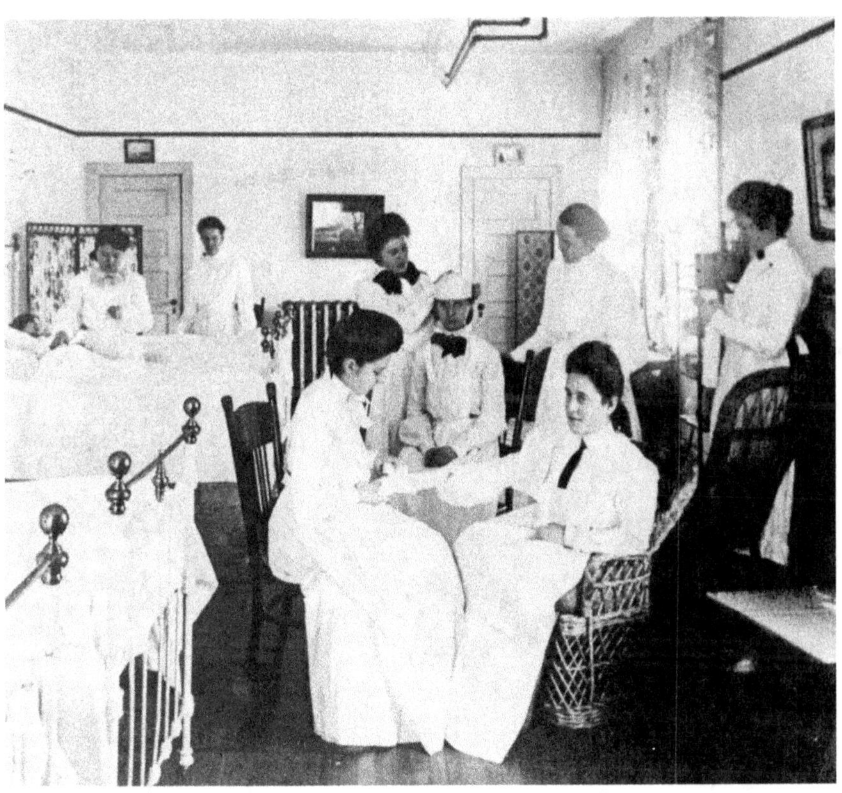

Ladies' college hospital, early twentieth century

Ladies' college fiftieth anniversary: former students of the first year return for the celebration.

The university faculty, 1902–3. Front row: Charles Stewart, David Allison (president), B.C. Borden, A.D. Smith, C.H. Paisley. Back row: J.M. Palmer, W.M. Tweedie, S.W. Hunton, H.A. Powell, W.W. Andrews

Football players of the class of 1903: H.E. Bigelow (seated) and Frank Parker Day

Women's hockey team, 1903

The first domestic science class, 1903–4

Ladies college 'lawn drill,' 1904

The campus, 9 November 1907. Mount Allison defeats Acadia at rugby 8–0. Major buildings visible in the background are (left to right): men's residence, Centennial Hall, Owens museum, and the ladies' college buildings (including the conservatory of music).

The conservatory orchestra, 1905. The instructor (top right) is R.C. Archibald.

The university dining hall, about 1907

The successful university debating team of 1908. Left to right: John S. Ashbury, Ivan Rand, Arthur Reynolds

Fawcett Hall, opened 1910

Ladies' college buildings, including Hart Hall (at right), opened 1910

Boating on the ladies' college pond: Lida Trueman Ford, 1910.

Football special, en route for Wolfville, 1911

The university faculty, 1913–14. Front row: H.E. Bigelow, J.M. Palmer, A.D. Smith, B.C. Borden (president), Howard Sprague, G.M. Campbell, C.A.S. Dwight. Back row: S.W. Hunton, W.M. Tweedie, J.W. Crowell, Frank Wheelock, F.W.W. DesBarres, W.G. Watson, H.W. McKiel

MOUNT ALLISON UNIVERSITY: A HISTORY, TO 1963
VOLUME I: 1843–1914

1

Introduction: A 'Liberal Offer'

On 30 May 1839, the Wesleyan Methodist ministers of the New Brunswick District held their annual meeting in Saint John. There was nothing remarkable in that, for several such meetings had been held there since the New Brunswick and Nova Scotia Districts had been separated in 1826, each remaining under the supervision of the Wesleyan Methodist Conference of Great Britain. Nor was there anything unusual in most of the business discussed at the 1839 meeting. Candidates for the ministry were approved, reports were received on the progress of the faith, and other routine matters were disposed of. When the meeting turned to 'measures to be adopted for the promotion of God's work,' however, a new element entered into the discussions. Charles Frederick Allison, a Methodist businessman from Sackville, a small rural town at the head of the Bay of Fundy, had made a proposal which he would shortly afterwards formalize in a letter written on 4 June to the district chairman, William Temple. Allison had been reflecting, he wrote, on a text from the book of Proverbs – 'Train up a child in the way he should go; and when he is old he will not depart from it' – and had become convinced of the benefits which could be derived from 'the establishment of Schools in which *pure Religion* is not only taught, but *Constantly* brought before the Youthful mind.' In order that such a school might be founded to serve the Maritime provinces, he offered to purchase land in Sackville, to have suitable buildings constructed at his own expense, and to provide an annual income of £100 for the first ten years of the school's existence. While the proposed institution would be 'altogether under the management and Control of the British Conference, in connexion with the Wesleyan missionaries in these Provinces,' Allison expressed no wish that attendance should be restricted to Methodists, and the scope of the curriculum he envisaged was shown in his hope that 'not only the Elementary but higher branches of Education may be taught.'[1]

Allison's proposal was warmly welcomed by the district meeting, though there was some initial disagreement over the site of the school. As was later recalled by Enoch Wood, one of the ministers of the district who would play an important role in the consolidation of the Sackville Academy, there were those who regarded the rapidly growing city of Saint John as a more promising location than the small country town of Sackville, for Saint John might well supply a large number of day scholars whose patronage would be a useful support for a school which would otherwise depend almost entirely on boarding students. The matter was decided, however, by Allison's insistence that the school should serve all of the Maritime provinces, and that Sackville's central location in the region made it the ideal site. There was also precedent for the selection of a rural or small-town situation for Methodist educational institutions, not only at Kingswood School in England, founded by John Wesley himself in 1739 and deliberately located at a safe distance from the distractions of the city of Bristol, but also at such other institutions as the Wesleyan Academy which had been established at Newmarket, New Hampshire, in 1818 and had been moved shortly afterwards to Wilbraham, Massachusetts.[2] At Sackville the school would be. The resolve of the New Brunswick District to accept Allison's 'liberal offer' was unanimous, and it was further ordered 'that as the contemplated establishment is calculated to meet the views and wants of our brethren and friends in Nova Scotia, the influence and assistance of the brethren in that District are affectionately solicited.'[3]

The decision to involve the Nova Scotia District was a logical one, and not only because of Allison's declared concern for the needs of the entire region. It had been at the annual meeting of the Nova Scotia District eleven years before that the idea of a Methodist 'Seminary of Learning' for the Maritimes had first been mooted, and a committee appointed to explore possible locations. By the time the committee reported to the following year's district meeting, held in Halifax in May 1829, proposals had been received from no fewer than four Nova Scotian centres – Halifax, Horton, Bridgetown, and Amherst – and with the optimism born of inexperience it was decided to proceed in any or all of these locations as soon as local fund-raising efforts should bear fruit.[4] The predictable result was that nothing was achieved in practice. In Halifax, it proved impossible to find a competent teacher, while in Horton the scheme was undermined by competition from the Horton Academy which had recently been opened by the Baptists; but the underlying cause of the failure was the diffusion of money and effort to so many separate localities.[5] None the less, one accomplishment of 1829 was the enunciation of certain important principles which were intended to govern the proposed schools. Curriculum and discipline were to be on the same lines as at the Wesleyan schools of England, and at Kingswood in particular. Pupils would receive 'in addition to a good English education, the Latin and Greek Classics, Mathematics, Natural Philosophy, Astronomy, Chemistry, &c.,' and if possible each school would be headed by a Methodist teacher from England. Thus, in accordance with the stress which had been laid by Wesley upon 'all useful learning,' the curriculum would include classical subjects but would not be dominated by them. Discipline would be tight, for 'the morals of the pupils shall be *strictly* attended to,' and the maintenance of these high standards would be ensured by the provision that a majority of the Trustees of each institution should be 'members of the Wesleyan Society.' What was not envisaged, however, and was specifically disclaimed, was any restriction upon pupils on religious grounds: 'pupils shall be at liberty to attend any place of worship, which their respective parents or guardians may deem most proper.' Methodism had begun not as a church but as a society made up from members of various denominations, and this element was intended to persist in its educational institutions in the Maritimes.[6]

These principles of 1829 were not forgotten in later years. Nor were the lessons of the failure of that year entirely ignored. A further proposal for a Methodist school in Nova Scotia was made in late 1832 by William Croscombe, a minister stationed at Windsor, Nova Scotia. After consultations between the Nova Scotia and New Brunswick Districts, and with the English-based Wesleyan Methodist Missionary Society, the project resolved itself into a plan for one institution in Lower Horton, to serve Nova Scotia, and one in Fredericton, to serve New Brunswick. Once again, though, resources were insufficient. Although subscriptions to the amount of £400 had been raised in Nova Scotia by May 1833, and a site selected in Fredericton and partially paid for, both schemes were soon abandoned, and the nearest approach to a Wesleyan school in the region would continue for the time being to be the Albion Vale school privately operated by a Methodist teacher, Andrew Henderson, at Annapolis Royal, Nova Scotia.[7] The failure of 1833–4, like that of 1829, was a revealing one. In this case, it was the advice offered from London by the Committee of the Wesleyan Methodist Missionary Society which raised important questions not only about the role of the committee itself, but also about the nature of Methodism in the Maritime provinces. John Beecham, one of the Society's general secretaries, responded to the Maritime proposal in a letter to the Nova Scotia District in 1834. 'The project,' he wrote, 'is fully approved of, and every assistance in our power, you may calculate on'; given prudent management, he saw every reason to hope for success. What Beecham could not offer, however, was financial assistance.

Furthermore, he warned, this was not a project for the clergy alone. 'You must distinctly understand,' he concluded, 'that the Committee [of the Society] cannot take the *responsibility* of the undertaking, nor can you as Missionaries; your object must be in all you do, to help our people to help themselves.'[8]

This admonition was characteristic of Beecham, and of the Missionary Society at the time, but it should not be interpreted simply as representing an idealistic desire to see the Methodists of the Maritimes run their own affairs. Since the formal inauguration of the Society in 1818, the Maritime provinces had come under its authority as a mission field. In earlier years, and especially during the late eighteenth century, Maritime Methodism had had close affinities with the Methodist Episcopal Church in the United States, but by 1800 a shortage of itinerant preachers had caused the pioneering missionary William Black to turn to the British Conference for assistance, and the region then came increasingly under the influence of British Methodism. This process was consciously promoted by the Missionary Society after 1818. Not only were matters of organization adjusted along British lines, but British missionaries came to dominate the ranks of the clergy. In 1833, the Society went so far as to insist that locally recruited preachers should not initially be given the full status of Missionaries, but should start with the lesser title of assistant missionary. This obviously discriminatory measure aroused deep resentment among those affected, including the young New Brunswick-born preacher Humphrey Pickard, who was later to become the first Principal of the Sackville academy. Writing in 1837 to Robert Alder, now Beecham's colleague as one of the four secretaries of the Missionary Society, Pickard complained of the particularly arduous tasks given to assistant missionaries. He was considering leaving for Connecticut to attend Wesleyan University, and bluntly informed Alder that 'I shall be the more willing to leave this District on account of the unjust distinction which is made by the Assistant Missionary plan between the young men taken out in this Country, and ... [those] out from England, during the earlier years of their Ministry.'[9] Where all the Methodist clergy of the region were on the same footing, though, was in the obedience to the Missionary Society's instructions which was expected of all, whether native or British-born. In 1832, for example, the Nova Scotia and New Brunswick Districts jointly founded a periodical, the *Nova Scotia and New Brunswick Wesleyan Methodist Magazine*, under the management of William Temple, by then a long-established British missionary. The venture had been undertaken, however, without the approval of the Missionary Society, which abruptly ordered its suppression after only four issues, on the ground that it might compete with British Wesleyan publications. It was not until 1838 that a further such magazine was attempted in the region, and not until 1840 that official approval was received from England.[10]

How could this authoritarianism be consistent with Beecham's clear call for local initiative in the matter of education? In part, the answer lay in the tension which had long existed within Methodism, between the spiritual freedom of believers and the strict regulation of organizational matters by John Wesley and his successors in the Methodist hierarchy. The theology of Wesley embodied an optimistic view of human nature, and of the relationship of human beings to God. Although he believed in the reality of original sin, he adopted the Arminian doctrine that salvation was open to all and added the further principle of 'assurance': that the individual believer could consciously be aware of the saving grace of God and could thus feel certain of personal salvation. Where Wesleyan doctrine differed most obviously from other evangelical faiths, however, was in the belief that an initial conversion experience, while important as the beginning of an individual's spiritual journey, was insufficient in itself to ensure salvation. Instead, it must be followed by a lifelong process of service to God, both through personal faith and moral uprightness and through service to others. For Wesley and the Methodists, there was nothing dull or sanctimonious about the Christian life. On the contrary, they believed that the true joy was spiritual joy, and all the more so because of the fellowship of believers in local groups. Methodist leaders, however, and especially the politically conservative Wesley, saw good reason to fear the consequences if this spiritual freedom were allowed excessive scope. It was not so much that individuals would become intoxicated with their own spiritual power. That problem, characteristic of the more extreme forms of Calvinism, was largely obviated in Methodism by Wesley's insistence on the need for lifelong self-discipline in order to maintain the assurance of salvation. Rather, it was the Methodist stress upon service to others as a means of serving God which was capable of leading to political radicalism and, in the highly charged political context of Britain in the eras of the French Revolution and the Industrial Revolution, to outright revolution. Furthermore, the network of local groups of Methodist believers – the 'class meetings' – could easily be adapted for political purposes, as indeed it was by radical and trade union organizations in late eighteenth-century Britain.[11]

For Wesley, and for the leaders of the British Conference after his death in 1791, political radicalism was a trap which Methodists must avoid at all costs, and this was the context of the increasing disciplinary control exercised by the Conference in the early nineteenth century. Through such leaders as Jabez Bunting, secretary of the Conference from 1814 to 1819, and again from 1824 to 1827, and four times its chairman, the Conference actively combated the radical influence in many major centres of British Methodism, despite the risk of dividing congregations and provoking secession movements. It was following one skirmish in Liverpool that John Beecham published his *Essay on the Constitution of Wesleyan Methodism*, in which he argued that the Conference, as the assembly of the clergy, was the legislature of Methodism and exercised sovereign power within the denomination. For Beecham, Bunting, and their supporters, the leadership of the central institutions of Methodism necessarily took priority over local organizations in matters of discipline and doctrine.[12] It was no accident that both Beecham and Bunting were leading figures in the Wesleyan Methodist Missionary Society. Bunting, in fact, had been instrumental in the organization of the Society in 1818, and was to serve as one of its secretaries until 1851, with the exception of only a few years. The foreign mission field was one into which the spiritual energy of Methodism, and its commitment to the improvement of the human condition, could be put to work not only without threat to the social fabric of Great Britain but also, the denomination's leaders hoped, with the result that divided congregations in Britain itself would regain their unity in support of this great overseas enterprise.[13] Thus, with regard to the Maritime provinces, the seemingly contradictory behaviour of the Missionary Society reflected a deep ambivalence that had influenced the expansion of British Methodist activity into foreign missions. On the one hand, it was perfectly consistent with the Wesleyan spiritual tradition that the initiative for such an evidently worthy cause as the foundation of a school should come from groups of local believers. On the other hand, in the view of the Missionary Society, it was only through unquestioned central authority that the integrity of the denomination could be preserved.

While considerations such as these explain how it was possible for Beecham to approve of local initiative in educational matters, while still taking an authoritarian view of the Maritime districts' overall relationship to the Missionary Society, he also had more mundane reasons for attaching such crucial significance to the role of 'your people themselves.'[14] Perennially short of money, the Society had no intention of adding to its existing responsibilities in the Maritime region, which consisted of supporting the general missionary endeavours of the two districts. Here again, there were elements of paradox. Thrift dictated that the proposed Methodist schools should depend upon the fund-raising activities of the local circuits, and therefore primarily upon the Methodists of the region itself. Yet it was thrift also which lay behind the low status accorded to locally recruited preachers, since although assistant missionaries in British North America were not penalized in terms of pay, they were not allowed to participate in the British pension fund.[15] The end result, as far as education in the Maritimes was concerned, was that the influence of the Missionary Society contained the seeds of its own ultimate decline. To be sure, the promoters of the Sackville academy proposed by Allison would continue to turn to London for advice, moral support, and for formal recognition within the Methodist denomination. The secretary Robert Alder, who had himself served circuits in all three Maritime provinces as a young missionary between 1816 and 1825, was a close and frequent adviser. None the less, Beecham's renunciation of responsibility for the establishment of schools in 1834 accurately presaged the importance of solid local support and patronage, while the contradictory and sometimes restrictive general policies of the Missionary Society ensured that effective leadership would come not from London but from individuals such as Allison, Pickard, Temple, and Wood, who were either native to the region or long-standing residents. The unsuccessful attempt of 1829 revealed the extent of British influence in matters of educational principle; but both it and the attempt of 1832–4 made clear the practical necessity that the enterprise should have deep roots in the Maritime provinces themselves.

The Methodist community in the region was indeed deep-rooted, though it was not large by comparison with other denominations. Yorkshire Methodists had begun to settle on and around the Chignecto Isthmus as early as 1772, and included such families as the Truemans and the Dixons, who would later play prominent roles in the development of the Sackville educational institutions. William Black was also a Yorkshireman, and it was in 1781 that he commenced his itinerant ministry, which was to expand and firmly establish the Methodist presence. Black faced serious obstacles, not least of which was the fact that he had to compete for adherents with the Newlight preacher Henry Alline, whose intense evangelism had begun in Falmouth, Nova Scotia, several years before. Although Alline's death in early 1784 was followed by the widespread disintegration of Newlight congregations, the assimilation of many of their members by the Baptists ensured that denomination a larger following in the region than Methodism.[16] A further difficulty was encountered by Black after the end of the American Revolutionary War, in the form of the strengthening of Anglican influence which accompanied Loyalist immigration. Despite the esteem in which Methodist leaders professed to hold the Church of England, out of which Methodism had sprung, such powerful Anglicans as Charles Inglis, consecrated Bishop of Nova Scotia in 1787, and the Loyalists who had prompted the foundation of the province of New Brunswick in 1784, looked upon Black and his followers with suspicion. At best, they regarded Methodism as a species of Dissent; at worst, it might be identified with the volatile and dangerous 'enthusiasm' of the

Newlights and other evangelical sects. The vigorous efforts of Inglis to nurture the Church of England as the established church of the region had enough success to impose limits upon the expansion of Methodism, particularly in New Brunswick. At the same time, the Scottish immigration of the late eighteenth and early nineteenth centuries ensured a large membership for the Presbyterian denomination, particularly but not exclusively in Nova Scotia; while the Roman Catholicism that already existed in Acadian communities was reinforced by the settlement of Highlanders on Cape Breton Island, parts of the Nova Scotian mainland, and the Island of St John (renamed Prince Edward Island in 1798) and then by the Irish immigration which had its greatest effect upon New Brunswick. There were profound divisions within both Presbyterianism and Catholicism, but the number of adherents in each case grew rapidly to outnumber the Methodists.[17]

By 1825, the records of the eighteen Methodist circuits in the Maritime provinces showed a total membership of 2134. Although the majority of circuits served rural areas through itinerant preaching, the largest in terms of membership was that of Halifax, and there were substantial congregations in other urban centres. The essentially rural Westmorland and Petitcodiac circuit, which included Sackville, was the third largest, with 153 members. The total membership represented approximately 1 per cent of the population of the three provinces, though this proportion is misleading, in that membership figures included neither children of members nor those who attended Methodist services without having formally joined the local Methodist society. Thus, for every member there were several other adherents. In the course of the next decade, membership would triple: although Methodism was the smallest of the major denominations in the region, by the 1830s its numbers were by no means insignificant.[18] Socially, the membership was diverse, within limits which William Temple defined in his journal by excluding 'the most wealthy and the most ignorant.'[19] From the time of William Black, however, there had also been a number of more eminent members, such as Judge Simeon Perkins of Liverpool, Nova Scotia, and later L.A. Wilmot of Fredericton, who as a young man was influenced in his conversion by Enoch Wood and shortly afterwards married Black's granddaughter.[20] Whether or not the winning of such recruits represented a conscious pursuit of respectability by a small but growing denomination, there is little evidence of social or political radicalism among Maritime Methodists of the kind which was developing at this time among Methodists in Upper Canada. Reform movements in the Maritime provinces would have the support of individual Methodists, of whom Wilmot was among the most prominent, but the denomination as such did not emerge as a political force. The social concerns which were so deeply rooted in Methodist theology were not abandoned, and would provide a base for the later success of the social gospel movement in the region. For the time being, however, attention was focused on social goals which could be pursued within the existing order. Both Methodist tradition and the needs of the Maritime region suggested that the development of education was an excellent example of such a goal, and in early 1842 each of the petitions which went from the various circuits in New Brunswick to the provincial lieutenant-governor to request support for the proposed Sackville academy carried an appendix which not only stressed the intellectual and social benefits of the scheme but also declared that 'the conservative and Loyal character and predilections of the Wesleyans are well known.'[21] It was a description which could have come from Wesley himself, and one which clearly showed the influence of the particular strain of Methodism which was characteristic of the Wesleyan Methodist Missionary Society and its missionaries.

As befitted a missionary endeavour, the Methodist denomination pursued social goals on the assumption that they were inseparable from the primary purpose of saving souls. Although the missionaries were suspicious at times of emotional excesses which seemed to recall what they regarded as the fanaticism of the Newlights and other such sects, their faith was ardently evangelical. The daily work of the itinerant preachers was highlighted from time to time by revivals on the various circuits, and it was at the behest of the secretaries of the Missionary Society that in 1836 a series of 'protracted meetings' was held in New Brunswick.[22] One of those who experienced conversion in that year was Charles Frederick Allison. For Allison, this was the culmination of a change which had been in the making for at least three years – it had been in 1833 that he had abandoned his Anglican background to take up formal membership of the Methodist society in Sackville – and at the same time it was the beginning for him of the search which he shared with all Methodists for Christian perfection.[23] Allison in 1836 was a forty-one-year-old bachelor, whose business career had prospered over a period of some twenty years. He was of Ulster Scottish descent; his grandfather had left Northern Ireland in 1769 intending to settle in Philadelphia, but had been shipwrecked on Sable Island and had stayed in Nova Scotia to establish a farm at Horton, and his father had become a farmer, fruit-grower, and merchant in the adjoining township of Cornwallis. It had been at the age of eighteen that Charles Allison had left home to work as a clerk in the store of Elias Ratchford in Parrsboro. In 1816, he had moved to Sackville to join the expanding merchant firm of his cousin, William Crane, first as a senior clerk and then as Crane's partner.[24]

The Crane and Allison concern operated both in the Sackville area, as a distributor of local agricultural produce and imported goods, and on the Miramichi River, where the firm's trading-house exported timber to Great Britain and distributed provisions and other imported commodities. As part of the local economy of Sackville, the foundations of the firm's prosperity were laid during the period before the transformation wrought by the growth of large-scale shipbuilding during the 1840s and by the development of the port of Sackville after the construction of the first public wharf in 1841.[25] Allison's active career, in fact, took place entirely in that earlier era, for he retired from business in 1840 to devote his full attention to the academy. Yet he was also a transitional figure, for the firm of Crane and Allison was among the patrons of the early shipbuilding activities which grew up in Sackville parish in the 1820s, chiefly in the coastal communities of Rockport and Wood Point. During that decade, the firm purchased three brigs from the yards of the Boultenhouse family at Wood Point, the largest being the *Hope*, of 332 tons.[26] After Allison's retirement, Crane would be a leading participant in the development of Sackville's economy, as might be expected of one who was also associated with Samuel Cunard in the initiation of regular steamship service across the Atlantic; he was also a member of the provincial House of Assembly from 1824, and was its Speaker at the time of his death in 1853.[27] Allison – shy, reserved, meticulous – was an effective counterpart for the ebullient Crane. His personal ambitions were different from those of his partner, for not only was his wealth limited by his early retirement – a contemporary later remarked that 'his fortune was a small one' – but in 1849 he also declined a proffered appointment to the provincial Legislative Council.[28] No less than Crane, however, Allison's career and the manner in which his wealth had been acquired made him a product of the evolving Maritime economy of the 1820s and 1830s. Just as important, the skills and the perceptions which he acquired, focused by the Methodist convictions at which he arrived in 1836, would influence his role in the establishment and operation of the Sackville academy.

Allison's church-related activity was not restricted to the field of education. He was also, for example, active in the cause of temperance, and in 1842 was elected president of the 'Middle Village [of Sackville] Temperance and Teetotal Society.'[29] None the less, education was a matter with which he had long been familiar, especially through the concerns of his partner, Crane. The development of schools in Sackville had a history which went back into the eighteenth century, but only on a small scale. A more significant development occurred in 1818: the opening of a Madras school in the adjoining settlement of Westcock. This school was one of several in New Brunswick sponsored by the English-based National Society for the Education of the Poor in the

Principles of the Established Church, and they derived their name from the fact that all employed techniques devised by the society's founder, Andrew Bell, while a missionary in India. By 1824, another Madras school had opened in Sackville itself, but both were to disappear by 1831. The Madras schools represented an effort to educate working-class children according to Anglican principles, and therein lay their principal limitations: they incorporated the Anglican catechism as a part of the curriculum, and thus were not necessarily acceptable to non-Anglican parents; with their concentration upon a large central school rather than small local ones, they were better suited to urban than to rural locations; and a curriculum aimed at imparting only basic knowledge to children destined to become workers in urban industrial locations could not satisfy a demand for more advanced, academic education.[30] It was particularly this last deficiency which was intended to be supplied by the opening of the Westmorland Grammar School in Sackville in 1820, at the behest of three of the county's wealthiest citizens, William Botsford, Edward Dixon, and William Crane. According to the proposal by which the three agreed to donate between them the £100 which was required in order to qualify for government assistance under the provincial County Grammar Schools Act of 1816, the school would offer instruction in 'English Grammer [*sic*], the Latin and Greek Languages, Orthography, the use of Globes and practical branches of the Mathematics.'[31] By September 1820 the grammar school was in operation, with Botsford, Dixon, and Crane associated with three others as its directors; the principal teacher, at least from 1822, was the Anglican rector of Sackville, Christopher Milner.[32] Although Milner was forced to resign in 1831, as a result of legislation prohibiting parish clergymen from serving as masters in grammar schools, the Westmorland school continued to operate at least until 1837, with Crane consistently serving as a director. The circumstances of its subsequent closure, and its later revival in Shediac, are unclear. However, its departure from Sackville at some time in the late 1830s undoubtedly left a gap in the educational facilities of the town and provided an additional, local, reason for the siting there of the proposed Wesleyan academy.[33]

As well as being familiar with the state of education in his own town of Sackville, Allison must have been aware also of developments elsewhere in the Maritime provinces. His family home at Cornwallis was located just a short distance from the Horton Academy which had been founded by the Baptists in 1828, and this was only one of several denominational endeavours of the time. Nova Scotia was especially prolific in such institutions, although the original intention of King's College, Windsor, at the time of its foundation in 1787 had been to serve the entire population of the province. It was in 1802 that regulations were adopted which required all students of the institution to subscribe to the Thirty-Nine Articles, and thus effectively restricted enrolment to Anglicans. Also a denominational institution, though not imposing any religious tests on its students, was the Pictou Academy founded by the Presbyterian Thomas McCulloch in 1816. In its earlier years, the Pictou Academy had a number of Baptists among its students; the decision of the Baptist denomination to establish its own school at Horton indicated both the erosion of traditional Baptist suspicions of education, and the influence of well-to-do converts from Anglicanism in Halifax during the 1820s. Each of these institutions functioned as an academy, though King's College also enjoyed degree-granting powers from 1802, and the standards of the Pictou Academy were such that several of its students were able to pass examinations to qualify for the MA degree at the University of Glasgow.[34]

In New Brunswick, the early history of academic education was profoundly influenced by the development of King's College, Fredericton. The first proposal for an academy in Fredericton had come from a number of Loyalist petitions in 1785, and by 1787 classes had begun in temporary accommodation. Largely because of the opposition of Bishop Inglis, however, who was unwilling to accept the existence of a rival to King's College, Windsor, chartering of the institution was long delayed. When finally chartered in 1800, it was as the degree-granting College of New Brunswick, although it continued for the time being to function purely as an academy and did not institute a degree programme until 1820. The charter of 1800 established the College of New Brunswick as an Anglican institution in unmistakable terms. Its president was to be an Anglican clergyman, its professors must be members of the Church of England, and its matriculants must subscribe to the Thirty-Nine Articles. By the time that the first college-level students matriculated in 1822, the trustees of the college had realized that the imposition of religious tests upon students was a source of weakness rather than strength; it not only restricted the potential number of students, but was also offensive, as the assembly leader Ward Chipman, Jr, remarked in 1825, to 'all classes of ... inhabitants, Churchmen, as well as Dissenters.'[35] Accordingly, a new charter was sought, and was granted in late 1828. Owing in large measure to the efforts of the provincial lieutenant-governor of the time, Sir Howard Douglas, who had successfully influenced the British Colonial Office in the face of strong opposing views, the religious test was no longer to be required of students or professors, other than in the field of divinity. It was on this basis that the reconstituted college was opened under its new name of King's College on 1 January 1829, and the retiring president of the old College of New Brunswick, James Somerville, declared on this occasion that henceforth 'no one is excluded from the Benefits of a Collegiate Education here, in consequence of his religious tenets.'[36]

Somerville was correct in his statement. Yet the matter was not so simple as he and his audience must have supposed, for they had no foreknowledge of the turbulent events which would characterize the following decade. Both in New Brunswick and in Nova Scotia, the 1830s would see developments which, while not creating the Methodist denomination's desire for its own academy, would intensify it and would thus add to the timeliness of Allison's proposal of 1839. The omission of the religious test for students and professors was a real concession in the King's College charter, but it did not in itself alter the Anglican nature of the institution. The president was still required to be an Anglican clergyman, while all members of the governing College Council were to be members of the Church of England. Most of the professors continued to be Anglicans, and even such an exception as the first professor of chemistry and natural history, James Robb, would eventually subscribe to the Thirty-Nine Articles in order to take up his seat on the Council four years after his original appointment in 1837.[37] The charter of 1828, in reality, had changed the nature of the institution remarkably little. Together with the narrowly classical curriculum with which King's College began, this fact prevented the college from enjoying the confidence of other denominations. It also led to the subsuming of the college question in a larger political issue, that of the effort of the provincial assembly to gain control of crown lands. King's College, for the leaders of the assembly, came to be identified as a bastion of complacency and of privilege. It was in this atmosphere that a Baptist school was founded in Fredericton in 1835, and subsequently sought provincial funding. Although this request was blocked by the Legislative Council until 1842, the favourable votes of the House of Assembly gave evidence of a sympathetic attitude towards non-Anglican denominational schools. Among the members who supported the Baptist application, and also an advocate of reform at King's College, was the Methodist L.A. Wilmot. The situation must have been clear too to his close associate, Enoch Wood.[38]

In Nova Scotia, the late 1830s also saw acrimonious controversy on the college question, though of a different kind. As early as 1817, the provincial governor, Lord Dalhousie, had advocated the establishment in Halifax of a non-denominational college which would be open to all those potential students excluded from King's College, Windsor. Acting with speed and vigour, Dalhousie assembled funds for the new institution, and the cornerstone of its first building was laid in 1820. Soon afterwards, however, Dalhousie departed for Lower Canada, to assume the misleadingly grandiose title of Governor-in-Chief of British North America, and the project languished. It was not until 1838 that it was revived in the Nova Scotia assembly. Supported by a fragile coalition of Presbyterians, Baptists, Methodists, and Roman Catholics, a bill passed which provided for the appropriation of £200 out of the normal £500 annual grant to Pictou Academy to the support of the non-denominational college in Halifax, and for the removal of Thomas McCulloch from Pictou to become its first president. McCulloch, whose consistent practice at Pictou had been to admit pupils of all denominations, had been weakened for more than a decade by the internal strife within the Presbyterian denomination between supporters of the Church of Scotland and the Free Presbyterians. The hopes he entertained for a more tranquil environment in Halifax were soon disappointed when the newly established board of governors of Dalhousie ruled that, while the college would be open to students without denominational restrictions, the professors must be Presbyterian. One immediate result was the breaking of an informal understanding with E.A. Crawley, a prominent classical scholar and a graduate of King's College, Windsor, prior to his becoming a Baptist, that he would be appointed to a chair. While many Nova Scotia Baptists might well have disapproved of Dalhousie College even if Crawley had been appointed, his rejection unified the denomination in its hostility, thus enabling Crawley to take the lead in the foundation of Acadia College, near the existing Horton Academy. Also influenced by the unexpectedly denominational character of Dalhousie was the effort of Halifax Roman Catholics to establish their own institution: begun in 1838, it was chartered three years later as St Mary's College.[39]

Both in New Brunswick and in Nova Scotia, therefore, efforts had been made to mitigate the Anglican exclusiveness of the two King's Colleges, but with limited success. The result had been the firmer establishment of the denominational principle of advanced education in both provinces during the 1830s. Though not attended by the same degree of controversy, the same was true of Prince Edward Island: a Roman Catholic Academy in St Andrew's operated between 1831 and 1845, and was the forerunner of the St Dunstan's College which was established in 1855, while Prince of Wales College originated in Charlottetown in 1836 under the title of the Central Academy and with an Anglican clergyman as its first principal.[40] By 1839, other denominations in the Maritimes were operating degree-granting colleges, or soon would be; the Methodists, despite their efforts in 1828–9 and in 1832–4, did not even have an academy.[41] If there was any lingering of the suspicious attitude towards education which had occasionally evidenced itself in North American Methodism – though alien to the Wesleyan mainstream – it was further weakened by the example of the successful opening of the Upper Canada

Academy at Cobourg in 1836.[42] The result of six years of planning by the Methodists of the Canada Conference, the Cobourg Academy was headed for its first four years by Matthew Richey, a missionary of the Wesleyan Methodist Missionary Society who was of Irish origin and had spent most of his career serving Maritime circuits between 1821 and 1835.[43] In April 1838, an issue of the *Wesleyan*, a periodical newly established at Halifax in anticipation of approval from the Missionary Society, carried a description of the Cobourg academy by W.E. Shenstone, minister at Lunenburg.[44] Four weeks later, an anonymous correspondent of the *Wesleyan* suggested that 'it would be a great blessing, if some friend acquainted with the resources of Methodism, would make a practical use of Rev. Mr. Shenstone's letter, and draw out a plan for such an Institution here.'[45] Whether this exhortation had a direct influence on the proposal which Charles Frederick Allison would make just over a year later cannot definitely be known. What is certain, however, is that Allison's initiative was not a haphazard act. It came at a time when a conjuncture of diverse circumstances had prepared the way for its ready acceptance.

The approval given to Allison's proposal by the New Brunswick District in May 1839 came some six weeks before an unusual event: a visit to the Maritime provinces by the Missionary Society secretary, Robert Alder. Alder's journey to North America was intended chiefly as an effort to bring about peace between contending Methodist factions in Upper Canada, but on 12 July he took the chair at a joint meeting of missionaries from the New Brunswick, Newfoundland, and Nova Scotia Districts, held in Halifax. It was an ideal opportunity for Allison to expound further on his educational project, which he did in person. He was, as Enoch Wood later recalled, somewhat diffident:

> I well remember [wrote Wood] his quiet and meek appearance as he stood in that meeting describing his feelings and intentions. One would have thought by his unassumed humility that he came there to ask some special favor, rather than to make a noble and generous offer for the benefit of others. One sentence of his address I have never forgotten ... – 'The Lord hath put it into my heart to give this sum towards building a Wesleyan Academy,' – and then he made a short pause, as though he was afraid he had spoken too strongly, resuming – 'I know the impression is from the Lord, for I am naturally fond of money.'

Allison's nervousness may have been all the greater as he had not yet informed his business partner, Crane, of his intentions.[46] Crane, however, would make no difficulties, and as for the reaction of the meeting of 12 July, it was predictable. A series of resolutions commented on the need for an educational institution which had been 'long and painfully felt,' styled Allison's proposal a 'munificent offer,' and set up committees to supervise its implementation.[47] At the same time, Alder was requested to assist in gaining the approval of the Committee of the Missionary Society, an easy task in which he succeeded at the committee's meeting on 12 February 1840. The committee noted that no claim would be made on its funds, but stood ready at all times to offer 'counsel and advice.'[48]

By February 1840, Allison had already made progress towards the building of the academy. The site was acquired from Christopher Atkinson, the son of one of the Yorkshire settlers, who had in turn purchased it from one of the first New England planters, Amasa Killam. No deed has survived to document the purchase, but its extent was a little over five acres, located near the centre of Sackville, on the rise of ground which would shortly afterwards come to be known as Mount Allison.[49] By the end of 1839, Allison had already expended some £350 on lumber and other necessary supplies for the start of the building, and at a meeting of the planning committee in Sackville on 17 January 1840 he announced his intention to spend a total of £4000 on the construction. On the basis of this meeting, Enoch Wood reported to London that the academy had had 'a very auspicious beginning.'[50] A more formal occasion came on 9 July, with the laying of the foundation stone at a service led by Temple, as Chairman of the New Brunswick District, and by Richard Knight, Chairman of the Nova Scotia District. The stone was laid by Allison himself, with the hope that 'the Education ever to be furnished by the Institution [shall] be conducted on Wesleyan Principles, to the glory of God, and the extension of His Cause.'[51]

As far as the building itself was concerned, the project thenceforward proceeded smoothly under the personal direction of Allison. The architect, Charles Bugbee, had already designed the Centenary Chapel in Saint John, and his design for the academy was quickly approved by Allison with the exception of a decorative tower which was deemed too expensive as well as too ornate: the characteristics of the building, as summarized by Wood, were to be 'respectability and comfort, blended with economy.'[52] One hundred and fifty feet long, forty-five feet in width, and four stories high including the basement, the academy would include accommodation for professors and a steward, a large lecture-hall and two classrooms, library and study space, a dining room and kitchen, and forty rooms each of which could accommodate up to four boarding students.[53] By the end of 1840, Wood reported to London that 'our generous brother Allison is getting on rapidly with the Academy at Sackville,' and his assessment is borne out by the fact that Bugbee was paid on 31 December 1840 for 234 days of work since the preceding

March.[54] By the summer of 1841, the outside of the building was complete, though work remained to be done on the interior, and the plaster on walls and ceilings – seven thousand yards of it – was expected to dry over the coming winter, assisted by fires kept constantly burning. The institution was expected to open in the spring of 1842, according to an article inserted in the *British North American Wesleyan Magazine* by Knight and Temple in October of 1841.[55] A short item in the same periodical the following summer proclaimed that the new building was 'probably unsurpassed by any wooden fabric, erected for similar purposes, on the American continent.' This claim may well have been extravagant and was certainly immodest. Just a little less so was the verdict of the minister at Point de Bute, William Leggett, when he wrote in a private letter in July 1842 that 'our new Academy at Sackville ... is a noble structure – superb, but plain and truly Methodistical.'[56]

The fact was, though, that the school had not opened as planned in the spring of 1842, and according to Temple's estimate of the likely response from parents of prospective students, this must have caused considerable disappointment: 'the Character which Wesleyanism sustains, through the uprightness and diligence of Wesleyan Missionaries employed from the earliest recollections of the provincialists, has given being to an influence in favour of the Institution, of which you can hardly be aware without witnessing it. Many persons are keeping their children at home rather than send them elsewhere.'[57] Temple's view is corroborated by a letter directed to Allison later in the year by James Ross, a Presbyterian minister and publisher of the newly established Pictou newspaper, the *Presbyterian Banner*. Reflecting ruefully on the disputes between Presbyterian factions which were threatening the ruin of the Pictou Academy, Ross commented on the various alternatives:

> We have no confidence in Dalhousie College and just as little in the Baptist seminary at Horton. We cannot think of sending our young men to Windsor and St. Mary's is utterly out of the question. Our attention is therefore directed with considerable interest to Sackville. If its management and the course of education pursued in it meet our approbation we will probably for a time at least gladly avail ourselves of its advantages.[58]

If the projected academy could draw such widespread interest before it had even opened, and not only from Methodists, what was the cause of the delay? In part, the answer lay in the difficulties of fund-raising. Allison's donations, while providing the land and the building, had not covered all the costs of beginning the academy. Nor had they been intended to do so. By the time the academy was completely fitted and finished, equipped with 'Chemical, philosophical and Astronomical apparatus,' and provided with the rudiments of a library, the total capital cost would rise to £8000, double the amount of Allison's expenditure on construction. Nor did this include the cost of running the academy from year to year, which was estimated at £1000 for the first year, offset only by an estimated £400 to be paid in tuition fees and by Allison's promised annual contribution of £100.[59] Clearly, there was a substantial gap to be closed, and appeals to the local circuits did not always bring the desired result. In August 1842, one of the principal fund-raisers for the academy, S.D. Rice, wrote to Allison from Halifax that 'it is certainly rather *slow* work. The impression here is that it is a bad time of year as the farmers cannot tell what kind of crops they will have and are therefore afraid to say what they will do.'[60] Later in the same month Alexander McNutt, another minister who was active in raising support for the academy, admitted to Allison that 'this is rather a dark time,' and was inclined to blame the cyclical depression which the region was then passing through, in common with Great Britain; Rice confirmed from Fredericton in October that 'the people here *feel* a good deal of interest but their embarrassment is such they *cannot show* it just now.'[61]

Yet the financial difficulties, while real, do not in themselves explain the delays which afflicted the Wesleyan academy, especially since fund-raising had proceeded successfully during the early part of 1842. By February of that year, Rice had raised £928 from Westmorland county and the adjoining Nova Scotia county of Cumberland, and his work was praised at the New Brunswick District meeting in May.[62] Furthermore, there was good reason to hope for substantial government aid from both the provinces of New Brunswick and Nova Scotia. In New Brunswick, Enoch Wood in Fredericton had been optimistic of government assistance from the start, counting especially upon support in the House of Assembly. On 17 March 1842 his hopes were justified by the voting of a grant to supplement private donations, as he took pleasure in reporting to Alder:

> The Legislature here have voted us £500 to assist in furnishing it [the academy], our friends in the Lower-House would have said a thousand, but the Province is poor just now, and the depressed state of trade will greatly affect the revenue. The vote passed the Council without a dissenting voice, a proof that the feelings of that body toward us have greatly changed within the last few years.[63]

This grant, in fact, was the result of a co-ordinated series of petitions which had been sent to each branch of the legislature during February from the various circuits in New Brunswick, which had carried a total of some 965 signatures, chiefly Methodist though also including non-Methodists such as Joseph Crandal, Baptist minister in Sackville.[64] The success of this appeal not only gave hopes of a continuing annual grant from the province, but also inspired the Nova Scotia District to initiate a similar campaign at its meeting in June. In Nova Scotia the principle of grants to denominational institutions was already well established, though it would shortly be challenged by Joseph Howe and others, and the petitions which reached the branches of the Nova Scotia legislature in January and February 1843 – again with over 900 signatures in total – resulted in the voting of a £200 operating grant to the Wesleyan Academy in March of that year.[65] It was a sum which was exactly matched by the province of New Brunswick just a few days later.[66]

When seen in context, therefore, the financial situation of the academy was not so gloomy. What posed a greater threat was a lack of cooperation from the Committee of the Missionary Society in London. The early 1840s were turbulent years for British Methodism, as conflicts over the strict connexionalism of Bunting and the British Conference became acute and were further sharpened by the more general economic uncertainty and social unrest of the decade. At the 1843 Conference, Bunting himself admitted 'the declining attendance of poor people at our services,' and blamed 'radicalism, infidelity and socialism.'[67] Inevitably, the secretaries of the Missionary Society found themselves preoccupied with these issues, and one result was the postponement of important decisions on the Sackville academy, and especially on the appointment of its principal. An obvious candidate from the start had been Matthew Richey, the former principal of the Upper Canada Academy who was now engaged in pastoral work in Toronto. Enoch Wood, who with William Temple conducted the correspondence with the Missionary Society on the matter, had doubts about Richey's capacity for work, and there was in any case strong support for the bringing of a candidate from Britain: in late 1841 Temple asked the secretaries to find 'a man who, a good classic and mathematician, would condescend to superintend the minor details of education, as well as be able to take the lead in all departments that are essential to a *good* education.'[68] Above all, however, Wood and Temple wished to avoid looking to the United States for a principal – 'New Brunswick and Nova Scotia Methodists and indeed others in the Provinces would rather have an Englishman, or perhaps one ought to say a *Briton*' – and by early 1842 they had decided that Richey would be acceptable at least as a short-term appointment.[69] Richey's reply when approached was encouraging, but he pointed out that the approval of the Missionary Society would be needed for his removal from Canada to New Brunswick, and he left the decision to its committee.[70]

For several months, Wood, Temple, and their colleagues in the two

Maritime districts waited in vain for a decision from the committee. By late August 1842 Wood informed Allison that they were 'looking very anxiously for news about the Academy Appointments'; some two weeks later he was 'sadly tried, perplexed, even chagrined about it.'[71] Even a visit to England by Temple failed to bring a decision, for he had trouble in gathering the secretaries together to consider the matter, and then was put off with vague suggestions of possible candidates in Ireland. 'While they are doing something,' wrote Wood bitterly to Allison on 7 October, 'they may *hit* upon the right path.'[72] The truth was that the crisis point had been reached, not only because of the general loss of public confidence which would inevitably result from further delays, but also for two very specific reasons. The first of these was the frame of mind of Charles Allison, who in the late summer had been brought to the point of despair by the delays and difficulties then occurring, and had even threatened to terminate his active involvement in the project. Alexander McNutt, no doubt amongst others, had urged that he should not 'persist in giving up your office' and he had eventually complied, but by 15 October Wood was warning Alder that 'Mr. Allison's mind is greatly exercised at the delay which has occurred about the appointment of the Principal ...'[73] The second particular reason lay in the matter of government grants. Carefully planned petitioning campaigns had been launched both in New Brunswick and Nova Scotia on the assumption that the opening of the academy was imminent. The petitions which had been submitted in New Brunswick in February 1842 had predicted its inauguration 'early in the ensuing Spring' – a confidence now proved unjustified – while the petitions to be presented in Nova Scotia early in 1843 would describe it as 'now in operation.' Wood's conclusion was that the hoped-for operating grants would be jeopardized if the academy did not open in January 1843 at the latest.[74]

There was now a real possibility tht the scheme proposed by Allison would suffer the same fate as those of 1828–9 and 1832–4. Wood, however, seized upon the only other recourse when he advocated to Allison on 24 October that 'we must now try and help ourselves' rather than wait for the Committee, and reported that a special meeting of the New Brunswick District was to be held the following week to 'see if we can get the institution into motion.'[75] On 2 November, the meeting convened in Saint John. No argument took place on the principle of proceeding with the academy, but rather a unanimous desire was expressed to open it as soon as possible. 'In attending to this duty,' the minutes of the meeting recognized, 'we may be obliged to interfere with some appointments in the District, contrary to our usages, without first obtaining the consent of the Secretaries and Conference; but the necessities of the case ...

induce us to cherish the expectation (if not of full confidence,) that the Secretaries will countenance and approve of the following decisions.'[76] The missionaries had no wish to be rebels; but neither did they intend to let constitutional niceties stand in the way of the opening of the academy. As 'governor and chaplain' – a non-teaching position involving oversight of the moral standards of the institution – they appointed Albert DesBrisay, a native of Charlottetown and a veteran minister, though one whose health had been suspect since his early retirement from itinerant ministry in 1836 as a result of nervous exhaustion.[77] The crucially important position of principal was to go to one of the few ministers who had a university degree, and one who was also a native of New Brunswick: Humphrey Pickard.

Pickard was undoubtedly an emergency choice. Not yet thirty years old, he had been received as a minister only the previous year and had never held a position at an educational institution. He himself was surprised at his appointment, for it was only five months since he had been appointed editor of the *British North American Wesleyan Methodist Magazine* and 'book agent' for the New Brunswick District, duties which he carried out in addition to his pastoral work in Portland, near Saint John.[78] As he confided to his journal, however, he interpreted the offer of the academy principalship as 'a providential call to a post more arduous and difficult.'[79] The eldest son of a Fredericton merchant, Pickard had left for Wilbraham, Massachusetts, at the age of sixteen to attend the Wesleyan Academy then headed by a prominent Methodist educator, Willbur Fisk. Almost immediately, he had had a conversion experience at a religious meeting held in the academy; this, along with the influence of Fisk, fixed in him the lifelong conviction that religious experience and education were, or should be, inseparable. Completing his studies at Wilbraham in 1831, he went next to Middletown, Connecticut, where Fisk had become president of the newly opened Wesleyan University, and studied there for a year before returning to Fredericton to work in his father's business. By 1835, however, he was seriously considering entering the ministry. On the recommendation of Enoch Wood, he preached in Sheffield, near Fredericton, and on the Miramichi before once again entering Wesleyan University in 1837; graduating two years later, he returned to New Brunswick despite receiving several offers of pastorates in New England. At the same district meeting in 1839 at which Charles Allison's proposal was first considered, Pickard was granted the formal status of candidate for the ministry and spent two more years on the Miramichi before his reception to the ministry and stationing in Portland in 1841.[80]

Thus the new principal, despite his youth, brought to his position a variety of experiences in education, in commerce and in the ministry. He had deep roots in New Brunswick, although he had also been influenced by his formative years spent in New England. As a friend and protégé of Enoch Wood, he was familiar with the British tradition of Wesleyan Methodism in the Maritimes, and yet his bitter protest to Alder in 1837 over his low status as an 'assistant missionary' had shown him untroubled by any undue reverence for the Missionary Society. Indeed, both Pickard's personal history and the manner of his appointment as principal made it clear that from the beginning the Wesleyan Academy at Sackville was an institution bound by the most strong and intimate ties to the three Maritime provinces which it primarily served. Its formal ownership by the British Conference could be seen as 'a sufficient guarantee to the Home Government and to the lovers of British connexion, and British principles in the Province [of New Brunswick], as to the character both of the Instructors who shall be employed, and the general principles which will be inculcated in the Establishment.' Such was the assurance given in late 1842 by Temple, Wood, and their colleague Sampson Busby, as trustees of the academy, in a petition to the lieutenant-governor of New Brunswick, Sir William Colebrooke, which was part of the campaign for an operating grant from the province.[81] Yet the institution was not an attempt to reproduce a British model on colonial soil. While at times receiving encouragement from the Missionary Society in London, its planning and inauguration had depended on initiatives originating within the Maritime provinces, and never more than in the final, crucial decisions taken in November 1842. Its financial support came from within the region, whether from the commercially generated wealth of Allison, from contributions raised on the local circuits, or from legislative grants. Naturally, therefore, its fortunes had risen and fallen with the economy of the region, and would continue to do so. Its declared interest was to serve the region without limitation. Allison's intention that the academy should draw pupils from all three Maritime provinces had been clear from the start. Also essential, and reaffirmed by Temple, Wood, and Busby in their petition to Colebrooke, was the principle that this 'will be no Sectarian Institution [and] Proselytism will be no object of its conductors'; it would therefore seek students of all religious denominations. It would seek also to draw students from a variety of social backgrounds: Pickard would affirm in his inaugural address in 1843 that 'in order to extend the benefits of the Institution as widely as possible, the tuition fees are made so low, that from these we can expect to derive scarcely half the necessary income to maintain its full efficiency.' His conclusion was that the academy must continue to depend for its survival upon provincial government grants, which would in turn confirm its obligation to serve the entire community. It would be, unmistakably, a Methodist institution; but it would be, equally unmistakably, an institution of and for the Maritime provinces.[82]

The formal opening of the Sackville academy would take place in late June of 1843. The resolution of the New Brunswick District, however, had been to have it in operation as soon as possible, and the date selected for the start of classes was 19 January 1843. Pickard and his family – his wife of less than two years and their four-month-old son – travelled by coach to Sackville in the intense cold of early January. Their first week was spent as the guests of Allison and his wife, for he too had recently married, and then they moved to their quarters in the academy. The first term began as scheduled on the 19th, with little ceremony. A short service of prayers and scriptural readings was attended by seven students, by one teacher – J.R. Hea, tutor in French – and by four ministers from nearby circuits, as well as by Pickard, Allison, and their wives, and was followed by tea in the Pickards' drawing-room. As observed by Hannah Maynard Pickard, 'Mr. Allison was, during all, the picture of quiet gratification.'[83] Well he might be. The implementation of his proposal of 1839 had taken more than three and a half years, and had not been easy. Even this opening was but a small and plain beginning. Yet it was only a few months before that he had been close to despair, and even a small beginning was better than that.

PART ONE

2

The Wesleyan Academy: 1843–1855

'We have assembled to-day on no ordinary occasion, and for the advancement of no common-place object.' So Humphrey Pickard began his inaugural address at the formal opening of the Wesleyan Academy on 29 June 1843.[1] His audience had gathered in Sackville by coach, by sailing vessel, and by steamboat from many parts of the Maritime provinces, and included not only the leading Methodists of the region but also members of the legislatures of both New Brunswick and Nova Scotia. By the time 70 guests sat down to 'a cheerful and abundant dinner' in mid-afternoon, the ceremonies had continued for almost four hours, with six ministerial addresses having been given in addition to that of Pickard. The *British North American Wesleyan Methodist Magazine* was careful to point out, however, that 'not the slightest manifestation of weariness or satiety was visible to the last.'[2] The event had certainly been eagerly awaited, and the proceedings contrasted with the informality with which the academy had commenced operations in the preceding January. In the interim, the number of students had grown from the original seven to 30 in the spring term, divided equally between day scholars and boarders.[3] The formal opening represented the beginning of the first complete academic year, and as Pickard reviewed the prospects for the future he did so in the expectation of further growth in student numbers and in the belief that 'the sympathies of the public are enlisted.'[4]

Pickard's address began in general terms, as he alluded to the long association of Methodism and education which had begun with the Wesleys' attendance at Oxford University. For himself, he ackowledged that his position was one 'in which riper scholarship, greater tact, and more experienced skill might be well employed.'[5] As he was no doubt aware, the idea of recruiting a principal from Great Britain had not altogether been abandoned even as late as March 1843, when William Temple had written to Robert Alder in London that 'could we get a principal from home we should be able to take a higher stand, even though he might be inferior in attainments to H. Pickard.'[6] Now, however, the position was undoubtedly Pickard's and he resolved to enter it 'most cheerfully ... , humbly but confidently depending upon God for assistance in the discharge of its duties.'[7] In Pickard's view – and here he showed the influence of his mentor, Willbur Fisk – this was an auspicious time to enter upon such duties, for the importance of education was now beginning to be recognized at all levels of society: 'it is now generally acknowledged that any plan designed to elevate the human race which does not practically recognize its [education's] importance is fatally deficient, whether religious, or philosophically benevolent, or political motives, may have prompted the formation of that plan.'[8] Without a belief in education, therefore, even religious motives were likely to miscarry. Yet equally, for Pickard, education without a religious and moral purpose was absurd. The true goal of education, he argued, was to bring out the noblest aspects of the nature of the individual and of mankind: 'to raise him from indulgence in gratification merely animal, to participation with the higher orders of beings, in refined and elevating happiness, – to rescue him from degrading intimacy with objects of the earth, and lead him to seek acknowledged connexion and realized communion with God!' Pickard thus affirmed, as his fellow Methodist Egerton Ryerson had done in his own inaugural address as principal of Victoria College at Cobourg in 1842, that reason and religion were inseparable and that a rational education could and should have an ultimately religious purpose.[9]

The remainder of Pickard's inaugural address followed closely from that general principle, and dealt with certain essential requirements upon which would depend the success of the academy in fulfilling its mission. Some of his observations identified obvious necessities that needed little elaboration. Students would be required, for 'without these nothing can be done.'[10] Adequate funding was necessary in terms both of initial capital investment and of a continuing income. In discussing the former, Pickard paid tribute to the generosity of the founder, and to other lesser donations, which had enabled the academy building to be constructed and furnished. He reminded his listeners, however, that the academy was 'yet entirely destitute of Library, Apparatus, &c,' and he estimated that a further £2000 would have to be raised in order to supply this need and to pay off other remaining debts; encouraged by 'the liberality of many whose aid has been already given,' he was confident that the task would be accomplished.[11] For operating funds, the academy would depend on two major sources, tuition fees and government grants:

In order to extend the benefits of the Institution as widely as possible, the tuition fees are made so low, that from these we can expect to derive scarcely half the necessary income to maintain its full efficiency. But as its claims have already been acknowledged by the Legislatures of both Provinces, and as we hope that these will be strengthened by its usefulness, we expect that what is lacking will be supplied by their joint liberality.[12]

Pickard's expectations were borne out by the practical development of the academy's financing in the early years. From the beginning until 1857, the combined annual fee for board and tuition was fixed at a minimum of £25 and a maximum of £30, depending upon the level of classes attended, and in 1844 the provincial school inspector James Brown remarked upon this 'moderate price of Board and Tuition' in his report to the legislature.[13] Brown's report, which contained other favourable comments, strengthened the academy's claim to government funding. In the first three years of operation, provincial grants from New Brunswick and Nova Scotia averaged a total of some £411 per year, as opposed to £323 brought in by tuition fees. Such grants, although outstripped by the proceeds of tuition fees as enrolment grew, would continue to constitute an important part of the institution's financing until discontinued by New Brunswick in 1872 and Nova Scotia in 1881.[14]

Also essential to the success of the academy were the recruitment of teachers and the settlement of curriculum and discipline, and to these matters Pickard devoted considerable time in his address. Teachers, he warned, must not only be well qualified but also 'able and willing to labour, and interested, almost enthusiastically so, in their work,' and he expressed confidence in the staff now on hand.[15] In addition to Pickard himself, there were two teachers. The first to be appointed had been Joseph R. Hea, a young Methodist from the Miramichi, as tutor in French. Whatever academic qualifications and experience Hea may already have had, he was also enrolled as a student in the academy and would ultimately win a non-resident degree of BA from King's College, Fredericton, in 1849. Eleven years later, he would briefly be president of that institution, newly renamed the University of New Brunswick, before leaving academic life.[16] Thomas W. Wood, English master, had been brought to the academy from a grammar school teaching appointment in Richibucto, in Kent County, and it was to him that Pickard referred when he spoke of 'one of our number [who] is a tried man for the work.'[17] With assistance in various years from pupil teachers, or 'ushers,' Pickard, Hea, and Wood would constitute the academy's teaching staff for its first five years.

They taught a curriculum which was intended to affirm the essential unity of knowledge and religious belief, and oversaw a disciplinary regime which concerned itself with both intellectual and moral training. Indeed, Pickard made it clear in his address that curriculum and discipline were inseparable matters:

According to our definition of the term [education], the human being is to be prepared by it for the labours and joys of existence, – the mental powers must be strengthened and expanded to maturity, – the mind must be enriched with stores of knowledge more or less extensive, – habits of prompt, energetic, well-regulated, mental action must be formed, and the dispositions and affections thoroughly cultivated, and disciplined for undeviating rectitude of moral action. Let these be carefully sought, even in all the minor arrangements, and success will seldom be wanting; – let any one of them be disregarded, and full success will never be secured. A well-formed educational system seeks then, at the same time, and always, to secure constant improvement to the pupil in all these respects, – thus leading him ever onward to the formation of a mental and moral character, perfectly symmetrical ...[18]

There was symmetry too in the general principles of curriculum which Pickard went on to enunciate. 'Wisdom from the past' would be sought through classical study, for the surviving literature of Greece and Rome provided 'arks richly freighted with the brightest gems of thought, and the most valuable creations of genius.' But this would not be an exclusive preoccupation, for 'we shall also listen to the invitations of nature to examine her vast volume': scientific subjects and philosophical intepretations of the nature of mankind and the world would comprise the second major branch of study. In addition, however, Pickard drew attention to what would be 'infinitely our most valuable textbook.' Classical authors or 'the laboritories [*sic*] of nature' might sooner be dispensed with than the revelations of the Bible, for it was only by attending to the word of God, he declared, that 'men [might] be prepared to do good service to the cause of truth in our fallen world.'[19]

This stress upon the pre-eminence of biblical truths did not imply a curriculum dominated by theological subjects. On the contrary, the 40 subjects listed in the first academy catalogue included only two which had a directly religious content: evidences of Christianity, and Greek Testament. Here again Pickard's purpose was to indicate that all knowledge, however gathered, was knowledge of a divinely ordered universe. It was a point made explicitly in the class on evidences of Christianity, which was undoubtedly based on the works of the Anglican archdeacon William Paley. Paley, whose conclusions on natural theology were widely taught not only in academies but also in almost every English-speaking college in British North America up until the 1870s, had argued that an examination of nature showed unmistakable evidence of an overall design, one that could only be divine in origin. In responding to the criticisms of Christianity which had been levelled by the Enlightenment thinkers of the eighteenth century, he had thus affirmed not only the harmony but also the indivisibility of empirical and revealed knowledge.[20] In this context, it was natural for Pickard to emphasize the religious purpose of an academy curriculum which was essentially literary and scientific. The same principle also provided additional substantiation for the important distinction between a denominational institution, which the academy avowedly was, and a sectarian one, which it equally avowedly was not: it was denominational not only in that it was operated by the Methodists but also in that it offered a Christian education; but its teaching would favour no particularly Methodist theological bent.

Both evidences of Christianity and Greek Testament, therefore, were integrated into more general curricular categories. There were three such categories, defined 'for the purpose of securing the advantages of method and regularity, and at the same time accommodating different Classes of Students ...' The primary course, initially the largest in terms of student numbers, consisted of basic instruction in six areas: geography, English grammar, arithmetic, parsing, history, and 'First Lessons in Composition and Penmanship.'[21] The second, or literary and scientific, course was based on mathematical, philosophical, and scientific subjects, and in the second catalogue, that of 1844–5, this was specifically described as a course occupying two years or four terms. In the first year, algebra, geometry, and French would be studied in both terms, together with chemistry in the first term and natural philosophy in the second. During the second year, the prescribed subjects comprised trigonometry, mensuration, mental philosophy, evidences of Christianity, rhetoric, logic, moral philosophy, astronomy, and political economy. Each of these would be studied for one term, while in the first term of the second year the student would exercise his only choice: whether to study French or mineralogy and geology.[22] The third, or classical, course was the most rigorous offered by the academy and no precise time period was specified for its completion. In addition to all the subjects studied in the two other courses, seventeen areas of classical study were prescribed, including exercises in Latin and Greek, Greek Testament, major authors in both languages, and ancient history and geography. In the academy's formal curriculum, therefore, classical study was prominent, though not dominant.[23]

In addition to the subjects which comprised the three courses, additional classes were advertised as available when requested by a sufficient number of students, chiefly in practical subjects such as bookkeeping, land surveying, and navigation. In the era of Sackville's development as a port, the navigation class must have seemed an especially appropriate venture, although enrolment was initially disappointing: only two students in each of the first two years. In 1845, navigation and surveying were combined and the enrolment reached 25 in the following year, before declining again; in 1849 navigation was dropped and the class continued in surveying only.[24] By 1850 a further practical subject had been added in the form of a course of lectures on 'Scientific Agriculture,' which drew praise from the *Wesleyan* as an example of the determination of the academy's officers 'to render the INSTITUTION as efficient as possible in the great work of education, popular, practical and scientific; and to maintain its just claims on the already well-earned patronage of the Public.'[25]

Thus, the Wesleyan Academy offered a wide range of possible studies. As Pickard had made clear in his inaugural address when discussing the matter of fees, it was intended also to attract students from a wide range of social backgrounds. To be sure, the more advanced courses were clearly preparing students for entry into the higher strata of provincial society. One speaker reflected on the day of the formal opening that at the academy 'the teacher will be fitted to take charge of youth, the minister to instruct his fellow men, the magistrate to enforce human law, the judge to decide upon legal cases in dispute.'[26] Some years later, when the minister Richard Knight addressed the academy students on the virtues of a liberal education, he defined such an education as 'an amount of attainment by which the student may be able, not merely to move on the common-place arena of life, *but*, should Providence so open his path, to move forward with ease, dignity, and advantage, in the higher walks of this life's activities and professions.'[27] Furthermore, the academy's governing committee was well aware of the value of attracting students from well-to-do families, as Enoch Wood made clear in a letter to Alder in late 1843, in which he rejoiced at the prosperity of the academy and noted that those attending included the sons of several prominent merchants who were not Methodists; among them was the son of Hugh Johnston, a Presbyterian merchant of Saint John who was a member of both the legislative and the executive councils of New Brunswick.[28] The claim of the academy to offer popular education did not represent any desire for social levelling. None the less, the claim was substantiated both by the deliberate effort to provide classes in practical subjects outside of the regular academic courses, and the stated aim of holding down fees so as to open the benefits of all the courses, as another speaker declared at the opening ceremony in June 1843, 'to the attainment of those who would aspire to them from the lower and humble vales of life.'[29] Lack of biographical information on most of the students precludes any confident statement as to how far this aim was translated into reality, though Pickard in 1848 described the academy as a 'large family made up of individuals from so many different families, and so many different places, and so many different ranks in our provincial society ...'[30] One of the students of the first year was James Dawson, a twenty-year-old Methodist carpenter from Bathurst who offered his carpentry services in place of monetary payment in order 'to come to the Academy for one term or two.' Dawson in fact took little time to complete the primary course, and he then proceeded to the literary and scientific course, in which he was enrolled for at least part of each year from 1844 to 1847.[31] In this case, the academy had certainly succeeded in its chosen role.

It was also the academy's purpose, as Allison had made clear from the start, to serve a geographically varied constituency, embracing the whole of the Maritime region. In early 1844 the *New Brunswick Courier* noted with approval that students had been attracted 'from a great variety of places from Kingston, Canada West, to Cape Breton.' The article looked forward too to the introduction of steam transportation links which would facilitate the attendance of students from Newfoundland.[32] In point of fact, the impression given by the *Courier* article was somewhat premature. The student referred to from Kingston was an exceptional case, the only non-Maritime resident of the 80 students who had attended the academy at various times during 1843; he was attempting to live down an unfavourable reputation gathered while attending the academy at Cobourg some years before.[33] The student body in the academy's first year was drawn in large measure from the immediate vicinity of Sackville: 27.5 per cent of the students came from Sackville itself, while the combined proportion from Westmorland County (including Sackville) and the adjoining Nova Scotia county of Cumberland was no less than 57.5 per cent. None the less, this left a substantial minority of those coming from elsewhere, and in the course of the first five years this minority would become a large majority. In each of the years 1845, 1846, and 1847, the percentage of students from Sackville was less than half of what it had been in 1843, while the proportion of those from the two local counties stood at a little more or a little less than 30 per cent. Most of the students came from New Brunswick, with large annual contingents from Saint John, though a substantial number – normally more than one-quarter and sometimes more than one-third – were from Nova Scotia. At least one student in each year came from Prince Edward Island, while the first Newfoundland student attended in 1845. Thus, the Wesleyan Academy was soon able to claim with good reason that it was a regional institution rather than purely a local or even a provincial one.[34]

In terms of student numbers, the institution prospered also, with the 80 students of the first year rising to 131 in the second year and thereafter continuing to rise gradually. Not all of these would attend at the same time, but in the third term of 1844 the attendance rose to a record figure of 93.[35] As early as October 1843, Enoch Wood had confided to Alder that 'the Sackville Academy prospers beyond the expectations of its best friends';[36] in the following year his optimism was confirmed by the favourable report of the provincial school inspector James Brown. Brown's arrival in the Sackville district in October 1844 came after he had spent several weeks inspecting schools in other parts of New Brunswick, and he visited several small private schools in Sackville and the adjoining parishes before proceeding to the academy. The first mention of the institution in his journal concerned the view across the marsh from the nearby settlement of Point de Bute, and his observation bore out the description of Sackville in the academy catalogue as 'a retired country village':[37]

From a rising ground near the residence of Mr. [Thompson] Trueman, had a fine view of the country. In front lay the great Tantramar Marsh covered with innumerable stacks of hay, and extending many miles in every direction. Far on the left, and bounded by the forest in the rear, and the great marsh in front, lay the settlements of Sackville, the Academy on Mount Allison conspicuous among the other buildings.[38]

A few days later, on 12 October, Brown visited the academy in the company of Charles Allison. It happened that the day was a Saturday, a half-day for the students, and also that the fall term had only just begun, so that Brown's observations were not made on a typical day. None the less, in his report to the New Brunswick legislature in the following month, he made detailed comments on those classes he was able to attend:

The class in Chemistry was taught by question, answer and explanation. Geometry, Algebra, and the higher branches of Arithmetic, were all orally taught and demonstrated; the Students by turn, under the eye of the instructor, and in presence of the class, drawing their own Geometrical Figures, or working out the Algebraic and Arithmetical examples, with chalk on the Black Board, and then severally subjecting the same to audible and ocular demonstration. Many useful portions of Arithmetic were performed mentally in answer to questions put by the Tutor, and much was also done with slate and pencil. Geography was taught chiefly by means of Maps and Black Boards; in the latter case, the most prominent features and outlines of certain portions of the earth were drawn out and represented with chalk by the students, and afterwards minutely pointed out and described. Reading and English Grammar were taught carefully and thoroughly. Writing was taught in the usual manner, and the specimens were generally very good.

The students, Brown observed, were well dressed, well fed, and cheerful, and he also gave an account of the ages of the 84 who were in attendance at the time of his visit: 'six are under 10 years of age, eleven are over 10 and under 12, thirteen over 12 and under 14, twenty four over 14 and under 16, fifteen over 16 and under 18, seven over 18 and under 20, and eight 20 years old and upwards.' Largely, therefore, this was an institution for teenage boys, though the primary department included a number of younger pupils, and there were also a few who, like James Dawson, were older and were making up for the lack of educational opportunity earlier in their lives. Brown had only one criticism – that the library, while sufficient for immediate needs, was 'yet small' – and he closed his report with generous praise. 'Taken altogether,' he wrote, '... the Wesleyan Academy is, perhaps, the very best Educational Establishment in the province.'[39]

For a new institution, James Brown's was a remarkably thoroughgoing endorsement from a neutral and well-qualified observer. By the time Brown's report was considered by the provincial legislature in 1845, however, the academy would be on the point of a crisis which would seem briefly to threaten its very existence. Enoch Wood had foreshadowed the episode when he had informed Alder in October 1844 that certain New Brunswick Anglicans were inclined to view the Sackville academy as a threat to King's College, Fredericton, and as 'an antagonist institution.'[40] Although the promoters of the academy had avoided public comparisons with King's, there was no doubt that the success of the Sackville institution had been used by the enemies of the college as a propaganda weapon, and there was thus some justification for the attitude described by Wood. In April 1844, for example, the brusque Chatham merchant and legislative councillor Joseph Cunard had taken the opportunity offered by the debate on the annual New Brunswick grant to the academy to declare that 'there was an institution in Fredericton which cost very large sums annually, and did not meet the views of the country; and which had but very few students; while the institution at Sackville had something like seventy, and gave very general satisfaction.'[41] In the following August, the comparison was again made publicly, in a letter published in the *Courier* under the pseudonym of 'Omega,' which discouraged parents from sending their sons to King's and urged the representatives of the Sackville academy to come out in opposition to the college's legislative grant.[42] This in turn evoked a bitter reply in the form of a letter to another newspaper, the

Loyalist and Conservative Advocate, in September. The writer, 'Homunculus,' denounced Omega as 'a puffer of the Sackville Academy' and went on to satirize both the academy and Humphrey Pickard. Surely, he suggested, the college students could be sent to Sackville instead: 'there the little dears would be made fat and sleek, and beautiful to behold; and, if we may believe the illustrious president, that Master of Rhetoric, – fitted in the twinkling of a bed post to instruct, not only the inhabitants of this lower world, but the very Saints in Glory.'[43]

In itself, this attack had limited significance, and the editor of the newspaper carefully dissociated himself from any adverse reflections on the academy. None the less, as the correspondence provoked by Omega continued during September and October 1844, it might well have been taken as a warning that any indiscretion, particularly one which concerned the religious character of the academy, would be seized upon as part of the ongoing college controversy. For Enoch Wood, and for his counterpart William Temple in Nova Scotia, such a warning was hardly necessary, in view of their experience in efforts to gain and secure legislative funding. In Nova Scotia, the principle of government aid to denominational schools and colleges had but narrowly survived the assaults of William Annand and Joseph Howe in the assembly in 1843, while in Fredericton the marshalling of political support for the academy was for Wood a constant concern.[44] No such inhibitions, however, weighed upon the governor and chaplain of the academy, Albert DesBrisay. In the spring of 1844, DesBrisay had been relieved of most of the administrative duties of his position as governor, for which, as Wood informed Alder, he had proved unsuited. In the future, continued Wood, 'he will now have only to attend to religious duties, with the exception of a General oversight of the Buildings and Grounds, an engagement most suitable to his habits and talents.'[45] How seriously DesBrisay took his now full-time chaplaincy became apparent on 5 March 1845 when A.E. Botsford rose in the legislative council of New Brunswick to describe 'a circumstance which had lately transpired at the Academy, which in his opinion must have a tendency to injure, very seriously, the character of the Institution.' Botsford had been informed that a revival meeting had been held 'and that all the Students had become converts to Methodism, with a few exceptions,' and he concluded that this was 'a species of "Fanatiscism" [*sic*] (he could call it by no other name) which he could not subscribe to.'[46]

Botsford, an Anglican and a member of one of Westmorland County's most prominent Loyalist families, described himself as having 'ever been a warm friend of the Institution,' and he had in fact been among those who had attended the opening ceremony in 1843.[47] Another councillor who had supported the academy was Hugh Johnston, the Presbyterian merchant whose son was enrolled in the classical course; Johnston still had words of praise for the institution, but admitted that if the report of the revival meeting were true, 'it would tend very much to destroy the character of that Establishment.'[48] Johnston's fear, in his own mind at least, was soon confirmed in a letter from E.B. Chandler of Dorchester, a colleague on the legislative council and himself an Anglican whose ten-year-old son was enrolled in the primary course at the academy. Drafting his reply to Johnston's appeal for information, Chandler on 22 March 1845 supplied a detailed description of what had taken place:

I fear that there is too much truth in the reports which have reached you in regard to the religious excitement at the Sackville academy during the present Winter. I have not yet [had] an opportunity of making any enquiries of Mr. Allison, but I presume the main facts cannot be denied. It is said that during the Winter several scholars had been in the habit of congregating together during evenings in some of their Private Rooms and then join aloud in praying and singing, in which if not directly instigated, they were at least encouraged by the Chaplain or Principal, Mr. DesBrisay, who altho I believe a very good man, yet is a great enthusiast, and consequently [illegible] of Revivals and excitements so called. Matters proceeded in this way for some time, when some of them would pray aloud in the lecture room at the close of the day when all the scholars as also Mr. DesBrisay were present. This led to further prayers and exhortations and an invitation by Mr. DesBrisay for all who *wished* to come forward to the *Altar* as it was called urging them I presume by the usual incentives ... and many, in fact nearly all went forward and professed to be moved. ... Your son Hugh however and a few others were impenitent and did not join. My little boy George ... went up with others [and] knelt at the *Altar* shed tears and thought he was Converted – and when he returned home a day or two after, appeared much dejected and unwilling to return, and after being home a day, called his Mother aside and told her, that he was Converted – and that he was *afraid he was a Methodist*.[49]

Chandler believed that the public discussion of this episode would effectively discourage any repetition and he decided therefore to allow his son, now 'thoroughly cured of his *conversion*,' to continue attending the academy for the time being.[50] The legislative council had apparently reached the same conclusion, and the actual threat to the academy's grant lasted only two days. It had already been approved by the assembly on 1 March, before the storm had broken; the council, having deferred its consideration on the 13th in view of Botsford's disclosure, assented on the 15th without a division.[51] Basic questions had been raised, however, about the academy's role and responsibilities, and the matter was not altogether clarified by the publication in the *Courier* on 22 March of statements agreed upon by a general meeting of the students a week before. The students agreed that 'more than usual interest has recently been felt and manifested on the subject of Religion,' but denied that this had been allowed to interfere either with the academic routine of the school or with the several denominational allegiances of those attending. No attempt had been made to make converts to Methodism, and as far as they knew no student had become a Methodist. They concluded that Botsford's information had been false and his informant 'shamefully careless or malignantly wicked.'[52] Enoch Wood, by the end of the month, harboured suspicions that the report had originated with John Black, the Anglican minister in Sackville, and expressed to Alder the hope that he could soon confirm the identity of the 'slanderer,' and 'try to improve ... [his] cautiousness if not his conscientiousness.'[53]

What to make of this direct contradiction of information which Chandler had investigated and found to be accurate? In part, the answer lay in Methodist theology. Conversion, for Wesley, had been a necessary stage in the spiritual development of all Christians, and did not necessarily imply that the convert would then join the Methodist denomination. It was entirely possible that he would continue in association with another denomination altogether and would progress towards sanctification in that context. Such was evidently the view of conversion held by DesBrisay when he reported to the New Brunswick District meeting in May 1845. In March, his health had again broken down; but by May he was able to 'record the loving-kindness of the Lord in visiting the Institution, during the past winter, with the awakening influences of the Holy Spirit – arousing attention of many of the youth to serious concern for salvation.' According to DesBrisay, there were several who had 'given evidence of a change of heart'; but he made no mention of any proselytes to Methodism.[54] Furthermore, religious revivals comprised an accepted part of student life at many contemporary Protestant colleges in the United States. Oberlin College in Ohio was the scene of an almost continuous series of revivals between 1836 and 1842, while those held at Wesleyan University in Connecticut were obviously of even more immediate significance to Mount Allison, since it was there that Pickard had undergone his own conversion.[55] Pickard himself entered the lists of the controversy on 18 March, with a letter to the *Courier* in which he denied any suggestion of proselytism, but also contested a reported assertion by Botsford that the academy had sought to downplay its religious character when applying for government funding. 'Christian parents of all denominations would have wisely feared to place their sons in an Institution where they would be "perfectly free from all religious restraint."' The academy, he continued, was 'a Christian – a Wesleyan Institution,' but that did not imply that pupils of other denominations would not have their beliefs respected.[56]

For all that, the controversy had touched upon a real ambiguity, for as Botsford remarked in a reply to Pickard's letter, 'it ever has been, and is a controverted question as to what extent religious instruction can be imparted in any Institution for the *general* education of youth of different Denominations. ...'[57] Ultimately, the episode did not seriously damage the prosperity of the Wesleyan Academy. It did, however, help to define its character. Revivals would continue to occur intermittently throughout the nineteenth century, and – despite Pickard's occasional expressions of discouragement in his journal at the indifference of the more 'thoughtless and careless' among the students – one former student would recall that in the 1850s, 'the Quaker's designation of the Methodist Chapel, a converting furnace, might be given to the old Academy. Dr. Pickard was accustomed to make powerful appeals to the students to decide for Christ.'[58] At the same time, efforts to attract recruits to Methodism were consistently disclaimed. For some non-Methodist parents such an assurance was unacceptable; so it was for Hugh Johnston, who withdrew his son from the academy in the spring of 1845. For others, the high academic reputation of the institution was enough justification for their children's attendance. More generally, the whole principle of public support of denominational institutions would continue to be debated both in New Brunswick and in Nova Scotia, and the eventual result in each province would be its discontinuance. As for the academy, Enoch Wood would later reflect that DesBrisay was lacking in tact; but even he would have agreed with Charles Allison when he assured a correspondent on 27 March 1845 that the officers of the institution 'have not ceased (and GOD forbid they ever should) to impress constantly upon the minds of the youth committed to their charge, the superior claims which Religion ought always to have upon their attention. ...'[59]

Much of the bitterness of the revival controversy of 1845 had proceeded from the issue which underlay all debate on educational matters in New Brunswick at the time: the state of King's College. Those who supported the college and saw the growth of denominational academies as a threat to its well-being could hardly avoid relishing the embarrassment of the Sackville institution. On the other hand, it was ironic to the Methodists that the academy should be vilified for its religious character when Anglicanism was so firmly entrenched at King's. This point was made in the *Courier* by Pickard during his increasingly acrimonious correspondence with Botsford in March and April 1845, and again shortly afterwards by a Saint John resident writing under the pseudonym of 'Observer,' who accused Botsford of wishing to preserve King's College at the expense of the denominational academies so as to retain power and privilege for 'the favoured class.'[60] Botsford, for his part, protested that he remained a friend of the academy despite 'the impertinence of its conceited principal.'[61] Furthermore, on 15 March, the same day on which the legislative council had passed the appropriation for the grant to the Wesleyan Academy, Botsford had been one of the legislative councillors who had successfully voted for the passage of a bill to amend the charter of King's College. Despite suspicions and recriminations which periodically arose, particularly between the assembly and the council, the need for reform of the college had come to be widely recognized, especially as some £47,000 in government grants had been invested since the re-establishment of 1829 without making the institution conspicuously successful. The meaure adopted in March 1845 – though its proclamation would be delayed for almost two years, to the distress of the assembly, on account of objections raised by the lieutenant-governor, Sir William Colebrooke, and the colonial office in London – was a moderate reform, relaxing the hold of the Church of England upon the college in a number of repects. Most important, it opened membership of the college council to non-Anglicans.[62]

Colebrooke's preference had been for a more radical reform, though one which would have effectively preserved the Anglican character of King's College. Since 1844, he had been advocating to the colonial secretary, Lord Stanley, that a central federated university should be established in the province, along the lines of the University of London. Under such a scheme, students from the various denominational institutions would be eligible, on equal terms with those of King's College, for degrees awarded by the university. In Colebrooke's opinion, both the Wesleyan academy and the Baptist school in Fredericton were 'respectable Seminaries,' and although he was himself a high Anglican he deprecated attacks upon them by 'the Church party.'[63] In the spring of 1846, Colebrooke confided his plan to Enoch Wood, who informed Alder that 'as to its proposed relationship to the Literary Institutions of Evangelical Bodies, differing from the Episcopalians, it exactly meets our views, provided the principle can be fairly and honestly worked out in detail.'[64] Ultimately, it was the reform passed by the legislature in 1845 which received royal assent in late 1846 and was finally proclaimed on 3 February 1847, and not the plan for a federated university. Even so, Colebrooke took the opportunity to give King's College a more representative character by including non-Anglicans in the composition of its reformed council. Among the new members were the Methodists L.A. Wilmot and George S. Hill. To Wood, Colebrooke 'stated distinctly he had appointed

Messrs. Wilmot and Hill to be Members of the College Council ... because they were Wesleyans.'[65] Also under the new regulations, provision was made for non-resident students to take examinations and obtain degrees at King's College, and Wood commented just over three weeks after the new act's proclamation that 'several of our Sackville Scholars have already entered.'[66] In anticipation of the change, the academy catalogue of 1846 had already added a 'collegiate course' to the existing three courses. It would comprise 'such Studies, in addition to those of the preceding Courses, as will prepare Students for the successive Annual Examinations, requisite for admission to the Degree of Bachelor of Arts, at KING'S COLLEGE, Fredericton.'[67]

The number of those students availing themselves of this opportunity was apparently not large, as students of the collegiate course were not separately listed in the academy catalogue until 1852. None the less, the change represented the beginning of higher educational instruction in Sackville. By 1851, Humphrey Pickard, in addition to his position as principal, carried the title of 'Professor of Mental and Moral Science, &c. &c.' His brother Thomas, who was also a graduate of Wesleyan University and had replaced Thomas Wood on the academy staff in 1849, was 'Professor of Mathematics, Natural Science, &c. &c.' Hea, by now a graduate of King's College, was 'Professor of the French, Latin and Greek Languages, &c. &c.' Thus, in this year the entire teaching staff consisted of university graduates. In 1852, when Hea resigned and opened a private school at Lower Horton, Nova Scotia, he was replaced by Alexander S. Reid, a Scot who until then had been principal of the Wesleyan day school in Halifax. Although not a graduate, Reid had attended the University of Edinburgh in his younger days, and would leave Sackville in 1859 to become principal of the newly established Wesleyan Academy in St John's, Newfoundland.[68] The catalogues for 1851 and 1852 also showed revision of the curriculum, by which the literary and scientific course and the classical course were no longer differentiated. Instead, their elements were combined to form a two-year intermediate course and a four-year collegiate course. The intermediate course included some training in Latin, but also stressed geography, history, English grammar and reading, arithmetic and algebra, along with practical subjects such as penmanship and bookkeeping. The collegiate course included the study of both Greek and Latin authors, although in each of the four years classical subjects were outnumbered by scientific or philosophical ones.[69]

In 1852, of a total student body of 128, the collegiate department accounted for 22, the intermediate department for 84 and the substantially unchanged primary department for 22. Of those in the collegiate department, however, not all were following the full course, as the catalogue listed nine students who were omitting one or both of the classical languages.[70] It was in the same year that the editor of the *Wesleyan*, in an angry protest against the drawing of the academy into the concurrent arguments over college education in Nova Scotia, made an important and revealing distinction: 'the Sackville institution *is not* a COLLEGE, nor does it pretend to be a College, in the properly understood sense of the word, though in effect affording a "Collegiate Course" of education.' From the start, the academy's curriculum had been sufficiently wide-ranging to invite comparison with those offered in the colleges of the region, and its success in attracting students from all three provinces and beyond had underscored the fact that this was no mere local institution. The introduction of collegiate work was a natural extension of the existing curriculum, but did not as yet betoken any fundamental shift in the character of the institution. As the editor of the *Wesleyan*, Alexander McLeod, implied, the academy offered a variety of educational services to its constituency, of which the collegiate course was now one. It would not be for some years, and only after much soul-searching and debate, that the matter of whether or not to found a college in Sackville would be resolved. In the meantime, as McLeod summarized in his editorial, the institution was 'an ACADEMY, with a competent staff of Professors and subordinate Teachers, designed from the beginning to give its students a *thorough*, *well-grounded*, *extensive*, and *systemaic* SECULAR EDUCATION, in connection with due attention to morals, and the fundamental principles of divine truth.'[71]

One person who professed the utmost respect for the academy and for its service to society was Amos Purdy, a student enrolled in the literary and scientific course in 1846 and 1847, who wrote to his father in Wallace, Nova Scotia, in late 1846 that 'this is most assuredly an elegant Institution and is doing a great deal of good to the young and rising generation.'[72] His verdict may have been influenced by the fact that he was writing the letter as a class exercise under the supervision of Joseph Hea; but Purdy's letters, along with a few others which have survived from the early years of the academy, provide rare glimpses of the students' way of life. Two years previously, in July 1844, the daily routine had been described by Allen Otty, whose literary style was effective although not altogether a credit to the literary and scientific course in which he too was enrolled:

I like this school very much they ar very srict we have to be up at half past five and have an half a hour to dress then we have for to go to prers which help is a bout an half hour after that we return to ourown bedrooms and stay ther till half past seven and then go to breckfast after breckfast play till nine then go to chool till twlve cumout to dinner go in chool a geen at one and stay ther till fore and then we have till seven to ourslevs then we have to go to our own roomes and stay ther till bed time all the lits must be put out by ten oclock.

For relaxation on the half-holiday which was observed each Saturday, Otty would occasionally borrow a gun and go off to shoot pigeons. More usually, though, he wrote, 'making flies is our chief amusement when we can get feathers.' His brother Robert, enrolled in the classical department, added a more pointed postscript: 'we have half a day in the week to ourselves and then can make flies as there is nothing els to do.'[73]

By the time Amos Purdy attended the academy, extracurricular activities were becoming more organized, and he himself participated in the inauguration of certain long-lived Mount Allison student traditions. In early 1847, he described the foundation of the first student newspaper, 'The Mount Allison Students Repository,' which had emerged out of Pickard's composition class. Published weekly, it consisted of two long sheets of paper, was read aloud to all the students each Saturday morning at 10:30, and opened its columns to 'all kinds of composition of different sciences; anything that is amusing; and also a corner for jokes; but all must be governed with a sense of propriety.' The editor was elected by secret ballot each month, though Pickard took the precaution of naming the candidates himself.[74] The foundation of a debating society in the following September was apparently an initiative of the students themselves, as Purdy was appointed one of a deputation 'to wait on Mr. Pickard to obtain his sanction to our proceedings and also to get his leave to occupy the classical school room as our regular debating apartment. ...'[75] Earlier in the year, however, Amos had been less enthusiastic about one of the first musical efforts at the academy: 'Mr. Hea is in the Lecture room trying to form a choir of singers and devote 2 hours every Wednesday evening during the term in displaying their vocal powers. I do not intend to join it.'[76] Nor was he impressed a few days later by the tea meeting which he attended at the Sackville temperance hall at a cost of one shilling and sixpence, for it was 'not to be compared to our tea meetings [in Wallace, NS] not by a long chalk either for regulations or order.'[77]

Amos did not elaborate on the nature of the disorder at the tea meeting, but he did go into detail on the dangers of the game of hurley, a forerunner of hockey. Hurley was played in the academy yard with sticks and a leather-covered ball which another student later described as 'a very ugly missile about one's shins.'[78] For Amos Purdy, the threat was not the ball but a high stick that caught him above the left eye and gave him a severe bruise. 'This however will be a warning to me for the future,' he reflected philosophically, 'and perhaps save me from greater misfortune by my determination not to engage in such games again although there is no other game at this season of the year that we can derive any exercise from.'[79] For all that, the students must have been kept fit not only by sports but also by cutting wood to fuel the small stoves which heated all the bedrooms. By Purdy's account, the amounts cut were impressively large, for he described 'such a pile of wood as I never saw before,' comprising some 300 cords. He himself expected to cut 20 cords during the winter season.[80] However, of all Amos Purdy's impressions of life at the academy, perhaps the most vivid was derived from Humphrey Pickard's class in natural philosophy:

This week [he wrote on 12 March 1847] has been occupied with the study of Electricity which is of a very curious nature. While we were performing some experiments today in the Lecture room with the Electrifying machine ... the school was dismissed for noon. The boys being anxious to share in our fun soon crowded into the room. Mr. Pickard after getting through with his class course requested them to join hands and form a ring around the room if they wanted to feel how it operated. Some were quite reluctant but he assured them that it would not injure them so they formed a ring with more than fifty boys. The machine was put in motion and the Electricity extracted from it by a box with brass nubs on the top which is called the battery as soon as he collected a sufficient quantity of Electric fluid he placed the battery upon a table placed between two of the boys in the ring. One of the boys took hold a nub for the purpose, and the boy on the other side as soon as the other boys of which the ring was composed had grasped each others hands presented his nuckle to the nubs on the top of the battery but no sooner had he done this the Electricity being attracted by the finger the shock was received by all in the ring with equal intensity. Some jumped, some hollowed, some rubbed their arms and others their legs which caused a merry laugh by Mr. Picard [*sic*] and our class. I have had two shocks myself and also each one in the class but I cannot tell you how it feels.[81]

Purdy was obviously not alone in his fascination with this particular experiment, for when a large number of former students assembled on 19 January 1853 to celebrate the tenth anniversary of the academy's opening, the account in the *Wesleyan* noted that 'in one corner of the lecture room a numerous party were receiving shocks from an electrifying machine. ...'[82] The electrical generator, of course, was never used as an instrument of discipline. Indeed, in the academy's early years, corporal punishment in any form was avoided, and a laudatory article in the *Courier* in October 1844 commented on this 'new principle of government [that] has been introduced here – that of *moral* instead of *physical* force.'[83] As years went on, however, this principle was evidently not strictly observed, as a former student recalled that Pickard had kept two riding whips in his office and had used them on occasion with 'judicial impartiality.'[84] Pickard's own thoughts on discipline had been summarized in his inaugural address: 'we do not promise to furnish the remedial appliances of a Penitentiary in order to restore to virtue and rectitude those who have been corrupted and ruined elsewhere, but we do promise that with most diligent prayerful care we will guard all from being qualified here as candidates for Penitentiaries.'[85]

Ironically enough, in the fall of 1847, two academy students were indeed unfortunate enough to be sent to jail in nearby Dorchester for non-payment of highway taxes. Some 20 of the students had refused to be assessed in Sackville, on the grounds that they were not Sackville residents, but had been unable to produce certificates that they had paid elsewhere. For the highway overseer, Captain Thomas Robson, this was not good enough, and two – including William Tuck of Saint John, a future chief justice of New Brunswick – were successfully sued. Still refusing to pay, each was sent to Dorchester for a week, and Amos Purdy recorded that the intention of 'the mean overseerers' was 'to sue one every week and send him over as soon as the other came out.' Apparently, though, the boys successfully called Robson's bluff, as no more of their number were incarcerated. It had not been an unduly rigorous confinement even for the two scapegoats: the first one jailed had been visited on Saturday afternoon by a group of his fellows, who discovered that 'he was not locked up but the goaler [*sic*] had given him full liberty of his house, he had plenty of company and in good spirits.'[86] Tuck himself testified almost fifty years later that he had congenial memories of the week he had spent at Dorchester, 'getting good food and enjoying the society of pleasant companions.'[87]

Underlying this episode, comical as it must have been at the time, was an important question: how would the residents of the small town of Sackville respond to the gathering in their midst of a substantial group of students drawn from across the Maritime provinces and beyond? The attempt to have the students assessed for highway tax in Sackville was clearly an indication of a determination to make the academy pay its way in the community, and it foreshadowed later arguments over whether the Mount Allison institutions should pay local property taxes. A more basic element of conflict was also begun in the earliest years, and would recur intermittently later on: an academy student of the early 1860s, who had grown up in Sackville, recalled skirmishes between academy boys and groups of boys from Upper Sackville and Westcock who 'resented the imaginary high-toned manners of the school.'[88] Nor were all local residents content to have the educational life of their community dominated by the academy, and an attempt to found a Mechanics' Institute in Sackville in 1848 – though short-lived – was interpreted by one contemporary as reflecting a desire 'not to be indebted to the Academy folks for "culture."'[89]

Nevertheless, there were also good reasons for town and academy to coexist harmoniously. For the academy, the choice of Sackville as a location had been no accident. Allison had particularly stressed the advantages of its geographical position, and its rural surroundings were frequently described with pride. Year after year, the catalogue declared that 'Sackville is a retired country village, pleasant and healthy, and easy of access from all parts of the Lower Provinces.'[90] To the community, the academy brought advantages of its own. The obvious ones were educational and cultural: the institution provided an inexpensive and thorough education for many local young people, and also provided public lectures and entertainments of a kind which would otherwise have been infrequent at best. Members of the academy, whether students or teachers, also participated in the church life of Sackville, as part of the Methodist congregation and by supporting events such as the missionary meeting in the winter of 1852 which was attended by 'the whole of the Reverend and Lay Faculty of the Academy.'[91] Furthermore, the academy brought economic benefits to the local community. While the number of local employees was small at first – in the second half of the nineteenth century, Mount Allison would grow to the point where it would be one of the major employers in the town – purchases of goods and services inevitably had a stimulating economic effect. The students themselves were not encouraged to spend large amounts of money, for the catalogue of 1844–5 contained an admonition that was repeated annually thenceforward: 'Parents and Guardians are *earnestly advised* that lads should be furnished *very sparingly*, if at all, with spending money.'[92] The academy accounts of the same year, however, showed an expenditure of £1031/3/2 for 'Provisions, Stewards Salary, Servants Wages, and other Expenses for Students Commons.'[93] Virtually all of that sum would find its way into the local economy, as well as lesser sums spent for such items as repairs to the building, and the amounts spent by staff members from their salaries. Since most of the institution's income – whether from government grants or from students' fees – originated outside the local area, there was clearly a substantial net gain. In later years, as the campus grew and demanded more extensive and costly services from the town, while maintaining exemption from property tax, the balance of advantage would be more difficult to define precisely, but the importance of Mount Allison and the overall benefits which it provided would continue to be generally recognized. Also not to be discounted were the efforts made to provide instruction in such areas as navigation, scientific agriculture, and bookkeeping, which had an obvious application to local pursuits.

Thus, there were links between the academy and the community that were important to both. They were reflected in the participation of academy members and local residents in events of mutual interest. The academy examinations were held twice each year, for after the first year the academic calendar had been divided into two terms, one from January to June and the other from August to December. The examinations were held in public and consisted of questions addressed to the students of the various classes for immediate answer. The examinations were concluded by the delivery of orations by the more senior students, for which they had been trained in classes held every two weeks in 'Public Declamation.' In June 1846, the declamations were given before a crowd which overflowed the main lecture room of the academy. The *British North American Wesleyan-Methodist Magazine* recorded that the room was 'literally crowded with Ladies and Gentlemen ... whilst large numbers were outside endeavouring to listen at the windows.' The session was followed by a public lecture by Charles DeWolfe, future theological professor at Mount Allison College and then a minister in Windsor, Nova Scotia, in which he expounded on the unity of science and religion. The attendance was no less than 700, and exemplified the popularity of the academy's closing exercises as an entertainment for visitors and townspeople alike.[94] Equally, the academy recognized major events in the life of the town. The launching of a large vessel from one of the shipyards, for example, was reason for a half holiday, and a few of the students were customarily allowed to be on board the vessel being launched. On at least one occasion, the older students assisted in dislodging a ship that had stuck on the ways.[95] The relationship between the Wesleyan Academy and the community of Sackville, despite its tensions and occasional conflicts, was a close one and conferred benefits on both sides.

The relationship between academy and community was also a dynamic one, evolving through time. The social and economic make-up of Sackville would change, as the shipbuilding industry rose and fell between the 1840s and the 1880s, and as the town was then affected by the short-lived development of heavy industry in the Maritimes in the last decades of the nineteenth century. The academy evolved too, and in 1847 a major change was first contemplated. On July 3rd, in Sackville, a joint meeting of the New Brunswick and Nova Scotia districts passed a resolution in favour of 'the necessity and desirableness of establishing an Institution under the controal [*sic*] of our Church similar to that we have in the case of the Sackville Academy for the religious education of

Females.' The resolution did not specify that the proposed academy for girls would be located in Sackville, but it did appoint Pickard in his capacity as principal to investigate the feasibility of the plan.[96] In the following year, the New Brunswick district heard and accepted a proposal by 'the Wesleyans and their Friends, in Sackville and its Neighbourhood' to provide £2000 and a lot of land for the establishment of the new institution. In fact, as Richard Knight informed the Wesleyan Methodist Missionary Society in London, £1000 was offered by Charles Allison, while the other £1000 was the total pledged by others in Sackville and district.[97] For North American Methodists the academic education of female students was not a novelty, for there were a number of precedents in the denomination's academies in the United States. There were precedents in British North America too. The Upper Canada Academy at Cobourg had admitted girls, though strictly segregated from the male students, between 1836 and 1842; this practice had ended with the institution's elevation to become Victoria College, but the work had been carried on by two schools founded in Cobourg at that time by wives of college professors.[98] In Sackville, the prosperity of the boys' academy, which in 1846 had prompted an enlargement to the building to accommodate another classroom, gave reason to hope that the proposed female academy would be assured of success.[99]

In practice, however, the establishment of the female academy was delayed by a series of difficulties and other preoccupations which diverted attention away from the new venture. The first of these was the economic depression which struck the Maritime provinces, and New Brunswick in particular, in the course of 1848, lasting for some three years. In New Brunswick, the timber trade upon which the province depended so heavily was seriously threatened by the adoption of free trade measures by Great Britain. Preferential access for New Brunswick timber to the British market was now severely curtailed, and it was widely believed that the shipbuilding industry, closely linked to the timber trade, would be jeopardized also. Overshadowing the concurrent inauguration of responsible government in the province, dire predictions of commercial ruin were heard throughout New Brunswick, and merchants and shipbuilders deliberately cut back their operations in anticipation of the adverse conditions to come. During 1848, the level of trade fell to one-third of what it had been in normal times, and to make matters worse the harvest failed for the second successive year.[100] The fortunes of the academy had always been closely linked to the economic state of the province and of the region, for not only the raising of funds for any new project but also the number of students in attendance from year to year was dependent upon the prosperity of the institution's constituency. In December 1848, Pickard informed Alder that 'the unprecedented business depression which is so painfully felt by all classes and by almost everybody in these Provinces has somewhat reduced our number of students during the year now ending, and will inevitably produce a similar effect for some time to come.' Pickard was not altogether pessimistic, but he warned that 'whether it will be judged prudent to proceed next spring with the Building for the Academy for Females is now, owing to the business state of the Country, somewhat doubtful.'[101]

The depression of 1848–50 had lesser effects in Nova Scotia than in New Brunswick, since the Nova Scotian economy was not dependent upon any single protected trade, although instances of trade decline and crop failure occurred there also. For the academy, the result was a steeper decline in the numbers of New Brunswick students than in those from Nova Scotia. No precisely broken-down figures were published for the years 1849, 1850, and 1851, but in 1850 the attendance for the year fell to 79; two members of the academy's governing committee remarked in a letter of early 1850 to Joseph Howe, Provincial Secretary of Nova Scotia, that the number of Nova Scotia students had in the previous year exceeded the number in attendance from New Brunswick.[102] This unusual situation did not persist, for the combined student attendance for 1849–51 showed 52.3 per cent from New Brunswick and only 34.9 per cent from Nova Scotia, and the New Brunswick proportion would again rise in the succeeding years, at the same time as overall attendance figures regained and surpassed their previous level. Nevertheless, the episode had demonstrated the extent to which shifts in the regional economy could affect the academy. Saint John, always an important catchment area, was especially hard hit by the depression, and between 1849 and 1851 the proportion of students originating from that city averaged 14.0 per cent, its lowest level since 1843. As prosperity returned, Saint John's proportion of the student body would recover and briefly in the early 1850s would exceed one-fifth. The decline in attendance from New Brunswick, however, and from Saint John in particular, made it clear why the years from 1849 to 1851 were unpromising for the inauguration of the academy for girls.

There were also administrative and political considerations that demanded attention in the late 1840s and early 1850s. None was more urgent than the need for a formal constitution. After Charles Allison had acquired the land on which the academy was to be built, he had deeded it on 26 May 1840 to three trustees, the ministers Sampson Busby, William Temple, and Enoch Wood. Their trust was intended to be temporary, pending a final settlement by the Wesleyan Methodist Missionary Society, and a draft constitution had been sent to London for this purpose. In this as in other matters the Missionary

Society had delayed; even the bold actions of late 1842, by which the institution had been set in motion, did not prompt any decisive action. In the meantime, the academy operated under the effective control of the managing committee appointed by the Nova Scotia and New Brunswick districts, but it was not formally incorporated and in 1845 Enoch Wood predicted to Alder that 'we shall have some difficulty before long, unless this Deed and the Constitution by which the Academy is to be governed be agreed upon and completed. …'[103] A year later, despite a further sharp reminder sent by Wood in January 1846, nothing had been done and the managing committee agreed that Pickard should visit England as soon as possible to attempt to bring about a settlement.[104] The soonest possible proved to be more than two years later, and Pickard carried with him a specific proposal. Rather than rely upon the Missionary Society to execute a final trust deed, Pickard was to ask the society's approval for the obtaining of an act of incorporation through the legislature of New Brunswick. Richard Knight, writing Pickard's letter of introduction to the Missionary Society in his capacity as chairman of the New Brunswick District, stressed that the proposed establishment of the academy for girls made action all the more urgent and noted the especial anxiety of Charles Allison that the institution should be put on a firmer foundation. After consultation with the provincial attorney-general, Knight and the managing committee had become convinced that a New Brunswick statute would be 'the more easy, yet we think not less safe settlement of the trust, and management of the affairs of our institution.'[105]

Pickard's transatlantic sojourn was fruitful. On 27 September 1848 he addressed the committee of the Missionary Society and evoked not only generous praise for the academy's success but also two important decisions. The committee recognized that the institution had been inaugurated through initiatives within the Maritime provinces and paid tribute to those 'native labourers whose piety, intelligence and zeal, would be an ornament and a blessing to any Church in any Country.' Permission was granted for the establishment of the new female academy on the familiar condition that the society would take no financial responsibility. As for the constitutional matter, the committee accepted the proposal to seek a New Brunswick act of incorporation, provided that legal advice were taken 'in order that such Act may be so framed as to secure in every respect the strictly Wesleyan character of that Institution a[illegible] that it may be secured in perpetuity for the connexion in accordance with the design of its Founder.' The committee was not so forthcoming on a renewed request for its approval of the launching of a new Methodist newspaper in the Maritimes; but on academy matters Pickard was well satisfied when he returned to Sackville in November 1848.[106]

The bill of incorporation was introduced to the provincial assembly by L.A. Wilmot on 12 February 1849, and quickly passed through both houses, receiving royal assent on 14 April.[107] Its major purpose was to constitute a new body of trustees as the permanent managing corporation of the academy. From each of the two Maritime districts, four trustees would be drawn – the chairman and secretary of each district and two laymen selected annually at the district meeting – while the academy principal would be the only other member. Thus there would be nine trustees for the time being, although provision was made for the number to be adjusted to allow for equal representation for any other districts which might be created in the future by subdivision of the existing two. The chairman of the New Brunswick District was designated as chairman of the trustees. The introduction of laymen to the management of the academy was not unexpected, since it had been envisaged in the earlier draft constitution upon which the Missionary Society had not acted.[108] Also not unexpected was the naming of Charles Allison as one of the laymen initially appointed. The act gave no direct powers over the academy to the Missionary Society, although it noted that the two districts were constituted under the society's authority, so that the society retained by implication an indirect power to influence the institution's government. The name of the institution was formally defined as 'the Wesleyan Academy, at Mount Allison, Sackville': for the moment, 'Mount Allison' remained a geographical term included to define the academy's location, rather than itself being part of the corporate name. On the institution's purpose, the act had little to say beyond summarizing the founder's intention that it should carry out 'the instruction of youth in the various branches of science and literature upon christian principles.' On one point, however, it went into greater detail, in an effort to define what the Missionary Society had referred to as the academy's 'strictly Wesleyan character':

> No person shall teach, maintain, promulgate, or enforce any religious doctrine or practice in the said Academy or any department thereof, or in any religious services held upon the said premises, contrary to what is contained in certain Notes on the New Testament, commonly reported to be the Notes of the said Reverend John Wesley, A.M., and in the first four Volumes of Sermons commonly reported to have been written and published by him.[109]

The negative phrasing of this article ensured that it did not conflict with the academy's professed avoidance of sectarian bias: it did not prescribe any body of doctrine to which students or teachers must adhere. Obviously, though, it was a restrictive provision and although it was never specifically reaffirmed in any future legislation it was not repealed until 1913. In the shorter term, it demonstrated the firm commitment of the academy to the denominational principle. At the very time when the act of incorporation was being discussed in the New Brunswick legislature, that denominational principle was under attack in Nova Scotia, and one of the major preoccupations of the newly constituted governing body would be to mount an effective defence. Once again, as in 1843, Joseph Howe was a prominent figure in the debate: he was now Provincial Secretary in the Liberal administration of James Boyle Uniacke that had taken office following the concession of responsible government. On 7 February 1849, the recently installed chairman of the Nova Scotia District, Ephraim Evans, informed Alder that 'we have had to make a general movement in behalf of the Sackville Academy.' It was well known that Howe was determined to revive Dalhousie College, which had fallen into decay after the death of its president, Thomas McCulloch, in September 1843 and had closed its doors in the spring of 1845, and in April 1849 a reconstituted Dalhousie Collegiate School was opened. What Evans feared was that public aid would then be withheld from denominational institutions, especially as the legislation upon which the academy's annual grant of £150 depended was due to expire in the spring of 1849. He had informed Howe directly that 'it will be a dangerous experiment for any Provincial Ministry to array themselves against the religious feeling of the country, in attempting to establish a godless system of public instruction,' and with the assistance of ministers from the various circuits of the district he had assembled 1214 signatures on a petition to be presented to the Legislative Council.[110] Evans himself, with his colleague Alexander McLeod, had petitioned the provincial assembly a few days previously on behalf of the academy's managing committee, and had stressed the important role of legislative aid in permitting the institution 'to extend the advantages of Academical instruction to many whose limited means would have otherwise precluded them from participating therein.'[111]

In the event, the threat to the Wesleyan Academy's grant from Nova Scotia was less than had been feared. Since 1843, Howe had become convinced that denominational education was well enough established in the Maritimes that its abolition was not feasible, and that the re-establishment of Dalhousie College must proceed in the context of the continuation of grants to denominational academies. By early February 1849 Howe had explained his position privately to Evans, and in the following month a motion to abolish the grant, was defeated in the assembly after he had refused to give it his support.[112] For all that, Howe's change of attitude did not in itself resolve the question, and the first volume of the *Wesleyan*, the newly established weekly Methodist newspaper for the Maritime provinces, conducted a series of editorial campaigns of behalf of the academy. In the spring of 1850 the issue was again debated in the provincial assembly, with the same result.[113] For the time being the annual grant from Nova Scotia was safe. So too was that from New Brunswick, although in April 1851 it was forced to a division in the assembly and passed by 21 votes to 10. At the same session, an attempt to reduce the amount of the grant to £150 from its previous level of £300 was also defeated.[114] The principle of legislative aid had been vindicated in both provinces, although the events of 1849–51 had shown that it was not unchallenged.

By the summer of 1851, with economic prosperity returning to the region, with the act of incorporation secured, and with the legislative grants successfully defended, the trustees of the academy returned to the question of the branch for female students. At first they proceeded cautiously, and although Allison formally renewed his offer to contribute £1000 in June 1851, the decision to proceed was postponed until fund-raising efforts should have yielded an amount close to the additional capital required, which was estimated at between £3000 and £4000. An appeal was therefore launched for donations, subscriptions, and 'scholarships,' a scholarship being a donation of £25 carrying the proviso that the donor was entitled to claim a £5 annual discount on the fees of any student of his choice for a period of seven years.[115] In the summer of 1852, special appeals were made in the cities of Halifax, Saint John, and Charlottetown. This was a prosperous year for the cities, as was reflected in the composition of the student body at the academy: the combined proportion of students from these three cities, which had never before reached even as high as one-third, stood at a wholly exceptional 42.2 per cent in 1852.[116] The results of the appeals were as hoped, and Pickard was able to announce shortly afterwards that the fund stood at £2500 and that 'the Institution which has been in contemplation several years, is (D.V.) [God willing], to be immediately established.'[117] By early 1853 work had begun, again under the personal supervision of Charles Allison.[118]

The fund-raising efforts of the early 1850s had an important by-product. In July 1853, Pickard wrote to the *Provincial Wesleyan* (as the *Wesleyan* was entitled from 1852 until 1875) to introduce three new agents who would be canvassing for funds in various parts of the region. Much of the letter went over old ground, as it affirmed the need for proper facilities in order to further the academy's work of education, especially in view of the projected addition of the academy for girls. What was new was the hope expressed that 'an Endowment Fund of at least from eight to ten thousand pounds should be secured to aid in the permanent support of the United Institution.' In the past, funds had been raised exclusively for initial capital costs, while current expenses had been met from tuition fees and government grants. The proposed endowment fund would not replace these customary sources of income, but it was hoped that it would provide a substantial supplement and, like the government grants, would help to ensure 'that the ordinary expense of students may be as low as possible.' Thus, in a time of economic prosperity the academy sought to raise funds to offset dependence upon the legislative aid which had been seriously even though unsuccessfully opposed in the provincial legislatures between 1849 and 1851. In point of fact, the plan was overambitious, and the academy's balance sheet for 1854, the year in which the branch for female students was opened, showed that the expenses of construction and equipment of the new building had exceeded the funds raised by just over £1000. Far from enjoying endowment income, the academy had a substantial debt of over £1100 by the end of the year.[119] In later years, however, endowment funds would supply an important portion, at times crucially important, of the income of the Mount Allison institutions.

By December 1853 the *Mount Allison Academic Gazette*, a new publication which for several years replaced the old *Catalogue* and provided news of the academy and printed versions of sermons and addresses given there, as well as the course descriptions and general regulations which the *Catalogue* had contained, was able to announce that the 'commodious and beautiful edifice' of the female academy was nearing completion.[120] A wooden building of three storeys, it was designed to accommodate 70 resident pupils. With many additions and renovations it would stand upon the Mount Allison campus for 115 years before being demolished to make way for more modern buildings in 1969. The experience with the original academy in the early 1840s had shown that completion of a building did not in itself ensure opening of an institution, and again now there were anxious moments as nominations to administrative offices proved problematic. Pickard, who had been dissuaded in 1852 from resigning his position as principal in order to return to 'the regular ministerial work,' was nominated as principal of what were now the two branches of the academy. Ephraim Evans was nominated as governor and chaplain, an appointment which would necessarily bring about the retirement of Albert DesBrisay who still held the position of chaplain.[121] Again, the approval of the Missionary Society was sought, for although it had no direct control over the academy, it still held authority over Pickard and Evans as ministers. Once again, there was delay, and in October Richard Knight warned the society that 'rival institutions are to be anticipated in these Provinces' and that if the nominations were not approved 'we shall be really placed in a very critical and trying situation.' His admonitions were apparently heeded, for on 20 December confirmation of the appointments was dispatched from London.[122]

The opening of the female academy was fixed for 17 August 1854, the day on which both branches were to open for the second term of the year, and a full programme of music and addresses was planned. In Saint John, however, early August marked the height of the disastrous cholera epidemic which would ultimately take the lives of some 1500 of the city's 30,000 residents. On the 10th, Humphrey Pickard announced in the *Provincial Wesleyan* that the general disruption caused by the epidemic had caused the formal opening ceremony to be postponed, although the academy would still start the term as planned. Reflecting the prevailing belief that cholera was not contagious, but rather was caused by unclean air, Pickard reported that 'the state of public health in Sackville is as usual, good' and assured parents of potential students 'that it is one of the healthiest places in the world.'[123] On the 17th, the new building was duly opened in the presence of 'an unexpectedly large company' of intending students, numbering between 80 and 90, and classes were immediately organized after a service of dedication lasting only an hour. A week later, the building had reached its planned capacity of 70 boarders, and 29 girls were enrolled as day scholars. In its first term, enrolment at the female branch would reach 118, surpassing by six that of the male branch. It was, as Pickard remarked, 'an auspicious beginning of the new epoch.'[124]

How new, in reality, was the new epoch? For the academy, the presence of more than a hundred female students and a staff of seven women teachers clearly altered permanently the hitherto male-dominated environment of the institution. Coeducation, however, was not the purpose. On the contrary, the *Mount Allison Academic Gazette* assured its readers in June 1854 that 'the Family and Class organizations [of the female branch] will be entirely distinct from those of the other Academy, and the Students of the different branches will not be allowed to associate or even meet, either in public or private, except in presence of some of the officers of the Institution.'[125] Charlotte Dixon, a student from Sackville who attended the female academy in its first term, later recalled that boys and girls would rarely meet even in the street, 'for the day the young men walked up the road the young women walked down the road and vice versa.' Social gatherings were infrequent, the major event being an annual 'Reunion' at the male academy at about the time of the New Year. Lasting from 6:00 in the evening to about 9:30, the reunion began with tea and continued with conversation, along with 'music and a general good time.'[126] Even at church, separate seating prevented contact between the students of the two branches. Thus, every effort was made to maintain a decorous distance between the sexes; but the very need for such regulations showed the magnitude of the change that had taken place in the social life of the institution.

The academy's clientele also changed as a result of the opening of the female branch. An early student recalled that 'many of the village girls attended the seminary as day pupils myself among the number although quite young in years.'[127] Analysis of the composition of the student body in the first three years of the female academy confirms her recollection, for there was a heavy concentration of pupils from the local area. In the second year, over one-third of the students came from Sackville itself, and almost half were from Westmorland County. As a result, when the total student body from both branches is examined, the proportions of local students were higher than at any time previous to the opening of the female branch, except for the opening year of 1843. Nor, in the case of the female academy, was this a passing trend. In 1856–7, fully 35 per cent of the female students came from Sackville; the proportion among the male students was only 16 per cent, so that the combined proportion was 24.4 per cent. In this respect, the characteristics of the two branches were at variance. Yet in another respect, the arrival of female students strengthened a trend that had already been apparent in the male academy. From the beginning, the academy had professed to serve the overall population of the Maritime region, and on this basis had been awarded legislative grants. That population was overwhelmingly rural; and yet substantial proportions of the students had come from the major cities of the region and especially from Saint John. In 1852, no less than 23.4 per cent came from Saint John, with a further 9.4 per cent each from Halifax and Charlottetown.[128] This, however, was the peak year of urban attendance, and in the male academy in 1856–7 these cities supplied only 19.1 per cent of the students. Clearly, 1852 had been an exceptional year, following the severe economic depression, but the figures also reflected the growth of alternative educational opportunities in the cities, and notably the operation of Methodist academic day schools in Halifax and Saint John.[129] The female academy, on the other hand, never had any such high proportion of students from the major cities, and thus its opening tended to accentuate the shift away from urban attendance. In the early 1850s, the academy had seemed briefly to run the risk of becoming an institution primarily for local and for urban students: in each of the years 1852 and 1853 some 70 per cent came either from Westmorland or Cumberland County or from one of the major cities. By 1856–7, the equivalent figure for the two branches combined was only 57.3 per cent, with students from the cities comprising only 18.8 per cent. Thus, the composition of the student body was coming more nearly to resemble that of the population it professed to serve, though with a confirmed bias towards those who originated from Sackville or nearby.[130]

The opening of the female branch, therefore, did make a difference to the Wesleyan Academy, affecting both the life of the campus and the constituency served. Did it also make a difference to the education of women in the region? Certainly, the institution did not claim total originality. Boarding schools for girls were by no means rare either in Great Britain or in the United Atates, where even college education had been opened to women at Oberlin College in 1837 and by other institutions soon afterwards.[131] In British North America, initiatives in Methodist women's education had been located chiefly in Canada West, the Upper Canada Academy at Cobourg being a major example. In the Maritimes, also in 1836, the Baptist denomination had taken the lead by opening its Fredericton seminary to both male and female students. Yet the Cobourg and Fredericton experiments were short-lived. Only a year after the 'female department' of the Upper Canada Academy had been discontinued in 1842 with the institution's acquisition of college status, the Fredericton seminary also allowed its female department to lapse in the face of competition from private schools in the city.[132] Private girls' schools in the Maritimes had existed since the late eighteenth century, and their number grew rapidly during the earlier decades of the nineteenth. In 1839, for example, a school in Halifax was advertised by 'the Misses Tropolet,' who offered instruction 'in English Reading, Writing and Arithmetic, Ancient and Modern History, Geography, Plain Needle Work, and Fancy Work, Music and Drawing, and the Use of Globes.' Eleven years later, a girls' school was opened much closer to Sackville, when Mrs C.E. Ratchford advertised a 'Female Seminary' in Amherst.[133] The scale of the female branch of the Sackville academy, however, made it at the time of its founding the major school for girls in the region. In June 1854 the *Mount Allison Academic Gazette* proclaimed that the female academy was 'designed to be in every respect, in proportion to its extent, equal to any public Institution devoted to the advancement of Female Education on this Continent.'[134]

As chief preceptress – the highest office in the school held by a woman, and carrying essentially the duties of a principal, though subject to the nominal authority of Pickard and Evans – was appointed Mary Electa Adams. A native of Lower Canada, Adams had grown up in Upper Canada and had studied both there and in the United States. She had finished her education at the Cobourg Ladies' Seminary, an institution which had been founded after the exclusion of women from Victoria College and which moved to Toronto in 1847 and became known as the Adelaide Academy. Subsequently, Adams had been lady principal of the Picton Academy, again in Canada West, and had spent four years teaching at the Albion Seminary in Michigan. Still only thirty years old when she arrived in Sackville in 1854, she none the less brought considerable experience to her position. Although she stayed only three years before family deaths forced her return to Canada, her influence was soon apparent not only in the devotion which she evidently evoked in her pupils, but also in the nature of the academy and particularly in the curriculum offered to female students.[135] When the trustees of the academy had petitioned the New Brunswick legislature in early 1854 for an operating grant for the female academy – an annual allocation of £300 was voted in the following year and thereafter – the expected curriculum had stressed training in the social graces rather than a rigorous academic programme. 'In addition to the Elementary Branches of Education,' the assembly had been informed, 'that of the French and other polite Languages, Music, Drawing, Painting, and other ornamental Branches, will be taught.'[136] By June 1854, although parents were assured in the *Academic Gazette* that 'the cultivation of refined taste and lady-like manners' would receive due attention, academic content was accorded a new prominence:

> The Course of Study in Literature and Science, the principles of Classification, and the general routine of the intellectual training will correspond, as nearly as may be, with the plan which is ... published for the other Branch, and which has been so successfully tried. There will be here as in the other Branch, three departments – the Primary, the Intermediate, and the Collegiate – each with its own appropriate portion of the course of study suitably modified.[137]

The nature of the suitable modifications was revealed when the detailed curriculum was published in the following year. The primary department curriculum was similar to that of the equivalent in the male branch, though with the addition of 'occasional Oral Instructions in Physiology, Domestic Economy, and Natural History.' The intermediate course also resembled its counterpart, though with the omission of Latin and certain subjects such as bookkeeping and surveying, and their replacement by classes in map-drawing and mythology. The collegiate course for female students was divided into three years, rather than the four years prescribed in the male branch: the difference lay chiefly in the omission of Greek language and literature, and of two out of six Latin authors; also omitted were political economy and mineralogy. Vocal music, along with English composition, was continued throughout the collegiate course, while instrumental music and fine arts were available to all students at added cost.[138]

Thus, the education offered to female students at the academy was characterized by a lesser concentration than in the male branch on classical subjects and on those subjects pertaining to careers which women were unlikely to pursue. The students were avowedly being prepared for their roles as 'the daughter, the sister, and the mother.'[139] The stress on music and fine arts was clearly in that vein too, although in later years the teaching of these subjects would go far beyond the mere inculcation of ornamental skills. Even in the first year of the female academy, the success of music was such that it was introduced as an option in the male branch in 1855. Yet it was equally clear that the courses of study provided for girls were not exclusively designed to cultivate good taste and the accomplishments of the drawing-room; this point was strongly made in an editorial in the *Academic Gazette* of December 1855 which clearly bore the imprint of Mary Electa Adams. Attacking 'the ordinary modes of female education' as tending to produce 'that impatience of thought, that tendency to the desultory and the superficial, which are proverbial failings of young Ladies,' the editorial advocated above all a systematic programme of study. 'It would be superfluous to advocate,' it declared, 'what must now be considered a settled principle, – that the introduction of the abstruser sciences into a course of study for females, is of the highest utility.' Accordingly, the subjects retained in the collegiate course for women included all the branches of mathematics, Latin language and literature, the major science subjects, and philosophical subjects in the form of mental and moral science and logic. Also retained was the philosophically important course in evidences of Christianity. 'The ornamental branches,' stated the editorial, 'without being depreciated or displaced, will always be pursued in subserviency to the solid studies.'[140] The Wesleyan female academy would aim to produce women of high moral character and good taste; but it would aim also to produce women of intellectual vigour.

The opening of the second branch of the Wesleyan Academy in the summer of 1854 was followed soon afterwards by the addition of other buildings to the campus on Mount Allison. One of these, opened in the autumn of 1855, was a small gymnasium by the side of the girls' academy: the female students were not expected to chop wood, but their physical health was henceforth to be safeguarded by 'a regular course of Calisthenics, comprehending all the movements required to develop every part of the muscular frame. ...'[141] Earlier in the year, on 30 January, a much larger building had been opened in the form of the New Hall, soon to be renamed in honour of the Saint John timber merchant, Bartlett Lingley, who had at first agreed to finance its construction although business setbacks had later limited his contribution to a small proportion of the final cost.[142] Providing an auditorium with seating accommodation for 700, as well as space for the library of the united institution and for a museum of geological and other scientific curiosities, Lingley Hall fulfilled an important purpose at an academy which now had well over

200 pupils at any one time. For some fifty-five years it would house meetings, lectures, concerts, and convocations. Architecturally, its six tall Ionic columns made a graceful counterpart to the plainer female academy building; it was, as a writer in the *Provincial Wesleyan* declared, 'a rather elegant-looking structure.'[143]

The opening of Lingley Hall afforded an opportunity for 'solemn exercises' of a kind which had been forestalled a few months previously by the Saint John epidemic, and later for celebrations with music, refreshments, and the customary delights of 'the Electric apparatus.' For those who had been associated with the academy from the start, it was a chance to reflect. Charles Allison took the chair for the formal dedication. Above him, specially fitted up for the occasion, were large inscriptions which recalled the hopeful tones of Pickard's inaugural address almost twelve years before: 'the words – SCIENCE, LITERATURE, RELIGION, appeared on a large triangle, with a Crown in bold relief, and the letters V.R. immediately under – and still lower – EDUCATION ON CHRISTIAN PRINCIPLES – THE BEST INHERITANCE.' Allison's first task was to introduce Pickard as once again the main speaker. Alluding 'briefly and delicately' to the difficulties that had been surmounted in previous years, the principal dwelt at greater length on the continuing success of the academy; that success had been crowned by the achievement of 'the long cherished purpose of erecting a Branch for Female Education' and now by the opening of the new building, 'so much needed for the effective and comfortable working of the united Institution.' It must be, he concluded, 'a Temple Sacred to Literature, Science and Religion combined!'[144]

Pickard spoke again later on, as the ninth and last speaker on a series of topics clustered around the general theme of Christian education. His own address started from the premise that 'a recognition of the *law of progress*, is essential to the efficiency and usefulness of Educational Institutions.'[145] Victorian belief in progress must certainly have seemed appropriate both in the general context of the prosperous Maritime provinces of the 1850s, and in the particular context of the academy. Twelve years before, a handful of students had been sparsely settled amidst the spacious recesses of the first building. Now, both branches were filled and more than filled, to the point that one of the larger rooms in the girls' academy accommodated six residents and was popularly known as 'the tower of Babel.'[146] Twelve years before, Pickard and J.R. Hea had constituted the teaching staff, shortly to be joined by Thomas Wood. Hea and Wood were now gone, and Pickard's most senior colleagues were his brother Thomas and A.S. Reid. Three other teachers had been added – including J.R. Inch, a future president of Mount Allison, as teacher in the primary department – while in the female branch Mary Electa

Adams headed a staff of seven. Like Pickard, she had a family member as a colleague, for her sister Augusta taught in the collegiate course.[147] To be sure, not all was progress and prosperity. A sceptic might have pointed out that there were increasingly severe disagreements between Pickard and Ephraim Evans. Evans, later described by Inch as 'a man of military bearing, holding himself erect as a soldier,' had entered actively into his role as governor and chaplain, and the spheres of authority of the two men had soon begun to overlap. David Allison, another future president of Mount Allison and a member of the academy teaching staff from August 1856, recalled that 'the chief annoyance and trouble fell on the ordinary teachers who were compelled to attempt the scriptural impossibility of serving two masters.'[148] Then again, there was the question of debt, for the accounts for the year ending on 1 January 1855 had shown an accumulated deficit of £1140/10/11 even assuming that all outstanding student accounts would be paid, and the debt would increase in each of the two succeeding years. For the year ending in June 1857, it would stand at the disturbing figure of £1888/6/8½, with a further £1293/0/7 tied up in unpaid student accounts.[149] Yet 30 January 1855 was not the day for worrying either about personal conflicts or about deficits. It was, rather, the day of celebrating progress. As the *Provincial Wesleyan*'s correspondent feelingly wrote, it was the day 'when every devout heart must have been ready to exclaim – "What hath God wrought!"'[150]

For Humphrey Pickard personally, the previous twelve years had brought their troubles. The death of his second son, an infant, in February 1844 had been followed by the death of his wife three weeks later. Some two years afterwards the first son also died, and although Pickard remarried in 1846 the loss of his first family was obviously one from which he did not easily recover.[151] As principal, he had been a controversial choice at the start, and he was never an entirely uncontroversial figure. His pugnacity was legendary and apparently was not always confined to the columns of newpapers. The story was told, for example, of the occasion when he accompanied some students on the steamer from Sackville to Saint John and found them being offered a drink of rum by – the story varies – either a butcher or two muleteers. When his verbal protest to the offender, or offenders, went unheeded, Pickard was said to have finished the matter rapidly with his fists.[152] His reputation as a scholar and teacher was a matter of dispute. One of his pupils of the 1860s, Benjamin Russell, wrote that 'I never heard anybody affirm that he [Pickard] was a scholar.' For Russell, Pickard was a forbidding figure, a disciplinarian who demanded respect from his students and obtained it through fear rather than love. By contrast, he found Pickard's brother to be a more inspiring teacher and a more sympathetic figure: Thomas was known to the students as 'bedbug,' because he once described the bedbug in the natural science class as a '"junkey little animal with red a head," which form of words was thought to be very happily descriptive of himself.'[153] Yet there was more to Humphrey Pickard than either the controversialist or the disciplinarian. Inch recalled that he was 'tender and sympathetic, deeply solicitous for the moral and spiritual welfare of the students,' while David Allison wrote that 'he did not aspire to the reputation of profound or versatile scholarship, but he was a clear thinker, with exceptional aptitudes for the exact sciences, for logic, and for philosophy.'[154] Perhaps the most revealing contemporary verdict on Pickard was a much earlier one, that of Enoch Wood. 'Pickard's time,' wrote Wood in a letter to Alder in 1846, 'ought to be occupied with literary engagements exclusively, for which he has great love, and much intellectual power to excel.' The fact was, however, that Pickard's position as principal gave him little opportunity to develop fully that side of his character. To steer the Sackville institutions through their first decades, as Pickard did, was a task in which pugnacity and stubbornness were at times just as necessary as piety and scholarship. Wood, himself no mean protagonist of the academy, recognized the nature of Pickard's contribution: 'justice to Mr. Pickard compels me to say, that it is to his talent, indefatigable exertions, and many sacrifices, with the Divine Blessing, the Academy owes its present distinguished position.' Pickard, he concluded, 'will never be showy; nature has not endowed him with the facility for display; but he is a thorough gem; or, as the Yankees would say, a "whole team" in himself.'[155]

Enoch Wood had left the Maritime provinces in 1847 to become superintendent of missions in the Methodist Conference of the province of Canada, and from 1850 to 1858 he served as president of the conference. In the summer of 1855 he returned to the Maritimes for a visit, the occasion being the inauguration of the new conference of Eastern British America. Relations between the Maritime districts and the British Conference, through the Missionary Society, had been conducted cordially by the individuals on either side, but had long been unsatisfactory in an administrative sense. The tendency of the Missionary Society committee to be preoccupied either with missions in other parts of the world or with the internal tensions of British Methodism had led to the delays and frustrations of which the academy had had its share. For the society itself, it was questionable whether scarce funds should continue to be expended upon the support of missionaries in the British North American districts, which were now well established in rapidly maturing colonial societies. The idea of a union of the Maritime districts with a view to greater independence had been broached by Alder as early as the 1830s, and it was discussed intermittently in the following decade. The objections had arisen chiefly within the region itself, from those who did not believe that the denomination could support itself without continued support from the Missionary Society, or who feared that a move towards independence would be a move away from British-style Methodism. In the early 1850s, however, the committee of the Missionary Society became more determined to cut back on its financial responsibilities. Furthermore, there were precedents for the foundation of conferences independent of the British Conference, though still in association with it. The Irish conference was a long-standing example, dating from the mid-eighteenth century. More recently, the Canada Conference had begun in 1840 through a full-scale revolt against the Missionary Society, but had been recognized in 1847. Five years later, in 1852, the French Conference had been inaugurated on a similar constitutional basis.[156]

By 1855, general agreement had been reached between the Missionary Society and the Maritime districts. John Beecham, now sixty-eight years old and the senior secretary of the society, was dispatched to found the new conference and to assist in winning over any remaining opponents; it was he who presided at the first meeting of 'the Ministers of the Wesleyan Connexion, or Church, of Eastern British America' in Halifax on 17 July 1855. The success of their first conference was testimony both to Beecham's able presentation of the plan to the district meetings in the previous weeks, and to his skilful drafting of the detailed provisions for the change. During an initial transition period, the Missionary Society would continue to give financial support; and a close connection with British Wesleyanism would be ensured by the powers retained by the British Conference to choose the president of the new conference and to disallow within one year any of its enactments which were considered contrary to Wesleyan doctrine or discipline. Thus the principal fears over the results of autonomy had been allayed.[157] Among the items of business transacted in Halifax was the formal adoption by the conference of Eastern British America of responsibility for the operation of the Wesleyan Academy, through an appropriately reformed board of trustees which would now be composed of the nominees of the conference rather than of the several Maritime districts.[158] The district structure itself had been altered, so that there were now seven districts within the conference, including one centred on Sackville. The area served by the conference did not solely include the Maritime provinces, since Newfoundland was also included. So too was Bermuda, which had been attached to the Nova Scotia District in 1851 and now became part of the new Halifax District. For the academy, Newfoundland had already supplied a regular, though small, contingent of students, while the first of a continuing flow from Bermuda would arrive in 1857.

Thus the academy, though continuing to draw its clientele chiefly from the Maritimes, would also undertake to serve a wider constituency.

Other things were changing in Maritime Methodism in 1855 besides constitutional structures. The membership was growing: the 1855 conference noted an increase of nearly 7 per cent in its constituent districts over the previous year. Economic prosperity was engendering a growing proportion of wealthy members, especially in the cities. Bartlett Lingley, despite the embarrassments which had followed his offer to finance the building which bore his name, was one example. The concern for social issues which had always been inherent in Wesleyan doctrine was becoming more explicit, especially in the gradual evolution of the temperance movement from its traditional emphasis on individual self-improvement to a greater preoccupation with social change through legislation. Though the urgent desire to save souls remained, the social gospel was in the making, and both concerns were evident at the academy. In the spring of 1854 a revival took place among the students that prompted Richard Knight, now chairman of the New Brunswick District, to comment that 'the Academy is turned into a Bethel.' It was a final achievement for the chaplaincy of DesBrisay and also for Pickard, whom Knight described as 'entirely overcome with the Light.'[159] In the following year, the new chaplain, Evans, chaired the inaugural meeting of the Sackville Prohibitary Law League, and Pickard was an active participant.[160]

Thus the academy shared in broader currents of Methodist concerns in the region. Undoubtedly, though, the constitutional innovations of 1855 had great significance. The practical operation of the academy was little affected, since the Missionary Society had long ceased to have any active involvement other than in the matter of appointing ministers to academy positions. Symbolically, though, the ultimate control over the institution had now passed to a conference established in British North America rather than in Great Britain. It had been Beecham in 1834 who had warned that the Methodist academy in the Maritimes must depend upon the resources of the region itself, and now in 1855 it was Beecham who presided over the formal adoption of responsibility by the new conference. He had visited the academy personally, and had generous praise for it when reporting to the British Conference later in the year.[161] At the request of the conference of Eastern British America, a full-length portrait of Beecham was soon afterwards painted by the English artist William Gush, and sent to the academy where it would hang above the platform in Lingley Hall from 1857 onwards. Shortly afterwards it would be joined by a similar portrait of Charles Allison, completed by the same artist. It was an apt tribute to the different but complementary roles which the two men had played.[162]

3

Sackville Institutions: 1855–1869

In 1855, the Wesleyan Academy was a single institution with two branches. Fourteen years later it had evolved into three autonomous institutions, including a degree-granting college. The intervening period was clearly one of significant changes in organization, although it was also one that made surprisingly little change in the fundamental character of the institutions. The alterations in corporate structure that flowed from the assumption of control by the conference of Eastern British America were made by act of the New Brunswick legislature in early 1856, and they implied no radical departure from the previous situation. Rather than depending upon appointments by the several districts, the board of trustees now depended entirely upon the conference, and both the president of the conference (or his delegate, since the nominal president was customarily a clergyman of the British Conference) and its secretary were members by virtue of their offices. Also ex-officio members were the principal of the academy, the governor, and the chaplain; although it was not so specified in the act, the last two positions were normally held by the same individual. The balance of the membership consisted of four ministers and seven lay members to be appointed annually by the conference. Thus, as had been true since 1849, the numbers of clergy and laymen were equal apart from the principal: if, as had always been the situation so far, the principal was a minister, then there would be a ministerial majority of one on the board.[1]

Necessarily, the act enumerated the names of those who were to be trustees until the next meeting of the conference; it revealed, as in previous years, an effort both to provide representation for various parts of the Maritime region and to include prominent and wealthy laymen. Among the ministers were three from Nova Scotia, including Matthew Richey of Halifax, who was also president of the board by virtue of being the delegate of the conference president. The other two were T.H. Davis of Newport, near Windsor, and Michael Pickles of Yarmouth. William Temple, now conference secretary, was one of the three clerical members from Sackville, where he happened to be serving as minister, the others being Pickard and Evans. Richard Knight of Saint John and John McMurray of Charlottetown were the two remaining ministers on the board. Of the lay members, Charles F. Allison was a natural choice, and he was joined by another Sackville resident who was also the only lay appointee who had never previously served on the board, the successful merchant and shipbuilder Mariner Wood. From Wallace, in the nearby Nova Scotia county of Cumberland, came Stephen Fulton, another merchant-shipbuilder who had enjoyed a modestly successful career in provincial politics but would lose his assembly seat in the general election of May 1855. More enduring was the political career of Charles Young, the lay member of the board from Charlottetown. A lawyer of Scottish birth, and the first in Prince Edward Island to receive the title of Queen's Counsel, he was in the midst of a long period of service on the provincial legislative council and also had recently been appointed as a judge of probate. Two lay appointees came from Halifax and were members of wealthy families – John H. Anderson and George H. Starr – while Gilbert T. Ray was from Saint John. All Methodists and all prominent in politics, in mercantile endeavours, or in both, the lay trustees evinced the wealth that had grown up within the denomination and the current prosperity of the region. Both the political maturity that had recently resulted in responsible government for all three provinces, and the economic development that would cause later generations of Maritimers to look back on this period as a golden age, were exemplified among them.[2]

In one respect, the act of 1856 made a significant change. The name Mount Allison had early been applied to the land donated by Charles Allison, and the formal title of the institution had been 'the Wesleyan Academy, at Mount Allison, Sackville.'[3] Over the years, the term Mount Allison had come to signify more than a geographical location, as had been symbolized in the title of the first student newspaper, 'The Mount Allison Students Repository,' and in that of the *Mount Allison Academic Gazette* from 1853. In 1856, Mount Allison became an official designation, for the corporate name was changed to be 'the Trustees of the Mount Allison Wesleyan Academy.'[4] Another name change that was effected some three years later was from 'female branch' to 'ladies' academy.' The former title had always been somewhat lacking in sonority – David Allison would later recall it as a 'most unmelodious and repulsive name'[5] – and was now rarely used. Instead, the custom grew up of referring respectively to the academy (for male students) and the ladies' academy. Although the change to two separate academies would not be embodied in legislation until 1875, the separation was already a reality by that time.

The change in the designation of the female branch was one of several that followed the appointment of John Allison to replace Mary Electa Adams in 1857. Allison, a thirty-six-year-old minister and a native of Newport, Nova Scotia, was technically the successor to Humphrey Pickard, for he was given the title of principal while his wife, Martha Louisa Allison, assumed the title of preceptress. The fact that Allison was a near cousin of Charles Frederick Allison no doubt played a role in his appointment, but he also brought with him a reputation as an outstanding preacher and held AB and AM degrees from Syracuse University, New York.[6] Martha Allison also possessed a combination of family association with the academy – she was the daughter of the minister and trustee Richard Knight – and formal qualifications. Also holding AB and AM degrees, from Genesee College in New York state, she was the first woman graduate to teach at Mount Allison. She was also the first woman to hold a professorial appointment, as in 1859 she was designated as professor of natural sciences, ancient and modern languages, within the ladies' academy. John Allison was professor of mental and moral science, belles lettres, and languages. The only other professorial position in the ladies' academy was that of the music professor, held by a number of successive incumbents from year to year. The staff was completed by six other teachers, including one in music, two in painting and drawing, and the others teaching English, mathematics, and languages. Thus, the early years of the women's academy had seen the development of a pronounced emphasis upon music and the fine arts, taught by four teachers out of a total staff of nine. The staff of 1859 also showed two other family connections: John Allison's sister, Louisa DeWolf Allison, taught English and mathematics, while Martha Allison's sister, Laura C. Knight, was only sixteen years old when appointed in 1859 to teach languages.[7]

At the male branch, the teaching staff also had a close-knit character. Humphrey Pickard and his brother Thomas continued to be the only staff members to hold degrees, and in 1857 the principal had received an honorary Doctorate of Divinity from Wesleyan University. The only other professorial appointment remained that of A.S. Reid, while Arthur McNutt Patterson and J.R. Inch were teachers in the intermediate and primary departments respectively. There were also temporary assistant teachers from year to year, and in 1856–7 this status was held by another cousin of the founder in the person of David Allison. David Allison rejoined the staff in 1860 as professor of the Latin and Greek Languages and Literature, following his own graduation from Wesleyan University. Patterson and Reid had left by this time, while

Inch was elevated to professorial rank as professor of French, and had also taken over the intermediate department. Together with John Allison, and a further appointee in the person of George S. Milligan, a former assistant teacher at the academy who had since been ordained as a minister and had graduated from King's College, Fredericton, this academy staff would also comprise the faculty of the Mount Allison Wesleyan College in its first year of 1862–3.[8]

At the ladies' academy, however, the prevalence of family connections apparently arose in part from a rapid turnover of the existing staff after the arrival of John and Martha Allison. A correspondent of the *Provincial Wesleyan* in October 1857 had high praise for the start which the Allisons had made on their new duties, and declared that they seemed 'providentially designated to their office.'[9] Yet a few months later rumours spread in Sackville of disagreements between Allison and the other teachers: 'they say all the teachers resigned in a body, in one day.'[10] Certainly by 1859 none of Mary Electa Adams's staff remained. Whatever the nature of these disputes – a surviving reference indicates only that 'poor Brother Allison finds it, not so very easy a thing to govern such an institution, as he formerly thought'[11] – the Allisons could not be faulted for inactivity. Almost immediately upon their arrival, they had instituted a revised curriculum, in which the number of courses offered was reduced to two. A new 'preparatory course' was based on the old primary course and included some of the subjects previously included in the intermediate course. The new 'graduating course for ladies' was a three-year programme obviously based upon the old collegiate course, but with changes in regard to classics and languages. Students could now study Greek as well as Latin if they wished, though no specific authors were now prescribed; and it was made possible to complete the course without any study of classical languages at all, by substituting French for Latin and German for Greek. Those who completed the full three years were promised 'a beautiful and appropriate diploma,' the forerunner of the Mistress of Liberal Arts diploma introduced in the early 1860s.[12]

The new ladies' academy curriculum provided, in addition to the specified subjects, that those completing the graduating course must have 'some knowledge of Music or Drawing,' and there was now clearly a deliberate effort to cultivate these already successful fields. In 1859, the catalogue informed its readers that 'during the last two years several new [musical] Instruments have been procured, of superior quality and tone, for lessons and practice.'[13] Eight pianos were available, some at least acquired by Allison second-hand from a dealer in Boston.[14] The ladies' academy also possessed an organ harmonium, and for more advanced purposes a large pipe organ was available in Lingley Hall. The organ, imported from the United States at a cost of £300, was the result of an initiative by a committee of students, assisted by alumni, and had been installed in 1857.[15] Also imported, in this case from London, were materials for the teaching of fine arts. 'No expense has been spared,' assured the catalogue, 'in procuring the greatest possible variety of the best copies for the pupils': most teaching was done through the copying of approved works of art by pupils, in the hope that the skills of the artist would thus be transmitted. The catalogue made clear, however, that explicit parental permission would be needed before any students would be allowed to register for fine arts, presumably because of the expense involved. The next paragraph remarked upon the low tuition fees in all branches, but went on to warn parents that 'if their children take many studies and add to these Music and the Fine Arts, with the materials required, their bills must run up to a pretty large sum.'[16] Both music and the fine arts were considerably more expensive than other subjects. In both academies the basic charge for elementary tuition and board was now £9/3/4 per term or £27/10/- for the academic year, having been raised for the first time in 1857. Each advanced subject cost an additional 6/8d. per term. Vocal music was abailable at the same rate of 6/8d., but instrumental music cost £2/13/4 per term, including a fee for use of instruments. The various branches of the fine arts, which would frequently be taken in combinations, ranged from 10/- for Grecian or Oriental painting, £1 for such subjects as watercolours and drawing, £1/6/8 for wax flowers or wax fruit, and to a maximum of £2 for oil painting.[17]

Despite the relatively high fees, however, the courses in music and fine arts were much in demand. Of the 153 students listed in the 1859 catalogue, no fewer than 120 were studying instrumental music and 105 vocal music, and of all the subjects taught these totals were exceeded only by composition (140) and penmanship (130). Even arithmetic (97), reading (86), and English grammar (78) were well behind. The fine arts enrolments are more difficult to assess, as they were divided into ten separate classes, but were substantial also, with the highest enrolments – in drawing and in 'coloured crayon' – reaching 36, and five others ranging between 21 and 27. Watercolours, monochromatic painting, and Grecian painting were less popular.[18] With more than one-third of the ladies' academy pupils continuing to originate from Sackville itself, it is probable that a considerable number of the students listed were attending solely to study music, and to a lesser degree the fine arts. Thus already the trends had begun which would result during the 1890s in the opening both of a conservatory and of an art gallery on the Mount Allison campus.

There were also other efforts to diversify the activities of the ladies' academy during John Allison's principalship, although with limited results.

In early 1858 Allison announced that the government of the United States had constructed an observatory on the institution's premises for puposes which he rather enigmatically described as relating to 'Coast Survey.' In due course, he hoped that it would be turned over to the academy and would be 'permanently useful in the instruction of students in astronomy.'[19] Since astronomy was already a part of the graduating course, his hopes were understandable enough, but lack of any further references to the observatory suggests that it may have been a temporary structure only. The ladies' academy also made some gestures towards providing training for teachers to enter the parish school system, no doubt prompted by the passage of the New Brunswick Parish School Act of 1858 and the expansion of the system it sought to promote. Another possible catalyst was the *Parish School Advocate and Family Instructor*, a journal started in 1858 by Alexander Monro, a land surveyor living in Baie Verte. Monro, as the title of the journal suggests, was dedicated to the social value of the parish school. He was also sceptical of denominational education, and in April 1858 he attacked the principle of government grants to institutions such as the Sackville academies, declaring that the total sum granted annually by the province of New Brunswick to denominational institutions – he included King's College in that designation – 'would, along with the usual local subscriptions, endow two hundred parish schools, and afford education to 4,000 children.'[20] Whether or not he had been stung into action by Monro, John Allison disclosed in a letter of late 1860 to Leonard Tilley, the New Brunswick provincial secretary, that 'we are now educating a few [students] at reduced rates who expect to become teachers.' The purpose of his letter was to propose that the ladies' academy should receive a special grant to finance expansion of its building and that it 'might make some return ... by educating 4 or 6 students free with the prospect of becoming teachers.'[21] No such grant was voted, however, and earlier in the year an attempt to obtain provincial sanction for an arrangement by which academy students could obtain parish school teaching licences by examination at the training schools of the province without actually having to attend classes there was given the non-commital response, 'each case will be dealt with according to its own merits.'[22] Academy students could apply for examination without attendance, as Mary and Alice Gallagher of Sackville successfully did in July 1860, but it would remain a privilege rather than a right.[23] Formal incorporation of Mount Allison into the provincial system of teacher training would be an innovation of the twentieth rather than of the nineteenth century.

The notion of expanding the facilities of the ladies' academy, of which

Allison had written to Tilley, was inspired by high levels of student attendance in the years 1859 and 1860. During the 1858–9 academic year, 153 students attended. This was already a large enrolment, but in 1859–60 the number rose to 189 and, Allison wrote, 'we became uncomfortably crowded.'[24] In April 1860 Allison broached the idea of an enlargement of the building in a letter to the *Provincial Wesleyan*, and he was supported by the board of trustees in May.[25] A wing was to be added to each end of the building, thus adding residential space for another 40 boarders as well as classrooms, music and painting rooms, and an enlarged dining hall; by the end of the year one of the two wings was complete at a cost of £600. To Tilley, Allison confided that fund-raising efforts had succeeded in raising only three-quarters of this sum, although he had hopes that Tilley's Nova Scotia counterpart, Joseph Howe, would work towards the securing of a special grant from Nova Scotia. Howe's views on denominational education had apparently evolved to the point that this was not an extravagant hope – his granddaughter would later attend the ladies' academy – but the grant did not materialize from either province.[26] As a result, only the north wing was added to the ladies' academy, and for fifteen years the building would present a lopsided appearance. Even this limited addition necessitated by the summer of 1861 the raising of a loan of £250, or $1000 in the currency system that had recently been adopted in New Brunswick.[27] The board of trustees had initially approved the expansion on condition that it would not add to Mount Allison's already considerable burden of debt. Especially in view of the efforts concurrently being made to begin the Mount Allison college, the necessity for the new loan was a disturbing portent for the future.

The first formal indication that a degree-granting college was being considered for Mount Allison had come at the Eastern British America Conference held in Sackville in June 1857. Following expressions of confidence in the academy and its officers, and the appointment of trustees for the year, a further resolution was adopted:

That the Conference earnestly requests the Board of Trustees for the ensuing year to direct attention to the important question, to the consideration of which God in His Providence seems to be now calling our Church, i.e., what measures should be adopted for the establishment of a College proper, to comprise a Theological Department, in order that adequate provision may be made to afford to youth of our congregations and others in the colonies, within the boundaries of this Conference, the privilege of securing the benefit and honours of a complete University course of literary and scientific study, and to candidates for our Ministry, a suitable Theological training; and to report to the next meeting of this Conference the results of their deliberations upon this matter.[28]

Little direct evidence has survived of the discussions that had led to the college proposal, but there were clear reasons for its adoption at this time. The autonomy of the conference, now entering its third year, was a reason in itself for extending the educational institutions and in particular for the addition of a theological school. Hitherto, the Missionary Society had held ultimate responsibility for ensuring the availability of suitably qualified ministers for the Maritime circuits, and the majority of those serving had been of British background. Now, however, the recruitment of ministers from Britain would all but cease, and responsibility for selection and training would fall entirely on the conference of Eastern British America. At the same time, as standards of education became higher in the provinces generally and among Methodists, the need for more formal training for ministers was increasingly apparent. There was also the argument that intellectual critiques of Christian doctrine were increasing in numbers and strength: the *Provincial Wesleyan* observed in an editorial in the early 1860s that 'infidelity comes before the world in a new guise,' and that defenders of the gospel 'must be armed not only with the panoply of faith, but with well burnished weapons.' Even the Baptists, traditionally the denomination which harboured the most suspicion of an educated ministry, had recently moved to establish a theological institution in connection with Acadia College, and their example underlined the need felt by the conference.[29]

As the conference resolution made clear, however, the proposed college was to include more than a theological school. Like the academy, it was to offer a general education to Methodists and non-Methodists of the region served by the conference. While the need for theological training may well have given the proposal its first impetus, there was no doubt that there was a real and expanding demand for higher education in literary and scientific subjects in the prosperous Maritime provinces of the 1850s. Furthermore, it could be argued that by inaugurating a degree-granting college Mount Allison would be enlarging only modestly upon the work it already carried out. Students from its collegiate department had already successfully taken examinations at King's College. Moreover, analysis of the age structure of the student body at the academy, drawn from reports submitted in various years to the governments of Nova Scotia and New Brunswick, reveals that a substantial proportion of male academy students were aged eighteen or over. In 1857–8, 47 students, or 36.7 per cent, were in that age category, and the proportion would never fall below 34.6 per cent in any of the ensuing years that preceded the opening of the college.[30] Given the fact that King's College still languished with very few resident students – it had only 15 in 1854[31] – the case for recognizing Mount Allison's contribution to higher education in the province, through the conferral of degree-granting powers, was a strong one.

So it was deemed by the New Brunswick legislature in early 1858. As the trustees of Mount Allison were well aware, King's College had been the subject of lengthy and often bitter debates in the assembly almost throughout the 1850s. The legislation of 1846 had temporarily abated the attacks upon the college, but within a few years its narrowly classical curriculum, its continuing association with Anglicanism, and its failure to secure large numbers of students were again attracting attention. Sir Edmund Walker Head, lieutenant-governor from 1848 to 1854, was a sympathetic critic, and it was he in 1854 who rescued the college from the dangers of a bitter assembly debate on the future of its provincial grant by successfully proposing the appointment of a commission of enquiry to recommend possible changes. Among the members of the commission, chaired by a member of the provincial government in the person of John Hamilton Gray, were the superintendent of education for Nova Scotia and future principal of McGill College, William Dawson, and Egerton Ryerson of Canada. The report was produced before the end of 1854, and its recommendations recalled the proposals of Sir William Colebrooke some ten years before, as well as reflecting the more recent suggestions of Sir Edmund Head himself. Admitting the shortcomings of King's College, the report none the less refused to recommend its abolition. Instead, it suggested the creation of a non-denominational University of New Brunswick which would exercise direct supervision over King's College, but would also examine candidates for degrees who had been trained at other collegiate institutions in the province. The proposed university would also regulate the normal, grammar, and parish schools, in order to ensure a co-ordinated system. 'Thus,' the commissioners believed, 'will the denominational seminaries, as well as other educational institutions of the country, become linked to the University in the bond of common relationship, co-operation, and interest; the independent self-government of those seminaries, will not, in the slightest degree, be interfered with, while their exertions and usefulness will be encouraged and honoured. There will be connexion and unity in the whole system, from the Parish School up to the University.'[32]

It was an intelligent report and a worthy ideal. The proposals were virtually identical with those that Enoch Wood had been prepared to welcome from the standpoint of the Wesleyan Academy a decade before. Yet political turmoil supervened, and the so-called 'Smashers' asserted their supremacy in the assembly during 1856 and 1857, and it was in this context of three years of inaction upon the commission's report that the Mount Allison college proposal went forward to the legislature. By now it was clear that a full-scale attack upon King's College was imminent, and the passage of the Mount Allison legislation through the assembly in February was a prelude to that assault: the trustees' petition and the resulting bill were both sponsored by Albert Smith, a leader of the Smashers and a bitter enemy of King's College, who was also member for Westmorland County.[33] None the less, the debate in the Legislative Council in the following month demonstrated that the institution of a college at Mount Allison was not simply a project of the Smashers. Several councillors expressed hopes for the establishment of a genuinely provincial university in the future, but were inclined to regard the Mount Allison proposal as, in the words of one, 'a distinct application to which the parties were entitled.' There was praise for the operation of the Sackville academies, especially from the Westmorland councillors E.B. Chandler and A.E. Botsford; evidently having long forgotten the controversies over the revival meetings of 1845, both stressed the importance of the zeal and organization which could be contributed to a college by the support of a religious denomination. Even W.H. Odell, a graduate of King's College and its strong supporter, did not seriously oppose the measure, although he warned that the new Wesleyan college would soon be applying for provincial funds: 'this would certainly be required unless the Wesleyans possessed the philosopher's stone, an article which he could not see when some time ago looking over their Musuem.'[34]

Shortly afterwards, with the lieutenant-governor's assent given on 6 April 1858, the Mount Allison trustees had their college charter. Its terms were simple. The trustees were constituted as the board of governors of the college. They would appoint the president and professors who would constitute the faculty, and the governors and the faculty together would comprise the college board which would regulate academic matters. As soon as the faculty consisted of the president and two or more professors, and as soon as ten or more students were duly matriculated, the college would have full power to confer 'the Degrees of Bachelor, Master and Doctor in the several Arts and Faculties.'[35] All had gone smoothly, especially when the fortunes of Mount Allison were compared with the travails of King's College: the opponents of the college had succeeded in having a measure passed, after lengthy debates in both houses, to discontinue its grant as from 1 February 1859. As one historian has remarked, 'outwardly, it seemed that the home of higher education in New Brunswick was to be transferred from Fredericton to Sackville.'[36] The minutes of the conference of Eastern British America, meeting in Halifax in June 1858, naturally made no reference to the apparently imminent demise of King's College, Fredericton; but they recorded the resolution that the conference 'rejoices to learn that the Legislature of the Province of New Brunswick, at its late session, granted a Charter for the establishment of ... [a college]; and recognizes it as an imperative duty to adopt measures for the accomplishment of this object at the earliest possible period.'[37] In reality, though, the conference minutes did not tell the whole story, any more than did the act discontinuing the King's College grant. Judging by the report in the *Provincial Wesleyan* that the passage of the college resolution had been preceded by 'an animated conversation,' the advisability of proceeding had not gone unchallenged in the conference. Then at a public meeting held at the Brunswick Street Church in Halifax a few days later, Pickard had indicated that an annual revenue of at least £1000 would be needed in order for the college to prosper. Since tuition fees and government grants were unlikely to yield any such sum, it was clear that a substantial endowment fund would be required, quite apart from the capital expense of constructing and furnishing a building. With the net debt of the academy standing at £1450/12/7 in the year ending 10 June 1858, this was obviously no easy undertaking.[38]

As for King's College, the events of early 1858 comprised only the first phase of a long campaign. Although the lieutenant-governor, now J.H.T. Manners-Sutton since Head's departure for Canada in 1854, felt unable to refuse assent to the bill directed against the college grant, for fear of provoking popular unrest, he soon began to seek constitutional means by which to frustrate its purpose. At the same time the provincial government, under the leadership of Charles Fisher, rallied support for a bill to transform King's College into a non-denominational University of New Brunswick. This measure adopted many of the principles and much of the phraseology recommended by the commission of 1854. The university would be governed by a senate consisting of eight laymen and the university president, while its chair in theology was abolished, and no reference at all was made to the established church. In order to promote the provincial character of the university, free tuition was offered to a set number of undergraduates from each county and from the cities of Fredericton and Saint John, while a broad curriculum was ensured by the continuation of instruction in engineering and the introduction of special courses in agriculture and in commerce and navigation. These courses, additional to the regular arts programme, had been recommended by the 1854 commission; so too had the provision, also now incorporated into the bill, that students from affiliated institutions in the province, designated as such by the lieutenant-governor, would be eligible for degrees conferred by the university. In one important respect, however, the bill differed from the commission's proposals. The commission had envisaged that King's College would remain as one of the federated institutions within the university, and thus that although the university would have special responsibilities for the administration of King's, it would none the less be a non-teaching body. As the bill was now drafted, the University of New Brunswick would in effect evolve out of King's College, which would disappear and be replaced by a non-denominational teaching university, and this point would assume great importance in the view of the prospective founders of the Wesleyan College. The University of New Brunswick Act was passed by the legislature in April 1859. Although it would be early 1860 before it was confirmed in London and finally proclaimed, its passage ensured that any decisions taken in regard to the proposed Sackville college in 1859 would be taken in a different context from that which had seemed to obtain in the previous year.[39]

In the meantime, Mount Allison had suffered a severe loss with the sudden death of Charles Frederick Allison on 20 November 1858. His funeral in Lingley Hall was attended by all the students of both academies, while in the *Provincial Wesleyan* he was described as 'a benefactor to his race, a blessing to his country, an ornament to the age in which he lived.'[40] Many of the tributes paid at this time might well have been deprecated by Allison himself, for he had never courted praise. Yet they represented a sense of grief that went far beyond the requirements of dutiful observance. Allison was not only the founder of the academy, but he had also been a familiar figure to all who lived and worked there, as well as to the Sackville community as a whole. The local newspaper, the *Borderer*, described his death as 'a public bereavement' and remarked upon 'the many ways in which his quiet influence will be so much missed in our neighborhood.'[41] In an address later delivered to the students, at their request, Humphrey Pickard declared that Allison's gift to Mount Allison had been his time as well as his money, and the point was taken up in a written tribute by Richard Knight. As treasurer of the academy, Knight recalled, as a working member of the board of trustees, and as a participant in 'the execution of every plan the Board devised for the extension and consolidation of our Educational Establishment,' Allison had added to his already remarkable contribution.[42] His passing was mourned not so much as the demise of a benefactor, which it was, nor yet as the severance of a link with Mount Allison's past, which it also was, but rather as the loss of an able counsellor and a loyal and constant friend of the institution.

Allison's will contained further provisions for Mount Allison, in the form of a bequest of £500 for the academy and one of £250 for the proposed college. Meeting in January 1859, the trustees determined that the latter bequest should be used as the beginning of the endowment for 'the Charles F. Allison Professorship,' and announced the intention of raising at least £2500 to ensure the perpetual maintenance of this chair as a fitting memorial to the founder.[43] But in order to institute a college professorship there must first be a college, and the trustees betrayed their awareness at this same meeting that there were serious obstacles to be overcome. The expense of beginning a college had always been potentially daunting, and now matters were made worse by another in the series of cyclical depressions which affected the region in the mid-nineteenth century. In this case, the crisis originated in Great Britain, where currency shortages and price fluctuations had a severe effect upon demand for New Brunswick timber, perceptible from late 1858.[44] Like its recent predecessors, this depression would prove to be only a temporary interruption of the region's prosperity, but it was enough to prompt the Mount Allison trustees to suspend all fund-raising efforts except those in aid of the Allison professorship.[45] By June, when the trustees met in Charlottetown during the sessions of the conference of Eastern British America, Pickard was able to report that £1070 had been given or promised. It was not a bad sum, but it was far from completing the fund, and gave no encouragement for hopes of proceeding at once with the college. Accordingly, the trustees voted 'to postpone further effort for the immediate establishment of a College proper,' although they also recommended that the conference should take steps 'to effect a provision [for] the Theological Education of Candidates for the Ministry.'[46]

Thus, the two purposes for which the college had been intended were now separated, and the initiative was thrown back to the conference. Though unrecorded in the minutes of either body, there was also the additional complication of the impending organization of the University of New Brunswick. The actual inauguration of the new university was still over a year away, but the effect it might have on the enrolments at Mount Allison and on the future award of government grants was unpredictable, and provided an additional reason for delay. The demand for theological education, however, depended upon the Methodist denomination itself rather than upon an appeal to a wider constituency, and there was no question of obtaining any government funding. The way was therefore clear for this aspect of the college scheme, provided only that sufficient initial funds could be raised. In deciding to proceed, the conference adopted a simple expedient: the Allison professorship would be in the field of theology. Accordingly, the subscriptions raised to date could be applied to the proposed theological school, and arrangements were made to appoint a fund-raising agent in each of the districts of the conference. With the double appeal of the need for theological training and the desire to commemorate the life of Charles Allison, the conference anticipated 'hearty co-operation.'[47]

When the conference reassembled in Fredericton the following year, its hopes had not been entirely fulfilled, although a report that fund-raising efforts 'in many places were very successful' led to the hope that the Allison professorship would be fully endowed 'at the earliest period possible.' It was also hoped that an appointment could be made to the chair a year hence, and in the meantime the superintending minister of the Sackville circuit was 'especially charged ... with the oversight of the Divinity studies of such Students in the Mount Allison Academy as may have been recommended as candidates for our Ministry. ...'[48] Whether by chance or design, a new minister was appointed to Sackville at this conference of 1860, Charles DeWolfe. A native of Wolfville who had been converted to Methodism from an earlier association with the Baptists, DeWolfe had studied at the Hoxton Theological Institute in England and had once declined the principalship of the Horton Academy. He was thus an obvious candidate for the oversight of theological students, and in 1861 was invited to assume the title of theological professor.[49] DeWolfe was not unreservedly enthusiastic – the conference had 'insisted on my remaining in this village as Professor of Theology,' he wrote to a friend – but he accepted. Nor did he have any illusions about the difficulties of his task, which forced him to '*attempt* a good deal – Theology, Homileticks [*sic*], Biblical Introduction, Church History and the Hebrew language.' With a low salary, and a 'very meagre' library, DeWolfe could only hope for better times in the future; 'it is,' he reflected, 'the day of small things with us.'[50] However, with the exception of a single year, when his health and that of his wife prompted him to retire to Shelburne, Nova Scotia, in 1862–3, DeWolfe would serve as professor of theology until 1868. For all that, the endowment fund for the Allison chair remained incomplete, leaving theological training to be funded for the time being from general conference funds. The theological professorship thus did not become the direct memorial to Charles Allison that had been intended; but the intention had none the less prompted the beginning of theological instruction at Mount Allison.

As for the 'college proper,' its postponement in the summer of 1859 proved to be a lengthy one. Throughout the 1859–60 academic year the proposal was lost to view, and the decision of the trustees in May 1860 to support John Allison's request for an enlargement to the ladies' academy suggests that the possibility of raising funds for a college was far from their minds. The conference of Eastern British America, meeting in Fredericton in June, apart from its actions on the theological professorship, confined itself to routine expressions of confidence in the management of the academies, and the appointment of trustees.[51] Life at the academies, in fact, had proceeded along familiar lines during the year. On 19 January 1860, a group of alumni had gathered to celebrate the anniversary of the opening in 1843, and to be entertained by 'multiplied electrical experiments.' In February, the correspondent of the *Provincial Wesleyan* had noted evidence in the end-of-term public examinations of both academies of 'a wise appreciation of the inestimable privilege ... [the students] enjoy at Sackville of obtaining education on enlightened and most approved principles, and that on the part of the Board of Instruction there had been a faithful remembrance of their responsibility. ...' In April, John Allison had written to the same newspaper to announce a great upsurge in religious feeling at the ladies' academy, all the while disclaiming any sectarian influence: 'it has been a subject of much anxiety with us to avoid unsettling the religious beliefs of those committed to our care.'[52] All agreed that it had been a successful and productive year – one of 'continued and unchecked progress of our Academy with those high educational and moral ends for which it was established,' as the trustees put it – but nowhere was there any mention of a college.[53]

It was in the columns of the *Provincial Wesleyan*, however, that the issue was revived later in 1860, and in controversial circumstances. The episode began quietly enough, with a letter written under the pseudonym 'Juvenis' in praise of the performance of the Mount Allison students at the terminal examinations held in late October. In conclusion, the writer remarked upon 'the large number of young men in attendance at the male Branch, and the advanced character of the studies pursued by a large portion of the students,' and inferred that a college education could be given at Sackville with little addition to the staff and few increases in expense. Surely, he hoped, 'the day is not far distant when the Church will discharge her duty in this respect.'[54] Juvenis offered no clue to his identity, except that he was returning to Sackville after a long absence, and thus was probably a former student of the academy. His call to action might well have gone unnoticed had it not been for the harsh reaction of the editor of the *Colonial Presbyterian*, a Saint John newspaper that had emerged as a strong supporter of the newly inaugurated University of New Brunswick. The *Presbyterian* had not supported every part of the university's constitution – it had, for example, attacked the exclusion of clergymen from the university senate – but its ultimate conclusion had been that this was a genuinely non-denominational institution and deserved support. The determination of the provincial government to demonstrate the magnitude of the change that had taken place had even led to the appointment of a Methodist as the first president: none other than Joseph Hea, much of whose teaching career had been spent at the Wesleyan Academy. Hea's departure from Sackville had been abrupt, and there had been hints of personal feuds and recriminations.[55] Certainly, the tone of his public utterances, as reported by the *Presbyterian* in early 1861, suggests that his memories of Mount Allison were not altogether warm. In the meantime, however, it was the *Presbyterian* itself which launched a full-scale attack upon Juvenis. All denominations, argued the editorial of 29 November 1860, should support the University of New Brunswick and should avoid competing with it. As for a college in Sackville, 'we have seldom heard of anything more absurd, unless it were the idea that the Government of this country, which has committed itself to the University education of the people, by means of one great and central institution, should lend any additional pecuniary aid to such a fantastic project.'[56]

The *Colonial Presbyterian* editorial brought a quick response in the columns of the *Provincial Wesleyan*, and from an evidently more formidable controversialist than Juvenis. 'Laicus,' though again affording little clue to his identity except that he was evidently a Methodist and, from his pseudonym, a layman, wrote first to denounce in general terms the editorial's 'insufferable arrogance.'[57] The following week, he wrote at greater length. Reviewing the history of the Sackville college proposal since its origins in 1857, he recalled that its implementation had only been postponed, because of 'the fearful financial depression from whose effects the Provinces have not yet fully recovered.' Defending Juvenis, he went on to praise the quality of instruction at the Sackville academy, and in the collegiate course especially:

> Although under existing circumstances very few students only have been induced to pursue the full course 'regularly and systematically' to its close, from one half to three-fourths of the work of instruction which would have been necessary to conduct a full set of College classes each year through an under-graduate course of study, has been done and *well done* at Sackville. Probably it would not be too much to claim that during the last seven years as many students have been receiving collegiate instruction at Sackville as at any institution in either Nova Scotia or New Brunswick; and had the 'small numerical additions of one or two' above contemplated, been made to the Professorial Staff at the commencement of this period, and had the institution then assumed its rank as a College, offering as an inducement to a full course of Collegiate study the honor of University degrees, it would, I doubt not, have had larger college classes than any other institution in the country.

The arguments of Laicus chiefly concerned the past, and aimed to establish only that the letter of Juvenis had contained nothing unreasonable. He pointed out that Joseph Hea himself had received his 'highest scholastic training' at Sackville. What Laicus carefully avoided was any suggestion of action that the Methodist denomination could or should take, although he called for a further discussion of 'Provincial Education' in the columns of the *Provincial Wesleyan*.[58] None the less, even his statements in the past tense were enough to fuel the fires of controversy. That the *Colonial Presbyterian* should take the fight back to Laicus on December 20th and 27th was to be expected. Even among the Methodists, the *Presbyterian* contended, there were few who really favoured the notion of instituting a 'sham college.'[59] But when J.R. Hea took the field in January, to attack Mount Allison in a speech delivered in Saint John, that was a different matter. His aspersions did not go unchallenged, for a reply was delivered shortly afterwards by J.R. Narraway, minister of the Carleton Street Church in Saint John, but at least one interested observer, the former academy teacher Thomas Wood, felt that Hea had had the better of the exchange. 'Poor Mr. Narraway,' wrote Wood in a private letter, 'has got into trouble in St. John.'[60] Be that as it might, for the president of the University of New Brunswick to become publicly involved in a controversy over a college proposal that had lain dormant for nearly two years obviously lent credibility to the notion that the project might be revived. Whether the Mount Allison college charter of 1858 would have been quietly forgotten if it had not been for this outbreak cannot be known with certainty. Even now, there was no return to the rather easy self-confidence that had been evident when the proposal had first been mooted in 1857. It was undoubtedly the controversy, however, that prompted a series of closely argued editorials in the *Provincial Wesleyan* in early 1861, a series which not only became a manifesto for the establishment of the Mount Allison college in the following year, but also accurately presaged its character for the first two decades of its existence.

All these editorials, the first appearing on 16 January, were anonymous. The editor was Charles Churchill, a minister and a trustee of Mount Allison, and it is possible that he himself was the author. However, Churchill had announced a few months earlier, at the time of his appointment as editor, that he would draw upon other leading members of the conference to supplement his own editorials, and it is hard to avoid the conclusion that the author may well have been Humphrey Pickard. What is certain is that the articles soon gained acceptance as representing the official views of Mount Allison, for two of them were reprinted with approval in the December 1861 issue of the *Mount Allison Academic Gazette*.[61] The first editorial dealt generally with the objectives of higher education, which should, it argued, 'be as widely diffused as possible.' Not that higher education should be universal in society – the article rejected this as impractical – but it ought to be 'accessible to all who may aspire to its attainment, and to all who, from position or profession, ought to have it in their possession.' Merchants, manufacturers, farmers, legislators, doctors, lawyers, journalists, schoolteachers: all should be 'men of large and liberal culture.'[62] As the second article added, an educated ministry was essential also, for 'the Christian religion wages successful war upon rudeness and ignorance.' The corollary, which the article expounded in terms that recalled Pickard's inaugural address, was that all knowledge was 'but the knowledge of God, of His works, and of the multiform operation of His power.' Education, therefore, could never be isolated from religion, and mental power should always be balanced by religious knowledge and moral strength.[63]

Thus far, the author of the series had restated principles already familiar at Mount Allison. The third article turned to means by which the principles might best be implemented, and identified three possibilities: a state institution; one founded and controlled by an individual; or one controlled by a denomination, with or without state aid. The first – and here the University of New Brunswick was clearly the target, though it was not named – had the fundamental defect that it could never guarantee that its tuition would not fall into the hands of adherents of a particular branch of Christianity or, even worse, of 'Arians, Socinians, and Deists, if not infidels.' It might be, through good fortune, that such a situation would be avoided, and it could also be ameliorated by such expedients as permitting clergymen of the various denominations to have regular access to the undergraduates for religious instruction. But the fact remained that a state institution could not positively ensure 'the effective presence of the religious element in Collegiate Education.' Institutions founded by individuals, the article continued, were usually then presented either to the state or to a denomination, and so needed no consideration in themselves. Denominational colleges therefore comprised the real alternative to state institutions. One form of the denominational college was the one which was sectarian, and imposed religious tests upon its students: such an institution might be morally justifiable, 'but it lies open to the charge of selfishness and unchristian exclusiveness.' A denominational college without religious tests and without proselytism, on the other hand, could offer all the advantages of the state institution in breadth of curriculum and extent of the constituency served, while at the same time guaranteeing a sound Christian education. Such a denominational college would also have the additional advantage of being able to attract private donations, whether from the wealthy or from 'the cheerful tribute of generous poverty,' would have greater incentives towards economical working because not entirely dependent on government funding, and would have a substantial natural constituency of students from its own denomination.[64]

Now, on 6 February, the penultimate article moved ahead to practical matters. A denominational college, it argued, had 'a most righteous claim' to state aid, provided only that it was 'doing work for the State by imparting literary and scientific culture,' and with the major exception that theological education should be entirely the responsibility of the denomination itself. One way of effectively regulating the relationship between college and state would be through a non-teaching university, such as the University of London, Queen's University of Ireland, or the University of Toronto. If such an arrangement could be replicated in New Brunswick, the fifth and last editorial affirmed, 'this plan, if honourably and justly carried out in good faith we perhaps would prefer.' Among other advantages, 'it would forever relieve us from the malicious imputation of attempting to palm off an inferior Collegiate education upon our Church and country.' Nevertheless, if 'a properly constituted New Brunswick University' proved unattainable, there was still the charter of 1858.[65] One way or the other, the author concluded with a ringing call to action, though also including a long and significant series of warnings:

It might be deemed *desirable* to crown some swelling eminence at Sackville with a gorgeous Collegiate structure, with cloistered courts and marble front; with turret, and pinnacle, and spire; with traceried windows, 'richly dight,' shedding, through many-tinted glass, a 'dim, religious light' on long-drawn corridors, on tesselated pavements, and through lofty halls. But what is needful is, a plain, substantial, comfortable, well-arranged building in which College Classes may recite, and College lectures may be delivered. It might be *desirable* to found an immense library, illustrative of the science and literature of all times and of all climes, rich in undecipherable manuscripts and marvellous typography. But what is *needful* is a sufficient number of books, treating in their totality exhaustively upon all the branches of proper Collegiate study, – procurable for a modest sum, and which may be steadily increased from year to year. It might be *desirable* that vast collections of objects in all departments of Natural Science should be accumulated at Sackville; that magnificent and costly Chemical, Philosophical and Astronomical apparatus should be procured; and that a lofty, cloud-piercing observatory should be reared, whence young Newtons and Herschels might watch the unrolling of the Celestial mysteries. But what is *needful* to begin with is, a sufficient number of natural objects, and a sufficiently extensive apparatus to illustrate the leading principles of the several departments of Natural Science; an introduction to which is all that can be attempted in a College course, without substituting certain easy flash studies, included in the inductive Sciences which are feeble developers of mind, for the difficult, deductive Sciences which are mind educators of the highest class. It might be *desirable* that there should be rich endowments by which world-renowned men of learning might be drawn to the Professorial chairs; and wealthy bachelors might be induced to wed themselves to the life-long pursuits of Science. But what is *needful* is, sufficient endowments or means to command men competent to do the work required – a class of men with which nine colleges out of ten, the wide world over, are compelled to be content – Scaligers and Newtons, Bentleys, Porsons and Parrs have never, at any time, been very plentiful. It might be *desirable* that multitudinous scholarships and captivating prizes should be provided to attract and stimulate the youthful minds, otherwise insensible to the charms of mental culture. But what is *needful* is, that the requisite facilities be provided for imparting a sound Collegiate education at Sackville, and then Methodism will find a way to bring her sons within its reach; and the prizes will come in good time.[66]

Thus, in accordance with his professed suspicion of the inductive sciences, the author of the editorials had argued from the general to the particular. The general principles – the desirability of wider access to higher education, and the need for intellectual training to be put in a Christian context – had yielded the conclusions that the University of New Brunswick was unacceptable as presently constituted, and that there should be a Methodist college, preferably within the larger framework of a non-teaching university. Furthermore, the Methodist college must define itself not according to grandiose institutional aspirations, but strictly according to what was necessary in order for it to fulfil the purposes that were again dictated by the more general principles with which the articles had begun. It was an impressive case, and certainly appealed strongly to the board of trustees at its meeting in June, held in Saint John in conjunction with the annual meeting of the conference. Two important decisions of the trustees looked forward to the inauguration of the college. The first was to appoint George S. Milligan as an additional professor – he would be professor of Latin – 'with the intention of establishing a class for undergraduate instruction.' Secondly, the board resolved unanimously that 'the establishment of a proper University Body – to be separate and independent of all teaching Institutions, and to be the sole source of University honours and degrees, would prove of essential advantage to the cause of liberal education in this Province'; it therefore requested the conference to appoint a committee to apply persuasion to the provincial government towards this end.[67]

This the conference immediately did, expressing full agreement with the trustees, and later in the summer Pickard and John McMurray, minister in Saint John and secretary of the conference, visited the New Brunswick provincial secretary, Leonard Tilley, to press their case. As the next session of the legislature approached, a petition was drafted, and on 17 January 1862 Pickard wrote a seven-page letter to Tilley in which he marshalled the general arguments in favour of a non-teaching university and contrasted the shortcomings of the current University of New Brunswick. 'Let the College at Fredericton remain with all its property, etc. intact,' he urged, 'only, requiring it to drop its recently acquired mis-nomer of University of New Brunswick and allowing it to resume its former and much more becoming title of King's College or any other *praenomen* which may be preferred.' Then King's, Mount Allison, and any other qualified college could enjoy equality and freedom under the provincial university.[68] Yet all was in vain. In the summer of 1861, it might not have been difficult to rally support for a further reform of university education, for the University of New Brunswick's first year had been a stormy one. The former president of King's College, E.F. Jacob, whose clerical status had barred him from continuing in that position in the new university, had refused to accept his reduction to the role of professor of classics and moral philosophy, and had obstructed Hea as much as he could. Hea had also become embroiled in acrimonious disputes with students upon whom he had attempted to enforce a strict disciplinary regime, and this had led to his forced resignation after only a year in office. However, his successor, William Brydone Jack, had greater success, partly because Jacob had retired at the same time as Hea had departed.[69] By early 1862 the University of New Brunswick was a solid reality, and it would clearly be difficult to justify yet another upheaval. On 13 March, the petition of Pickard and his colleagues on the conference committee was introduced into the assembly by a former academy student who was now member for Albert County, A.R. McClelan. It was read by McClelan, received, tabled, and considered no further.[70]

The response of the Mount Allison board of trustees was not long delayed. Meeting on 10 May 1862, the board heard 'that the Government, though quite favourable to the proposed University Scheme, yet under existing circumstances, decline for the present to entertain such project.' After some debate, it was then resolved to proceed to establish a college under the 1858 charter and authorization was given to start the construction of a suitable building. The one proviso was that the inauguration of the college should not involve the incurring of any further debt: the building was to be funded by subscriptions raised for the purpose, while faculty members would be salaried only for their teaching duties at the academy and their remuneration for college teaching would be drawn directly from 'class fees' paid by the college students. Indeed, no additions to the existing staff were contemplated, and Humphrey Pickard was appointed as president of the college in addition to his existing role as principal of the male academy.[71] Pickard entered on his new duties with gusto: Charles DeWolfe, now completing his first year as theological professor, wrote in a private letter of 20 May that 'Dr. P. is full of the

College and has already commenced with the foundation of the New Hall, which will be open in the Autumn.'[72]

There was just one important detail, however, which had not been finalized, and that was the approval of the conference. Given the resolution of 1861, in favour of a college within a federated provincial university if possible, but under the 1858 charter if necessary, it may have been assumed by Pickard and the trustees that their actions would be automatically ratified. It is also possible that the hasty beginning of the college building in May represented an attempt to present the conference with a *fait accompli*. In either case, the college proposal did not have a smooth passage when the conference met in Halifax in late June and early July. There had always been resistance within the denomination to the notion of beginning an independent college. It would be an expensive project, and now that it was no longer possible to think of operating within the framework of a non-teaching university, there was the likelihood of competition with the University of New Brunswick. What if the *Colonial Presbyterian*'s jibes about 'sham colleges' should be proved all too apt? As DeWolfe was to reflect a few months later, 'the political strife to which some of our Colonial colleges have given rise, has rather frightened some of our timid people at the very name of such a thing.'[73] On the other hand, it could be argued that the past record of the academy gave reason for confidence in the academic success of the proposed college, and that the trustees had made their arrangements with expense cut to a minimum. Such were the contentions undoubtedly advanced by Pickard, who happened also to be president of the conference in this year, during the 'lengthened debate' on the college question which occupied two complete sessions of the conference, from the beginning of the evening session on 1 July until midday on the following day.[74] The fact was too that plans for the college were already well advanced, and the building partially constructed. According to one observer, it was this last point that was ultimately decisive, as made by John Brewster, minister in Halifax:

> Who that was in that Conference when Dr. Pickard read a balance-sheet of a building just erected, and asked permission to go on, can forget it? A College? A College at Sackville? The witty Brewster turned the current of doubt and prejudice by asking if the Conference was prepared for the contempt which must come to Methodism if the traveller, passing that way, should wag his head and say – 'This man began to build and was not able to finish?'[75]

Accordingly, the conference resolved to give its 'cordial sympathy' to the college scheme, although it did so with a preamble which reflected the nature of the preceding debate. The previous year's resolutions, including that in favour of a provincial non-teaching university, were reaffirmed, despite the recognition that 'the application to the Government and Legislature, as ordered in the recent resolution, was unsuccessful.' Furthermore, the actions of the board of trustees were approved with an explicit understanding that they 'do not involve the necessity of any general appeal throughout the Circuits for additional funds.'[76] The college was now clear to go ahead, but the manner of its approval gave important clues to its future character. When the proposal had first been put forward in 1857, it had been in prosperous times and with King's College in a state of decay. Neither of these circumstances had persisted. When the project had been revised in 1861, even its staunchest advocates, such as the author of the *Provincial Wesleyan* articles, had expressed a preference for a federated provincial university, with an independent college as a second choice, and with sombre warnings that in either case the institutional aspirations of the college must be strictly limited. On that basis the scheme had proceeded, but even so had nearly foundered in the face of scepticism within the conference of Eastern British America. The result was a mandate for a college which would serve the educational needs of the population of the region, and of Methodists in particular. It was not a mandate, however, for institutional aggrandizement, nor even a commitment to institutional independence except in so far as there was no acceptable alternative. The decision had been taken, and as a measure in the interests of Christian education it had been taken wholeheartedly; but the choice of an independent, degree-granting college had been a reluctant one.[77]

The decision once taken, of course, there was no reluctance about the opening of the college, although it, like the academy nineteen years before, had a quiet start. Despite the rapid progress made during the summer, there was no chance that the building would be ready by the beginning of the academic year on 24 July, and so classes were apparently held at first in the male academy. In the year 1862–3 there would be 20 students, of whom eight were special students, pursuing only certain subjects, while 12 were enrolled in the three-year degree programmes. Of the 12, two – Josiah Wood and Howard Sprague – had already completed sufficient work in the academy to be classed as senior students, while four were juniors and the remaining six were freshmen.[78] By October 1st, the college building was close enough to completion to allow its use for what was advertised as a 'great tea meeting,' open to the public at the modest admission fee of 37½ cents. The third storey, as yet 'unencumbered by any partition walls,' would provide space for no less than 500 people to sit down to tea at one time; perhaps necessarily in view of the numbers expected, the advertisement also guaranteed 'adequate arrangements for the preservation of becoming order throughout every part, so that the safety of both person and property may be ensured, and the comfort of all promoted.' Not least through the over $300 profit realized, the day was evidently a great success, and it supplied a fitting prelude to the formal opening on New Year's Day, 1863.[79]

With a platform party including local Anglican, Baptist, and Presbyterian clergymen, the opening ceremony was designed to demonstrate the absence of sectarian rivalry, to remove, as the *Provincial Wesleyan*'s correspondent put it, 'the jealousy ... with which the enterprise had been regarded, by a number of the friends of education, both lay and ministerial.' Sixty-eight by forty feet, and standing beside Lingley Hall, the three-storey college building was plain and unpretentious. Its interior was functional, containing a lecture-room, a library, and four classrooms on the ground floor, with a large students' meeting-room and sixteen individual studies on the other two floors. Although the third storey was not yet complete at the time of the opening, it was undoubtedly 'a respectable addition to the previously existing set of Academic Edifices. ...'[80] Less than five months later, the Mount Allison Wesleyan College was ready to confer its first degrees, as Sprague and Wood delivered their senior orations in Lingley Hall on May 19th, prior to receiving their Bachelor of Arts degrees. Sprague, a future dean of theology at Mount Allison, spoke on 'the Changelessness of Human Nature,' while Wood, later to be lieutenant-governor of New Brunswick, addressed himself to 'Modern Delusions': the two presentations were no doubt complementary. The first graduation was an event of obvious importance, and the trustees, meeting on the same day, saw every reason to expect that the college would 'speedily take permanent rank with the best Colonial Collegiate Establishments.'[81]

Just how far this was a realistic hope would of course depend upon the strength of the foundations laid for the new college, both academically and administratively. The faculty, consisting of five professors and J.R. Inch as 'Teacher in French' – not yet a graduate, Inch was enrolled as a student as well as being a faculty member, and would graduate in 1864 – gave ample evidence of the truth of the later aphorism that a Mount Allison professor occupied not a chair but a settee. Humphrey Pickard took responsibility for 'Logic, Ethics, Evidences of Christianity, &c.,' while his brother Thomas taught 'Mathematics, Natural Philosophy, Astronomy, &c.' John Allison was professor of 'Rhetoric, Mental Philosophy and German,' while the two classical professors each had non-classical responsibilities as well. David Allison taught political economy as well as Greek, and G.S. Milligan both Latin and Hebrew. Of the five professors, each held the degrees of AB and AM, although in practice the requirements for the Master's degree would customarily have involved but little beyond the course of study for the AB. Humphrey Pickard's Doctorate of Divinity, the only degree held by any faculty member higher than the AM, was an honorary degree. Predominantly, the faculty members were Maritime-born: the two Allisons in Newport, Nova Scotia, the Pickards near Fredericton, New Brunswick, and Inch in the small community of Jerusalem, in Queen's County, New Brunswick. The only exception was Milligan, who was a native of Scotland but had come to New Brunswick as a young man. Conversely, Milligan was also the only graduate on the faculty who had not received his training in the United States: he had graduated from King's College, Fredericton. Humphrey and Thomas Pickard, and David Allison, were all graduates of Wesleyan University, while John Allison had at one time attended classes at Dalhousie, but had graduated from Syracuse University.[82] Thus, the faculty members represented the tendency which it was hoped the inauguration of the Mount Allison college would bring to an end: of the fourteen resident students at the college in August 1864, wrote Humphrey Pickard to the minister W.B. Boyce in England, 'almost every one ... would be, had it not been for our College's organisation, prosecuting his course of study under influences alien either to Methodism or to British Institutions.'[83]

For their work, the Mount Allison professors were not generously paid. In the year 1862–3, Humphrey Pickard's salary was $900, compared with that of $2000 enjoyed by Brydone Jack at the University of New Brunswick. With a single exception, the other professors in Fredericton were paid $1200, whereas Thomas Pickard, David Allison, and Milligan had salaries of $700. The salary of John Allison was paid through the ladies' academy, and was not separately itemized in its accounts, but was probably comparable to that of the other three professors; Inch, as a more junior member, had a salary of only $400. To these salaries were added the 'class fees' paid by students at the rate of $3 per subject per term, to a normal maximum of $36 for a regular student. Given the small numbers attending the college in the 1860s, this may have added a little over $100 to a professor's salary in a good year. Salaries, in fact, comprised one manifestation of the extent to which the college in its early years was a relatively small outgrowth of the academy.[84]

The curriculum too showed clearly its close kinship to the collegiate course in the male academy, which it had now displaced. The ladies' academy still offered a collegiate course leading to the diploma of Mistress of Liberal Arts, and would continue to do so even after women became eligible in 1872 to enrol in the college, but the male academy now offered only the primary and intermediate courses. Successful completion of the intermediate course constituted the matriculation requirement for the college, and most of the college students in the early years did come out of the academy. There were others, however, and all applicants who were 'of good moral character, and of, at least, fourteen years of age' were entitled to write matriculation examinations at the beginning of the academic year. Once admitted to the college, there were two principal degree programmes from which to choose, the Bachelor of Arts (BA) and Bachelor of Science (BS); from 1864 the degree of Master of Arts was open to 'any Bachelor of Arts of three years' standing, who shall satisfy the faculty that his course, subsequent to graduation, has been such as to entitle him to this distinction.'[85] The BA was advertised at first as a three-year degree, and essentially remained as such until the 1880s. However, from 1867 onwards it was set out as a four-year programme which 'may be completed in three years, by such students as can prepare well for four recitations daily.' The subjects of study were specified term by term:

Freshman year, First Term:	Horace; Homer's Iliad; Chemistry
Second Term:	Horace and Livy; Herodotus; Chemistry
Third Term:	Livy; Plato's Gorgias; Physiology
Sophomore year, First Term:	Cicero de Officiis; Aeschines de Corona; Algebra
Second Term:	Tacitus; Demosthenes de Corona; Geometry
Third Term:	Juvenal; Greek Tragedy; Trigonometrical Analysis
Junior Year, First Term:	Advanced French *or* English Constitutions; Analytical Geometry; Rhetoric
Second Term	Advanced French *or* Political Economy; Calculus; Rhetoric
Third Term:	Advanced French *or* International Law; Optics; Logic
Senior Year, First Term:	Mental Philosophy; Geology and Mineralogy; Analytical Mechanics *or* German *or* Hebrew
Second Term:	Moral Philosophy; Zoology; Analytical Mechanics *or* German *or* Hebrew
Third Term:	Evidences of Christianity; Wood's Botany *or* Paley's Natural Theology; Astronomy *or* German *or* Hebrew[86]

The curriculum was thus divided perceptibly into two halves. In the first half, classical study was paramount, although the student was also introduced to certain aspects of science and mathematics. In these respects, the Mount Allison curriculum was unexceptional among other BA programmes in British North America. The second half, however, was unusual both in the disappearance of classical studies and in the inclusion of options which enabled a certain amount of specialization. Modern languages were made readily available, as were legal and political studies, and Hebrew for the aspiring minister. Also available as options were more advanced scientific subjects in the form of mechanics and astronomy, although these, like all science subjects, must have been hampered by what one student of the 1860s later described as 'a sad want of apparatus for all kinds of scientific study.' Certain scientific subjects were compulsory in the later years, as were advanced mathematical subjects in the third year, but major emphasis was placed on philosophical studies. One conspicuous omission was English language and literature: English language training was in fact catered for outside of the prescribed classes, in that each student in the first three years was obliged to prepare a weekly exercise, 'alternately in English composition and elocution,' while senior students were required to prepare and deliver two 'original orations' each term.[87] English literature, however, did not enter the curriculum at Mount Allison until 1881.

The Bachelor of Science curriculum – or the Bachelor of Science and English Literature, to give its full and somewhat misleading title, since English literature as such was absent from this programme also – bore close similarities to that for the BA. Set out specifically as a three-year programme, it included all the subjects prescribed for the BA except for the classics and Hebrew. There were no options, and all the subjects optional in the BA curriculum (except for Hebrew) were compulsory for the BS. Added were two terms of 'Practical Mathematics,' the first emphasizing 'Mensuration &c.' and the second 'Surveying and Navigation,' and two terms of 'General History.'[88] As the three-year pattern implied, the BS was regarded as a somewhat lesser degree than the BA, and from 1869 onwards the college catalogue remarked that it was designed for those 'of our British American youth [who] either do not appreciate the importance of classical learning, or lack the time necessary for its acquisition.'[89] What was undoubtedly common to the two courses was a stress on the unity of all knowledge, as was made explicit in the final year through the use of such textbooks as Wayland's *Elements of Moral Science*, for moral philosophy, and Paley's *Evidences of Christianity*. As the catalogue also made clear, 'the fullest recognition ... is given to the truths and claims of the Christian religion; the Bible is publicly honored as the Word of God, and no pains are spared that the education imparted may be suitably leavened with religious principle.'[90]

A similar leavening was evident in the disciplinary regulations provided for the college students. Obviously the full rigours of the academy regime could not be enforced upon students who were necessarily assumed to be older and wiser, but stern and explicit warnings were given against the pitfalls to which even a college student could fall prey. 'The use of tobacco,' reminded the college catalogue, 'or of any kind of intoxicating liquour or drug, resorting to any tavern or place where intoxicating liquors are sold, every species of gambling, and all games of chance, as well as all profanity, are, of course, strictly prohibited.' So too was any absence from the campus in the evening or overnight, unless permission had been obtained in advance; and in case there should be any suspicion of untoward behaviour in the college itself, 'every student's room is considered as always subject to the entrance of any member of the Faculty.' None the less, discipline at the college was not an end in itself, but according to the catalogue was seen rather as a means 'to aid the student in the formation, for himself, of a truly manly character,' and extracurricular hours could be spent on a variety of pursuits towards this end.[91] Some of these were necessary tasks common to both academy and college: all students, for example, still had to cut their own wood. Sporting activities too had changed but little from the earlier years of the academy, with handball and cricket the major sports in the warmer seasons, skating on the marshes in winter, and hurley the year-round game in which the players 'swept the play-ground from end to end like a herd of stampeded buffaloes.'[92] Although baseball was making its first appearance during the 1860s, and hurley was soon afterwards to evolve into hockey, sports at Mount Allison retained as yet their more traditional character.

One activity that had evolved considerably from its origins in the academy, and was recognized as an appropriate and beneficial pastime for the students, was debating, now carried on under the auspices of the Eurhetorian Society. When the society had first been organized by senior academy students in 1861, however, it had run into faculty opposition. One of the charter members later attributed this to the failure of literary societies at the academy in past years, as a succession of such endeavours had apparently risen and fallen since the pioneering days of Amos Purdy, but the fact that a literary society was already successfully operating in the ladies' academy would seem to make this an unlikely explanation. It is more probable that it was the paganistic undertones of the society's first name, 'The Pantheon,' that had caused the trouble. Even the members of the society admitted in late 1861 tht this was 'very inappropriate,' and the name 'Eurhetorian' was adopted in early 1862 at the suggestion of the classics professor, David Allison. It was not unusual for North American college literary societies to enjoy sonorous Greek titles, and this one was probably an adaptation from the 'Philorhetorian Society' at Allison's own *alma mater*, Wesleyan University.[93] The first public meeting of the Eurhetorian was held in Lingley Hall in February 1862, consisting of a debate on the state of the civil war in the United States; so favourable was the impression gained by the faculty, and especially by Humphrey Pickard, that a room in the new college building was set aside for the society's exclusive use, and the college catalogue from 1864 onwards gave official recognition to 'this ... voluntary Literary Society which embraces most, if not all, the members of the College, and also some of the Senior students of the Academy.'[94] The weekly Eurhetorian meeting was not devoted entirely to debates, as fifteen-minute orations by members were also included, but from the beginning it was the debates that lent colour and drama to the occasion. One participant, Benjamin Russell, recalled debating resolutions ranging from whether plants have sensations to the merits or otherwise of trade tariffs imposed by the United States on British North American goods. As a correspondent of the *Provincial Wesleyan* remarked in 1863, the Eurhetorian was a society 'for the mutual improvement of its members,' and he went on to describe it as 'well fitted to be a preparatory school for those who in pursuing a course of study, look forward to forum, bench, or pulpit as the future scene of their labors.'[95]

This anonymous correspondent was in fact entirely correct, not only as to the skills fostered by Eurhetorian debates, but also as to the ambitions of the early generations of students at the Mount Allison Wesleyan Academy. Of the 27 graduates of the 1860s, 25 are known to have entered upon particular careers – one died before he could take up any occupation, while on another no record has survived – and no fewer than 19 out of the 25 became either ministers or lawyers. Not all, of course, followed the same career all their lives, and one of the lawyers first pursued a teaching career, while one of the ministers spent his younger years as a merchant in Yarmouth, Nova Scotia. Conversely, several of the lawyers began new, though related, careers in the course of their lives, either in politics or in teaching law; and of the six lawyers who did not eventually pursue political careers, four became judges. Of the other graduates – those who did not enter the ministry or the law – one was a doctor, one a schoolteacher, one a journalist, one an engineer, while the remaining two went on to have long professorial careers at Mount Allison.[96]

The preponderance of professional or ministerial careers, often leading to positions of influence in church or in state, would have come as no surprise to the author of the editorials in the *Provincial Wesleyan* in 1861, who had argued the need for educated persons in such occupations. There was also another respect in which the careers of the graduates were fulfilling expectations. The *Provincial Wesleyan* had observed on 27 August 1862 that in the past many academy students had been forced to seek out other institutions for their college work, and had often gone outside the Maritime region, perhaps to be 'lost to these Provinces.' This, it was hoped, would be prevented by the opening of the college at Sackville. Similarly, the author of the 1861 editorials had begun from the assumption that 'Eastern British America is our home' and that 'our love for our common country' formed an important part of the justification for the college proposal.[97] To a great extent, the college in the 1860s was indeed producing graduates who would pursue their careers within the region. Of the 25 graduates whose careers are known, 19 remained in the Maritimes; one other, Seward Toddings, was a Bermudian who returned to work in Hamilton. Three of the graduates went to the United States, all as ministers and after spending several years in the Maritimes in each case; the remaining two also began their careers within the region, but eventually took up federal civil service positions in Ottawa. None at all are known to have left Eastern British America on graduation.[98] This does not, of course, imply that Mount Allison must necessarily have bred in its graduates an altruistic desire to serve the Maritime provinces: at a time when the region was producing few college graduates, the route to the highest professional levels lay open to those few, giving them a clear incentive. None the less, in a region which was beginning to feel the effects of out-migration, the fact was that Mount Allison was making good on its claim that it would encourage trained and talented Maritimers to stay.

For all that, the 1860s were not without their crises. One major area of concern was the financial condition of the ladies' academy. The shortfall of $1000 on the construction of the new wing, which had become apparent by the summer of 1861, was serious in itself. What was much worse was that the ladies' academy now began to lose money at an alarming rate on its year-to-year operations. The balance of debt shown on the financial statement for 1860–1 was almost $6500, although the fiction was maintained that unpaid student accounts compensated for some $5300 and that the rest of the debt was more than offset by provisions, stationery, and other materials on hand. In the next three years, the debt mounted, and in 1863–4 the attempt to disguise it was abandoned: the financial statement simply recorded that it stood at just over $16,000.[99] There was no doubt that, as Humphrey Pickard informed Boyce, 'that branch of our Institution is in a very distressing state of embarrassment,' and it was in an atmosphere of crisis that the board of trustees met in May 1864. J.R. Inch later recalled that one trustee had seriously argued for the closure of the ladies' academy; but rather than abandoning the effort to provide woman's education the board decided instead to accept the resignation of John and Martha Allison, who shortly afterwards moved to the United States, and to put both branches under the principalship of Pickard. Inch was appointed vice-principal, and would provide the effective day-to-day leadership for a reduced teaching staff of only five. Inch himself was teacher of languages, in addition to his similar appointments in both of the other institutions, while the other teachers specialized respectively in natural science, mathematics and calisthenics, drawing and painting, and music.[100] This was obviously an unwelcome curtailment, since the staff in 1863–4 had numbered seven, but the result of this and other economies was evident in the accounts for the following year, which showed that the debt had been virtually stabilized, having increased by the relatively small amount of just over $500. As the minister George Butcher remarked in a letter in February 1865, 'the crisis is past with the Female Branch. It may scarcely pay its way this year, but it is making some progress and is gradually, we trust, recommending itself to our people.'[101]

As Butcher hinted, the crisis had not only been financial, but had also involved a loss of public confidence in the ladies' academy. To what extent this had been the personal responsibility of the Allisons is difficult to gauge, but there is no doubt that they bore the brunt of whatever blame was being attributed in 1864. Their initial plans for the ladies' academy had been ambitious, as demonstrated by efforts to diversify the curriculum, by the increase in teaching staff to a peak of nine between 1859 and 1863, and by the expansion of the building. The assumption had been that enrolments would continue to maintain the high levels which they had reached in 1859 (an assumption ultimately proven unjustified), and by early 1861 at least one observer, the former academy teacher Thomas Wood, was privately expressing doubts as to the quality of the Allisons' management. Ill health on the part of Martha Allison certainly had not helped, and was given as the reason for the Allisons' resignation in 1864. Another factor had been persistent personal rivalry between John Allison and Humphrey Pickard: John Allison himself wrote emphatically in late 1862 of 'the *other* side of the *road*,' where '*I have no influence*,' and David Allison later recalled that relations between the two academies in the years from 1857 to 1864 'were not always of the most harmonious character.'[102] To be fair to John Allison, the limited evidence which has survived suggests comparisons between these disputes and those which had occurred between Pickard and Ephraim Evans before the latter had resigned as governor and chaplain in 1857. Both apparently involved overlapping spheres of influence in areas where Pickard had previously enjoyed overriding authority. What was unquestionable, though, was that by 1864 the number of students in the ladies' academy had slipped alarmingly. The beginning of the 1863–4 academic year had been delayed by seven weeks – partly because of the illness of Martha Allison, but also as an attempt to economize on teachers' salaries – and the insertion in the *Mount Allison Academic Gazette* of June 1863 must have conveyed its rather defensive tone to parents of prospective students as it declared that 'the expenses [of ladies' academy students] will be less than usual, and the period of the pupils' absence from home will be shorter. It is hoped that with increased efficiency and attention on the part of the Faculty of Instruction there will be ample opportunity for a successful year's work.' In fact, only some 20 resident students were attracted, and although about 30 local day students added a modicum of respectability to the number, the severe financial deficits clearly could not be allowed to continue.[103]

The financial embarrassment of the ladies' academy inevitably had serious implications for all of the Mount Allison intitutions. The theological branch was experiencing difficulty in attracting candidates for the ministry, and DeWolfe and Pickard commented jointly in a letter of 1863 on the urgent need for endowment funds not only for the Allison professorship but also to provide scholarships for potential students. In early 1866, DeWolfe still regarded his efforts in this field as 'comparatively feeble and tentative,' and complained that most of the candidates lacked the financial resources to stay at Mount Allison for more than one or two years. As Pickard commented shortly afterwards, 'many of them come from the lower walks of life or poorer classes of society.' By December of the same year, DeWolfe was raising the possibility that 'we shall have to go back soon to the old system and import our ministers from England. ...'[104] This was scarcely a serious suggestion, especially in view of the fact that the Missionary Society was now in the process of phasing out its subsidies to the Eastern British America Conference. 'Our constituents,' the secretary W.B. Boyce had warned in 1864, 'will not tolerate any longer that money contributed to the general fund for Missionary purposes should appropriated to a Colonial Pastorate.'[105] Thus, DeWolfe's concern was a clear indication of the need for additional funds from within the region in order to secure the continuation of theological training at Mount Allison.

The same might also be said of the more general work of the college. Throughout the 1860s, the college continued to be carried financially by the academy, which paid the salaries of the professors and administered the boarding arrangements of the students. With its larger enrolment the academy proved able to take the load, and its debt was in fact reduced between 1862 and 1865, from almost $3900 to just over $2100.[106] It was hardly a satisfactory arrangement, and as Pickard later remarked to Boyce, it was 'always regarded by us as proper only as a temporary one, while the Academy was financially able and the College in its infancy.'[107] One obvious answer to the problem of enabling the college to support itself was the raising of government grants. In New Brunswick, however, the launching of the university had precluded any possibility of grants to other colleges. The annual grant of $1200 to each of the academies continued, and the college benefited from this in that its financial welfare was so closely tied to that of the male academy. In the year 1864–5, for example, the expenditures at the male academy and the college, other than the 'boarding hall expenses' which were directly covered by students' payments, amounted to $4882.61, and of this $1687.50 or 34.6 per cent was covered by the combined government grants from Nova Scotia and New Brunswick.[108] These grants, though, were the same as the academy had been receiving before the college opened, and so the college was in effect cutting into the academy's resources rather than bringing in any funds of its own. Another possible solution was to attract private endowment, and the Eastern British America Conference, meeting in Yarmouth in the summer of 1865, directed a suggestion 'to the wealthy members and adherents of the Methodist Connexion, capable of the exercise of a patriotic and far-seeing munificence, that no object within the range of their benevolence would be fraught with richer advantages to their Church and country, than the efficient and permanent endowment of the various professorial chairs of Mount Allison College.'[109] Yet endowment funds took time to build up, and there was always the knowledge that the income from any funds that were subscribed would have to be reckoned against the crippling burden of maintaining the debts incurred by the ladies' academy.

In 1865, the college did receive its first specific government grant, from the province of Nova Scotia. It came at the end of a lengthy political battle over the reorganization of Dalhousie College which had been initiated by the newly formed United Presbyterian Church in 1862. Dalhousie had yet again discontinued university work in 1857, and in 1860 even high school work had come to an end. The Nova Scotia Act of 1863 which revived the college provided for it to be non-denominational, in that no religious test could be required of faculty or students, and in that any religious denomination – or any individual or secular group – was free to endow a professorial chair and thus to gain the right to nominate not only the professor but also one member of the board of governors.[110] Despite the equal status of all denominations in theory, however, the first three professorships were endowed by the Presbyterians and the position of principal was given to a Presbyterian minister in the person of James Ross, and it was these arrangements that led to furious protests from the Baptist denomination in early 1864 to the effect that the property and the status of a supposedly provincial college had been put in the hands of the Presbyterians to the detriment of the other denominations. In June 1864, the Methodist conference joined in and formed a committee to co-ordinate petitions against the new Dalhousie experiment, which it described as 'professedly Provincial, virtually denominational.' An issue which made the matter even more contentious was the forgiving by the province of a £5000 loan which had been given to Dalhousie many years before, in 1823, and had never been repaid: it could be argued that this amounted to a grant of $20,000 to Dalhousie, and conferred an unfair advantage over all other colleges.[111]

In important respects, the Nova Scotia college question which arose in 1863–5 resembled that which had recently been debated in New Brunswick. In late 1863, the *Provincial Wesleyan* angrily rejected a suggestion by its Halifax competitor the *Presbyterian Witness* that denominational colleges should move to Halifax and affiliate with Dalhousie. The Methodists, the *Wesleyan* proclaimed, '*will never for one moment entertain the idea of partnership in Dalhousie*.' What could and should be implemented, the newspaper added in a further editorial three months later, was a federation of colleges: 'the time may not be far distant ... when provincialists will be able with the highest satisfaction to point to our UNIVERSITY OF PROVINCIAL COLLEGES.'[112] The resemblance of this concept to the federated University of New Brunswick for which Mount Allison had vainly argued in 1862 was obviously not accidental. For the time being, however, the best that could be obtained from the Nova Scotia government was a reorganization of grants to denominational institutions as a means of offsetting the advantages gained by Dalhousie through the cancellation of the old £5000 loan. Accordingly, King's, St Mary's, Acadia, St Francis Xavier, and Mount Allison all received an annual increase of $400 to their existing grants of $1000. At Mount Allison, the increase was regarded as a specific grant to the college, while the original $1000 continued to be divided equally between the two academies.[113] It was undoubtedly a useful addition to the college revenues, and in the mid-1860s, approximately equalled the amount brought in by the $24 per annum tuition fees paid by the students. Towards making the college self-supporting, however, it was only a short step, and the dangers of too great a dependence upon the academy would soon become all too clear when the academy building burned to the ground on the evening of 16 January 1866.

The evening of the fire began normally: the college and academy students sat down to their meal as usual, and dispersed to their rooms for a study hour immediately afterwards. Just before 6:00, the alarm was given that fire had broken out in the kitchen, after a cinder from an overheated flue had ignited a pot of grease. As it happened, the preceding autumn had been a time of drought and no water could be found to fight the flames; within a few hours the building was entirely destroyed. The disaster had its redeeming features, notably that no lives had been lost. David Allison, who was living in the academy at the time, lost all his possessions and according to the report in the *Provincial Wesleyan* he 'narrowly secured the escape of his infant child.' Some of the students also lost all but the clothes they wore, while a few were able to rescue books and other personal effects, but there were no deaths or injuries. Another consolation was that there had been no wind to carry sparks to any of the other buildings. The fact remained, though, that a disaster it was. In part, the sense of shock came from the sudden destruction of the building where Mount Allison had begun almost exactly twenty-three years before. Charles DeWolfe and Charles Stewart, a member of the board of trustees who was at this time minister in Amherst, wrote jointly to the Missionary Society secretaries on the 17th with news of the fire, and described the old building as 'a Hall of Education based on Scriptural principles, and second to none for Efficiency in these Provinces; the birthplace of many souls. ...' Now, they went on, 'the sacred Edifice is gone – entirely burned down!' As DeWolfe and Stewart also pointed out, the financial loss of the fire posed a threat to Mount Allison's very existence, troubled as it already was by some $20,000 of debt.[114] The editorial in *The Provincial Wesleyan* of 31 January 1866 was entitled, 'Shall Mount Allison be Rebuilt?' It was a question worth asking.

In posing his question, of course, the editor of the *Provincial Wesleyan* had no doubt as to what the answer should be, and it soon emerged that his hopes were well justified. Not for the last time, Mount Allison would discover that a major emergency could bring forth resources that were not otherwise available, and from a variety of directions. The fire gave an early opportunity to the alumni association, founded in 1864, to come to the assistance of the academy. On 14 February, a correspondent of the *Provincial Wesleyan*, signing himself simply 'Alumnus,' recalled that from Sackville 'the merchant has gone forth ... to his counting-house; the lawyer to his chambers; the physician to his practice; the farmer to scientific agriculture; and the clergyman to his pulpit.' He called upon all of them to 'co-operate in the great work' and to 'answer back in tones of thunder – "It shall rise again!"'[115] In the meantime, the same message had been addressed by representatives of the trustees to all ministers and members of the Methodist denomination in the region, in terms that recalled the donations of Charles Allison and asked, 'cannot our hundreds of congregations unitedly accomplish as much as one gentleman himself did twenty-four years ago?'[116] By the time the trustees met in emergency session on 21 February, over $10,000 had been promised to the rebuilding fund, including $6250 in Saint John and $3000 in Halifax. A further $6250 was confidently expected from Westmorland County. The trustees therefore took the formal decision to rebuild, and dispatched agents to all parts of the

Maritimes, to Newfoundland, and to Bermuda. By May, the subscriptions had reached $19,000, and the trustees took the further step of requesting the conference to appoint George Butcher as full-time agent for the coming year.[117] This the conference did when it met in June, and it was also able to announce a special grant from the Wesleyan Methodist Missionary Society in London. Three years earlier, the conference had made a formal request to the Missionary Society for a grant to Mount Allison from the Jubilee fund set up to celebrate the fiftieth anniversary of the society. At that time it had been estimated that £8000 was needed to pay off debts and establish endowments, and that double that amount could be used to advantage. No action had been taken by the society, and when Pickard appealed to Boyce in March 1866 he pointed out that what was at stake now was not 'the comfortable working of the Institution,' but its continued existence. On 1 June, Boyce dispatched £1000 taken from the insurance fund of the society, as the Jubilee fund was already spent. It was the first – also the last – direct financial contribution of the society to Mount Allison, and it could not have come on a more timely occasion.[118]

In the following year a further source was tapped, as the legislature of New Brunswick voted a special grant of $1000 for the purchase of apparatus. By the time the trustees met on 7 August 1867, the day before the opening of the new academy, Pickard was able to report a remarkably favourable financial situation. Over $17,000 had been collected from the subscriptions received, while the Missionary Society grant amounted to almost $5000 and insurance had realized $12,000. Assuming that $4500 would come from hitherto uncollected subscriptions, the total of over $38,500 was enough to pay for the building and furnishing of the new academy, which had come to $25,000, to pay the expenses of campaigning for funds, and to reduce the combined debt of the institutions to only $7500 as opposed to the total of $20,000 before the fire. It had been, in fact, an unexpectedly profitable exercise, and the trustees also recorded the view that the new building was 'far superior in every respect to the former one, and wholly unequalled by any other similar Institution in the Lower Provinces of this Dominion.'[119] Their phraseology anticipated a point made by more than one of the speakers at the formal dedication of the new academy on the site of the old one the following day, when they remarked that the opening of the new building at Mount Allison coincided with the opening of a new era for the Maritime provinces, as they entered the newly confederated Dominion of Canada. It was less than three years since Lingley Hall had resounded with the partisan arguments of those for and against confederation: E.B. Chandler, Leonard Tilley, Albert Smith. Now, however, the theme of the dedication address by S.D. Rice, a veteran minister and formerly the successful fund-raiser for the Wesleyan Academy in the 1840s, was 'our present position as subjects of the New Dominion, and our duty to the cause of christian education as arising out of that position.' Millions of new inhabitants, he argued, would soon populate the great open spaces of Canada, and Christian education must be made available to them. As for the new academy, reported the *Provincial Wesleyan*, it was 'a stately structure.' Lacking the Doric columns of the old academy, it none the less presented an appearance of handsome simplicity, with its arched front entrance surmounted by a balcony. Those who attended the opening would no doubt have agreed that 'the new edifice well sustains the comparison naturally instituted between it and its predecessor.'[120]

The opening of the new academy and the reduction of the debt represented an enormous achievement, given the dire circumstances that had obtained at the time of the fire, although it did not solve all the problems of the Mount Allison institutions. In late 1866, DeWolfe worried that the college had not yet attained 'that amount of popular interest and sympathy which are so desirable for any such institution, especially in its nascent condition,' and it was true that student numbers fell in the late 1860s from a total of 31 attending at various times in 1866 to 21 in 1868.[121] On the other hand, reduction of debt was a move towards the obtaining of much-needed endowment, and an indication of future possibilities came with the announcement of the first endowed scholarships in 1868: a $60 scholarship was endowed by the minister D.D. Currie for award to a candidate for the ministry, while two $30 scholarships were offered annually by the alumni association for competition among former academy students matriculating in the college.[122] More worrying was the decline in student numbers at the male academy in the late 1860s. No precise term-by-term figures were published for the year 1867–8, but in November 1868 the alumnus Josiah Wood wrote to his brother that 'there has been some increase in the No. Students – Male Branch now numbers about 50 and female 30 Boarders.'[123] In part, the small numbers could be explained by the undoubtedly depressed state of the Maritime economy, as the traditional staple trades and industries of the region felt the prelude to their decline in the 1870s. The conference of Eastern British America, meeting in Fredericton in 1868, noted with regret that for Mount Allison 'the past year has been one of unprecedented trial and difficulty, chiefly arising from the great and very general depression in business circles, which has prevented the enrollment in its classes of so large a number of pupils as may be reasonably anticipated in future years.' Apparently unwittingly, though, the conference resolution then touched upon a deeper problem faced by the academy, as it hoped for 'a much larger number of students, from the recently improved common schools of our country.'[124] Improvement in public schools might indeed qualify more pupils to take an academic course; but the increasing ability of the public school systems to cater for the demand they created meant that an academy such as Mount Allison must now face increasing competition.

Thus, analysis of the student body for the year 1868 shows total attendance figures of 21, 84, and 87 for the college, the male academy, and the ladies' academy. Attendance at any one time would of course have been substantially lower, and the proportion of resident students lower still. As compared with the mid-1850s, student numbers were now smaller. The geographical origins of the students, however, had undergone no radical alteration. The proportion from New Brunswick students had declined somewhat, and that from Nova Scotia had risen; but still 58.9 per cent of the combined student body originated from New Brunswick and 30.7 per cent from Nova Scotia. The male academy had come to rely rather more on local students than it had done in the mid-1850s, 29.8 per cent of its students coming from Sackville itself and 40.5 per cent from Westmorland county. Correspondingly, the proportion attending the male academy from the major cities had decreased considerably, and with the percentage from Saint John now having dropped to only 3.6, but this was partially offset by a larger number of Saint John and other city students at the female academy. In the overall proportions, therefore, the changes were not drastic.[125] Nor, as yet, had the college grown large enough to have a major impact either upon the composition of the combined student body – proportions at the college were rather different from those at the academy, but the numbers were too small to be significant – or in determining the more general character of the Sackville institutions. The college had begun as an outgrowth of the academy, its curriculum evolving from the old collegiate course, its faculty virtually the same as that of the academy, and its professed purpose the same as that which had always been claimed for the academy: to make the benefits of a Christian education as widely available as possible in the Maritime region. Thus, the college had not yet established a clearly distinguishable identity from that of the academy. The ladies' academy did have such an identity, arising not only from the strict separation of female from male students, but also from the importance of music and fine arts in its curriculum. Yet in the late 1860s, as the ladies' academy gradually recovered from its near-disaster in 1864, it was no longer as isolated from the male academy as it had been in the days of John Allison. Under the administration of Pickard and Inch, in fact, the old terms 'male branch' and 'female branch' had been revived, and appeared annually in the catalogue. The years between 1855 and 1869 had seen many changes in the Sackville institutions, but under the direction of Humphrey Pickard there had also been important continuities.

By 1869, however, Pickard's long period in office was moving towards its close. It did so by his own choice, albeit a choice influenced by ill-health. The fire of 1866 had brought Pickard new troubles at a time when the financial strains of the previous years were already taxing his capacities severely. Described by the *Provincial Wesleyan* in the wake of the fire as 'toil-worn and indefatigable,' Pickard did not spare himself in the successful efforts to recoup Mount Allison's position during 1866. By the early months of 1867 he was suffering from what, in the minutes of the trustees, was described simply as 'diminished health,' and asked in May to be relieved of his duties. Instead, the trustees created the new position of vice-principal of the male academy – taken up later in 1867 by Cranswick Jost, a minister and a graduate of Wesleyan University – and persuaded Pickard to retain his positions as principal and president with reduced duties.[126] In October, Pickard himself made public his desire to retire, in the last paragraph of an article in which he appealed emotionally for more students:

> My apology for the unstudied earnestness of my appeal above, if apology is deemed necessary, is this, – it is now within two or three weeks of a quarter of a century since I was unexpectedly called to commence the work in this Institution; I then estimated the object for which it had been founded as of very great importance or I should not have listened to the call; but now when failing strength and an over-tasked, if not shattered, nervous system, tell me in language to which I must listen, that my share of that work is about done, it seems to me of far greater importance than it did twenty-five years ago; and, therefore, although I am fondly looking for a speedy release from the responsibilities of the position which I have so long held in the Institution, I do most earnestly desire for it ever increasing prosperity and efficiency; and to ensure this an abundant supply of students at all times is indispensable.[127]

It was not until May 1869 that Pickard ultimately had his resignation accepted by the board, which had hoped rather to persuade him to recover his health through a trip to Europe at the expense of the college. Pickard, however, procured an appointment as steward of the Methodist Book Room in Halifax, and editor of the *Provincial Wesleyan*, and on this basis the board had no choice but to accede. In so doing, it singled out for especial praise 'the indomitable application and perseverance, the high business ability, and the earnest Christian aim by which Dr. Pickard has been animated during the whole period of his service in the government of these Institutions.' It was an apt tribute, for it was these qualities above all which had sustained Pickard and Mount Allison through the crises of the previous quarter-century. Nor were his talents entirely lost to Mount Allison as he moved on to other areas of responsibility within the denomination. Still only fifty-six years old, he would be a constant advocate of the institutions until his death in 1890. In the service he rendered to Mount Allison even after his retirement from office, as well as in his exertions while in office, lay the measure of his dedication to the institutions he had done so much to establish.[128]

Pickard's successor, both as president of the college and as principal of the male academy, was David Allison. Tall, full-bearded, renowned for his booming voice and for his love of using long and complex words, Allison was a popular figure. In the nine years since he had joined the Mount Allison staff, he had made a reputation as a brisk and inspiring teacher, not only in his main field of classics, but also in his classes on constitutional history, political economy, and international law. Allison's teaching evidently had much to do with the choice of law as a career by so many of the graduates of the 1860s, at least according to one of the graduates, Benjamin Russell: both Russell and his lifelong friend and colleague R.C. Weldon, who played crucial roles in the establishment of the Dalhousie Law School in Halifax, began their legal education under Allison's tuition.[129] Thirty-three years of age and a layman, although a powerful preacher, he would certainly be a very different president from his predecessor, but if any doubts were entertained within the denomination on that score they were soon laid to rest. A Halifax newspaper article in 1870 reported that Allison, 'although a younger man [than Pickard] and a layman, has fairly earned his laurels. ...'[130] Along with Allison's appointment came the appointment of J.R. Inch as principal of what was now designated 'the female academy,' and this represented the renewed separation of the two academies. Also vacant at this time was the position of theological professor, which DeWolfe had resigned in 1868 on grounds of ill-health, although he continued to be active on the board of trustees. In this case, the choice of a replacement was the responsibility of the conference, and was delayed until the appointment of Charles Stewart in 1870.[131] Once that position was filled, each of the institutions was under a new head.

The sense of a new regime impending was undoubtedly one reason for the exhilaration which prevailed at the ceremonies that marked the end of the 1868–9 year at Mount Allison. Another reason was the sense that the worst dangers of the past three years had been averted. The Saint John *News* commented that 'Dr. Pickard ... leaves the Institutions at Sackville in an excellent position generally,' while the *Provincial Wesleyan* remarked on the perception that 'steadily, after years of struggle with huge and complicated difficulty, Mt. Allison was asserting its power and its dignity as one of the most reliable and really successful institutions of learning in the land.' A third reason was the presence of the Methodist and long-standing friend of Mount Allison who less than a year before had become the first native-born lieutenant-governor of New Brunswick, L.A. Wilmot. Greeted with spontaneous cheers as he entered the hall, Wilmot spoke not only of the importance of higher education but also of the opportunities opened up to young people by the Dominion of Canada. He himself had been a staunch advocate of confederation, and he looked forward to the day when Sackville would hear 'the whistle of the Locomotive on its way from Halifax to Vancouver's Island.' The *Provincial Wesleyan*'s correspondent was not entirely convinced, and wrote that 'some might, perhaps, question the good taste of some of his remarks in reference to the recent political changes in the country. He seemed to forget that there were some around him who differed from him on this subject although, perhaps, as honest and disinterested as himself.' Yet, the item concluded, 'his remarks ... were so good that no one could possibly take offence'; Wilmot's speech was greeted with prolonged cheers before the company adjourned for a meal of roast beef and plum pudding in the dining hall of the academy. There was still room for debate over the benefits of confederation for the Maritimes, and there was still room for doubt over just what role Mount Allison could and should play within the region and within the new dominion. But now was not the time for either doubt or debate, or at least not until the hard-won consolidation of the Sackville institutions, not to mention the elevation of a Methodist to be lieutenant-governor, had been properly celebrated.[132]

4

Questions of Identity: 1869–1881

Despite the exuberance that greeted the lieutenant-governor's visit in 1869, the next twelve years comprised a period of profound self-examination for all the Mount Allison institutions. The 1860s had bequeathed difficulties not easily solved, especially as the ensuing decade was one of economic decline in the Maritime provinces. The two academies faced the problem of defining their role as the college gradually assumed its position as the most prestigious, although not yet the largest, of the institutions. For the male academy, this was an especially urgent question, as the collegiate department had been entirely taken over by the college in 1862. The ladies' academy retained its diploma course, but faced the same problem to a more limited extent after the decision of 1872 to admit women students to the college. The college itself continued to struggle for financial security and academic recognition, and still aspired to become part of a larger, federated, non-teaching university. This ambition was realized in 1878, with the foundation of the University of Halifax, modelled on the University of London, but within five years the experiment had failed despite the support given to it by Mount Allison. The theological institution also underwent important developments during the 1870s, particularly its integration into the college in 1875 as the faculty of theology. The period was one of change, and in many respects one of achievement; but even the achievements contributed to the uncertainty over Mount Allison's future which would prevail in 1881.

For the college, as for the other institutions, the change of headship in 1869 was accompanied by a general turnover of teaching staff. The college faculty now assumed a character more clearly distinct from that of the academy, and the arrival of professors who would serve for twenty, thirty, or more years began to define what that character would be. David Allison and J.R. Inch retained their professorial appointments, while Cranswick Jost continued in

1869–70 as professor of Hebrew and also took over temporarily the responsibilities of Thomas Pickard as professor of natural science. In the following year, however, Jost resigned to return to the regular ministry, and as science professor he was replaced by John Burwash. Burwash would hold this position for most of the next twenty years, with the exception of short periods when he too – also a minister – returned to pastoral work. A graduate of Victoria University at Cobourg in 1863, he came to Mount Allison without teaching experience except for a year spent as a tutor at Victoria in 1866–7, where his elder and ultimately more famous brother Nathanael had just begun his own six-year term as professor of natural science. Bluff and forthright in manner, John Burwash also carried out geological survey work for the New Brunswick government, and geology, physiology, and chemistry were among the science subjects he taught at Mount Allison. By students, he would be remembered for 'his remarkable experiments and explosions.'[1] As a scientist, Burwash left little direct indication of the philosophical bent of his teaching and study, although as a minister and from 1875 as professor of homiletics in the faculty of theology he clearly did not accept the aspersions cast upon Christian doctrine by empirical scientists and by Charles Darwin in particular. Like Sir William Dawson, the eminent geologist and principal of McGill University who vigorously combated Darwin's evolutionary theories during the 1870s, Burwash recognized that the history of the earth must now be seen in the context of geological time but regarded divine creation not only as a revealed truth but also as the most reasonable explanation of the appearance of plants, animals, and mankind. As he remarked in a sermon in 1883, for example, the purpose of teaching botany was to evoke 'the forms and relations of the beautiful *things* that God has placed in forest and field.'[2] Burwash was certainly not untouched by concurrent scientific developments. Like his brother Nathanael, he maintained that 'the scientific method is as applicable to religion as to science,' in that a Christian life could be lived only by a willingness to be guided by experience in living out scriptural truths: 'to go from the book to heart and to life, and from experience of heart and life back to the direction of the book.' That scientific truth could be learned in isolation from Christian doctrine, however, he denied: 'the bane of our age is doubt; not open opposition to the truth, not positive disbelief, but doubt, – harassing, paralysing doubt.'[3]

Charles Stewart, the professor of theology who also came to Mount Allison in 1870, agreed. Addressing students in 1878, he argued that 'the danger of the 19th century education' lay in 'training the intellect but neglecting, perverting, destroying the moral sympathies and capabilities.' All knowledge, he believed, must be based upon 'the rock of eternal truth.'[4] Stewart was a Scot, forty-three years old at the time of his appointment, who had come to Nova Scotia from Glasgow as a probationary minister in 1852 and had since served on circuits in various parts of Nova Scotia and New Brunswick. He was no stranger to Mount Allison, having been minister at Point de Bute from 1863 to 1865 and chairman of the Sackville district in 1864 and 1865. Without teaching experience and without formal academic qualifications – his knowledge of systematic theology and biblical languages had been acquired by dint of prolonged private study, and was recognized by Mount Allison in the award of an honorary degree of Doctor of Divinity in 1870 – Stewart had mixed feelings about his new position. First nominated at the 1869 conference, he had asked for a year's delay in order to prepare, but as late as April 1870 he confided to A.D. Morton, his nephew, that 'I shall certainly be very awkward, and am afraid very inefficient.'[5] Once he had arrived at Mount Allison, however, he was more optimistic, and was especially cheered by the contrast between 'the dusty streets of St. John,' where he had had his last ministerial charge, and 'the salubrious lanes and avenues of Sackville.'[6] Stewart would remain at Mount Allison for forty years, until his death in 1910, and would head the theological faculty until 1903. As professor and also as college chaplain, his overriding concern would remain the same as it had been during his years in the active ministry: the saving of souls. 'You will not, I am sure,' he had written to Morton in 1865, 'suspect me of indifference to systematic Divinity; yet, after all, as much is to be learned in the actual presentation of the gospel, as in private studies over it. And of a surety, "He that winneth souls is wise."'[7] Stewart's intense dedication to his task ensured the vigour of theological teaching at Mount Allison. It also at times made him seem a stern figure to those students whom he taught – both as theological professor and as professor of moral philosophy in the regular Arts work of the college – or who received his pastoral visits as chaplain. This side of his character, however, was assessed at the time of his death by H.A. Powell, a graduate of 1875 and a lawyer and politician not given to sentimentality: 'as a youth at college I did not understand him, regarding him as austere and unsympathetic, [but] closer friendship wrought a perfect transformation in my views and revealed his wealth of human kindness and affection. I have long looked upon him as the most lovable man of my acquaintance.'[8]

Also remembered with affection by his former students was A.D. Smith, who began in 1871 his forty-five-year career as professor of classics. Both of Smith's parents were Bermudians, though he had grown up for the most part in Newfoundland, where his father had been a Methodist minister. After graduating from Mount Allison in 1867, he taught for four years in Yarmouth, Nova Scotia, before returning to take his MA degree and join the faculty. Famous for his flaming red beard, and for his detailed knowledge of the family histories of the generations of students who attended his classes, 'the genial doctor' – he received an honorary LL D from Victoria University in 1888 – impressed students with the breadth of his knowledge and his infectious love of books and learning. He was most renowned, however, for his wit in the classroom, one instance of which he himself described to a student:

> One of the most satisfying experiences I have had as a teacher was one day years ago, when Doctor [David] Allison had a donkey, and used to keep him sometimes in the field here. ... It happened that in my senior Latin class, there was a young chap who was what you would call a real smart aleck. He would interrupt me and spoil my jokes and sometimes ask ridiculous questions just to raise a laugh. On the day I spoke of, he had just asked one of those silly questions, when Doctor Allison's donkey raised his voice in a resounding bray. That was my chance. ... I raised both hands in the air, and said 'One at a time, *please*, one at a time.' The laugh that followed wasn't the one that he had been fishing for, and it held him for quite a while afterward.[9]

Smith had been appointed as an 'adjunct professor' to relieve David Allison of part of the responsiblity for classical instructin, but during the year 1873–4 he also fell heir to the task of teaching chemistry, while Burwash had temporarily returned to ministerial work in Ontario. The other subjects normally taught by Burwash – botany, zoology, and geology – were taken over by Richard C. Weldon, professor of mathematics and political science. Weldon was also a graduate of Mount Allison, having taken his BA in 1866 and his MA in 1870. He had first taught at the college between 1869 and 1871, but then had gone to study at Yale University and returned in 1873 with his PH D degree. A year later, Weldon again departed for further study in Europe, studying international law at the University of Heidelberg before returning to take up his position at Mount Allison in 1875. He was, until his move to Halifax eight years later to become founding Dean of the Dalhousie Law School, the first holder of the PH D degree to teach at the college, and he remained the only one until the arrival of H.E. Bigelow in 1911 as professor of chemistry.[10]

At the academies too, there were changes in the teaching staff in 1869 and the ensuing years. Changes at the college affected the male academy, since all of the professors also held positions there, with the exception of the theological professor and J.R. Inch as principal of the ladies' academy. This close relationship did change, however, during the 1870s. In 1874 the board of trustees abolished the old system by which professors were paid for their college work by means of class fees, and ruled instead that fixed salaries would be paid specifically for teaching in the college. From then on, the faculties of the college and the male academy were largely separate. The teaching staff of the ladies' academy had already been separate from that of the college, with the exception of its principal, but there too there were extensive changes in 1869. Among the new additions was Mary E. Mellish, a recipient of the MLA diploma at Mount Allison in 1867, who came as teacher of mathematics and natural science and thus began a long and influential career at the ladies' academy. Theodore Martens arrived from the Leipzig Conservatory as professor of music, the sixth individual to hold that position in the ladies' academy in the previous fifteen years. Martens himself stayed only three years, an indication of the difficulty of holding well qualified staff in the field of music in the years before a separate conservatory was built.[11]

Also in 1869 was the appointment of the first professor of drawing and painting, the landscape artist John Warren Gray. The details of Gray's early life are the subject of conflicting evidence, but it seems clear that he had grown up in England, had attended classes at the South Kensington School of Art in London, and had then come to New Brunswick while still a young man. Settling in Sackville, he worked on a farm and as an employee in the timber trade, before spending some time in Saint John, and pursued both woodcarving and painting on a part-time basis before his appointment at Mount Allison. Gray's approach to the teaching of fine art was clearly influenced by his primary interest in landscapes, and also reflected the religious concern which was characteristic of the teaching of all subjects at Mount Allison. In a lecture given in August 1869, as he was about to enter upon his duties, Gray affirmed the spiritual as well as the materialistic character of mankind and went on to declare, as reported in a Sackville newspaper, that 'it is from the study of nature that we cultivate the taste. As we cultivate the taste, we refine and exalt the feelings – "turn from nature to nature's God."'[12] Gray, who also taught 'Drawing, Mechanical and Architectural Drafting, &c.' in the male academy, prompted the adoption of a new and more detailed description of the fine art programme in the ladies' academy, and one that qualified the previous reliance on copying as a means of tuition:

> The method of instruction is that employed in the best European schools. Copying, under the eye of a skilful teacher, is regarded as the first means of acquiring correct ideas of the Art; but, from the beginning, the pupil will be taught that Nature is her ultimate guide, and as early as possible will be accustomed to make studies and sketches directly from natural forms.[13]

The appointment of John Warren Gray, therefore, not only inaugurated the professorship of painting and drawing and brought to Mount Allison an artist of considerable and growing stature, but it also indicated a new awareness of the philosophy and methods of art teaching. In this respect, the appointment of Martens from Leipzig was complementary to that of Gray, and on his resignation in 1872 he was replaced by another European musician, Saverio d'Anna of the Naples Conservatory.[14] The circumstances of Gray's departure in the following year, however, were quite different. At the meeting of the board of trustees on 28 May 1873, it was announced by Inch 'that he considered it undesirable to continue the services of Mr. Gray as Teacher of Painting, his salary being greater than the profits yielded to the Institution financially,' and accordingly Gray was allowed to leave.[15] Gray's own career apparently suffered little, for he moved to Montreal and prospered both as a teacher and as a practising artist, but it would be twenty years before Mount Allison would again have a professor in the field of fine arts; in the meantime, tuition was normally carried out by an assistant teacher. The decision indicated that 'the ornamental branches,' as they were still described in the catalogue, were expected to pay their own way, as musical instruction undoubtedly did. It was also a symptom of a more general climate of uncertainty that was shared at this time by the college and both academies, in the wake of the withdrawal of the New Brunswick legislative grant.

The financial state of the Mount Allison institutions in the early 1870s had improved markedly since the crisis of the previous decade. Detailed financial records for this period have not survived, but in May 1869 the trustees saw reason to hope 'that by persevering effort the straitened circumstances of the past may soon be succeeded by the total removal of pecuniary encumbrance.'[16] In the following year, a measure towards this end was introduced by the conference of Eastern British America in the foundation of a conference Educational Society. Of the money the society hoped to raise through the donations of Methodists in the region, most would find its way to Mount Allison directly or indirectly: one third was to be paid to the college as a grant, one third to be used to provide scholarships for theological students, and the remaining third to provide scholarships for children of conference members studying at the Sackville institutions or elsewhere. The results of the society's first year of operation were apparently not entirely successful, as the conference of 1871 called for wider co-operation from the circuits, but a worthwhile beginning had been made, and four scholarships had been awarded.[17] In restoring the financial stability of Mount Allison, however, the trustees did not intend to rely exclusively upon the church. Rather, they hoped also for an increase in the New Brunswick grant, and a petition of 1870 from the trustees to the provincial government declared not only that the existing grant to the two academies was 'indispensable to their proper maintenance' but also that a grant 'of moderate amount' directed specifically to the college would provide timely assistance.[18]

As events proved, this was not a good time to be applying for provincial aid. The New Brunswick election of 1870 brought to power a government, under the leadership of George Hatheway, which was committed to the introduction of more effective legislation on common schools, and in particular to the principle of free access to schools for all children, financed through taxation; the previous act of 1858 had stopped short of implementing this principle, since it had made a local property tax optional for each school district. When the legislature met in early 1871, the lieutenant-governor's speech maintained that the provision of an improved public school system was the most important matter to be considered during the session. It was a declaration that was fully in accordance with Wilmot's personal views, for he was a long-standing advocate of free public education. Accordingly, the Common Schools Act was rapidly passed into law. Its provisions did not apparently impinge upon the grants customarily awarded to Mount Allison and to other denominational academies. Indeed, it would have been surprising if they had done so, for not only did Wilmot have close connections with Mount Allison, but also the likely author of the act, the attorney-general George E. King, was a Methodist and had attended the academy in the 1850s. The act set forth a detailed scheme of administration for free schools in the province and for their financing by a combination of provincial, county, and local taxation, while a clause was added during the assembly debate which provided 'that all Schools conducted under the provisions of this Act shall be non-sectarian.'[19]

Opposition to the act quickly ignited, particularly among French-speaking and English-speaking Roman Catholics. On the basis of an ambiguous clause in the previous act of 1858, which had allowed considerable freedom to each school in regard to religious services and instruction, the Catholics argued that the 1871 act deprived them of an established right to separate schools; the conflict became even more embittered with the adoption under the act of detailed regulations which forbade the displaying in schools of symbols of any political or religious group. In the course of the next four years, the issue was argued in the Dominion parliament, was referred to the Privy Council in London, and prompted riots in the northern part of the province, before a compromise solution was reached in 1875 by which the act was retained in force but Roman Catholic schools were informally recognized in certain parts of the province.[20] At the beginning of the controversy, however, damaging accusations had been made as to the allegedly anti-Catholic bias of the 1871 act, and the Saint John *Morning Freeman* had gone so far as to proclaim the existence of a Methodist conspiracy led by Wilmot and King.[21] Mount Allison, owned and operated by the Methodist denomination, was obviously not 'conducted under the provisions' of the 1871 act; but as controversy mounted in late 1871 and early 1872 it became equally obvious that the continuation of its provincial grant would be politically impossible. Thus, when the government presented its estimates to the legislature on 25 March 1872 they contained only a 'special grant' of $400 to Mount Allison, intended to assist in the process of adjustment to the loss of the previous annual grant of $2400.[22]

According to the Mount Allison board of trustees, meeting on 29 May, the decision had been entirely unexpected. The trustees, recorded the minutes, 'feel compelled to place on record a strong expression of their astonishment at the summary manner in which these Institutions have been deprived of public aid, which this Board, in common with a large portion of their fellow countrymen, believe to have been judiciously expended in thus fostering higher education. ...' The board also recorded its view that maintenance of the New Brunswick grant would have promoted the success of the common school system.[23] By this time, however, expressions of regret had little practical purpose; representations had already been made by David Allison and had been rejected, and the reality was that the grant would no longer be available. In purely financial terms, the loss was substantial. In the year 1870–1, the New Brunswick grant had represented 18.1 per cent of all the expenditures of the college and academies other than boarding hall expenses, and the trustees noted that its withdrawal would 'at once cause such embarrassment in the finances of these Institutions as will seriously mar their efficiency as Seminaries of learning. ...'[24] Even more disturbing was the implied rejection by the government of the principle that a denominational institution might deserve public support in return for the services it offered to the community as a whole. From the beginning, Mount Allison had sought government support in order to allow it to offer an inexpensive education to students from a wide variety of backgrounds. In turn, the receipt of the grant had reinforced the institutions' obligation to the community, and Humphrey Pickard had accordingly affirmed in his inaugural address in 1843 that 'the Institution is established neither for private purposes nor for local ends, but for public utility and the benefit equally of all parts of the Provinces.'[25] Now, however, the provincial government had effectively declared that the Mount Allison college and academies were indeed private institutions, and it remained to be seen how far this unwanted status would change their nature and ideals. There was, of course, still the smaller provincial grant from Nova

Scotia, and it was no accident that Mount Allison now more than ever before began to turn its attention eastward. Yet the abrupt withdrawal of the New Brunswick grant could only be seen as a heavy blow to the original self-concept of Mount Allison.

One temptation that was resisted was that of denouncing the government's action publicly and mounting a campaign against the Common Schools Act. David Allison noted in May 1872 that the trustees 'had been invited to join in a crusade' against the act and 'had refused to do anything of the kind.'[26] Instead, they concentrated on the most immediate problem, which was to find alternative sources of funding. Inevitably, fees were raised: the annual fee for board and basic tuition in either academy now went from $120 to $135.[27] For the balance of the required funds there were two obvious possibilities: private endowment and the church. Accordingly the trustees determined to raise a minimum of $60,000, or up to $100,000 if possible, and this message was carried to the church conference in the summer of 1872 by David Allison and Charles Stewart. The immediate results were encouraging, as members of the conference personally pledged to donate some $12,000, and by May of the following year Allison was able to report to the trustees that $45,000 had been raised.[28] The target of $60,000 was reached in 1875, after Humphrey Pickard had been temporarily delegated by the conference to act as fund-raising agent, and it was with good reason that the trustees congratulated him on his achievements at a time of 'commercial embarrassment and business pressure.'[29] By 1878 the endowment fund was yielding about $3000 annually: it was not enough to alter radically the financial situation of the institutions, but more than replaced the New Brunswick grant.[30]

In the meantime, funding by the church had become more formalized with the foundation of the Methodist Church of Canada in 1874. Formed by the union of the Eastern British American Conference with the Canadian Conference and the smaller New Connexion Methodist Church, the new church served areas including the whole of the Canadian Dominion as well as Newfoundland and Bermuda. It was not a comprehensive Methodist organization as several groups, including the Episcopal Methodist Church in Canada, retained their independence until the further union of 1884. Henceforth, though, the Methodists of the Maritimes would look westward to Toronto for headquarters of their church. A corollary of the arrangement was that the few remaining formal ties with the British Conference were cut off, and in 1873 Humphrey Pickard and Charles Stewart visited London in a successful mission to obtain the support of that conference for the union. During the nineteen years of the existence of the Eastern British American conference, the number of its circuits had increased from 70 to 181; the membership had risen from just over 13,000, with a further 587 on trial, to some 17,500 and over 3000 on trial; the number of ministers had gone from 69 to 145.[31] This growth in itself contributed to the reasons for union, for the area served by the old conference was now divided into three separate conferences: that of New Brunswick and Prince Edward Island; that of Nova Scotia, including Bermuda; and that of Newfoundland. They, along with the Montreal, Toronto, and London conferences, were now constituent parts of the new church, subject to the authority of a quadrennial general conference.[32]

One result of the union of 1874 was the replacement of the educational society of the Eastern British American Conference by a new educational society of the Methodist Church of Canada. Mount Allison thus became one of ten Methodist educational establishments from St John's, Newfoundland, to Winnipeg that were listed in the society's first annual report in 1875. Mount Allison's combined attendance of 242 put it among the largest of the ten, although it was exceeded by the 300 at the Wesleyan Female Academy in Hamilton, Ontario, and by the 251 at the Wesleyan Methodist Academy in Charlottetown. Along with the attendance of 110 at the Wesleyan Academy in St John's, Newfoundland, the existence of this large school on Prince Edward Island provided part of the explanation for the inability of the Mount Allison academies to attract as many students in the 1870s as they had done twenty years before.[33] The amount of the funds distributed by the educational society varied from year to year according to how much was raised on the circuits, but in the initial year 1874–5 Mount Allison received $800 and in 1878 the approximate value of the annual grant was estimated by a committee of the Mount Allison board at $1000.[34] Still at that time the institutions had an accumulated debt of nearly $10,000, and the Mount Allison report to the general conference of 1878 pointed out that a further increase in endowment funds would be necessary in order to ensure continuing financial health.[35] The immediate crisis brought about by the withdrawal of the New Brunswick grant had, however, been surmounted.

The financial strains of the early 1870s brought significant change in areas beyond the specific matter of funding. One such change was the formal recognition of the role played by alumni in the legal incorporation of the Alumni Society in 1874 and the right given it to appoint two members to the board of trustees. The purpose of the society was described in the act of incorporation as 'the promotion of sound education and the advancement of the interests of the Mount Allison Educational Institutions,' and the presence of alumni representatives on the board clearly indicated that the assistance rendered by the society would not be restricted to fund-raising, but would imply an active interest in the financial and other affairs of the institutions.[36] This would not have been an unnatural development in any case, but in the context of the intensive campaign for endowment funds in 1874 it was obviously all the more desirable. The first two alumni representatives, the minister H.D. Cowperthwaite and the lawyer and future provincial politician A.A. Stockton, accordingly took their seats on the board in May of that year.[37] Stockton, as well as being a graduate of 1864 and an officer of the Alumni Society for several years, was also the son-in-law of Humphrey Pickard; his wife, Amelia Pickard Stockton, had been the prime mover in the foundation in 1871 of an independent Alumnae Association for former students of the ladies' academy. It had been she who had chaired the meeting of the new association, she who wrote its constitution in 1872, and she who declared in a speech at the closing exercises of that year that the Alumnae Association would in future 'rely altogether on its own resources.'[38]

Not until 1895, by that time under the leadership of Mary Mellish, would alumnae representatives join their male counterparts on the Mount Allison board. Amelia Stockton's confidence in the future of the Alumnae Association, however, was well justified in the context of a decision that had been taken the day before her speech: to admit women as regular students of the Mount Allison College. For such an important departure, the change was accomplished with little ado. It was sponsored in the college board by Inch, whose position as principal of the ladies' academy clearly made him an appropriate mover of the resolution, and by Charles Stewart, whose daughter Harriet would ten years later become the second woman to graduate from the college and the first to receive the degree of Bachelor of Arts. The minutes recorded the occasion tersely:

> Moved by Prof. Inch seconded by Dr. Stewart that: Ladies having regularly matriculated and completed the course of study prescribed by this board shall be entitled to receive the degrees in the arts and faculties upon the same terms and conditions as are now or may hereafter be imposed upon male students of the college. Carried nem. con. Moved by Mr. Pope seconded by Dr. Stewart that such measures as may be necessary to give effect to the resolution be managed by Faculty and Examining Committee. Carried nem. con.[39]

If there was any opposition to this crucial change, it did not show itself. David Allison was known to hold rather different views from those of Inch on the matter of women's social role. Several years later, when they shared the platform at the ladies' academy closing exercises of 1880, Inch declared that 'years of experience had taught him that young ladies can compete with the sterner sex in either intellectual acuteness or the power of acquisition,' whereas Allison's view was that 'any woman's best and highest sphere [was in] ... aiding some good, honest, faithful man in discharging the duties of life.' Even Allison, however, acknowledged that 'any Education that differentiates between the sexes is wrong,' and although he believed that relatively few women would ever desire to go to college he gave no support to any obstruction of those who did.[40] It is possible that the decision to admit women was hastened by the financial emergency of 1872. One historian of higher education in the United States has remarked that in the late nineteenth century 'coeducation helped to save many one-time men's colleges of the small denominational type from being put out of business,' by increasing student enrolment.[41] While there was no immediate influx of women students to Mount Allison, the college was certainly widening its constituency by permitting their attendance. Also, the decision was often cited in appeals for endowment. Inch declared publicly on 28 May 1872 that in 'this liberal policy' Mount Allison now 'led all Seminaries in these Provinces'; while the editor of the Saint John *Globe* shortly afterwards praised it as an action 'in keeping with the spirit of the times' and called upon wealthy individuals to contribute to the endowment fund 'on patriotic grounds.'[42] Thus, the admission of women students undoubtedly had its practical advantages. None the less the origins of the decision taken in 1872 went back much further than the immediate crisis of that year.

The roots of the change lay in reality in two previous decisions. The first was the determination in 1854, heavily influenced by Mary Electa Adams, that the new female branch of the Wesleyan Academy should impose rigorous intellectual standards upon its pupils and should emphasize systematic study.[43] Thus were the foundations laid for the 'collegiate' programme which provided the evidence to Inch and others that female students were as capable as males. The second was the decision taken shortly after the opening of the Mount Allison College to allow senior ladies' academy students to attend college classes as part of their own collegiate course. Exactly how and when this was arranged was never recorded, and was not publicized, no doubt to avoid the denunciation of those who believed that male and female students had no business in the same classroom together. None the less, the *Provincial Wesleyan* pointed out in June 1872 that 'we have seen ladies in those college classes years ago maintaining their ground in the most spirited scholastic contests,' and the Saint John *Globe* recalled that the custom went back to the very beginning of the college's existence.[44]

The *Provincial Wesleyan* drew the conclusion that the change made in 1872 was 'not a new decision,' and claimed that if the women students of past years had not taken degrees 'it was not owing to any restrictions in the rules of the college.'[45] This assertion, designed as it was to allay any lingering opposition to coeducation, was not as ingenuous as it seemed. It was quite true that there was nothing either in the college charter or in the catalogue to say that women should not matriculate and graduate; but neither was there anything to say that they could, and the very action of the college board in 1872 showed that a deliberate measure was required in order to supply the omission. From 1872 onward, the catalogue provided explicitly that students were 'admitted irrespective of sex.'[46] The argument that the decision was not new, however, helps to indicate a further aspect of the origins of Mount Allison's action. Less than a year previously, in the summer of 1871, the board of trustees of Wesleyan University in Connecticut had similarly resolved that there was 'nothing in the charter to prevent ladies from being admitted to the privileges of the University,' and in view of the close ties still existing between that institution and Mount Allison it was certain that this precedent would not go unnoticed.[47] Along with the concurrent discussions of coeducation at Cornell University – which decided favourably in 1872 – and other United States institutions, it obviously impressed the anonymous correspondent who described the Mount Allison examinations of November 1871 in the *Provincial Wesleyan*:

> One fact, in view of the various 'new departures' in modern education, deserves here to be noted in respect to the lady students. It is their marked success in the College classes with which they have been associated. This success they have striven to make the rule and they have done it. No comment is needed.[48]

The extending to women of eligibility to enter Mount Allison College as regular students, therefore, was a genuine and far-reaching change, but it had antecedents both in the previous arrangements at Mount Allison, and in American precedents which had been known and discussed in the Maritimes. Elsewhere in Canada, on the other hand, and throughout the British Empire, women's struggle to gain access to higher education was more protracted.[49] Thus it was a Mount Allison student, Grace Annie Lockhart, who in 1875 attained the distinction of being the first woman to be awarded a Bachelor's degree at any institution in the British Empire. A native of Saint John, Lockhart enrolled in the ladies' academy in 1871 at the age of sixteen. Most of her courses were in fact taken while she remained a ladies' academy student, and it was only in her final year, after obtaining her MLA diploma in 1874, that she was officially registered as a student of the college. Her graduation on 25 May 1875 with the degree of Bachelor of Science and English Literature – no woman had as yet enrolled in the full Bachelor of Arts programme – apparently passed with little comment. The Halifax *Herald* noted that her graduating oration on 'The Literature of the Moon' was 'a chaste and finished production, and displayed literary ability of a high character,' and that 'this was the first occasion on which the College had conferred a degree on a member of the female sex.'[50] The newly inaugurated student magazine, the *Eurhetorian Argosy*, was only a little bolder in asserting that 'Miss Grace A. Lockhart ... is, we believe, the first lady in these provinces to receive a college degree.'[51] She herself made little mention of her academic achievement in later years. J.R. Inch, however, recalled in 1880 that 'while other institutions were halting and hesitating and putting the door ajar, ... [Mount Allison] had boldly opened its doors to all irrespective of sex.'[52] Even he was probably unaware that Grace Annie Lockhart's graduation had been so great an innovation throughout the British Empire; but his pride was evident – and justifiable – all the same.

Grace Annie Lockhart was, during her student career, the only woman student at the college. In 1877, Harriet Starr Stewart, daughter of the theological professor Charles Stewart, enrolled as a special student, and in the following year she became a member of the regular freshman class; when Stewart graduated in 1882, she was to be the first woman at Mount Allison and in Canada to receive a Bachelor of Arts degree, and she was followed by three other female graduates during the 1880s. It was not until the 1890s that the proportion of women graduates – 31 out of 152 in the decade from 1891 to 1900 – became substantial.[53] The admission of women to the college, therefore, did not have such a perceptible immediate effect upon the social life of Mount Allison students as had the opening of the female branch of the academy some twenty years before. One awkward question that did arise was whether Lockhart, as a college student, could be a member of the Eurhetorian Society, or whether as a woman she should be disqualified. The difficulty was neatly solved by electing her to 'honorary' membership, and the same expedient was adopted in the case of Harriet Starr Stewart in 1880.[54] With that exception, to judge from the columns of the *Argosy*, coeducation had not yet seriously disturbed the male ethos of the college.

For all that, the presence of the ladies' academy ensured that women's aspirations could not safely be slighted. In December 1877 the editors of the *Argosy* rashly suggested that 'careful and scientific instruction in cooking ... [should] form a fundamental part of female education,' and that all those completing such a course should attain the degree 'FFW – FIT FOR WIVES.'[55] The reaction from 'our readers, particularly the female portion of them,' forced retrenchments by the editors in two successive issues of the magazine in early

1878, and although the light tone of the exchange was preserved some substantial points were won. 'The same quantity and quality of work should,' admitted the editors in the context of the differential salaries paid to male and female teachers, '*ceteris paribus*, receive the same amount of remuneration, whether performed by a man or a woman. That it does not is a fact the unblushing iniquity of which human society will, we hope, one day realize.' Even worse was 'the pretentious and abominable arrogance with which men take it on themselves to decide that women are not fit for this profession or that.' None the less, the law of averages and 'the immortal passion of love,' the final editorial argued, would ensure that the majority of women would become wives, just as the majority of men would become husbands; and the repective roles of each, once married, were not brought into the debate. 'In fact,' declared the concluding paragraph. 'all the editors of the ARGOSY are possessed by the most unalterable determination to get married as soon as it may be practicable. Who wants a husband?'[56]

At the Mount Allison of the 1870s, though, there were limited opportunities to find the answer to that question. Except under careful supervision, access to the students of the ladies' academy was restricted to members of family, and even correspondence 'beyond the home circle' was allowed only with special permission; failing such permission, the catalogue prescribed, the principal had power either to destroy offending letters or to send them to the parents of the student involved.[57] It was not for nothing that the *Argosy* speculated in late 1877 that the advent of the telephone would provoke new restrictions, 'to prevent little conversations between the College and Academy.'[58] Officially, the chief occasion on which male and female students could meet – other than in classes and at church, which offered little chance for conversation – was the reception held every second Saturday night in the ladies' academy. From 1877 onwards, this was even recognized in the catalogue as improving the students' manners and social graces.[59] If the *Argosy* editorial of November of that year is to be believed, the receptions must have succeeded in that among other things:

There the lofty Senior stalks round 'with a smile on his pale face,' philosophically surveying the scene, and 'thinking of the days that are no more.' There, too, the gallant Junior, arrayed in purple and fine lines, gazes with admiration on a spectacle which no other educational institution in the country can present. There the high-souled Sophomore looks with emotion on a scene, surpassing all the imitations of the stage. There the downy Freshman, blooming and verdant, drinks in the sweet poison at every pore. There the grave Theologue, 'o'erlaid with black, staid Wisdom's hue,' studies fallen human nature in its most seductive forms. There the Academician, reckless, swift of foot, talks affectionately to somebody else's sister. There, are seated round the room the fair young daughters of the New Dominion, 'clad in white samite, mystic, wonderful,' or radiant in 'colors costly as the blood of kings.' There the stringed instrument or the voice of song 'moves the vocal Air to testify his hidden residence.' There all is enchanting, all delicious. Young men and maidens talk as though they were never to grow old. Alas, that ever they should! But *eheu! fugaces labuntur anni.* Yet a little while and we shall all have passed away from the spacious halls of Mount Allison, never perchance to meet again on earth.[60]

It was an impressive vision, but not necessarily a realistic one, as the gossip column of the *Argosy* often revealed. Excessive formality was a frequent complaint, and the constrained awkwardness of conversation at the receptions was a standard joke. 'Reception. Gentleman, after tedious silence, coughs. Young lady: "Beg pardon, sir, what did you say?" Gent., feebly: "Nothing, Miss."' One bored female listener, asked for her views on Darwinism, was quoted as replying that 'I am more than ever at this present moment convinced that the Darwin theory is correct, because I *now* and again see a man looking so much like a monkey.'[61] At times, though, receptions were not so dull – one in September 1878 was described as 'unusually free from hateful formality'[62] – and in any case in winter there was always the rink, and the tobogganing ground. The opening of the Tantramar Skating Rink each December from the time of its construction in 1876 was customarily welcomed by the *Argosy* with an admonition to all students to buy season tickets, and if occasionally the advocates of tobogganing would respond with a defence of the merits of their own sport, it did not mean that participation in the one necessarily excluded the other.[63] Winter sports, although duly chaperoned, provided the most relaxed social setting that Mount Allison had to offer, and it was not surprising that the advent of winter was greeted enthusiastically.

In the days before the introduction of hockey, organized team sports were characteristic of fall and spring rather than winter. Games of hurley might still be improvised in the academy yard, and handball remained a popular individual pastime either indoors or in an open court when weather permitted; but cricket and, increasingly, baseball and rugby football were the major interests. The era of intercollegiate competition lay still in the future, and the greatest rivalries were those between Mount Allison and the village cricket clubs in Sackville, Amherst, and Dorchester. That the college team was defeated by the Cumberland club – presumably of Amherst – in the fall of 1875 prompted the *Argosy* to reflect upon the lack of systematic practice that was apparently to blame: '"One secret of education," says Herbert Spencer, "is to know how wisely to lose time." We do not know of any place where the secret can be better found out by collegians than in the Cricket-field.'[64] Cricket flourished at Mount Allison well into the 1880s, reaching its height in 1885 when the college team defeated both of the Sackville clubs – the Tantramar club, which according to the *Argosy* included several professional players, and the Mechanics – in matches that attracted large crowds. Cricket, described as 'this truly national game,' was praised in an *Argosy* editorial of 1884 for its value in 'strengthening the mutual feelings of friendship between town and gown'; certainly it was one major college sport that provided for regular contests between Mount Allison and teams from the local communities.[65]

Other than on the sports field, the collective spirit of the students continued to be fostered at meetings of the Eurhetorian Society and of its equivalent at the ladies' academy, the Eclectic Society. The public meetings of the Eurhetorian Society continued to offer their customary programmes of orations and debates on matters of current interest. The standard of debate was variable, at least in the opinion of the local newspaper the *Chignecto Post*, which complained in 1877 that 'the old fire has gone out. ... The debaters are no longer gladiators.' Probably written by W.C. Milner, the owner of the newspaper and a member of the society during his own student days in the previous decade, the article mourned the passing of the time when the Eurhetorian had been able to 'secure public attention and respect.'[66] What could not be denied was the success of the Eurhetorian Society's major innovation of the 1870s, the launching in 1875 of the printed version of the *Eurhetorian Argosy*. For several years the *Argosy*, following the previous tradition of Mount Allison student publications, had been read aloud at meetings of the society rather than circulated in printed form. The *Eclectic Journal*, its equivalent at the ladies' academy, continued even now to be publicized in the old way. The *Argosy*'s opening editorial hinted that the change to its new form was an effort to emulate the already established *Dalhousie Gazette* and *Acadia Athenaeum*, a task which the editors modestly declared to be enough to make their courage sink.[67] By the time the second issue appeared, however, they had recovered sufficiently to enter a spirited controversy with the *Gazette* over an editorial in that newspaper which had attacked Mount Allison's academic standards and had particularly impugned the qualifications of J.R. Inch and Charles Stewart as professors. Petty, insolent, undeserved, unnecessary, narrow, bigoted, discourteous: such were the terms applied to the *Gazette*'s article, although at the same time the *Argosy* disclaimed any intention of 'thinking or speaking ill' of its sister publication.[68] Eurhetorian debates might no longer be gladiatorial, at least in Milner's view, but there was no lack of pugnacity in the early issues of the society's magazine.

Nor was the *Argosy* timid in its treatment of issues within the college. The prominence of classical study in the curriculum, for example, was questioned in an editorial of May 1875. The classics should not be abolished altogether as part of the curriculum, the writer argued, but those whose inclination was towards modern languages should be allowed to draw their inspiration from Molière, Racine, and Goethe rather than from 'weary hours' spent on classical authors. 'Invention and originality,' he warned, 'are being starved to death by want of individuality, and by a too servile imitation of models.'[69] This was a point returned to several times during the next five years by successive editorial writers, and by March 1879 it had been incorporated into a vigorous call for better teaching of English language and literature in place of 'digging among Greek and Latin roots.' The weekly 'Saturday class' in composition and declamation still survived, having originated in the first year of the academy, and the editorial observed that this was the one duty regarded among the students 'with perhaps more antipathy than any other.' For students inexperienced in writing to be forced to write compositions was useless, it maintained, in the absence of the encouragement to read widely in English literature; similarly the reciting of memorized declamations, often consisting of 'long harangues of some old one-sided politician,' was equally sterile.[70] What the *Argosy* editorials essentially identified was the continuing difficulty of offering a college course with a faculty of only five, especially in an era of rapidly expanding knowledge and at the very time when the principle of a wide choice of elective subjects was being introduced at many institutions in the United States, including such a prestigious university as Harvard. The problem of adjusting to the new era would be attacked seriously at Mount Allison during the 1880s; in the meantime, the complaints of the *Argosy* revealed that the students were neither ignorant of the issues at stake nor indifferent to them.[71]

The *Argosy* also vigorously put the students' point of view on other issues. In January 1880, for example, it protested against the exploitation of theological students who might be requested for several successive Sundays 'to supply the pulpit, or more correctly, to do the work of some neighbouring circuit.' Losing the chance of relaxation during the weekend, and often missing Monday morning classes because of travelling time, such students should, the editorial argued, at least be paid for their time.[72] At a more mundane level, the magazine drew attention on another occasion to the broken water pump in the college building, which was forcing all students to make a perilous trip to the basement cistern in order to draw a pail of water. 'We want a new pump,' it demanded, 'or the old one fixed.'[73] Living conditions for residents of the college certainly lacked some amenities, especially when compared with the ladies' academy in the same period. Whereas the ladies' academy enjoyed steam heating from 1872 onwards – in 1875 it also gained more space through the addition of the south wing which had first been contemplated fifteen years before, and a mansard roof containing a fourth storey – the college students still stoked the wood fires in their rooms. At the academy, meanwhile, as one former student recalled sixty years later, the students of 1873–4 complained that their straw mattresses and pillows were too hard: 'we were ... told by those in authority, that it was good enough for us, would make us study harder; it did.'[74]

Apart from its interventions on matters of concern to students, the *Argosy* obviously reflected the students' perceptions and interests in its content. Its literary columns were made up for the most part of essays on a variety of subjects ranging from 'the True Economy of Study' (May 1875) to 'Slang' (November 1875), from 'Utility of Mental Philosophy' (October 1877) to 'Conversation' (March 1879), and from 'the Curse of Autograph Albums' (December 1879) to 'the Opportunities of the Age' (October 1880). The tone was usually light, often humorous, but rarely frivolous. Occasional book reviews and travelogues were interspersed, usually with a single poem on the first page. Virtually all the poetry, however, was the work of only two writers: Sarah E. Smith, an alumna from Saint John who had attended the female academy in the 1850s, and 'Harry Halifax,' whose pseudonym effectively preserved his anonymity. Apparently there was little poetic writing among the students. Nor did the *Argosy* contain fictional stories, although an essay on 'Novels' in November 1880 admitted that works of fiction were 'found everywhere and ... read by everybody,' and that they comprised 'the works of such noble minds as Scott and Dickens' as well as 'the short love stories of our weekly papers and the sensational dime novel.'[75] For the *Argosy*, the publication of essays rather than short stories evidently avoided the risk of coming too close to the latter category.

Also normally avoided in the *Argosy*, despite the fact that the largest single group of Mount Allison graduates in the 1870s chose to enter the ministry, was material of a directly religious or theological nature. As an editorial of February 1880 remarked, there were many other publications dealing with 'these very important matters.' On this occasion, though, the rule was breached, as the editor commended a reawakening of religion then taking place throughout the Mount Allison institutions and in the Sackville community. Earnest enquiry rather than excitement was its manifestation, and the editorial expressed 'pleasure and pride that our college not only represents a good share of intellectual ability, but that that talent is consecrated.'[76] The cause of temperance was also given prominence from time to time, as in the support offered in May 1880 to the provisions of the recently enacted Canada Temperance Act.[77] More often, however, religious matters, and especially theological controversies, appeared through indirect humorous references. The evolution question, for example, was frequently touched upon. An essay of October 1879 examined a variety of explanations for the existence of the Egyptian pyramids, and concluded that they had not been built, but had evolved: 'we may ... express our great surprise that this theory has not occurred to Mr. Darwin or Mr. Spencer, believing, as these gentlemen do, that evolution accounts for everything.'[78] Then again, another issue recorded that at a recent football game 'the Professor of Science came into violent contact with a theologue, affording a practical illustration of the conflict of science and religion.'[79] The *Argosy* was not essentially a religious publication; but it was written and read by students for whom religious concerns were familiar and important.

Geographically, the students continued to be drawn from various parts of the Maritime provinces, with a few coming from outside the region. In the year 1870–1, in fact, the three Maritime provinces were equally represented among the 17 undergraduates, each supplying five, with the remaining two being Newfoundlanders. As yet, however, the numbers were too small to support any general conclusions; and in any case the number of students coming from Prince Edward Island in that year was exceptional. More typical of the emerging pattern was the composition of the undergraduate body ten years later, when eleven of 25 came from New Brunswick, twelve from Nova Scotia, one from Prince Edward Island and one from Newfoundland. In the same year of 1880–1, the institutions as a whole showed a larger proportion from New Brunswick than did the undergraduates alone: 88 of 181, or 48.6 per cent. A further 40.3 per cent came from Nova Scotia, and 2.8 per cent from Prince Edward Island, while the remainder (of those whose origins were recorded) was divided between Newfoundland, Bermuda, and the United States. The greater proportion from New Brunswick was largely accounted for by the more local appeal of the academies as opposed to the college: no fewer than 35 students originated from Sackville in 1880–1 out of the overall student body, but only two out of the 25 undergraduates. What the academies and the college had in common was that they drew their students predominantly from rural communities or small towns, although with substantial minorities from larger, incorporated towns or cities. Of those attending from the Maritimes in 1880–1, 62.5 per cent of the undergraduates and 72.3 per cent of the students as a whole came from communities not incorporated as village, town, or city (in which category Sackville was still included) or from incorporated places with a population of 1000 or under. At the other extreme, 16.7 per cent and 16.8 per cent respectively came from towns or cities with a population of over 5000. Thus, although the student population at Mount Allison was not as overwhelmingly rural as was the population of the region – the census of 1881 showed just under 715,000, or 82.1 per cent, living in unincorporated communities or those with a population of 1000 or under, and 12.0 per cent in towns or cities of over 5000 people – it none the less reflected in general terms the characteristics of that population.[80]

With a student body drawn so largely from the Maritime provinces, it was to be expected that the economic and political interests of the region would be discussed frequently at Mount Allison. Editorials directly concerned with such topics were rare in the *Argosy*, but one issue that did not escape comment was the prevalence of migration out of the region, particularly among young people. These were 'hard times,' admitted the *Argosy* in April 1880, and had produced 'quite a mania ... for emigration out West and to some of the United States.' It was a trend, the editorial continued, that did not do justice to the potential prosperity of the Maritimes:

> We are prepared to say that these Provinces have in themselves all that is requisite to build up a splendid country. Taking into account the maritime interests, the mining, agricultural, lumber, and other industries, we have every feature that is necessary to ensure success. It is true, we labor under difficulties, but only such as are common to all new countries, and which can only be overcome by continued perseverance. It is a mistake to think that there are no chances to rise in this country; men have risen from mean positions to good stations in society; still, it was only through industry and pluck. We allow that at present, irrespective of any political reasons, the western part of our Dominion seems to be more attractive, but eventually a reaction will take place.[81]

Yet, analysis of the later careers of Mount Allison graduates of the decade from 1871–80 shows that few were entering business pursuits: only three out of 50, or 6.0 per cent. The largest single group, 38.0 per cent, entered the ministry, while 20.0 per cent made careers in education, 16.0 per cent in the law, and 8.0 per cent in medicine. Thus, the students were not practising what the *Argosy* preached, or at least not directly. Nor were as many staying in the region as had been true in the previous decade. A substantial majority still did so – 58.0 per cent were still in the Maritimes in 1903, and a further 6.0 per cent in Newfoundland – but western Canada and the United States were increasingly attractive. The Mount Allison college students of the 1870s were, for the most part, Maritimers, and they were concerned about the future of their region and its industries; but not many of them aspired to become entrepreneurs, and as a group they were not immune to the pressures that contributed to out-migration during the later decades of the nineteenth century.[82]

One issue that did attract frequent attention in the columns of the *Argosy* was the quality and future potential of higher education in the Maritimes, often discussed in a social and economic context. As early as the magazine's second issue, in February 1875, an editorial regretted that 'our Provinces are in a situation very unfavourable to a sound and comprehensive collegiate education.' Learned individuals comprised but a small percentage of a sparse population, the writer argued, and so the merits of higher education were not generally known or appreciated:

> When education is so little prized, it can be no matter of wonder to find our Colleges little better than German High Schools, and our graduates in some essential branches only fit for honorable European matriculation. We would exonerate our Colleges, however, from the charge of inefficiency. They perform the work allotted to them well. If Bonn, Oxford, and Heidelberg, were transferred to New Brunswick and Nova Scotia, they would completely fail. In their place they are grand engines of education, but here they would speedily be abandoned as useless and extravagant. A University must be the outgrowth of the country in which it is situated. As *society* improves, it gains in vigor and influence, and any *great* movement towards the beau ideal will prove short-lived and reactionary.

The solution proposed by the editorial was to establish 'an Examining Board with university powers': that is, a non-teaching university within which all of the colleges could function and could be encouraged to raise their standards. The proposal was similar to that for which Mount Allison had argued in Fredericton in the early 1860s, and the editorial specifically recalled those discussions. Now, in the 1870s, the issue was no longer the future form of higher education in New Brunswick, but that in Nova Scotia.[83]

At Mount Allison, the concept of the central, non-teaching university had not been forgotten despite the failure of 1862. At the opening meeting of the educational society of the conference of Eastern British America in 1870, A.A. Stockton had declared that 'he would be pleased to see Sackville College affiliated with kindred institutions in the lower provinces with one grand degree conferring university.'[84] In the following year Humphrey Pickard, as editor of the *Provincial Wesleyan*, took the matter a step further when he praised the alumni society of King's College, Windsor, for advocating the foundation of such a university. 'We believe ...,' he continued, 'that ...

[Mount Allison's] Board of Governors will readily consent to a suspension of its degree-conferring power, whenever its sister institutions shall be found prepared to severally agree to a similar suspension, in order that this common power may be centralized in a single independent University Board.'[85] That these views reflected the position of Mount Allison was clear, although no official statement was made as yet by the college itself on the Nova Scotia college question. Debate had been ignited in late 1870 when Charles MacDonald, professor of mathematics at Dalhousie College, had advocated the merging of denominational colleges into a central, non-denominational teaching university, with the strong implication that Dalhousie would be the natural focus of such a union. In newspaper columns, the resulting controversy was long-lived. As late as the winter of 1872, an acrimonious feud was being fought out in Halifax newspaper columns as to the merits or otherwise of denominational colleges, and as to whether Dalhousie was in reality the provincial institution it claimed to be, or whether it was, as the *Provincial Wesleyan* believed, essentially a Presbyterian college.[86]

The real beginning of the college question as a practical issue, however, came in early 1874 with the appointment of G.W. Hill to the Dalhousie board of governors to replace the recently deceased Joseph Howe. Hill, an Anglican clergyman in Halifax, was a staunch proponent of co-operation among Nova Scotia colleges; he also had political influence through his brother, P.C. Hill, a member of the provincial assembly who was to become provincial secretary later in 1874 and premier in the following year.[87] At his first meeting of the board in January 1874, Hill successfully proposed that an effort should be made to consolidate the resources of the colleges, and in the following May a letter drafted by him was circulated on behalf of Dalhousie to all the colleges, including Mount Allison. The letter proposed a conference of college representatives to discuss 'the advisability of endeavouring to form one general University for education in the Arts, by the concentration of the talents of the different faculties ...'; in the highly charged atmosphere that still persisted in the wake of the controversies of the previous years, it was this phrasing which doomed the proposal to failure, for it implied a central teaching university rather than a non-teaching federation. The Mount Allison trustees, meeting on 27 May, took a predictable view of the newly arrived communication from Dalhousie, 'in which this Board is requested kindly to abandon its distinctly declared policy in reference to the work of University Education.' Dated 29 May, the board's reply declined to attend the proposed conference, although declaring its belief in the merits of 'a supreme degree-conferring University with affiliated teaching branches,' as opposed to a 'centralized College,' and its willingness to participate in a conference on 'true University Reform.'[88]

Mount Allison was not alone in its response, and the general refusal of the other colleges to attend the proposed conference prompted a further initiative by Dalhousie. Heavily influenced by G.M. Grant, prominent Presbyterian minister of Halifax, member of the Dalhousie board, and future principal of Queen's University, the new proposals called for an increased government grant to Dalhousie and an enlargement of its board of governors in order to ensure a wider representation. Both were attained through the provincial legislature in 1875: the grant increase of $1800 for the year, and an act to amend the existing college legislation. As well as increasing the size of the board from nine to fifteen, the 1875 act conferred the additional power 'to affiliate to Dalhousie College any other Colleges desirous of such affiliation, or any schools in Arts, in Theology, in Law or in Medicine.'[89] Interpreted as an overt attempt to assert supremacy over the other colleges of the province, these measures produced a furious response, including co-ordinated protests from Mount Allison, King's and Acadia. These three colleges, pointed out the Mount Allison petition of early 1876, had seen their provincial grants remain at $400 – the other $1000 given annually to Mount Allison was granted in respect of the academies – while that of Dalhousie had now been raised from $1000 to $2800. This was – the petition showed as little faith in the legislators' arithmetic as in their educational policy – 'just seven times the sum accorded to Institutions which shrink from no fair comparison with the recipient of the larger favour, in capacity to provide the youth of the Province with a liberal education.' Furthermore, it was recalled, Mount Allison had 'earnestly and publicly striven to secure the Establishment of a Central Degree-conferring University, distinct from the teaching Colleges as its affiliated branches.' That fact, the petition concluded, showed in itself that Mount Allison was unafraid of comparison with other colleges, for such an arrangement would expose the weaknesses of any college whose students could not adequately compete in the centrally administered examinations.[90]

The petition, along with the similar arguments made by the other denominational colleges, won its point. On 8 March 1876, two related measures were introduced into the provincial assembly with government sponsorship. The first provided the levels of college grants for the next five years, and while it did not espouse the principle of equal grants to all colleges, it did move substantially in that direction: Dalhousie would receive an annual sum of $3000; King's, Acadia, and Mount Allison would each have $2400; and the two Catholic colleges, St Mary's and St Francis Xavier, would each be granted $1500. The second bill, which along with the other gained passage on 4 April, created the University of Halifax. The new institution was explicitly modelled on the University of London, both in that it was a federation of affiliated colleges for which it was empowered to prescribe curricula and administer matriculation and degree examinations, and in that it was also intended to examine candidates who had been trained at non-affiliated institutions or through private study. Its tasks were those of 'raising the standard of higher education in the Province, and of enabling all denominations and classes, including those persons whose circumstances preclude them from following a regular course of study in any of the existing colleges or universities, to obtain academical degrees.' It was, in short, exactly what Mount Allison had long favoured, both in its administrative arrangements and in the values which informed its stated purpose.[91]

It was true that there was more to the University of Halifax than appeared in the university act. P.C. Hill, now provincial premier, warned during the assembly debate on the University of Halifax proposal that it did not necessarily betoken the abandonment of the concept of the central teaching university. At the end of five years, during which the experimental University of Halfax would 'test the feeling of the people of this country with regard to a central undenominational university,' the grants to denominational colleges would have expired and the government and legislature might then proceed to institute a teaching university. They might, on the other hand, decide to 'perfect that which they found in existence, if it better suited the opinions of the people.'[92] This last phrase obviously gave hope to those who wished the University of Halifax to persist in its initial form. So too did the appointment of G.W. Hill as Chancellor. Despite Hill's role in the unsuccessful attempt by Dalhousie College in 1874 to promote a teaching university, his experience and his political influence were undoubted, as was his commitment to a co-ordinated higher education system for Nova Scotia. As for Mount Allison, its first and consistent response to the passage of the university act was to support the University of Halifax in the hope that it would indeed become a permanent institution. On 31 May 1876 the college board declared 'its readiness, to the fullest degree compatible with the interests of our College and the rights and privileges of the students of Mt. Allison, most cordially to cooperate with the proposed University of Halifax.' Praising 'the soundness of the principle of direct representation on the Senate of the University of all affiliated Colleges' – a principle not specifically embodied in the university act, but implied by an invitation to Mount Allison to nominate two members of senate for appointment by the lieutenant-governor of Nova Scotia – the board designated Allison and Inch as nominees.[93]

In its support for the University of Halifax, Mount Allison was not typical. The proponents of the central teaching university were obviously dissatisfied with what they regarded as a 'paper university.' Proponents of independent denominational colleges were also suspicious of the plan, but for the opposite reason, seeing it as an indirect means of undermining the colleges through state intervention. Acadia College inclined particularly to this view, and resolved in August 1876 to have nothing to do with the University of Halifax, but instead to guard against the withdrawal of government grants in five years' time by raising a large addition to its existing endowment. The *Wesleyan*, however, firmly supported the principle of the non-teaching university, and in its editorial of 13 May 1876 it adduced not only the example of the University of London, with its affiliated denominational colleges, but also that of the University of Calcutta, which it cited as operating successfully with colleges representing not only different Christian deonominations but also the Moslem and Hindu faiths.[94] Addressing the Nova Scotia Conference in the following month, David Allison did not reach so far afield, but, as reported in the *Wesleyan*, took the opportunity to expound the spirit in which Mount Allison had responded to the Nova Scotia experiment:

He defined the position of [the Mount Allison] Board of Governors in reference to the University of Halifax. It had expressed its approval of the scheme, not, however, as anticipating a Central Teaching University, but as a finality. It was also in favor of taking from the Government the additional thousand dollars, not with the idea that it was to be taken from them at the end of five years. It was fully committed to the principle of Denominational Collegiate Education, and deemed itself entitled to this sum as an acknowledgement in part of their service in the educational field.[95]

Allison's speech to the conference reaffirmed certain principles that had had a long history at Mount Allison. The notion of the government grant as a deserved reward for service to the community at large, and as an incentive for the offering of such service, had been fundamental to the launching of the academy in 1843. The notion of the denominational college as a constituent part of a larger, non-teaching university – committed by virtue of that status to maintain high standards, and yet free to maintain a regime based on particular religious beliefs and moral values – also went back to the 1840s, when Enoch Wood had supported the plans of Sir William Colebrooke, and had been espoused by Mount Allison in the New Brunswick college question of the early 1860s. Mount Allison had argued strongly for both principles in the New Brunswick context, and had ultimately been defeated. Now that success seemed to have been achieved in the context of Nova Scotia, Allison's remarks indicated a determination that this achievement should not be lost. Yet still the Mount Allison college faced grave difficulties, both academic and financial. Attacks on its academic standards by members of other denominations were frequent during the 1870s. The skirmish between the *Argosy* and the *Dalhousie Gazette* in early 1875 over the qualifications of Mount Allison professors was just one manifestation of the aspersions cast upon Mount Allison, and upon other denominational colleges, by supporters of Dalhousie as a provincial university. Strong words had also been used by the editor of the Saint John-based Baptist newspaper, the *Christian Visitor*, as he described the *Wesleyan*'s vehement support for Mount Allison as reminiscent of 'the pompous dialect of strolling pedlars of quack medicines.' It was a discredit to the cause of education, he went on, for Mount Allison 'to send out young men from High schools bearing the diplomas of A.B. and A.M.'[96]

Mount Allison did not lack for defenders against such attacks. Yet it was questionable whether the college had solved the academic problems that had arisen from its recurrent financial crises. At the beginning it had been grafted on to the academy and had had no financial independence, and since then it had had to survive the difficulties created by the ladies' academy's near-bankruptcy in 1864, the academy fire of 1866, and the withdrawal of the New Brunswick grant in 1872. Survived them it had, thanks to the efforts of its supporters and to the skills of Mariner Wood, who had succeeded Charles Allison as treasurer of the institutions in 1858; but inevitably there had been a heavy cost. One casualty was the library, which was among the smallest college libraries in the region. According to figures supplied to the Nova Scotia government in 1876, the Mount Allison college library contained only 950 volumes, less than the 1373 of the arts library at Dalhousie, the 1430 of St Mary's and the 2108 of St Francis Xavier, and much less than the 3477 of Acadia and the 7000 of King's, Windsor. It was true that the Mount Allison academies shared a library of some 3200 books, so that the overall availability of books was incrased thereby, but the fact remained that the library set aside for college use was very small.[97] Nor was the college generously supplied with scientific apparatus. Benjamin Russell, a student of the 1860s, recalled that his generation of Mount Allison students 'learned our chemistry out of a book exclusively'; with the exception of the ageing electrical generating machine and some surveying equipment, there had been no apparatus whatever.[98] Under Burwash, some changes had been made, but in June 1878 he felt obliged to present in person an urgent appeal to the board of trustees for an immediate grant. He was successful in obtaining $250 and in November the *Argosy* reported that the science laboratory had been renovated so that students themselves could now be seen in long white aprons, 'putting into actual practice what they have learned from text book or lecture on a previous day.' Thus, at least a start had been made in supplying the deficiency, although one student of the era later recalled that there had still been little equipment when he had arrived at Mount Allison in the fall of 1878, and that he did not remember ever seeing a microscope during his undergraduate years.[99] As for the library, some new sources of support were found: in 1877 the Alumni Society resolved to purchase reference books, and its vote of $150 was supplemented by $50 from the Eurhetorian Society and $100 from the trustees at their meeting in June 1878. The catalogue of 1878 was able therefore to predict 'valuable additions' to the library. None the less, there was much to be done, and it was not until 1881 that even a part-time librarian was listed in the catalogue, in the person of R.C. Weldon.[100]

Another area in which financial constraint was felt was in the recruitment and payment of professors. Although from 1874 onwards the professors were paid salaries for their work, rather than relying upon a combination of academy salaries and class fees, they were not conspicuously well off. The salary of Burwash, for example, was fixed in 1874 at $1000, and that of Smith at $900. Even allowing for the fact that Smith, though apparently not Burwash, also received the use of a house, their salaries were inferior to those paid at the University of New Brunswick, where the professor of classical literature and history was at the time receiving $1200, and the professor of chemistry and natural science $1400.[101] In the following year, Smith and Burwash took the unusual step of writing a joint letter to the board to ask for a pay increase, and although they were refused 'in view of the present financial position of the Institution,' they were promised careful consideration the next year. The board kept its word, and in 1876 each member of the college faculty received an increase of 15 per cent, facilitated by the income from the growing endowment fund and by the increased Nova Scotia grant.[102] Thus faculty salaries were brought more nearly into line with those elsewhere.

The problem of staffing the college, however, was too complex to be solved by a simple raise in pay. Given the limited financial resources available, and with student enrolment small – just 25 were registered in the regular degree programmes in 1880–1, and a further ten in theology – there was no question of recruiting a faculty large enough to encompass all of the disciplines that were burgeoning in the late nineteenth century. Professors had no choice but to continue teaching in a variety of areas, and the result was that they had little chance to develop real expertise in any. Even as it was, as the *Argosy* pointed out, there were necessarily areas neglected, such as that of English literature. These difficulties were not peculiar to Mount Allison, but were shared in varying degrees by all Canadian universities of the period, and by many others in the United States and elsewhere. In the Maritimes, Mount Allison's faculty of five was typical of the colleges of the region. According to information supplied to the respective provincial legislatures in 1876, Acadia had the largest faculty with its seven professors, and the largest student enrolment of 58; Dalhousie had a faculty of six and a student enrolment of 52; King's, Windsor, and the University of New Brunswick had, like Mount Allison, faculties of five, for student enrolments of 19 and 45 respectively; St Mary's had four professors for its 25 students, and St Francis Xavier three for its enrolment of 12.[103] At Mount Allison, however, matters were further complicated by the responsibilities which the professors also carried in regard to the academies: senior students from both academies attended certain college classes. It was, in fact, essential to the financial health of the college that they should do so, for a subcommittee of the board of trustees charged in 1878 with the task of defining the financial relationship between the college and the male academy estimated that of an annual college income of $6000, no less than $1000 should consist of a payment by the academy for the teaching services of the college professors.[104] Although, therefore, the academy and the college were now separately administered, the professors were not yet able to confine their teaching duties to the college students.

Furthermore, from 1875 onwards the majority of the college professors also held appointments in the faculty of theology. As Mount Allison reported to the general conference of the Methodist Church of Canada in 1878, the inauguration of this new division of the college had been prompted by 'the full persuasion that it was alike required by the progress of the College and the circumstances of the times.' A better-educated ministry would be, it was hoped, 'a means of doctrinal strength and proficiency in this day of religious indifferentism and controversialism.'[105] At the last meeting of the conference of Eastern British America in 1874, David Allison had optimistically expressed his hope 'to see the day when they would have a Theological Hall with a full teaching staff, instead of one overworked professor.'[106] In the following year, with Charles Stewart as Dean, the faculty of theology was indeed begun with a staff of six. None, however, was a new appointment. David Kennedy, a minister and at the time vice-principal of the male academy, became professor of Biblical literature and ecclesiastical history, while Burwash as the other minister on faculty became professor of homiletics. Stewart himself was professor of Old Testament exegesis and systematic theology. There were also three laymen: Allison was professor of New Testament exegesis, while Inch taught logic, and Smith taught Greek. Between them, they were responsible for the training of ministerial candidates sent by the three eastern conferences, who might or might not also be undergraduates in arts, and also for a new three-year programme towards the degree of Bachelor of Divinity, offered only to arts graduates of two years' standing.[107] There was no doubt that the initiation of the faculty of theology represented a genuine effort to provide a broader and more rigorous education for potential Methodist ministers in the region. It was also an emulation of the similar step which had been taken by Victoria College – with which Mount Allison would now obviously be compared, since they were the two major collegiate institutions of the new Methodist Church of Canada – two years before. Victoria's faculty of theology had 55 students by 1875, although as at Mount Allison most of its four instructors also had other duties within the college.[108] At Mount Allison, given the responsibilities already carried by the professors in regard to the academies and given also the more general problem of offering a full college curriculum with limited manpower, the decision to elaborate and modernize the programme of theological instruction without any new appointment to faculty clearly implied an additional burden to be carried by the existing professorial staff.

Inevitably, there were limitations on what faculty members could achieve in this situation. There was little question as to their teaching skill, and none at all as to their personal dedication. A Presbyterian clergyman, C.B. Pitblado, visited Mount Allison in 1880 and came away favourably impressed with 'the careful, accurate and emphatic way in which Dr. Stewart drilled his Hebrew scholars,' and with the 'light and vivacity which Professor Weldon threw into the class of mathematics'; of Smith's teaching of Horace 'in the regular peripatetic fashion,' he professed that he did not remember 'ever hearing a recitation that interested me more,' while Inch's mental philosophy students explained '[with] clearness and accuracy ... the different theories that had been held by the great philosophers, Spinoza, Kant, Berkeley, Hamilton, &c., concerning the sphere and reliability of consciousness.' The college, he believed, furnished an excellent and thorough education to its students.[109] Very different, however, were the recollections of J.C. Webster, a graduate of 1882 who had gone on to medical school in Edinburgh and had had a distinguished medical career in the United States before retiring to Shediac and devoting his energies to the study of Canadian history. Webster, writing in 1926, had warm praise for Smith and Weldon but scathingly questioned the competence of Burwash and Inch to teach the wide variety of subjects which they had attempted. In general, Webster went on, he had realized on his arrival at Edinburgh that he had been 'starved and cheated' at Mount Allison. 'Was it not dishonest on the part of an institution,' he asked, 'to waste the time of boys in such primary school procedure and to designate it as College Education?'[110] To be sure, Webster was not an impartial judge, for his harsh verdict was delivered while he was in the midst of a bitter quarrel with Mount Allison over the question of university federation during the 1920s. He might have remembered too that both Smith and Weldon, whom he lauded for having a 'masterly grasp' of their subjects, were both graduates of the same Mount Allison which he despised. Yet F.W. Nicolson, a graduate of 1883 who had gone on to a successful academic career at Wesleyan University in Connecticut and had since maintained a friendly contact with Mount Allison, privately informed the president of the Carnegie Corporation also in 1926 that he agreed with the contents of Webster's letter. Webster himself had moderated the tone of his pronouncements but not their substance by the time he published in 1944 the autobiography in which he referred at some length to the limitations of 'a small country college.'[111]

Certainly, the Mount Allison professors of the late 1870s and early 1880s had scant opportunity to develop their professional skills through research, since heavy and varied teaching loads left little time, and since adequate library resources and scientific apparatus were lacking. Again, the problem was not peculiar to Mount Allison, but was shared in varying degrees by other institutions in the region and throughout Canada. At the University of New Brunswick, W. Brydone Jack had admitted in 1876 that, although it was a worthy ideal for faculty members 'to devote their time and talents to original investigations and the prosecution of fresh discoveries in the branch of their study in which they have become famous,' his own institution could approach this goal only 'humbly and laboriously.'[112] Yet the University of New Brunswick did achieve distinction in scientific research, both through Jack himself as professor of mathematics, natural philosophy, and astronomy, and through Loring Woort Bailey, who published over a hundred scientific papers and several books during his long career as professor of chemistry and natural science.[113] That Mount Allison did not at this time develop a similar area of scholarly expertise was due in part to its denominational status. It was no accident that the author of the articles in the *Wesleyan* that had preceded the inauguration of the college had expressed a mistrust of the inductive sciences: the truth was that there was no strong tradition of unrestrained critical enquiry at Mount Allison. Instead, the goals of the college had been religious and educational, rather than stressing intellectual activity for its own sake. Not that such goals excluded critical thought. Indeed, the effective defence of religious doctrine in the 1870s required that empirical scientists be met on their own ground. In June 1875, for example, a recent graduate of Mount Allison, the minister Ralph Brecken, declared in the columns of the *Argosy* that 'science points to the traditions and superstitions which beclouded the vision of the church for centuries,' and admitted the possibility that evolution was the method employed for the divine creation of flora and fauna on earth, while attacking Darwin's attempt to exclude God's will altogether. For Brecken, religious faith had 'very little to fear from the contradictions of hypothetical science.'[114] Nor did educational goals preclude research, although the professors' responsibilities for teaching academy as well as college students implied that time and effort was spent in less advanced areas of knowledge. As a group, however, the Mount Allison faculty had little training for purely scientific or philosophical endeavours and little time to devote to private study. Only Weldon had a formal training in research, and his career would later mature not at Mount Allison but at the Dalhousie Law School. As for publication, Charles Stewart was accustomed to encourage his theological students to write 'short essays, narratives, or biographies for our own periodicals,' and 'to use the pen for the good of the church,' and this view prevailed beyond the confines of the theological faculty: publication was seen less as a means of communicating the results of scholarly enquiries than as a skill to be used in the direct service of the religious and educational goals of Mount Allison.[115]

By the late 1870s, the time was fast approaching when Mount Allison would have to face the question of how far the educational merits of the college could be preserved unless scholarly research was indeed undertaken as an end in itself by at least some of the professors, as part of their preparation for teaching if not as a prelude to publication. Likewise, it was uncertain how long the college could go on paying its faculty members salaries which were mediocre at best, while expecting them to maintain their enthusiasm, dedication, and versatility on a campus that had limited library and laboratory facilities. And yet, what was the alternative? Mount Allison was not rich, and it had a responsibility to discharge both to the Methodist denomination and to the wider community of the region. One possible solution lay in the concept of a central teaching university, for the standard argument in favour of such an institution was based on the limited resources of denominational colleges and the way in which wasteful duplication prevented any college from attaining the highest of academic standards. The letter circulated by Dalhousie to the other colleges in 1874 had called accordingly for 'one general University for education in the Arts, by the concentration of the talents of the different Faculties and its invariable results [*sic*] the gathering together of students in large numbers.'[116] The reasons for Mount Allison's rejection of this option, however, had been clear and conclusive. Mount Allison college was one of the three Sackville institutions that offered an avowedly denominational education, the principles of which were defined each year in the *Catalogue*: 'the general denominational control, under which it is placed, furnishes a sufficient guarantee that sceptical license will never be allowed to run riot within its walls, but does not imply the existence of a purpose or a wish to intefere with the conscientious convictions of any.'[117] Such assurances, the

Wesleyan remarked in April 1881, could not be given by a central non-denominational university which might base some or all its teachings on atheistic premises. This *Wesleyan* editorial also identified a second major reason for rejecting the merger of Mount Allison into a larger teaching university:

Now even in a physical point of view, the country possesses vast superiority over the city. Fresh air, field exercise, and the comparative freedom from the low attractions of the theatre and the drinking saloon which the Denominational Colleges in our land enjoy, do certainly place their pupils in a more highly favoured condition for the prosecution of their studies than is to be found amidst the bustle and fascinations of a populous city.[118]

To be sure, Sackville was not as isolated a community now, since the completion of the Intercolonial Railway in 1876, as it had been when Mount Allison had been founded. The academy *Catalogue* no longer maintained after that year, as it had since the start, that Sackville was 'a retired Country Village,' but noted instead from 1877 onwards that it was 'situated on the line of the Intercolonial Railway, midway between Halifax and Saint John.'[119] Yet it remained a small town, a more familiar environment for a student population of predominantly rural origin than a large city would have been. Furthermore, for Mount Allison college to merge its identity into a centralized university in Halifax would render it unable to serve satisfactorily the New Brunswick constituency from which it had drawn such a large proportion of its students in the past. For these reasons, the concept of the central teaching university could not seriously be entertained by Mount Allison, no matter what its merits might be on strictly academic grounds.

Yet the notion of complete independence had little appeal either. The academic and financial difficulties faced by the college gave grounds for doubt as to whether it could maintain self-sufficiency, and in any case the idea of the private college had never been regarded as an ideal at Mount Allison. The college, like the other institutions, had been founded in order to serve the needs of the Methodist denomination and the needs of the Maritime community as a whole, and temptations towards exclusiveness or institutional self-aggrandizement had been resisted as far as possible. David Allison had reaffirmed in a speech in Saint John in 1870 that Mount Allison was not only for the wealthy:

The sons of the wealthy will be welcome to its classes, and ought to furnish a goodly proportion of its graduates. But we are eager to help those needy youths whose souls are a glow with an ardent desire for a liberal education, who toil hard both mentally and manually for the attainment of the worthy object of their desire.[120]

Yet Allison's statements carried the undertone that it was questionable whether this professed openness of access which – even though there was no likelihood that attendance at Mount Allison, any more than at other academic institutions, would be fully representative of the social classes of the region – had been proclaimed from the beginning, was being maintained in practice at the college. At the time he spoke, the tuition fees normally charged for a complete Bachelor of Arts programme at Mount Allison were estimated at $200 in figures published by the Nova Scotia government, as compared to $77 at Dalhousie and $53 at Acadia; seven years later the difference had narrowed only slightly, as fees at Mount Allison had stayed the same while those at Dalhousie and Acadia had risen to $82 and $100 respectively.[121] Tuition fees were not the only criterion of an expensive or inexpensive education, but it was clear all the same that Mount Allison was having difficulty in living up to its historic ideals. Within the University of Halifax, with a substantial Nova Scotia government grant, its financial ability to do so might at least be prevented from deteriorating. In short, it seemed clear when the university began that this was the framework within which Mount Allison could best face the future. Neither its denominational character nor its small-town location were threatened by the university as it existed. At the same time, there would be no chance that Mount Allison could allow its standards to slip, for its students would, if the university succeeded, be competing with those of other colleges.

Already by 1877 affiliation with the University of Halifax had resulted in changes in the Mount Allison curriculum so as to bring it into line with the requirements the university had adopted on the recommendation of its own curriculum committee, which had been composed of representatives from the colleges, including David Allison. The result was a more rigorous requirement, organized on the basis of four years of two terms each; the old Mount Allison curriculum had been designed for four years of three terms each, but the catalogue had admitted that in practice it could be completed in three years.[122] The new curriculum also put a heavier emphasis on classical study than had the old. Previously, a BA student took at least 12 and no more than 15 classical studies out of a total of 36 termly classes; now the number was 24 or 25 out of 47, depending upon an option in the third year between a mathematical and a classical subject. During the first two years, 13 out of 22 classes were on classical subjects, together with four terms of chemistry, one each of algebra, trigonometry and 'conic sections,' with the balance being made up of one class in English language and literature and one in logic. The last two years, contrary to the former practice at Mount Allison, continued classical study, along with physics and mechanics, as compulsory subjects. In each of these years, the student was invited to choose two from three options: a language; mental and moral philosophy; or complementary classes in constitutional history and political economy. The new curriculum thus broke with Mount Allison's own previous curriculum in a number of respects, and not least in the disappearance of evidences of Christianity as a college subject. The magnitude of the changes was in fact reflected in favourable comments in the press: the Saint John *Telegraph* praised Mount Allison for its 'intelligent and loyal support' of the university, while the Halifax *Chronicle* stressed that it was 'leading the way in the good work.'[123] Students who successfully completed the programme now had the option of taking their BA degree from Mount Allison, or of taking the two series of BA examinations of the University of Halifax, which were administered by local examinations in Sackville each July: 'First BA' taken at the end of the second year, and 'Second BA,' at the end of the final year. Not all chose to register at the university, but of six members of the sophomore class in the year 1879–80, four chose to take the first BA examination in July 1880. All passed the examination, and three won prizes, including William Morley Tweedie, who won first prize and would later go on to a long professorial career at Mount Allison, and J.C. Webster, who took the fourth prize. In that year, therefore, although Mount Allison had not given up its degree-granting power, there was reason to believe that the majority of its undergraduates might well in future choose to take their degrees through the university.[124]

There were also other, less promising, indications. For one thing, apart from the four Mount Allison candidates in July 1880, there had only been one entry for the first BA examination, a clear sign that other colleges were not encouraging their students in that direction. There had been only one candidate for the second BA examination in that year and he, Sawdon Dunn Scott of Mount Allison, would be the university's only BA graduate during its short career. Even at Mount Allison, student opinion was not unreservedly favourable. The heavy classical content of the curriculum and the need to invest four years in its completion were drawbacks. So too was the practice of holding examinations in July, which obviously broke into the summer. Tweedie later recalled that when he and his colleagues came to Sackville two weeks early in the summer of 1880, 'the hospitality of the Sackville people with a round of picnics and entertainments prevented us from breaking down our health by too arduous study'; but it was not a popular arrangement, and in a letter to the *Argosy* later in the year the university registrar, F.C. Sumichrast, promised to consider a change.[125] The *Argosy*, in fact, continued to support the principle of the University of Halifax consistently and strongly, declaring in January 1881 that its establishment was 'one of the best educational acts of the Nova Scotia Legislature.'[126]

As for the college administration, a measure of its commitment to the university was the disappearance of the Bachelor of Science and Literature course from the catalogue of 1877. As in the case of the old BA curriculum, those students already enrolled in the programme were permitted to proceed, but in 1877 the only regular undergraduate programme advertised was the BA according to the university requirements. The university did offer a more purely scientific B SC, but Mount Allison did not offer courses towards this degree. Mount Allison retained the Bachelor of Divinity degree, since it was never intended that theological study should be conducted outside of the direct supervision – and funding – of the Methodist denomination. The Master of Arts was also retained, although in 1878 the procedures for this degree were elaborated by the addition of the requirement of 'a satisfactory thesis.' There was no suggestion that the thesis should involve research, or indeed that it should be anything more than an essay, but it was the first specific requirement for the degree other than that the candidate must be a BA of three years' standing.[127] These being the only other degrees offered, and with allowance for students already enrolled in the old programmes to proceed to completion, the fact now was that the only regular undergraduate programme advertised by Mount Allison was the BA according to the requirements of the University of Halifax. According to J.R. Inch, whose views were reported by the Presbyterian minister C.B. Pitblado and printed in the *Wesleyan* in early 1880, the university was 'an honest endeavour to unify the interests of higher education in Nova Scotia,' and through its framework 'the colleges might harmonize their courses of study.' They might also, he added, 'be kept under the fostering care of government. ...'[128]

Inch was speaking by this time as president of the Mount Allison college, a position he assumed in 1878 following the resignation of David Allison. In November 1877, Allison had been appointed to the position of superintendent of education for Nova Scotia, a post made vacant shortly before by the death of the previous superintendent, A.S. Hunt. Allison's appointment took immediate effect, although he continued to be president of Mount Allison until the end of the 1877–8 year, discharging the duties of both offices at the same time.[129] Allison's unexpected resignation was accepted 'reluctantly' at a special meeting of the board of trustees on 12 December 1877, together with expressions of high appreciation for his 'faithful and successful discharge of the onerous duties of his office' over a nine-year period. On the matter of his successor, the board was divided between two chief candidates. Inch was one, while the other was Howard Sprague, a member of Mount Allison's first graduating class of 1862 and now minister of Centenary church in Saint John. After an inconclusive ballot, Inch withdrew his name; Sprague was declared elected, and the appointment publicized in the Saint John evening papers the following day.[130] The only difficulty was that Sprague had not been consulted, and it soon emerged that he was in fact unwilling to serve, on grounds of ill-health. Accordingly, on 6 March 1878 the board met again in special session, and this time Inch was the only candidate. On motion of Humphrey Pickard, he was unanimously elected.[131]

Inch was a popular choice. The *Wesleyan* noted that he had 'grown with the growth of the Institution over which he is now to find himself installed as principal officer,' and that 'in every interest entrusted to him by our church, he has succeeded,' while the Saint John *Globe* praised what it termed a 'judicious selection.'[132] The *Argosy* referred to 'strong public feeling in favor of this appointment,' and assured Inch of a warm welcome from the students; he was, the editorial went on 'not a *novus homo*, but a gentleman who has been tried by years of faithful and successful educational service.'[133] Like his friend and predecessor, Inch was tall, full-bearded, and enjoyed a high reputation as a public speaker. His style, however, was not the booming oratory of Allison, but was characterized by quiet precision and clarity of argument and thought. The two men, whose careers paralleled and overlapped one another for over half a century, differed also in personal background. Allison was a close relative of the founder of Mount Allison, and had graduated at the head of his class at Wesleyan University. Inch, forty-two years old at the time of his appointment as president, was the son of parents who had emigrated a few years before his birth from Northern Ireland to the small rural community of Jerusalem in Queen's County, New Brunswick. Inch attended public schools, and taught in the public school at Keswick before coming to the Mount Allison academy as a teacher in 1854 at the age of nineteen. Ten years later he became vice-principal of the ladies' academy, and principal in 1869, and his achievement in pulling that institution out of its disastrous financial predicament comprised one of his chief recommendations as a potential college president. His BA and MA degrees were both from Mount Allison, and shortly after his appointment as president he became the first recipient from Mount Allison of the honorary dgree of LLD. He was also the second layman to be president. Had Sprague accepted the office, the presidency of Allison might have come to be seen as a brief exception to a normal succession of clerical presidents; as it was, the tradition of lay presidents was now established and remained characteristic of Mount Allison, with only two exceptions, in the future.[134]

As well as marking a change of administration at Mount Allison College, the inauguration of Inch as president also necessarily had its effects on the two academies. At the ladies' academy, Inch was succeeded as principal by David Kennedy, a minister who was a graduate of Victoria College and had been brought from the Montreal Conference in 1875 to serve as vice-principal of the male academy. Kennedy's move across the road created a vacancy at the male academy, where David Allison had been titular principal, but where the day-to-day administration had been carried out by Kennedy. At its meeting in June 1878, the board of trustees decided to act on a previous decision to separate the presidency of the college from the principalship of the academy, and Benjamin Longley, also a graduate of Victoria and also a minister in the Montreal Conference, was appointed principal. Now for the first time, each of the three institutions was separately administered, under the general authority of the trustees, or as they had formally been styled since 1875, 'the Board of Governors of Mount Allison Wesleyan College and Academies.'[135]

The new academy principals faced demanding tasks. Of the two, Kennedy had fewer immediate difficulties, for Inch in his last year at the ladies' academy had reported a profit of $2712 and had thus made substantial inroads into the institution's net debt, which now stood, in the summer of 1878, at just over $5000. Considering that a new heating system and a new wing had been added during the 1870s, it was a healthy state of affairs. The attendance of 82 students during the 1877–8 year was satisfactory also.[136] It was not as many as during the initial years of the institution, but was a great improvement on the situation when Inch had become vice-principal in 1864, and had been achieved in the face of competition not only from the public schools but also from such competitors as the Wesleyan Academy in Charlottetown, and the Acadia Seminary which had evolved during the 1870s from a private boarding school first opened in Wolfville in 1857.[137] Even the ladies' academy, however, had its problems. Competition from other schools was a continuing concern, and student numbers were not growing: 76 attended in 1878–9, 74 in 1879–80, and again 76 in 1880–1.[138] There was also considerable room for doubt as to the very nature of the school's future role. Beginning as a primarily academic institution for girls of all ages, the ladies' academy had tended in later years to cater for older pupils. Between 1870 and 1872, the average age had reached as high as nineteen, although by the mid-1870s it dropped to seventeen. The age-group under fifteen had not been abandoned entirely, but a large majority of the pupils were aged fifteen or over.[139] Now that the degree courses of the college were open to women students, there was an obvious possibility that the ladies' academy would be left with a dangerously narrow clientele of students, or that it would become in effect a 'finishing school' for students who did not aspire to a full college education. As a response to this situation, the 1879 catalogue carried a new series of descriptions of the courses of study offered, stressing their diversity. Of the six programmes, the first two corresponded to the old primary and intermediate departments, with the latter described specifically as 'the College Preparatory Course.' The old collegiate programme was extended from two to three years, and the Mistress of Liberal Arts diploma described as a 'title and degree,' rather than simply as a 'title.' The fourth programme, although the ladies' academy was not strictly entitled to regard it as its own, was the regular BA course through the college. Fifth and sixth were courses in instrumental music and vocal culture – with a specific curriculum laid out for a diploma in pianoforte – and in drawing and painting.[140] The ladies' academy, like the other institutions, faced questions of identity; but it did enter the 1880s with a well-defined series of programmes for its students.

The problems faced by the male academy were even more deep-seated. While there might be fear that the ladies' academy would become too much of a finishing school, the male academy did not even have that option. The loss of its collegiate department to the college in 1862 had been final, and it had no equivalent of the MLA programme. Yet it too faced severe competition, especially from the public schools, and by the early 1870s its primary department was sparsely attended. As in the ladies' academy, most pupils were now aged fifteen or over, and the average age in most years was seventeen.[141] A major effort to diversify the academy's appeal was begun in 1874, with the introduction of a commercial department under the direction of S.E. Whiston, described as 'a most skilful penman and accountant,' to offer instruction in 'the arts of merchandise, railroading, banking, &c.'[142] Welcomed by the *Chignecto Post* as showing 'a progressive spirit,' the commercial department, or commercial college as it was soon designated, was pronounced successful in the academy catalogue of 1875 despite the economic difficulties of the region: 'young men cannot employ these dull times better,' the catalogue urged, 'than in preparing to take full advantage of the revival of business soon to come.'[143] The trustees showed their confidence by authorizing in April 1875 the construction of a small building for the commercial college, adjoining the main academy, at a cost of $5000, and in early 1876 the *Wesleyan* pronounced that the new venture had succeeded 'far in advance of the expectations with which it was founded.'[144]

The commercial college did indeed assist the academy to prosperous years during the mid-1870s, and the total academy attendance reached over 100 in three of the four years between 1874 and 1878.[145] As David Allison remarked in a speech in 1877, the commercial college did not necessarily 'learn people how to become rich'; but it helped its students in that direction, and it helped the academy to maintain itself. In 1878, however, came a change for the worse. A major factor was the departure of Whiston, whose imaginative teaching had included the printing of Mount Allison banknotes: on occasion these even passed for genuine bills in local transactions, as the former academy teacher Thomas Wood found out in 1879 when he was 'cheated ... in a Mount Allison bill, amt. $2.00.'[146] Probably due in part to Whiston's departure, attendance at the academy fell to 71 in 1878–9, as compared with 109 in the previous year. Still, matters deteriorated. By April 1879, one Sackville resident mentioned in a letter to her brother that a teacher had had to leave the academy temporarily because of family illness and that 'they have so few students that his classes can be easily provided for.'[147] In the following month, she described an incident which indicated clearly a breakdown in discipline at the school:

> Poor Mr. Longley still has to battle with his boys – last Monday about fifteen of them started off to have a holiday at Fort Cumberland, without leave or license – and the poor tormented man has had to invent chastisements for the offenders.[148]

The summer of 1879 brought Longley's resignation, and his replacement by C.H. Paisley, a minister of the New Brunswick and Prince Edward Island Conference. There was also serious discussion by the trustees of the future of the academy, as a result of which the commercial college was abolished as such, although in the catalogue of 1880 a more limited programme in 'Book-keeping and Penmanship' was instituted.[149] The virtual collapse of commercial instruction, and the poor reputation for discipline which the academy had acquired during the previous year, had a predictable result. When the school year opened in August, the male academy had an attendance of only 16 students. Under Paisley's administration, a gradual recovery took place, and the total number for the year eventually reached a minimally respectable 51; in the following year of 1880–1 it improved to 70.[150] Despite the improvement, these were unhappy times for the academy. David Allison, in his new post as superintendent, was in a position to know the unpleasant facts when he spoke at the closing exercises in May 1880 of 'the recent development of the great free Common Schools system, which was tending to supplant such institutions as the Mount Allison Academy.' Allison himself still had faith in its future, appealing to alumni to come to its aid. The academy, he believed, 'had a larger representation in the persons of its old students in the Senate and the House of Commons of the Dominion than any other Educational Institution in these Provinces.'[151] Whether that fact could cure the academy of its current malaise, though, was very much open to question, despite the optimism of its former principal.

Also open to question in 1880 was the future of the Mount Allison college within the University of Halifax. The influence of the university upon Mount Allison had clearly been demonstrated in the curriculum changes adopted to conform with the university's requirements. Mount Allison had also influenced the university, not only through the service of Burwash, Smith, Stewart, and Weldon as examiners, but also through the participation of Allison and Inch on the university senate.[152] Inch had taken the opportunity to take up again an old cause: the admission of women to full status as students of the university. Harriet Starr Stewart, a daughter of Charles Stewart, was in her second year at Mount Allison in 1879–80, and wished to take the first BA examination of the university in July 1880, along with Tweedie, Webster, and their classmate H.A. McKeown. Accordingly, Inch began his campaign at the senate meeting in Halifax on 6 January 1880 by proposing that all statutes of the university in regard to admission of examination candidates and the conferral of degrees should be read as applying to either sex; the ensuing discussion was described by the Halifax *Herald* as 'the most spirited and interesting ... of the Session.' Despite his citation of 'movements in other countries where artificial barriers based on sexual distinctions were being broken down,' Inch was unable to carry his point against the opposition of, among others, Senator L.G. Power, and the matter was referred to a committee.[153] It was not until December that the committee formally brought forward a favourable recommendation. But in the meantime the provincial attorney-general, John S.D. Thompson, had ruled in May that there was nothing in the university statutes to prevent women from being examined and taking degrees. Harriet Stewart took her examinations in July 1880, and passed.[154]

Yet Mount Allison's co-operation with the University of Halifax was not typical of all the colleges, as G.W. Hill gloomily admitted in his chancellor's report in December 1880:

With the exception of Mount Allison College, we may say that not one of the six colleges, specially referred to in the Act of the Legislature, have considered it wise or advantageous to take advantage of the opportunity afforded them of having their students tested by examiners outside of their own institutions – that not one College, except that already named, has taken any practical interest in furthering the project of trying by one general touchstone the acquisitions of the youths whom they have been instructing. ... [The University], for some reason or other, has failed to enlist the practical sympathies, and even the luke-warm co-operation, of the chartered colleges of Nova Scotia.[155]

Hill's comments were accurate; but there was also another serious threat to the university's continuation. In the Nova Scotia election of 1878, the Liberal government of P.C. Hill was defeated by the Conservatives under S.H. Holmes. The future of the University of Halifax after its initial five-year period had never been clear, and the demise of the government which had sponsored the experiment was a further complication. The university registrar, F.C. Sumichrast, confided to Inch in November 1878 his hope that 'the new Government will recognise the fact that the University is useful and will therefore foster, and not injure it. The last I believe they would not do.' But he was clearly not sure.[156]

Even at Mount Allison, in 1878 and after, there were signs of uncertainty. The board of governors' report to the general conference of the Methodist Church of Canada in that year referred pointedly to the limited five-year term of the existing Nova Scotia grants to denominational colleges and to the need for increased endowment funds.[157] In 1879, measures were taken to offset the exclusive reliance upon the curriculum of the university in Mount Allison's course offerings. References in the minutes of the college board for 31 May 1879 to 'difficulties arising out of the adoption of the curriculum of the University of Halifax by Mt. Allison College' indicated that attention was now being paid once again to the development of curricula designed to appeal to Mount Allison's own constituency rather than only to conform to the university's requirements.[158] The results were embodied in the college catalogue for 1879, in which two new courses of instruction were provided, in addition to the existing BA programme. The PH B course was a three-year programme with no classical content except for one year of Latin. The rest of the subjects included were divided between science, mathematics, philosophy, modern languages, and related classes in political economy and constitutional history. Evidences of Christianity also reappeared in this course. The degree of PH B was unknown elsewhere in Canada, although it had precedents in the United States, and was probably borrowed by Mount Allison from Wesleyan University, where it had been introduced in 1873. Although it differed in a few respects from Mount Allison's former BS degree, it clearly was intended as a successor to that programme, and was so described by Inch at a meeting of the college board in 1880. The PH B curriculum also bore a close resemblance to the new three-year MLA offered by the ladies' academy, although the relationship of the two, if any, was not mentioned in the catalogue of either institution.[159] The other new course offered by Mount

Allison college in 1879 ws not a degree programme, but a six-month course in scientific agriculture: designed for farmers and scheduled to run from November to April, it included classes in chemistry, soil classification, drainage, the use of fertilizers, and bookkeeping. It was an imaginative concept, but was implemented hurriedly and attracted little interest among local farmers. In 1880 it was advertised to be given only 'if required,' and in the following year it was quietly omitted from the catalogue.[160]

As the five-year term of the University of Halifax act, and of the associated grants to denominational colleges, came towards its close, debate began once again on these matters. In late 1880 and throughout the early months of 1881, battle was joined between the advocates of a central teaching university and those of the denominational colleges. As for the University of Halifax, it attracted little strong support, as it was well known that it had failed to win the co-operation of its affiliated colleges. Even A.D. Smith, who wrote a series of letters to the *Herald* in January 1881 to take issue with the Dalhousie professor J.G. MacGregor over the latter's support of a consolidated teaching university and to defend the denominational colleges, was not notably optimistic:

> I do not feel called on to champion the University of Halifax. If all the colleges lay hold of it, it will probably live, and may, with some alterations, do good work after all. If they do not, it will just as probably die.[161]

In late February, the Nova Scotia government floated a possible solution to the matter, when Holmes wrote to each college to suggest that all should surrender their degree-granting powers to a 'General Examining Body of a representative character, in which your college would be represented.'[162] While such a course would have implied the abolition of the University of Halifax as such, it would have safeguarded the principle of the non-teaching central body, and Inch replied for Mount Allison that he had no doubt that the college would agree. Without having put the matter to the board of governors, he could not speak authoritatively; and it may be, as the *Herald* suggested in an editorial, that a college with a New Brunswick charter would have faced legal difficulties in foregoing its degree-granting power in favour of a Nova Scotia organization. None the less, Inch's letter of 2 March 1881 was a final gesture by Mount Allison in favour of the principle to which it alone had given strong support during the active life of the University of Halifax.[163]

St Mary's and St Francis Xavier Colleges gave their support to Holmes's proposal. Acadia, Dalhousie, and King's refused. The notion of the non-teaching central institution was now obviously doomed, and on 17 March

1881 the Nova Scotia government introduced legislation to abolish the University of Halifax. It did not, however, adopt the principle of the central teaching university; instead, as Mount Allison and the Nova Scotia Conference had requested in petitions to the legislature, it proposed the continuation of grants to be denominational colleges, albeit at a reduced level that would have given the Mount Allison institutions $1400 annually instead of the previous $2400. This was a disappointment, as was the proposed abolition of the university, but the measure was by no means a disaster. It had been clear for some time that the University of Halifax lacked widespread support, and the *Argosy*'s editorial of April 1881, with its tone of resignation and only mild regret, probably typified the prevailing mood:

Had those institutions which possessed the best local advantages for availing themselves of a competitive test been as ready to establish their superiority as they have been to boast of it, the University of Halifax might have lived longer and perhaps had a different history. But there is now no reason that the university should longer exist, if the denominational Colleges are determined not to use it. The sudden dissolution is rather inconvenient for about a dozen of our students who have been preparing for the examinations; but after all there is not much fun in the students of Mt. Allison going up to Halifax to compete with each other for prizes and honors. There was a spice of interest in these examinations when we were expecting the polished Acadian and the erudite Dalhousian to join battle for the pre-eminence. The former, however, never ventured forth, and the latter sat in his fastnesses, glorying in his might, but only appearing in companies of one, and then to no great advantage.[164]

Worse, however, was to come. The college bill had a smooth passage through the assembly, and was sent on to the legislative council on 6 April. There, it had first reading and passed routinely to the select committee on bills, which reported favourably to the council two days later. The legislative council, however, was still dominated by Liberals, as opposed to the Conservative majority in the assembly. Despite the fact that the assembly had voted almost unanimously in favour of the bill, the opposition councillors saw an opportunity to obstruct a government measure, and on 8 April they won a narrow majority – ten votes to nine – on a motion to defer consideration of the bill for three months. Since the session was now within a few days of ending, this refusal to grant passage effectively destroyed the bill.[165] In a technical sense, the University of Halifax was reprieved, although it could no longer function, since there was no provision for its funding. The last letter of F.C. Sumichrast as university registrar, written to the lieutenant-governor on 11 May, complained that 'no official communication' had been received as to the university's fate; it was an appropriate epitaph.[166] Nor could grants to denominational colleges be continued. For Mount Allison, this was the most serious consequence of all. In the draft college budget that the trustees had prepared in 1878, the Nova Scotia legislative grant had supplied some 23 per cent of the anticipated annual income. The reduction of the grant which had been envisaged in the rejected government bill would have been difficult enough to overcome. Now, almost one-quarter of the budget had suddenly been cut off. The board of governors met in emergency session on 3 June 1881. Of the fourteen who attended eight had also been present nine years before when the board had discussed the crisis arising from the loss of the grant from New Brunswick. They must have had a certain sense of *déjà vu*.[167]

PART TWO

5

Restoring Foundations: 1881–1891

'Brethren,' declared J.R. Inch in an emotional appeal for support to the New Brunswick and Prince Edward Island Conference during the summer of 1881, 'our college – your college – must not go down.'[1] Coming in addition to the other problems bequeathed by the 1870s, the loss of the Nova Scotia legislative grant seemed indeed to threaten Mount Allison College with extinction. That the threat was not realized, and that the 1880s became in reality an exhilarating decade of expansion for Mount Allison, was due not only to the strenuous efforts of college officials but also to changes occurring in the economy of the Maritime provinces. The days of shipbuilding, and of the large merchant fleets which had operated from Maritime ports in the middle decades of the century, were numbered. Although these activities, and the related lumber industry of New Brunswick, had survived the immediate crisis that had followed the British economic depression of 1873 and the associated decline in imperial trade, the prosperity of Atlantic shipping and shipbuilding was to decline in the later years of the decade. Instead, a new form of prosperity was initiated in certain areas of the Maritimes in the 1880s, based not on marine trade but on the industrial opportunities offered by the Dominion of Canada. From 1879, with the adoption of the 'National Policy' by John A. Macdonald's federal government, Maritime industries enjoyed the protection of a large tariff barrier against foreign imports, and benefited too from the favourable freight rate structure of the Intercolonial Railway. Able to compete effectively in both central and western Canada, Maritime firms dramatically increased their production of such commodities as textiles, sugar, and iron and steel products during the early 1880s. Ports and shipbuilding centres such as Yarmouth, Saint John, and St Stephen saw their economies transformed. Newer centres attained prosperity based on their railway location, including Moncton and Amherst. The prosperity was not evenly distributed throughout the region, and time would reveal that it was not as securely based as it first seemed. The decline of the older industries continued to cause business failures and out-migration from the region, and even the recent industrial developments were threatened by a commercial depression during the mid-1880s. But the early years of the decade were good years; Mount Allison's latest financial crisis could not, in this sense, have come at a more opportune time.[2]

At the special meeting of the board of governors on 3 June 1881, however, there was little if any trace of such optimism. The combined debt of the three institutions stood at over $12,000. In the year 1880–1, during which three-quarters of the Nova Scotia grant had still been available, an operating loss of just over $400 had been sustained: a small profit shown by the college had been offset by losses at the two academies. Endowment funds, it was true, stood by the end of 1880 at $34,524, with interest being collected also on a further substantial sum that had been subscribed but not yet paid. There could be no question, however, of using endowment funds to pay off debt, and in any case it was the endowment interest of over $3000 per year which was enabling the college to maintain a break-even situation from year to year. With the Nova Scotia grant – $1400 retained by the college, and $1000 divided between the academies – the institutions had been holding their own, even allowing for serious losses by the male academy. Without the grant, the prospect of annual deficits of over $2000 was grim and immediate.[3] The first possible solution considered by the board was to co-ordinate the work of the three institutions in order to ensure the survival of all, and on 6 June, after a three-day adjournment, it decided on a series of basic principles. The first of these was an obvious but necessary resolution that the overall budget of the institutions must be balanced from year to year, 'so that the alarming evil of an increasing *Debt* may be avoided'; the others were means of achieving this end. The academies must henceforth be self-sustaining, and the male academy should have as its chief object 'the preparation of students for matriculation in our College,' although continuing as a sideline to offer commercial training. Thus the primacy of the college over the male academy, which had been developing in practice since 1862, was formally recognized. The ladies' academy was not subjected to such a limitation, but the principle was reaffirmed that its students would continue to attend college classes when they wished to take advanced subjects, to avoid the organization of duplicate classes in the ladies' academy itself. Furthermore, a new 'Committee of Consultation and direction' was henceforth to co-ordinate, on behalf of the board, the working of the institutions.[4]

As for the college, the board declared that its continuance could be ensured only by the raising of a further $50,000 of endowment, and appointed a committee to study ways and means, and to report when the board met again two days later for its regular annual meeting. The spokesman for the committee was Humphrey Pickard, who proposed appeals to the three eastern conferences and nominated representatives of the board to carry Mount Allison's cause to each of the three. There was nothing new in that, for such appeals had been the traditional source of endowment funds for the college. The other recommendations, however, were less predictable. A year before, Josiah Wood – who had been appointed treasurer of the institutions in 1876 after the death of his father, Mariner Wood – had offered to contribute $10,000 towards the construction of a new college building, on condition that $50,000 was raised in new endowment funds. The old building was certainly too small and in poor repair, and the committee recommended that now was the time to act on Wood's proposal. Furthermore, it suggested that 'applications for aid be made to the few rather than to the many,' and that even the appeal to the conferences should be directed particularly to 'the leading friends of our principal circuits.' Thus, the committee put forward a bold plan to save the college, based not so much on the customary appeal to the collective generosity of the Methodist community as a whole, but rather on the anticipated donations of a small number of rich benefactors. After 'considerable discussion,' the new approach was adopted by the board. Regaining some of the optimism which had been absent at the earlier meetings, it also reflected on the high quality of educational work carried out at Mount Allison despite financial difficulties and concluded that such achievements gave ground 'for grateful acknowledgment of God's good hand upon us for good, and vindicate the right of the College with its affiliated Institutions to continued existence.'[5]

Pickard and his committee had not miscalculated. As an expanding religious denomination during a period of economic prosperity, the Methodist Church in the Maritimes, and in Canada as a whole, now included members whose mercantile and industrial pursuits had brought them wealth. One analysis of the social origins of leading Canadian industrialists of the early 1880s has found that Methodists comprised 19 per cent of this industrial elite, as compared with the 18 per cent of Methodists in the general population, while in the Maritime provinces no less than 30 per cent of the leading native-born industrialists were Methodists.[6] That such businessmen would respond generously to the call of Christian stewardship was quickly indicated when 'a few gentlemen in Halifax,' led by the merchant and former member of the board of trustees George H. Starr, quickly subscribed over $2000 to replace the Nova Scotia grant for the year 1881–2. Added directly to the operating funds of the college, this sum staved off the prospect of a serious deficit in that year.[7]

The long-term future was quickly made more promising by the success of the endowment campaign. The conferences gave ready assent to the campaign, and raised substantial sums among their own members: the New Brunswick and Prince Edward Island Conference, for example, immediately raised some $700 in a collection, while that of Nova Scotia raised $1400.[8] The success of the fund-raising effort was then made certain by substantial contributions from leading Methodist businessmen of New Brunswick. Josiah Wood agreed that his gift of $10,000 should be credited to the endowment campaign rather than used for building, and the amount was matched by a donation from Alexander Gibson of Fredericton. Another large contributor was Zechariah Chipman of St Stephen, who also left a bequest of $10,000 to Mount Allison on his death in 1883.[9] Each of these three donors personified in his own way the shift in the regional economy from staple industries to secondary manufactures. Wood had taken over the mercantile firm established in Sackville by his father, M. Wood and Sons, and by the mid-1870s had emerged as a successful merchant in his own right. The firm owned its own farm and sawmills, from which it exported agricultural goods and lumber, in its own vessels, in return for imports of manufactured goods. By the late 1870s, however, Wood was beset by the general weakness in marine trade, and also suffered serious losses in a series of shipwrecks; it was in 1879 or 1880 that he began to invest in manufacturing industry in Moncton. By 1882, his interests included sugar refining, cotton manufacturing, and an iron foundry.[10] Alexander 'Boss' Gibson, at the time of his large gift to Mount Allison, was still primarily a lumber exporter, basing his massive output upon large timber reserves on the Nashwaak river which he had bought from the provincial government in 1865. In 1883, Gibson undertook the beginning of his large cotton mill at Marysville, and by the end of the decade had formed his varied business interests into a joint-stock company with its capital of $3,000,000 controlled by himself and members of his family.[11] Zechariah Chipman, older than either Wood or Gibson, had attained considerable wealth as a shipbuilder in St Stephen, but was now a leading participant in the large St Croix cotton mill, constuction of which began in 1881.[12] The donations made by these three men were sufficient to bring Mount Allison within easy reach of the amount of funding which it needed survive. The prosperity of the institutions during the 1880s was thus built upon wealth generated by the more traditional economic activities of the region and now being increased by the new manufacturing industries: once again, Mount Allison's fortunes had proved to be intimately linked to those of the region it served.

The early days of 1882 brought a setback, though one which was soon turned to good account. In the early morning hours of 8 January, fire was discovered in the male academy. By daylight, the building was entirely destroyed. The fire, like the one in 1866, had begun in the kitchen, apparently from an overheating furnace, and comparisons were inevitably made between the two fires. It was, as the *Argosy* remarked, the 'second sacrifice to the fire-Fiend, at Mount Allison'; in the quadrennial report of the board of governors to the church general conference, it was described as 'a calamity – the second of its kind within a period of sixteen years.' In reality, however, it was questionable whether the fire was as calamitous as the report suggested. Certainly the editor of the *Wesleyan*, in the issue published five days after the fire, did not give that impression, although admitting that it was a 'sad event.'[13] There were a number of redeeming aspects of the situation. For one thing, no lives had been lost and much of the personal property in the building had been saved. The only injury had been sustained by a theological student, A.D.McCully, who had had the misfortune to break his ankle when his horse fell as he attempted to ride for help. Also, the adjoining commercial college building had not taken fire, partly because wet carpets had been spread over its side to extinguish sparks. The main building had been insured for $16,000, which was sufficient to cover four-fifths of the cost of replacement. Thus, the practical damage done by the fire had been minimal. Nor did the second academy building have the same historical significance as its predecessor: its loss could be accepted with more equanimity than had been possible when the very first Mount Allison building had been destroyed in 1866. In these circumstances, the fire produced little or no demoralization, but rather a determination to redouble the already successful fund-raising campaign so as to rebuild without delay. There was, of course, disruption and inconvenience. The operation of the academy had to be compressed into the limited space of the commercial college building, and the academy and college students had to take their meals at the ladies' academy: an arrangement which the *Argosy* seemed to regard as no great hardship.[14] Yet the prevailing mood was confident, even cheerful. The *Wesleyan* noted the sympathetic remarks of newspapers throughout the region, and quoted some good advice from the Saint John *News*:

> Were it our province to counsel the governors of the Institutions in the emergency, we would advise them to club together all the objects connected with the Institutions specially needing realization, in one grand scheme, and place it fairly and fully before the public in every part of the field to which, on any ground, they may be entitled to look for help. The country generally is now in a prosperous condition, and would

probably be more inclined to promote one comprehensive plan in aid of the Institutions than a succession of little schemes.[15]

Meeting in special session in early February, the board of governors decided to follow the approach advocated by the *News*, and appointed a fund-raising committee to provide for completion of the additional endowment of $50,000 – not a difficult task, as most of that sum had already been raised – and for construction of buildings for the academy and the college. Although a motion to build two college buildings as well as the new academy, proposed by Josiah Wood and David Allison, was defeated, the board did resolve that the new college building would be used for academic purposes only, while the existing one would serve as a student residence. Expansion was in prospect, not just the salvaging of an emergency. Later in the month, the *Wesleyan* carried the board's appeal for $30,000, together with editorial endorsment, while the local *Transcript* commented that 'there is now every prospect that the educational work in all its branches – Academic and Collegiate – will be carried on here with continued and increased efficiency.'[16] The campaign for building funds was carried on along more traditional lines than had been the previous year's endowment campaign. The appeal itself recalled that the achievements of 1881 were due to 'the few princely men' who had given large donations, while 'the great mass of the friends of "Education on Christian principles," including many former students of Mt. Allison, have not yet had an opportunity of offering assistance in the present crisis. ...'[17] Now they would have their chance.

The rebuilding of the academy was quickly put in hand, with the laying of the cornerstone by Josiah Wood on 5 June 1882. The day was cold and wet, and Wood's wife, Laura Wood, commented in her diary that the ceremony was funereal, 'as they sang a solemn hymn and prayed.' The *Wesleyan*, however, was characteristically enthusiastic, especially on the 'capital and timely address' delivered by Humphrey Pickard on the development of the academy in its two previous buildings.[18] By late 1882, the new academy was ready for occupation. On the same site as its predecessors, it was taller than they had been, with four storeys and a finished basement. As was carefully pointed out, the ovens and furnaces of the kitchen had been so designed that 'they shall have no contact with any wood work.' Also stressed in the description carried in the *Chignecto Post* was the hot water heating system, and up-to-date plumbing, both of which were improvements on the old building, and the *Post* concluded by congratulating the contractor, J.F. Teed of Dorchester, on his achievement.[19]

By the time the new academy opened on 4 January 1883, Teed had another large contract from Mount Allison, for the new college building. Serious practical discussion of this venture had begun at the meeting of the board of governors in the previous June, when John Lathern, a minister in Yarmouth and a member of the board, had pointed out that the Nova Scotia Conference was planning a celebration of the centenary of the beginning of William Black's ministry, and had suggested that 'some means might be raised by that effort for the benefit of Mt. Allison.'[20] Accordingly, when the board met again in December to authorize the letting of the contract, the new college was designated as 'the Centennial College Hall,' and it was to contain a large chapel named in honour of William Black. The architect, G.E. Fairweather of Saint John, had also designed the new academy, but there was to be a major difference between the two buildings: Centennial Hall was to be built in red sandstone, in Gothic style, and would thus be Mount Allison's first stone structure. After discussion of the site of the new college hall, the decision was taken to locate it a short distance to the south-west of the existing college site, and there the cornerstones were laid on 5 June 1883.[21]

A year later, Centennial Hall was complete. Ninety-five feet long by fifty-two wide, it was two storeys high above the basement, with a central tower standing seventy feet. As well as offices and classrooms, it contained science laboratories in the basement, and on the second floor a museum room for scientific exhibits, and a library with space for 10,000 volumes. The Black Memorial Chapel was also on the second floor, and was dominated by two large memorial windows, one commemorating William Black and the other Charles F. Allison. The official opening took place on 9 October, attended not only by a large gathering of Methodists from throughout the region, but also by the lieutenant-governor of Nova Scotia, M.H. Richey, the son of the Matthew Richey who had been sought in 1842 as the first principal. Also present was the principal of Dalhousie, James Ross, who responded at dinner in Lingley Hall to the toast proposed by Inch to 'our sister colleges.' Harmony was characteristic of the day. So too was faith in progress. J.R. Narraway, a veteran minister and supporter of Mount Allison throughout the previous forty years, stressed in one of the major addresses at the opening of Centennial Hall that Mount Allison had moved 'steadily onward' despite the difficult obstacles in its way. He went on in optimistic vein:

> At this moment the outlook is exhilarating. True, the sky is not all brightness, but nowhere is it overcast darkly. ... What has been solidly accomplished presages the greater things destined to be achieved.[22]

Narraway had retired from the board of trustees many years before, and so he had not been present at the meeting the previous afternoon when Inch had estimated the combined debt of the college and the male academy at almost $28,000. The centennial appeal had been adopted by both the New Brunswick and Prince Edward Island Conference and the Nova Scotia Conference, and the donations received amounted to approximately $18,000, much of this sum raised in small donations from the circuits.[23] The bequest of $10,000 from the recently deceased Zechariah Chipman was added to the fund, as was the $16,000 received in insurance on the burned academy building. Still, however, there was a shortfall of some $12,500 on the buildings – including their furnishing, and the cost of moving and refitting the old college – and this figure combined with the existing accumulated debts of about $6200 on the college and $9000 on the academy to produce Inch's overall estimate. It was a large burden of debt to carry, and its maintenance cost the college almost $1500 in the year 1884–5. None the less, there were good reasons not to be unduly alarmed. The endowment fund had reached a subscribed value of almost $100,000, of which some $73,000 had already been received and invested; the yield in the year 1884–5 was no less than $6120. With the help of this income, the college was now making a profit each year, and by 1886 had reduced its debt to some $4600. The academy was consistently losing money, but in amounts small enough to be more than counterbalanced by the equally consistent profits of the ladies' academy. Furthermore, as was pointed out in the Mount Allison report to the church general conference of 1886, the institutions now had an excellent physical plant, and the total value of land, buildings, and endowment was about $230,000. Set against that large figure, the debt no longer seemed so unmanageably large.[24] In the long term, it would be brought home forcibly to the administrators of Mount Allison that debt could not be taken lightly. Yet in the prosperous 1880s, with the crisis of 1881 surmounted and with the proven support of Methodists both rich and poor, there was ample justification for the belief in progress which Narraway evinced. Even those of his hearers who had attended the board meeting on 8 October no doubt joined feelingly in the applause that greeted his speech.

The mood of confidence that characterized Mount Allison at this time was also reflected in certain important administrative changes introduced by provincial legislation. In the spring of 1883, the membership of the board of governors was expanded to 26, with the provision that eight additional members would be co-opted by the board itself to serve until the next general conference of the Methodist Church of Canada. Thenceforth, the general conference would appoint 24 of the members quadrennially, while the alumni society would continue its annual appointment of two members.[25] Expansion of the board was an effective way of reinforcing and diversifying Mount Allison's range of contacts with its regional constituency, and this intention was clear in the co-option of the additional members at the board's meeting of 6 June 1883. In accordance with past practice, equal numbers of ministers and laymen were appointed. Of the ministers, two were from the Nova Scotia Conference: W.C. Brown, minister at Horton, and S.F. Huestis, the regional book steward, based in Halifax. The other two were from the New Brunswick and Prince Edward Island Conference: Howard Sprague, now minister in Fredericton, and Edwin Evans, minister in nearby Marsyville. The appointment of Evans was given added significance by the fact that 'Boss' Gibson was among the four lay appointees. Marysville was the milltown newly created by Gibson, and his co-option along with that of Evans was evidently an effort to nurture the interest in Mount Allison which had been shown in his recent large donation. Gibson would remain on the board until 1899, although he was not a regular attender at meetings. Of the other laymen brought on to the board, two were former members: J.L. Black, prominent merchant of Sackville and until recently a member of the provincial legislature, and G.H. Starr of Halifax, long-standing supporter of Mount Allison and a generous donor to its funds. The other member appointed was a newcomer from a prominent Charlottetown family, Lemuel L. Beer. Of the four, therefore, one was from Sackville and the remainder distributed evenly among the three Maritime provinces.[26]

The act that had expanded the board became, technically, outdated just over a year after its passage into law. Effective on 1 July 1884, the Methodist Church of Canada was replaced by a new 'Methodist Church' formed by union with the Methodist Episcopal Church and two smaller bodies, the Primitive Methodist Church and the Bible Christian Church in Canada. Thus the two major Methodist traditions in the Dominion – the British-influenced Wesleyan tradition and the American-influenced Episcopal – were brought together to form a united and distinctive church for Canada, Newfoundland, and Bermuda. For the Maritime provinces, the union of 1884 produced fewer immediate changes than had that of 1873, although the theological and organizational implications of union with the episcopal Methodists were hotly debated prior to the conclusion of the agreement to unite at a special conference in September of 1883. The Methodist Church of Canada had been the only major Methodist organization in the Maritimes, and the only change in membership brought about by the union was the incorporation into the New Brunswick and Prince Edward Island Conference of some 560 Bible Christians on Prince Edward Island.[27] The conference structure within the region remained the same under the terms of the union, with the three eastern conferences continuing to be the administrative units for the Maritimes, Newfoundland, and Bermuda, and therefore also delineating the constituency chiefly served by Mount Allison. There was, however, one major change. No longer did these three conferences represent half of the overall structure of the church, as they had before union. In addition to the existing Toronto, London, and Montreal conferences, three new conferences were created for Ontario – those of Niagara, Guelph, and Bay of Quinte – and a single one for Manitoba and the North-West. The area which up until 1873 had comprised the conference of Eastern British America now represented only three-tenths of the whole.[28]

For Mount Allison, the union necessitated few immediate changes. The work of the educational society of the Methodist Church of Canada was taken over by a similar body under the new church. The appointment of members of the board of governors would obviously devolve upon the general conference due to be held next in 1886. Technically, though, this would require an amendment to the existing college legislation, which specifically named the old Methodist Church of Canada as the appointing body. Accordingly a new act was passed by the legislature in the spring of 1886, with a preamble stating that it was a consequence of the church union. One of its clauses vested the power of appointment to the board in the general conference of the new Methodist Church, with the exception of the two alumni society members. Yet the act went far beyond this simple amendment of procedure. Most strikingly, it conferred university status under the new title of 'the University of Mount Allison College.'[29]

The origins of this change can be traced back to the board of governors' meeting of 10 June 1885, at which Inch and A.A. Stockton had been appointed as a committee 'to consider the propriety of making a change in the Corporate name,' and had been given full power to act upon their conclusions.[30] By early 1886, the new title had been proposed in a petition of the board to the legislature, which was presented in the assembly on 26 February by Stockton, now Liberal member for Saint John. The petition linked the title change directly to the Methodist union, in that it would 'harmonize its [Mount Allison's] designation with that of the Institution in Ontario.'[31] This was certainly a genuine reason, especially since Albert College, the institution of the Methodist Episcopal Church at Belleville, Ontario, had been united with Victoria and reduced to junior status under the terms of the church union. In the Ontario legislation giving effect to the new relationship of these colleges, the term 'Victoria University' had been formally inaugurated – although it had been in informal use for some years already – and it was stated that it should be the 'one university ... maintained by the said

Methodist Church.' There was talk at the time of a federated Methodist university for the Dominion, with which all existing institutions would be affiliated – a concept strongly supported, for example, by Josiah Wood in his speech at the opening of Centennial Hall – and there was an obvious case for ensuring that Mount Allison would enter into any negotiations for such a scheme on equal terms with Victoria.[32]

Yet there was more even than that to the Mount Allison act of 1886. The governors' petition noted that, apart from giving equal status with Victoria, the purpose was 'to express more fully the educational position and status of said College.'[33] The bill which Stockton introduced, also on 26 February, contained one especially noteworthy clause:

> The said Governors or Regents, in their corporate capacity, shall have power to affiliate to the said University [of Mount Allison College] any other College desirous of such affiliation, or any schools wheresoever situated, in arts, in theology, in law, in medicine, in agriculture, in civil engineering, or in any other department of science or knowledge. ...[34]

The bill, which passed into law on 2 April 1886, was both a necessary amending measure to the existing legislation, and an instrument of defence against any future pressures from Victoria; but it was also an overtly expansionist document. During the committee stage, Stockton was questioned on this clause and, according to the report carried in the Saint John *Telegraph*, 'explained the powers of the different universities throughout Canada and said the present bill gave no additional authority. Under it, however, [he continued] a law or medical school located at Halifax, or Fredericton, or elsewhere, could take its degrees from the university whose college is situated at Sackville.'[35] The prosperous years of the early 1880s had wrought a great change in the way in which Mount Allison perceived itself and its role. It was only five years since Inch had formally declared himself in favour of surrendering degree-granting powers to a central board esablished by the government of Nova Scotia, and had predicted that the board of governors would take the same view. Now the situation was reversed. Not only had Mount Allison's traditional avoidance of institutional expansion been thrust aside, but the affiliation of other institutions was openly contemplated.

How seriously was this change intended? Was such expansion really being considered, or was the clause simply included as a way of stressing Mount Allison's new university status? The answer to these questions lay in part in the events that had followed the collapse of the University of Halifax in 1881. In the spring of that year, a number of proponents of the concept of the central teaching university, whose hopes had been disappointed during the legislature session, had called for a conference of alumni of the various colleges in order to discuss 'university consolidation.' The alumni association of Dalhousie agreed to make arrangments for the conference. Predictably, the alumni of Acadia brusquely declined.[36] The proposal came before the Mount Allison alumni at their annual meeting of 7 June and provoked a debate which lasted from 10:30 p.m. until 2:30 in the morning; the issue was, as the *Chignecto Post* noted, 'very vigorously contested.' Although no motion was put forward in favour of university consolidation, there was strong support for sending delegates to the conference in order to explore the possibilities. The opposite view, and the one which prevailed by the narrow majority of 12 votes to nine, was that no countenance should be given to the proposed conference but that the alumni would be willing to 'send delegates to meet delegates from other Alumni Societies to discuss the desirability and feasibility of reviving the University of Halifax.' The supporters of this side of the argument included Inch, Stockton, Charles Stewart, J.L. Black, and A.D. Smith: an impressive list. The opposing side, however, also included influential members: R.C. Weldon, Benjamin Russell, H.A. Powell, David Allison, and the only BA graduate of the University of Halifax, S.D. Scott.[37]

Just over two weeks later a meeting was indeed held in favour of university consolidation, and an association formed to promote the cause. Among its officers were R.C. Weldon, vice-president, and Benjamin Russell, secretary. By the time the association held its annual meeting, in late December, it had circulated 12,000 copies of a pamphlet stressing the advantages of consolidation: a greater concentration of students and professors, leading to higher educational standards; more opportunity for professors to explore their subjects in depth; better library and laboratory facilities; the easier development of specialized schools in such areas as medicine, law, and applied science; the enabling of the churches to concentrate upon improving their theological education without the burden of other educational work. The pamphlet closed with the telling arguments that only through consolidation could Nova Scotian educational standards be raised to match those of 'the Upper Provinces,' and the most able Maritime students thus encouraged to remain in the region rather than seek their education and their careers elsewhere. The case was a strong one; and among the guest speakers at the association's meeting at the Halifax Hotel on 29 December 1881 was the provincial superintendent of education, David Allison.[38]

The university consolidation movement apparently made little more headway. As far as Mount Allison was concerned, it came up against the longstanding suspicion of a central teaching university, especially as its support was obviously strongest in Halifax. The suspicion was not lessened by the fact that Dalhousie was now enjoying the benefactions of George Munro, a native of Pictou who had become a wealthy New York publisher and would ultimately donate some $350,000. It was his endowment of the chair of constitutional and international law in 1883 which resulted in the attraction to Dalhousie of Mount Allison's best-qualified professor, R.C. Weldon.[39] Suspicion, though, could not obscure certain realities. A strong and influential minority of the active alumni of Mount Allison were convinced that university consolidation was at least worth considering. They included former supporters of the University of Halifax who had decided that a centralized university was better than having no co-ordination at all in the region's higher education. And their arguments were too persuasive to be easily dismissed, as the case of Weldon clearly indicated: it was too facile to suggest that he had been lured away by the material wealth of Dalhousie, when his advocacy of university consolidation had shown many months before that he, with his rigorous scholarly training, felt the need for the specialized opportunities that only a larger institution could provide.

Nevertheless, there was an answer which could be offered to the advocates of university consolidation. It was a simple one, though for Mount Allison it meant the reversal of the traditional aspiration to be a constituent part of a larger body, and it was implied in the expansionism that prevailed during the 1880s: Mount Allison must itself become a larger institution, and seek to embody the advantages enumerated by the pro-consolidation pamphlet. In part, this might simply mean the growth of the college along the lines that it had traditionally followed. Recalling the small beginnings of the Mount Allison college, Inch proclaimed to the Nova Scotia Conference in June 1885 that 'the history of the past twenty years is nothing to be ashamed of, and whoever is living twenty years hence will find Mount Allison one of the strongest and best of colleges. It is to go on for ever. *Esto perpetuata*!'[40] It was a good, rousing speech. But, as Inch well knew, it was tempting to go yet further. Rather than merely expanding its operations, why should Mount Allison not itself become the site of a central university for the region? The context of such thoughts was the concurrent discussion in Ontario which would lead to the University Federation Act of 1887. Although that legislation would make the University of Toronto a teaching university in science and social science subjects, the principle was established that constituent colleges would move physically to Toronto, but would retain their distinctive identity and character and would have responsibility for teaching in arts subjects.[41] In early 1885, in a letter to the Halifax *Evening Mail*, Inch himself suggested that the same model might be applied to the Maritimes. The central university, he believed, must serve the whole of the region, and must not be located in Halifax; the implication was that Sackville would be a much better site.[42]

Sackville, it might reasonably be objected, was not the same as Toronto. There was a simple answer to that point, though, and it was given emphatically in a letter to the *Wesleyan* of 22 January 1885 by 'J.L.' – almost certainly John Lathern – who wrote that an institution serving the three Maritime provinces must be situated within easy reach of them all. Thus, he argued, '*a location less central than that of Mt. Allison could not of course be thought of for a Maritime University.*'[43] In the course of the next two years, others echoed the call. S.D. Scott, one of the alumni who had been attracted in 1881 by the idea of university consolidation and now editor of the *Evening Mail*, spoke at the 1885 alumni dinner of the possibility that Mount Allison would 'grow mighty till we fill the Maritime Provinces, and King's and Acadia and Dalhousie and our Provincial University come and lodge in our branches.'[44] At the end of the following year, the Moncton *Times* declared that Mount Allison now had the strength to stand alone as a university as long as it chose to do so. In the case of a Maritime university federation, the newspaper saw a glowing future:

> The central position of Mount Allison, its spacious grounds, its beautiful climate and surroundings, the proximity of the preparatory Academy and the Ladies College, its inspiring history, and its facilities for expansion, make it an essential element in the settlement of the question, and point to Sackville as an eligible and not improbable site of our future Oxford or Cambridge.[45]

It was easy enough, of course, to have colourful dreams. It was enjoyable too, for such advocates of Mount Allison as Inch and Lathern to take the arguments for a central university and turn them upside down: in all of the grand visions of Mount Allison during these years there was a certain element of puckish delight in the notion of Sackville as the site of a great federated university. Underneath, however, and clearly shown in the university act of 1886, was a serious determination to ensure that Mount Allison should never again be open to the accusation that it was too small to be a college in anything but name. On the contrary, it would be a university both in name and in deed.

One field in which Mount Allison had already attained further distinction during the 1880s was that of women's education. Although Harriet Starr Stewart's progress as a student of the University of Halifax had been halted by the demise of the institution, she completed her course in 1882 through

Mount Allison's own examinations, and graduated with the degree of Bachelor of Arts. Mount Allison, and not the University of Halifax, thus became the first institution in Canada to confer this degree upon a woman. 'Whatever Canadian colleges may outstrip ours in producing famous graduates,' declared the *Argosy*, 'none shall win from Mt. Allison the honor of having trained the first lady B.A., and none shall win from Miss Stewart the honor of being that B.A.'[46] Harriet Stewart's graduation, unlike that of Grace Annie Lockhart seven years before, was not the first of its kind in the British Empire, for women had attained BA degrees in the interim in both Great Britain and New Zealand. Stewart, however, was the first woman at Mount Allison and in Canada to undertake and complete the arts programme. She also went on in 1885 to take the degree of Master of Arts, thus giving even fuller effect to the original intent of the college board in 1872 – according to the resolution seconded by her father – that all of the college's degrees should be taken by women on equal terms with men.[47]

Nevertheless, there was as yet no steady flow of women students in the degree courses at Mount Allison. The next woman graduate was Bessie Narraway in 1885, followed in 1888 by Annie Burwash and Sarah H.L. Shenton. Not until the 1890s did the numbers increase substantially, and in 1884 J.R. Inch publicly expressed regret 'that more young ladies had not availed themselves of the opportunities offered.'[48] The ladies' academy was still the main centre of women's education at Mount Allison. In 1886, with the college having adopted the title of university, it too changed its designation, and was known thenceforth as the ladies' college. The new title, adopted by the board of governors at its meeting on 3 June, implied that the ladies' college would be 'an affiliated Branch of the University' as envisaged by the university act; but the change in itself made little practical difference to the institution's development. What the new title did signify was the greater importance attached at this time to the ladies' college than to the male academy. Throughout most of the 1880s the academy continued to lose money, despite the proposal of a variety of possible solutions ranging from putting the institution under the direct management of the college to negotiating with the New Brunswick government for its inclusion in the public school system as a 'District School.'[49] In 1884, after a substantial annual deficit had once again been announced for the academy, it was put under the direct management of a committee of the board, chaired by Humphrey Pickard – it must have been a task undertaken with mixed feelings by the man who had become the academy's first principal forty years before – while the day-to-day running of the school was carried out by a 'head master,' T.T. Davis.[50] Some progress was apparently made, and in 1887 Davis was elevated to the title of principal, a position in which he served for three years. By 1891, however, the academy debt had risen to some $10,000, and the board of governors resolved that the university and the ladies' college should each take over one-third of this sum. The academy was able, by virtue of this assistance, to survive; but it had not been a good decade for the senior of the three institutions.[51]

The ladies' college, on the other hand, was flourishing. Under the principalship of David Kennedy, it had had annual enrolments of over one hundred from 1881 onwards, and had eqully consistently shown a substantial annual profit. When Kennedy departed in the summer of 1885 to become principal of Stanstead College in Quebec, his resignation was marked by expressions of regret and appreciation not only from the governors of Mount Allison but also from over two hundred citizens of Sackville who described him in a special address as 'one of ourselves, rather than one who, a short time ago, came among us a stranger. ...'[52] The ladies' college, with its large contingent of local students, was especially close to the Sackville community and Kennedy's seven-year regime had clearly reinforced this relationship. Even greater growth was to take place under Kennedy's successor. As principal, he was succeeded by another minister, Byron C. Borden. A native of Avonport, Nova Scotia, Borden had taught in Nova Scotia public schools before attending Mount Allison and graduating in 1878 prior to entering the ministry. For seven years, he had been active in pastoral work in Nova Scotia and Bermuda, and in 1880 he had married a Bermudian. He was thirty-four years old at the time of his appointment.[53]

The selection of Borden had been made by the governors from among seven nominees, all of them male. The notion of a woman principal had not yet been seriously considered, although Mary Electa Adams and Martha Allison had both exercised considerable influence despite being nominally subject to the higher authority of Humphrey Pickard and John Allison. During the principalships of Inch and Kennedy, the position of chief preceptress – the highest open to a woman – had been held by a series of younger teachers for periods of only a year or two, and none had attained the stature of either Adams or Allison. In 1885, however, the situation changed. Among the teachers at the ladies' academy during Inch's regime had been Mary Mellish, who had taught mathematics and natural science between 1869 and 1873, and had been chief preceptress during the last two of those years. In 1873 she had left to marry A.N. Archibald of Halifax; but following her husband's death she returned in 1885 to become once again chief preceptress.[54] Just a year older than Borden, Mary Mellish Archibald had both the experience and the determination to make a large and distinctive contribution to the development of the ladies' college. The partnership of Archibald and Borden, in fact, was to last through a successful period of some sixteen years, before it was ended by Archibald's early death in 1901.

They inherited the prosperity of the school; but they also inherited difficulties that were inseparable from that prosperity. The ladies' college, like the university, was affected by the increasing wealth of prominent Methodist families as the Maritime economy developed during the 1880s. At the ladies' college, the most obvious result was that more families could afford to educate their daughters, even to the extent of sending them to Mount Allison to be taught the finer details of ladylike manners and accomplishments. As the decade went on, student numbers rose appreciably. 'The attendance during the past year of 140 students,' declared the ladies' college catalogue for 1887–8, 'a number not equalled in the previous history of the Institution, – many of whom came exclusively for Music and the Fine Arts – is evidence of the unrivalled excellence of these departments.'[55] By 1890–1, the total student attendance had climbed to no less than 176, more than at the university and the male academy combined, competition from the Acadia Seminary and elsewhere notwithstanding. As a correspondent of the *Wesleyan* commented in 1889, 'it doesn't seem to make any difference what other seminaries or colleges arise, lady students continue to flock to Mt. Allison.'[56] It was all very satisfactory, and some of the problems of growth were easily solved. Improvements were made to the now-crowded ladies' college building, including the installation of a new water system powered by a windmill which pumped water from a spring on the adjoining property of the former college professor Thomas Pickard.[57] The administration of a burgeoning school was a growing task, and Borden's brother wrote to him in late 1886 to warn him not to overwork: 'you can have very little time to yourself and it will wear on you.' Wearing or not, though, Borden certainly agreed with Mary Mellish Archibald when she remarked to the alumnae society in 1888 on the need to keep the ladies' college 'constantly growing'; this was a time when expansion was not only facilitated by the state of the economy, but was also deliberately sought by those in charge of the institution.[58]

Yet there were problems associated with growth which were more deep-seated than the need to improve the student accommodations, or the strain of administration. The expansion of the 1880s was of such a nature that it challenged two of the long-standing characteristics of the ladies' college: that it was not exclusively for the rich; and that it was not primarily a 'finishing school.' The suspicion that the traditional clientele was being replaced by students from wealthier families was given public voice during the summer of 1884 by a correspondent of the *Wesleyan*, using the pseudonym 'A Lover of Mount Allison.' While praising Mount Allison's achievements, the letter complained that the dresses worn by the ladies' academy students at the recent closing exercises had been too elaborate. 'Apart from the love of display engendered,' it continued, 'we object on account of the heavy expense to parents. If allowed to continue it must end in excluding from the academy all but the daughters of the richest.'[59] The same concern was raised in a different context two years later by E.E. Rice of Bear River, Nova Scotia, in a letter to Borden. He was debating, he wrote, whether to send his daughter back for another year at Mount Allison, as he had heard that she would have a new room-mate, and feared that she might have a similar experience to that of his son at Acadia, who had been led astray by the bad company he had fallen in with there. 'I expected Sackville was stricter in carrying out dissiplin [*sic*] but have great fears in regard to it as there is to many rich folks children goes and they must have their way as at home or leave and the School cannot spare them.'[60]

Rice was apparently satisfied by Borden's reply, for his daughter was once again registered in the year 1886–7; but he had raised an important question. If the ladies' college were to be, or even to seem to be, an institution that was inaccessible to the ordinary Methodist people of the region – those who had subscribed in large numbers for the building of Centennial Hall – or one where their children would be alienated from them, great damage would be done to the standing of Mount Allison in its constituency. Yet as Rice implied, there could be no question of discouraging wealthy families from enrolling their daughters. Each year, as it had done for many years past, the catalogue carried the admonition that 'it is especially desired that the dress of students shall be simple and inexpensive.'[61] During 1886–7, Borden also made an effort to enforce a strict adherence to disciplinary rules. In early 1887 he informed one aggrieved university student, denied the privilege of 'private reception' with a ladies' college student, that 'students have been detained from the institutions' on account of suspicions that males and females were allowed to associate too freely.[62] Although the difficulty of keeping a decorous distance between men and women students was not a new one, that Borden should have to make a conscious effort to deny by word and deed that the ladies' college was a playground for children of rich families was evidence of the changes in clientele which were arising from the expansion of the 1880s. One parent who was not troubled was James Taylor, Methodist minister in Kingston, Nova Scotia, who wrote cheerfully to Borden that he was not sure tht he could pay his daughter's fees. 'If I conclude to send her,' he continued, 'you must not push me for payment – should know the Institution is so very prosperous – and prospects of unending popularity so cheering.'[63] It was true that prosperity might enable fees to be kept down and payments to be deferred; but the concerns expressed by Rice were evidence that prosperity also had its dangers.

There was also the question of whether the ladies' college was becoming a finishing school: Thomas Hart for example, minister in Berwick, Nova Scotia, wrote to Borden in early 1887 to express concern that the daughter of a family on his circuit had 'in some way formed the opinion that some of the Lady Students care more for a little finish than for a good Education.'[64] Such a perception certainly went against the stated intentions of the institution, as shown both in the diversity of the courses offered and in the statement carried each year in the catalogue that 'the ornamental Branches ... [are] regarded only as the accessories and embellishments of learning – not its substitute. ...'[65] The ideal of a rigorous academic education for women was also strongly advocated in an essay read to a combined meeting of alumni and alumnae in May 1887, by Jessie Troop Woodbury, who had attended the ladies' academy during the 1870s. Looking forward to the time when women would be freed from 'the inexorable thumb screw of society,' which had kept them untrained in science, literature, and political matters, she praised the role taken by Mount Allison:

> All praise to our *Alma Mater* which was in the very van-guard of our Institutions of learning to open the doors for woman to a Collegiate Education, and a more practical preparation for life than she had previously enjoyed. Certainly every member of the Alumnae Association experienced a thrill of pleasure when for the first time we read LADIES' COLLEGE on our catalogues. And it simply needs the idea as embodied in the *name* carried to full fruition to realize for our sex results which will make us the peers of our protectors in the various avenues of intellectual pursuit.[66]

Intellectual pursuits, or the accomplishments of the drawing-room? The challenge faced by the ladies' college in the late 1880s was to find a way of accommodating the demand for the teaching of subjects which would enhance social skills, while still remaining true to its original character as a school of high intellectual standards. It was a perplexing dilemma, and yet the answer was surprisingly simple. As the 1887–8 catalogue recognized, much of the institution's growth was owed to the demand for music and the fine arts; this did not imply, however, that these must necessarily be taught as purely ornamental subjects. On the contrary, if high intellectual standards in the literary departments – the primary, matriculation, and MLA courses – could be matched by the highest of artistic standards in the other departments, then the entire institution would be strengthened, and would have the opportunity to find new fields of distinction. Already in the summer of 1887, new developments were under way in the art department. The Moncton *Times* reported at length upon the unprecedentedly high quality and 'endless variety' of students' paintings and drawings in the exhibition mounted during the closing exercises of that year. 'The Mt. Allison Art School,' it maintained, 'now stands unrivalled in this part of the world.'[67] Shortly afterwards, it was announced in the *Wesleyan* that Elizabeth Wilmot, widow of L.A. Wilmot, had offered an annual prize of $25 for the best oil painting completed at Mount Allison, on condition that the ladies' college should acquire the winning entry; 'in this way a beginning has been made in the formation of an art gallery.'[68] Then, in the fall of 1887, a new four-year diploma course was introduced which provided for the first time a coherent and graduated programme of art study. The first year would be devoted to pencil drawing, and the second to charcoal and crayon drawing or water colours. The third and fourth years would be occupied primarily with oil painting, first by copying or from still life, and then painting from life; in the final year, instruction was given in design and composition, and there was provision also for 'China Modelling and Decorative Work.'[69] There was still much to be done in this field, and there had been no professor of art since the departure of John Warren Gray in 1873. None the less, the late 1880s saw developments which comprised a prelude to the much more radical changes of the following decade.

In the field of music, the second half of the 1880s marked a crucial period at Mount Allison. Music had attained a more prominent place than fine arts in the previous years: there had been a continuous succession of professors of music since 1855, and a diploma course in piano had been instituted as early as 1875. For many years also, the ladies' academy had advertised 'an admirable suite of rooms adapted to the Conservatory system.'[70] Yet, as one historian has observed, 'the teaching of Music on a higher plane began [at Mount Allison] in 1885.'[71] In part, this was due to the expanding student numbers; but it was also the result of the arrival of a new professor from the United States, Albert A. Mack. Previous professors of music had tended to stay for short periods, four years being the longest time served by any. Mack's eight-year term, on the other hand, was long enough to encompass substantial developments. Twenty-nine years old when he arrived at the ladies' college – at the same time as did Borden and Archibald – Mack was a native of New York but had spent fourteen years of his life in Germany. In 1880 he had graduated with distinction from the Stuttgart Conservatory, and had spent the intervening period teaching music in Garden City, New York.[72] On his arrival at Mount Allison, Mack certainly received encouragement to expand the range of musical instruction offered. In June 1887, the Moncton *Times* credited Borden with 'the expressed ambition ... to make this department the *Conservatoire* of the Maritime provinces. ...' In the ensuing fall, a further step was taken towards this goal with the beginning of a diploma course in violin; by that time, there were four teachers of music on the staff, including Mack.[73]

Yet a small suite of rooms in an overcrowded ladies' college building did not provide ideal surroundings for an aspiring conservatory, and the solving of this difficulty provided an excellent example of the effectiveness of B.C. Borden and Mary Mellish Archibald as managers of the ladies' college. It was Archibald, on 27 May 1888, who brought before the Alumnae Society 'a matter ... which had presented itself to her during the year': that the growth of the ladies' college necessitated the building of a distinct musical conservatory, and that the society should take the initiative in raising funds from its members and from the public. On her motion, the society resolved that the board of governors should be approached for its support. Four days later, Borden addressed the board, evoking 'considerable conversation and expressions of gratitude ... at this enlightened interest of the Alumnae Society.' The board's endorsement given, the alumnae met again on 4 June to plan their campaign for funds, and the conservatory project was now seriously launched.[74] Writing to the *Wesleyan* in August, Archibald announced that the alumnae had undertaken to raise half of the anticipated cost of the new building; and by February 1890, the campaign had succeeded to the point where tenders were called. According to Borden's later recollection, the board had by that time begun to have second thoughts about the expense involved, but was too far committed to the scheme to withdraw.[75]

The official opening of the conservatory on 2 June 1891 was the major event of the ladies' college closing exercises of that year. Joined to the south wing of the main building, its turrets and spire added a more ornate appearance to a structure already much changed from its original form of the 1850s. The conservatory contained thirty-five teaching rooms, while the ground floor comprised 'an Assembly Room and Gymnasium' which could be opened up to be used as a single large room for recitals. The prospect of an expanded programme of recitals, both by faculty members and by students, was just one of the developments facilitated by the new building. The musical curriculum was extended through the formalization of courses in vocal culture and pipe organ; classes were provided for all students in musical history and elementary harmony; a musical library was begun; and an orchestra was organized among violin students, 'for the practice of ensemble playing, studying and performing selections, and accompanying the singing class in recitals and other public performances.' Overall, declared the ladies' college catalogue for 1890–1, the new conservatory would offer facilities unexcelled anywhere in Canada. The intention was, it continued, 'to make it unnecessary for persons wishing to obtain a thorough and complete musical education, or to prepare themselves to teach music, to go outside of the Maritime Provinces.'[76]

There were other developments at the ladies' college in the late 1880s. Changes in the career opportunities open to women were reflected in the introduction in the 1889–90 year of 'courses in shorthand and typing ... designed to meet the needs of those who wish to fit themselves for employment in business offices.'[77] Although tending to be overshadowed by the more extensive commercial training offered by the academy, this programme continued in the ladies' college until 1905. A less formal innovation, though one which inaugurated a long tradition, was the formation of the 'Alamo Guards,' a group of ladies' college students who performed a series of military drill manoeuvres at the closing exercises of 1889. Calisthenics had long been considered an essential aid to health for the female students, as was further illustrated by the setting aside of a gymnasium room in the new conservatory, and the public 'lawn drills' performed at closing time now became a popular attraction for large crowds of spectators each year.[78] Undoubtedly, however, the greatest significance of this period for the ladies' college had lain in the effort necessarily made to cope with the difficult choices that were inseparable from the concurrent growth in student numbers. The solution adopted by Borden and Archibald was to make use of the prosperous condition of the institution so as to accommodate the demand for tuition in such subjects as music and fine arts without adversely affecting the offerings in literary courses, and the conservatory was a prime example of the benefits of providing distinct facilities for musical study, with a view to encouraging the highest artistic standards. As the catalogue of 1890–1 had indicated, the conservatory could also offer training for teachers of music; together with the course in shorthand and typing, this enabled the ladies' college to add a practical element to the education it offered to its students. By thus diversifying its curriculum, the ladies' college was able to face with confidence the competition that would inevitably arise as other institutions attempted to meet the increased demand for women's education in the region. Borden, in fact, commented some years later that 'the erection of this Conservatory of Music at the critical time when three new colleges for the education of young women were being opened in the Maritime Provinces, was the saving of this institution.'[79] Prosperity did not justify complacency: that Borden and Mary Mellish Archibald recognized this truth was the foundation of their success in the operation of the ladies' college.

Curriculum diversification during the 1880s was not confined to the ladies' college, but was characteristic also of the university. The basis of the BA curriculum during this decade was a revised version of the old Mount Allison curriculum which had been dropped between 1877 and 1881 in favour of that prescribed by the University of Halifax. Now once again, classical study was confined to the freshman and sophomore years, while science, philosophy, and modern languages predominated in the junior and senior years. Now once again, although the curriculum was arranged on a four-year basis, the catalogue advised that it was possible to complete the course within three years. None the less, the curriculum of 1881–2 was not altogether a restoration of its predecessor of the 1870s, but also incorporated certain new elements. Developments in the field of physics, for example, were recognized in the inclusion of molecular physics among the compulsory science subjects of the sophomore year, and the introduction of mathematical physics as an option in both terms of the senior year. Also introduced was a series of classes in English language and literature. English had first appeared in the curriculum in the previous year, under the regulations of the University of Halifax, but only as a single class in the first term of the sophomore year. Now, a class in English grammar, composition, and rhetoric was prescribed for both terms of the freshman year, while English literature was one of the compulsory subjects in the first term of the junior year. The literary works to be studied would vary from year to year, but would consist of a Shakespeare play and one of Macaulay's essays: in 1881–2, *King Lear* and the *Essay on Milton* were specified.[80]

As the decade went on, further changes were made in the basic BA curriculum in order to accommodate developments in particular disciplines, including recognition of the social sciences. In 1884–5, the existing courses in constitutional history and political economy were grouped together with logic, in the programme for the junior year, under the new rubric of 'logic and political science.' In the following year, political science was separated from logic, and by 1888–9 the class in logic had spawned another social science: in that year, the teaching of a class in logic as such was accompanied by another class in psychology.[81] The study of history was not yet included as a distinct subject, although interest was stimulated in 1888 when Josiah Wood offered a prize of $25 for the best essay on the history of Westmorland County written by an alumnus, alumna, or student. When Wood's offer was announced, it led to comments at the board of governors' meeting of May 1888 on 'the necessity of historical study,' and there was talk of instituting a new chair in history and political economy; but the formal teaching of history to undergraduates at

Mount Allison lay still some years in the future.[82] In general terms, the subjects offered by the BA curriculum of the 1880s were assessed fairly by the Moncton *Times* in late 1886: 'the authorities of Mount Allison while sufficiently conservative to retain in their curriculum the time-honoured mathematical and classical studies which for centuries have constituted the chief part of a college course, have not lost sight of the *new education*, so called.'[83]

Apart from the widening of the range of subjects taught at Mount Allison, the 1880s also saw important reorganizations of the university curriculum, again aimed at ensuring that it met the rapidly developing academic standards of the time. One anachronism that was finally abolished in 1884 was the practice of examining all students orally as part of the annual closing exercises. Dating from the earliest years of the college, this custom had been regularly attacked in the columns of the *Argosy* as a needless harassment of students who had already passed their courses by virtue of written examinations. In early 1884, an 'Old Student' declared that Mount Allison was almost certaintly the only institution in Canada to retain such examinations, and described their futility with evident feeling:

> The poor students, tired with the heavy work of the term, and the additional work in connection with the exams, has [*sic*] to pass through another fiery ordeal. They are required during the two or three days that follow to present themselves from time to time, to be gazed at by numerous visitors and a wondering and admiring (?) throng of Seminary ladies and Academy boys, and to submit to the oral examination by the members of the Faculty, and what is far worse, by kind-hearted and sympathetic friends of the Institutions, who seem to take especial delight in propounding dark and badly worded questions; and then, if opportunity presents itself, in snubbing the students when they have little chance of defending themselves.[84]

To parade the accomplishments of the undergraduates before such an audience had been considered twenty years before to be an appropriate way of publicizing the achievements of the college. In the growing Mount Allison of the 1880s, however, it was clearly more of an affront to the academic endeavours of the students than a means of displaying them, and in May 1884 the college board responded to student requests by abolishing the practice without a dissenting vote.[85]

More profound in its implications than the abolition of oral examinations was the institution of honours degrees in 1883. In introducing this form of specialization, Mount Allison was following many other Canadian institutions, including several in the Maritimes: the University of New Brunswick, for example, had adopted honours programmes as early as 1862. More recently, the lead given by the University of Toronto had brought about increased specialization in the curricula of the Ontario universities, and in 1884 Victoria University added more elaborate honours courses to its existing honours programme.[86] At Mount Allison, honours courses in five fields were promised in the catalogue of 1883–4 and were fully specified in the following year: classics, mathematics, English, natural science, and philosophy and logic.[87] Each honours course prescribed advanced work to be undertaken primarily in the junior and senior years, although also including certain classes during the two earlier years. The honours work was not to be taken in addition to the regular BA curriculum, but rather as a substitute for certain portions: the catalogue noted that honours students 'may omit any Pass subject not in that Department [i.e. the honours subject] except Logic, Mental and Moral Philosophy, and Evidences of Christianity.' Accordingly, it was still possible to complete any BA programme within three years. Also retained was the option of taking the degree of PH B, which was no longer defined by a special curriculum but consisted simply of the regular BA pass course with the substitution of modern languages for Latin and Greek.[88] It was a natural development, however, when the BA and PH B were defined from 1889 onwards as outright four-year degrees, as was implied by the dropping from the catalogue of the note advising that the work of the four years could be compressed into three. At the same time, the concept of 'senior matriculation' was recognized: students could enter the sophomore year directly by means of passing both the regular matriculation examinations and examinations deemed equivalent to those required of freshmen students.[89] Thus, the four-year programmes did not necessarily mean that every student would spend four years at Mount Allison. But any shortening of the prescribed period would be achieved not through compression of work but by a demonstrated level of accomplishment prior to entry to the university. This change, along with the others introduced during the 1880s, represented a strengthened commitment to intellectual rigour in the courses offered by Mount Allison. The curriculum, declared the Mount Allison report to the general conference of 1890, had been revised 'so as to adapt it more perfectly to the changed demands of the times as recognized by the older universities in Europe and America.'[90]

The same concern was evident in changes in the concept of post-graduate study. In June 1882, David Allison expressed concern to the college board that the existing requirements for the MA degree did not provide any genuine test of candidates' ability, and recommended that changes be made. At a further meeting in the same month, the board resolved 'that Faculty be instructed to prepare courses for degrees higher than that of Bachelor.'[91] It was a year before the faculty decided upon a course of action, and a further year before the new arrangements were embodied in the catalogue.[92] When they did appear, however, the changes made were considerable. The MA degree was henceforth to be directly linked to the new honours courses, in being available to 'any Bachelor of Arts of three years standing, who shall have taken (during his Undergraduate Course or subsequently), the full Honours in any Department, and who shall have prepared ... a satisfactory thesis on some subject connected with his courses of study.' No longer, therefore, could all BA graduates qualify for their Master's degrees by waiting three years and fulfilling certain easy requirements; instead, the degree was to be tied to specialized study in a given field.[93]

Mount Allison's new emphasis upon post-graduate study was not confined to the Master's level, for at the same time a Doctor of Philosophy degree was also introduced. There was no doubt of the college's power to adopt such a programme, for it had been envisaged in the original legislation of 1858, and several honorary doctorates had already been conferred; but the institution of a PHD by course work and examination was a radical departure. Mount Allison was in fact among the first Canadian universities to enunciate such a programme: it had apparently been preceded only by the University of New Brunswick, which had adopted statutes for the degree in 1867 and had conferred its first two PHDs in course in 1870. Queen's University established its doctoral programmes in 1889, while the University of Toronto had approved the idea in principle in 1883, but did not implement it until 1897.[94] The Mount Allison PHD involved no thesis, and apparently owed little to contemporary developments in research scholarship in Germany and the United States. It was a philosophy course in more than name, for the curriculum comprised the study of twenty-three prescribed works in history and philosophy, although the history side predominated. The fourteen historical works included several on Greek and Roman topics, including Gibbon's *Decline and Fall* and works on classical literature and law. There were also works on medieval Europe, including Hallam's *History of the Middle Ages*. The more modern period was represented by Macaulay's *History of England*, T.H. Green's *History of the English People*, Guizot's *History of France*, and Carlyle's *History of the French Revolution*. The philosophical side of the curriculum was headed by G.H. Lewes's *History of Philosophy*, and also included firsthand reading of Plato's *Republic*, Kant's *Critique of Pure Reason*, Descartes's *Discourse on Method* and *Meditations*, Locke's *Essay on the Human Understanding*, and works by Sir William Hamilton, W.B. Carpenter, and George Berkeley.[95] It was an eclectic combination, and no indication was given in the catalogue of the nature of the examinations by which candidates would be assessed, except for the provision that all candidates should already hold the MA degree. Nor was the PHD programme ever put to the test, for there were no graduates, and there is no evidence of any student even beginning the course of study. It continued to be advertised in the catalogue until 1894–5, after which it was quietly omitted. The Mount Allison PHD programme was neither long-lived nor successful; but it was among the first to be attempted in Canada.

Mount Allison's concern for the post-graduate education of its students extended also to their prospects of further study at other universities. R.C. Weldon's successful period of study at Yale had been exceptional for Mount Allison graduates of the 1860s, but since that time it had become more common for the most able students to attend major universities in the United States or Great Britain. One avenue leading to study either at the University of London or at the University of Edinburgh was the prestigious Gilchrist scholarship. Arising from the bequest of John Borthwick Gilchrist, a Scottish doctor who had spent much of his career in India, the Gilchrist Trust provided scholarships of £100 a year for three years to students from various parts of the British Empire. In Canada, one scholarship was awarded annually from 1868 to 1884, and was the object of keen competition from candidates throughout the Dominion. The chief intention of the scholarships was to provide education for non-graduates, although some of the Canadian winners were already graduates, and Mount Allison's first recipient was W.L. Goodwin, a freshman when he won the scholarship in 1877. He went on to take the BSC degree at London in 1881, after study at Edinburgh and in Germany, and later received the DSC degree from Edinburgh.[96] Mount Allison's second and last Gilchrist scholar was W.M. Tweedie, a graduate of 1882. Tweedie's success was announced in September 1882 by Goodwin, who had by now returned to Mount Allison as professor of chemistry and experimental physics, and caused wild rejoicing. The *Argosy* described Tweedie as 'our latest hero' and reported on the dinner held by the university in his honour on the eve of his departure for London.[97] The students' immediate reaction had been more robust; as A.D. Smith informed Tweedie by letter, it had caused some anxious moments to Charles Stewart, who as chaplain was responsible for discipline:

> The boys went nearly wild yesterday on receipt of the news. Last night they rang Lingley Hall bell at midnight for about half an hour. Poor Dr. Stewart was racing about the College after them until about three o'clock this morning. Twenty or thirty of the villagers put in an appearance and wanted to rush into the College and bulldoze the offenders, but Dr. Stewart, like Horatius of old, 'kept the bridge.'[98]

Tweedie's success in open national competition was clearly an achievement worthy of celebration, and he went on to gain the MA degree from the University of London after study in England, France, and Germany. Yet he was by no means the only member of his class to study overseas, for both J.C. Webster and Gaius Smith – the first recipient of Mount Allison's PHB degree – went to Edinburgh and enjoyed successful careers there as medical students.[99] An increasing proportion of Mount Allison graduates, in fact, were entering the field of medicine: although most graduates of the period 1881 to 1890 chose either the ministry or the law, a substantial minority of 11.7 per cent went into medicine.[100] Increasingly, though, as the 1880s went on, the United States became more attractive than Great Britain for those who contemplated post-graduate work, in whatever field. The Gilchrist scholarships were suspended in Canada in 1885 and 1886, and then finally withdrawn after 1887, ostensibly because the progress of Canadian higher education had made them unnecessary, but also because of the number of graduates who were competing for what had been intended as an undergraduate scholarship.[101] By contrast, the availability of post-graduate fellowships in the United States combined with the rising prestige of American graduate schools to attract students from Mount Allison as from other Canadian universities. By 1890 an informal arrangement had been reached with Harvard: F.W. Nicolson, himself a Mount Allison graduate and now an instructor in Latin at Harvard, was quoted by the *Argosy* as announcing 'that all graduates of Mount Allison, University of New Brunswick, Dalhousie and Acadia who have completed a four years' course will be admitted without examination into the junior year of that University. Honors and post-graduate work if satisfactory, will be sufficient for admittance into [the] senior year.' Mount Allison graduates were not yet accepted on equal terms with those of American universities, but such an understanding nevertheless provided opportunities for advanced study at a large university.[102]

With the increased emphasis at Mount Allison in the 1880s upon high academic standards and the prospect of further study beyond the Bachelor's degree, there were certain obvious requirements which had to be met. Improvement of the library and scientific laboratories was one such need, and the later years of the decade saw effective efforts towards its fulfilment. An important role was played by Ralph Brecken, a Methodist minister and a Mount Allison graduate of 1871, who made a donation of $7000 to the university in 1889. Of this sum, $1000 was to be expended on the library and $1000 on scientific apparatus, and $5000 was to be invested to provide income for student scholarships.[103] Especially as Brecken had already donated 600 volumes from his personal library, the $1000 gift made possible many important additions to the library. The college catalogue of 1889–90 reported that works had been purchased 'in History, Philosophy, Science, Poetry, etc., ... and books on local history, a department to which in the future special attention will be devoted, are being collected as opportunity offers.' Historical works, in fact, evidently predominated among the volumes selected for purchase from the Brecken fund, for two years later the catalogue noted that of the 728 volumes acquired no fewer than 277 had been in this field; 126 came into the category of literature, 24 were dictionaries or works of reference, 50 were in philosophy, 77 in science, and 174 in theology.[104] There were also other substantial additions to the library at this time, including 116 volumes of Latin and Greek classics presented in 1889 by the Macmillan publishing company of London, an annual donation 'of considerable value' from Alexander Gibson, and a number of smaller gifts each year from alumni and others. By 1890, the university was claiming in its report to general conference that it had one of the best college libraries in the Maritimes.[105] The *Argosy*, appraising the library in an editorial of late 1889, was not quite so firm in its praise. It was, the editorial suggested, 'a good library for ordinary purposes containing all the standard English authors and a good representation of modern historical, philosophical, and scientific works'; the next step should be the acquisition of more specialized works in connection with the honours departments. 'Although not a great library,' the *Argosy* believed, 'it is one for which present students have reason to be thankful and on which the *alumni* of the University may look with some degree of pride.'[106]

The purchase of scientific equipment was also an important purpose of the Brecken fund, although its implementation was apparently delayed until the arrival of W.W. Andrews as the new professor of chemistry and experimental physics in 1890. In November 1890, the *Argosy* reported that Andrews had ordered a number of gas generators, 'Hoffman's apparatus for the decomposition of water,' and a Crookes radiometer, as well as chemical and geological specimens, and 'a set of Microscopes for use in the classes.' Old equipment was being repaired and restored to working order, and the *Argosy* commented that 'we hope to have in a year or two well appointed chemical and physical laboratories.'[107] The balance of Brecken's gift, devoted to scholarships, enabled Mount Allison for the first time to offer financial assistance to students enrolled in the regular programmes: small bursaries had already been available to theological students, but the Brecken awards were open to all who maintained good academic standing and good general conduct, and who had need of aid. The maximum annual award to any student was $50, which could be continued throughout the recipient's student career. Thus, since the annual income amounted to some $600, the university could now offer assistance to at least twelve students each year.[108] Brecken's donation was applied, therefore, to a number of areas which particularly needed attention if Mount Allison was to sustain its growth and make good its claim to be an institution of high academic quality; it was, as the university reported to the general conference in 1890, a 'timely gift.'[109]

Also essential to Mount Allison's development in the 1880s was the recruitment of capable and well-qualified professors, preferably including several who were young enough to have had their training in the context of the profound intellectual developments which had taken place in so many disciplines in recent years. A measure of the success of Mount Allison in this respect was the fact that three of its new faculty members during the decade had been Gilchrist scholars. The first of these was Mount Allison's own first Gilchrist scholar, W.L. Goodwin, who returned from Britain to join the faculty in the fall of 1882, after John Burwash had resigned to return once again to pastoral work. Goodwin was invited to deliver the customary opening address of the college year on 28 August 1882, and he devoted much of his time, characteristically, to the practical value of scientific education. In particular, he called for more education for farmers, and cited German and Scottish examples of fruitful co-operation between universities and agriculture. 'What a splendid result,' he believed, 'might we expect from such well-directed labor expended on our rich soils.'[110] Goodwin's views were evidently in harmony with the thinking which had produced the unsuccessful attempt in 1879 to make agricultural study one of the major programmes offered by Mount Allison; in November 1882 he commenced a series of fourteen lectures on scientific agriculture by lecturing on 'Scientific Chemistry' to an audience of 'about a hundred farmers and others.' According to the *Chignecto Post*, the audience was 'very much gratified'; the *Post* itself had generous praise for Goodwin's efforts, and printed the text of each of the fourteen lectures which he gave during the months up until April 1883.[111] The *Argosy* was enthusiastic also. 'We are essentially an agricultural people,' it declared: 'manufactories have not as yet a very strong hold upon the masses, though at present manufacturing industries are springing up all over the Dominion.' The Maritimes, it continued, offered few educational opportunities to farmers, and most could not afford to travel to the Ontario agricultural college; thus, Mount Allison was to be congratulated on its leadership 'in the movement towards instituting regular courses of study in this branch.'[112]

This successful revival of the agricultural course did not, however, survive the sudden departure of Goodwin for Queen's University in 1883. There he would have a distinguished career as professor of chemistry and geology, and in accordance with his lifelong interest in the practical applications of science he later became director of the school of mining at Queen's and dean of applied science.[113] In 1886, addressing the Nova Scotia Conference, J.R. Inch referred once again to the need for agricultural education when he affirmed that 'there ought to be an Agricultural College connected with Mt. Allison.'[114] In reality, this prospect had suffered a mortal blow with the loss of Goodwin. Together with the departure of Weldon for Dalhousie in the same year, thus removing at once the only two Mount Allison professors who had had formal post-graduate training, there could have been no clearer indication of the difficulty faced by Mount Allison in maintaining an adequate faculty, and thus of the need for the tightening of academic standards which was about to be undertaken. Goodwin was replaced at short notice by a young recent graduate of Victoria, G.J. Laird, who stayed for two years before John Burwash returned for a third term as science professor. Laird shortly afterwards obtained an appointment at Wesley College, Winnipeg, and commenced a long career in that institution and the University of Manitoba.[115]

Weldon's replacement stayed longer. The new professor of mathematics, Sydney W. Hunton, was a BA graduate of the University of London, having gone there as a Gilchrist scholar after his early studies at McGill; his teaching career at Mount Allison would span no fewer than fifty-one years.[116] Hunton, in fact, had met both Weldon and Goodwin while studying in London, and – as Goodwin later recalled to G.J. Trueman, president of Mount Allison from 1923 to 1945 – they had successfully thrown their support behind his candidacy, despite narrowly avoiding a disastrous blunder. When the question was raised at a meeting as to whether Hunton was a regular churchgoer, Weldon had been about to reply that he was not when Goodwin sharply kicked him under the table. 'That kick,' reflected Trueman in 1940, 'meant a great deal to our department of Mathematics, and Dr. Hunton has been an officer in the church here and a regular attendant for nearly sixty years.'[117] When Hunton arrived in Sackville, he and Laird apparently had an immediate impact upon Sackville society as eligible bachelors: they were, as one ladies' academy teacher noticed, 'the sensation of the evening' at a social meeting of the WCTU in August 1883. Hunton did not remain a bachelor for long, for in December 1884 he married Annie Inch, daughter of the president.[118] Hunton's first major professorial task at Mount Allison was to begin the teaching of the new honours programme in mathematics. Including advanced courses in various areas of geometry, algebra, and trigonometry, it also introduced specific courses at the senior level in differential and integral calculus: clearly important areas of study both in themselves and in view of concurrent developments in the field of physics.[119] Also an enthusiastic supporter of university athletic teams, Hunton was best remembered by his students as a benevolent but exacting teacher. 'Unlike Dr. Smith,' recalled one, 'he spent no time in the class telling stories, and very rarely did he seem to notice any lack of attention, but when he did a blistering sentence was enough to correct it.'[120] Hunton was reported to have received frequent offers of positions in larger universities, and to have turned them down. His length of service to Mount Allison remains the longest by any full-time professor.

In 1887, Hunton was joined on the faculty by yet another former Gilchrist scholar, W. Morley Tweedie. Tweedie's active career as a Mount Allison professor would be just one year shorter than that of Hunton, although even after his retirement in 1937 he would return several times for temporary teaching or administrative duties. Since his departure for Great Britain in 1882, Tweedie had pursued his studies in English language and literature in London, at Heidelberg, and at other European centres before obtaining his MA degree from the University of London in 1887. During these years he had maintained contact with Mount Allison and had contributed articles on his travels to the *Argosy* under the pseudonym 'Tamawa.'[121] Inch was clearly anxious to recruit him for the faculty, writing in July 1887 to offer him a temporary appointment in modern languages with a view to creating a permanent chair in English language and literature in the following year. Thus, Tweedie's initial appointment was in English and German, while English language teaching was also shared by B.C. Borden, professor of rhetoric in the university as well as principal of the ladies' college. From the fall of 1888, Borden became professor of political science, while Tweedie took full charge of English language and literature.[122]

No doubt recalling the early departure of Goodwin, Inch had impressed upon Tweedie that if he was not prepared to stay at Mount Allison on a permanent basis he should not come at all. 'It must be plain,' he had warned, 'that your leaving us at the expiration of one year's service would seriously weaken us with the public.'[123] By the beginning of the 1888–9 year, Tweedie was not only still at Mount Allison, but gave in early September an inaugural address as professor of English which attained wide publicity in the press and comprised the most thorough review of modern scholarly developments which had yet been delivered at Mount Allison. Directing his remarks particularly at the students, Tweedie began by identifying a 'utilitarian wave' in contemporary attitudes to education. 'To this spirit is due,' he continued, 'the most striking feature of modern education, viz: the utter breach with the hereditary ideas respecting college or university work, and the tentative and often somewhat blind groping after something to fill the vacancy. Hence we have college courses made up largely of elective studies, so that students may look to the future and choose subjects which bid fair to help them in their profession or business; we have the founding of technical schools, and the increasing attention to the natural sciences and modern languages.' In some respects, Tweedie believed, these trends had gone too far, and he went out of his way to dissociate himself from any move to abolish classical study, although admitting that the present popularity of English was due in part to a reaction against the classics. Where Tweedie would admit no compromise, however, was in the nature and purpose of the study of literature. He attacked the notion that literary study consisted of compiling lists of great writers, with perfunctory assessments of each. Instead, literature must be understood as part of the larger study of man in society, and must be studied in the light of other disciplines, notably history. Furthermore, he argued, students must read critically and for themselves:

> Whether our study of literature is meagre or extensive let us be honest and not try to cheat ourselves into believing that to read about a book is the same as reading the book itself. We live now in an age of reviewing and criticism, and talk about books, so that it is especially needful for us to be on our guard. Let us make sure that we are looking with our own eyes.

Tweedie's last major point concerned the study of language. Like other disciplines – he mentioned medicine, the natural sciences, psychology, and political economy – the study of language had been revolutionized by modern scientific techniques. The English language must be studied not according to fixed preconceptions, but as it had evolved from the earliest Anglo-Saxon dialects to the present state of the language. 'Usage,' he suggested, 'is the one great law in language. ...' Studied with all the insights offered by nineteenth-century scholarship, Tweedie believed that English language and literature could contribute to what he saw as the two great functions of a university: to give training to students, and to promote an appreciation of culture in all its complexity. He closed by appealing to the students for their encouragement in attempting to ensure that it did so at Mount Allison.[124]

The honours curriculum in English which Tweedie introduced in 1888 showed clearly the impress of the principles he had enunciated in his address. Replacing a much shorter and less exacting honours programme, it included language study – focusing particularly on Anglo-Saxon and Middle English – in each of the final three years. Also in each of these three years, honours students would study the history of English literature in a specific period, accompanied by the study of the history of England during that period and by reading of selected authors. During the sophomore year, the focus was upon the Elizabethan period, with study of works by Spenser, Marlowe, Greene, and Bacon, as well as Shakespeare. In the following year the period was from 1714 to 1760, with detailed attention to such authors as Pope, Swift, Johnson, and Gray. The senior year was devoted to the Romantics, primarily to the poets – Burns, Wordsworth, Coleridge, Keats, Shelley, and Byron – but also including works by Burke and Scott.[125] In his early years at Mount Allison, Tweedie was a demanding teacher and students recalled that his criticism was often caustic. Nor was he averse to levelling criticism outside of the university, as on the occasion in 1894 when he presented a paper to a teachers' convention in Moncton in which he deplored the low standards of spoken and written English shown by matriculants at Mount Allison.[126] Tweedie's demands upon others, however, were always matched by his demands upon himself, as was evident in his continuing study of his subject: the summer of 1890, for example, he spent at the University of Berlin studying Old English and Gothic.[127] In 1912 Winthrop Bell, a former student and engaged at the time in post-graduate study in Germany, summed up Tweedie's achievement in the teaching of English at Mount Allison: '[to] give well-systematized, thorough and scholarly courses, as good, if not as numerous, as those open to the students of the larger Universities. ...'[128]

In 1890 came the final departure of John Burwash as science professor and his replacement by W.W. Andrews. Burwash was now returning to Victoria University to take up a position in its theological faculty, and the *Argosy* recalled both his personal popularity among the students of Mount Allison and the interest aroused by his classes: 'after his lucid explanations, the mysteries of molecules, monads, morphology, muscles, minerals and mastodons rapidly vanished away.'[129] His successor was also a native of Ontario, a graduate of Victoria, and a Methodist minister. Thirty years of age at the time of his appointment, Andrews had gone to school with Hunton in Ottawa during the 1870s. He had then spent five years in missionary work in Manitoba before attending Victoria and graduating in 1887. In the same year he married Nellie C. Greenwood, who in 1884 had become the first woman to graduate from Victoria's degree programmes: for her, there must have been a certain immediate affinity with Mount Allison. Most recently, Andrews had been minister of a large Toronto church.[130] When he arrived in Sackville, he quickly established a high reputation, and the *Argosy* looked forward in October 1890 to 'a strong union between teacher and students' in science classes.[131] Andrews, in fact, ascribed a more active role to the student in the classroom than had been customary in previous science teaching at Mount Allison. The conducting of experiments by students had been introduced to a limited extent during the 1880s; but for Andrews this was central to his teaching method, as he explained to a teachers' convention in Amherst in 1894:

Professor Andrews spoke on 'Research Work.' He compared at length two methods of studying science. In one the student read books, and took notes on lectures, watching an experiment at times. The result was that he acquired a general scientific knowledge, and some facility in note-taking. The student proceeding by the second method engaged in practical scientific work. They became truth-seekers and truth-finders. ... The pupil also learned by the latter method not to place dependence on the book alone. He might even down the book if necessary. Little flowers and crystals became his teachers however. This begets a humble spirit.[132]

For Andrews, the humility evoked by discovery of the intricacies of natural phenomena was the essential link between his roles as scientist and minister. He could see no conflict between science and religion, for he had been profoundly influenced by idealistic concepts of the ordered and purposeful development of the universe which had been current at Victoria University during his studies there, and in the writings of such prominent Canadian philosophers as John Watson of Queen's. Scientific knowledge, he believed, was the key to an understanding of the full power and beauty of the divine order, all the more so because science illuminated the evolutionary dynamic through which God worked. The scientific method was not an anarchic force, tearing at the fabric of revealed truth; on the contrary, it was the means by which the scientist was able, as Andrews wrote in the *Argosy* in 1894, 'to perceive facts in their true relations, and to reveal the hidden order of the world.' He went on to stress, like Tweedie but from a different perspective, the affinity between science and literature.

If scientific discovery is to trace the lines of those laws upon whose sublime curves are strung innumerable hosts of phenomena. If the mission of science be not only to provide the loaves and fishes for the multitudes, but also to exhibit the splendors of that intelligence and will which is revealed in the movements of every atom, if it is to show how the nearest and the infinitely remote, the infinitesmal and the immeasurably vast are related in subtlest bonds of brotherhood then 'the finer breath of scientific knowledge' must be poetry, and only the poetic soul is capable of waking to the manifoldness of relation and the suggestiveness of the isolated acts.[133]

During his career of more than twenty years at Mount Allison, Andrews' beliefs and abilities would lead him in a number of directions. He was an inventor and an agriculturalist. He was a social reformer, for in common with many other Methodists of his time he believed that society, as well as the natural universe, was evolving according to the divine will. At the university, he was a tireless advocate of growth and new directions, particularly in various aspects of applied science. By his students, however, he was remembered chiefly for his two essential preoccupations: science and Christianity. 'It fell to Dr. Andews,' recalled J.W. O'Brien, a student who later became a minister, 'as a college lecturer and an ordained minister of the gospel, to orientate the teachings of Christianity with the new light science had focussed on some traditional beliefs. That he did this with a minimum of friction was due not merely to his scholarship but to the beauty, simplicity and shining sincerity of spirit which he instinctively revealed.' H.E. Bigelow, on the other hand, a student of Andrews who later succeeded him as science professor, remembered best 'his native curiosity, the most important characteristic of a scientist. ... He had, indeed, the essence of true science.'[134]

By the year 1890–1, the arts faculty at Mount Allison had grown to eight members, as opposed to the five of ten years before. Two of the new appointments were in effect only part-time: Borden was principal of the ladies' college; while the appointment of Ralph Brecken in 1890, the same who had given the substantial donation in the previous year, was primarily as professor of homiletics in the faculty of theology, although he also taught the history of philosophy in the arts faculty. Inch and Stewart continued to teach in the arts faculty, as well as discharging their other duties, so that the four full-time professors in the university were Smith – since 1886 the incumbent of the recently endowed Josiah Wood Chair in classics – Hunton, Tweedie, and Andrews. There was no doubt that the faculty had been strengthened by the appointments made during the decade, although increasing student numbers ensured that the university was by no means overstaffed. The number of full-time undergraduates had grown to 62 by 1890–1, as opposed to 25 ten years before; growth in the number of theological students, ladies' college students, and part-time special students also tended to raise the numbers attending university classes. A correspondent of the Halifax *Herald*, visiting Mount Allison in the spring of 1888, reported that he had heard no complaints, but that 'I thought I could hear the college professors, thinking that they could do better work for those in the regular course if they were not quite so much encumbered with general students.'[135] As the *Wesleyan* noted a few weeks later, Mount Allison prided itself on the close contact between professor and students in its classes, by which 'character is moulded by personal influence.' Lectures and examinations comprised one part of the method of instruction and testing, but were supplemented by 'the drill of the classroom.'[136] Now that numbers were rising – Tweedie's freshman class in 1889, for example, had 45 members[137] – there would obviously be difficulty in maintaining this approach as thoroughly as before. Yet given a young and enthusiastic faculty, this kind of difficulty was not daunting: rather, it was further evidence of the exhilarating growth of the time.

Also necessarily affected by the growth of the 1880s was the way of life of the students themselves. Distinction between students of the different years had existed from the start, but had had little practical significance when the college was small and the student body close-knit. Initiation ceremonies for freshmen, for example, were not usual. In his report on the year 1886–7, however, Inch commented upon a case of hazing which had involved 'some of the best students.' The matter had not been pursued further after the students had agreed that the episode would not be repeated.[138] In the following year of 1887–8, it became apparent not only that initiation was not so easily dispensed with, but also that it represented a conscious belief in a hierarchy among the students. College-educated men and women, argued the *Argosy* in an editorial of February 1888, were accorded a high place in society because of their intellectual attainments; but while students, they should have the due humility to defer to those above them:

> In their desire to put a stop to hazing we think the faculties of our institutions have often overstepped the mark, and discountenanced even the slightest trace of class-distinction. Now this is not as it should be. Never should a man from a lower class be favoured or allowed the privileges of those above him. To bring the Freshmen, and even the Sophomores, too much to the front, tends to annihilate what love the Juniors and Seniors may have for their *Alma Mater*.[139]

Implied in the *Argosy* editorial was the distinction between hazing – with its connotations of violent or humiliating treatment – and a decent respect for hierarchy. How far the one could be separated from the other would be a concern of both students and administrators for many decades after. More generally, the outbreaks of hazing illustrated the greater problems of discipline that existed in a growing institution. In early 1887, rumours circulated that students had been going to the Brunswick Hotel in Sackville to drink, although to judge from the hotelier's angry reaction when enquiries were made it was a difficult matter to prove.[140] The faculty had in fact had a recent opportunity to rid itself of at least some of the responsibility for such cases, when it had considered the possibility of 'self control by Students,' presumably on the basis of a request from the students themselves. On 15 January

1886, however, the faculty minutes recorded that the question of 'Home Rule for Students' – A.D. Smith, the secretary, had obviously been keeping up with current events in Ireland – had been deferred pending consultations with some of the older students, and it was apparently then allowed to drop.[141]

Despite changes induced by growing student numbers, some things remained unaltered. Complaints about heating in the old college building, for example – used entirely as a residence after the building of Centennial Hall – were frequent in the *Argosy* during the 1880s. 'The season of the year has come,' commented one editorial in November 1883, 'in which it is necessary for the college students to resume the use of the axe and the buck-saw.' At some future time, it hoped, college rooms would be heated by more modern methods, and in the meantime students should be relieved from the need to cut, split, and carry their own wood.[142] The students' frustration was none the less for the evidence around them of the many technological achievements of the Victorian age: from the fall of 1887 they could be summoned to class by an electric bell, while May 1890 saw the introduction of electric light at the ladies' college.[143] On a grander scale, the Chignecto ship railway, in the process of construction in 1890 from Tidnish to Fort Lawrence, gave evidence of the material progress of modern times; and yet the Mount Allison students had to continue to stoke their stoves. By this time, some changes had been made in that the students were no longer responsible by 1890 for cutting and splitting their wood but only for fetching it from a woodshed. Even so, the *Argosy* wearily remarked, 'it is needless to say the the Lodge should be heated by steam or hot water. Every body knows that.'[144]

The *Argosy* also mounted other campaigns during these years. A frequent target was the practice by which students delivered orations at the closing exercises each year, as a requirement for graduation. Especially after the abolition of oral examinations, this custom seemed anachronistic, and in April 1891 a long editorial, observing that it was saying nothing new, noted that other institutions had abandoned the imposition of such ordeals upon their students and asked why Mount Allison should lag behind. 'We are sometimes gently reminded,' it went on, 'that the older sons of our Alma Mater possessed greater oratorical powers than the men of to-day'; in that case, why should not these alumni be invited to give the orations, and leave the present senior students to enjoy their graduation?[145] However, there was praise as well as blame in the magazine's columns. One innovation which received a hearty welcome in January 1891 was the 'Topic Reception.' Rather than simply putting together a large number of students in a room, the ladies' college receptions now provided a list of discussion topics to each person attending ; as the allotted time came for each topic, couples would walk and discuss together. It was, in fact, an impeccably moral substitute for dancing, even involving 'topic cards' on which to reserve partners for particular discussions. 'This term' commented the *Argosy*, 'the usual possibility of a young gentleman monopolizing one young lady throughout the entire evening will be removed and an opportunity afforded of becoming acquainted with more of our lady friends without being considered as "bounced."'[146] So popular was the topic reception that it would remain as the major regular social event on campus until finally displaced by dancing thirty-six years later.

Another campaign waged by the *Argosy* during the 1880s was for improved playing fields, and it reflected an increased interest in team sports. In November 1882, an editorial commented that Mount Allison students were obliged 'to play cricket and foot-ball literally on the side of a hill,' and called upon the board of governors to provide better facilities. As a competitive sport at Mount Allison, cricket reached the height of its popularity in the mid-1880s, while rugby football enjoyed a rapid rise in the following decade. The first intercollegiate match played by Mount Allison, however, was in baseball: it took place in the nearby town of Memramcook on 27 September 1887, the opponents being the students of the Collège St-Joseph. The visiting Mount Allison team was apparently decisively defeated – the *Argosy* did not record the exact score, but reported that 'the St. Joseph team proved too much for our boys' – but the occasion ended with a convivial dinner and entertainment by the St-Joseph college band. Eleven days later, the return match in Sackville ended with a similar result and once again a successful dinner in honour of the visitors.[147] Mount Allison thus had its first experience of intercollegiate sport, even though it still awaited its first victory. It also had its university colours, as 'cardinal and old gold' had been selected at a students' meeting some months before.[148] Here, as at many other North American universities, competitive sport was on the point of gaining rapidly in importance. An article in the *Argosy* in early 1891 predicted that 'as our political and social institutions become progressively more democratic, popular games will dethrone field sports, which in older and more populous countries can be enjoyed merely by a few.' Despite allegations that intercollegiate rivalry tended 'to develop muscle at the expense of brain,' the article cited examples from ancient Greece to assure potential participants that they would be doing nothing that was 'inconsistent with the character of a student or philosopher.'[149]

A characteristic of many Methodist students and philosophers at this time – at Mount Allison as elsewhere – was an increasing preoccupation with the social implications of Christianity. The Methodist theological tradition, with its doctrine of Christian perfection, had always put heavy emphasis upon service to mankind and the achievement of personal sanctification thereby.

Now that evolutionary theory had given support to the possibility of progress towards a more perfect society, the optimistic Wesleyan doctrines could readily be applied to the sanctification of society. These currents of thought, later known as the social gospel, were not confined to Methodists; in Canada, as in the United States, the movement encompassed a number of Protestant denominations. Methodists, however, took a leading role.[150] The term 'social gospel' did not become current until about 1910, but its forerunners were apparent much earlier as responses to the various social issues of the late nineteenth century. The temperance movement was an example of a cause which had moved steadily from its original stress upon personal sobriety to a greater awareness of alcohol as a social evil. At Mount Allison, temperance had long been a point of contact between college and town, and so it continued: in March 1890 the *Argosy* thanked the WCTU for sponsoring social gatherings for the students, and offered support for 'the noble and glorious enterprise in which they are engaged. ...'[151] Nor did the political implications of the social gospel escape the students' attention. An article on socialism in April 1886, for example, had no sympathy with communism, anarchism, or fenianism, and was doubtful of socialism even in its milder forms. None the less, it argued, the fact was that socialism was here to stay, and was supported by 'some of our best men.' Since 'it is bad to have Capitalism as at present,' the article concluded that 'the good tendencies of Socialism' should be welcomed: 'little by little it will be won over to our way of christian living, and the whole world will see the value of that truly golden rule, "Do to others as you would they should do to you."'[152] Five years later, a theological student took up 'the labour question,' praising the trade union movement and citing the settlement of the London dock strike of 1889 as a model for what could be achieved for underpaid workers. 'When employers not only say "Our Father,"' he concluded, 'but also treat their employees as brethren; when men generally, aye and women too, not only pray, "Thy kingdom come," but also put their shoulder to the wheel and hasten it forward, then will strikes darken our social horizon no more.'[153]

The social strains brought about by industrialization comprised the essential context for the development of the social gospel. Mount Allison students did not, in fact, have to look as far afield as Great Britain for evidence of the social costs of heavy industry, as they must have reflected in late February 1891 as they held a collection for relief of the families of the many victims of the disastrous explosion at Springhill colliery in nearby Cumberland County, Nova Scotia.[154] Nevertheless, the social gospel was an optimistic doctrine, and the 1880s an optimistic decade for the students of Mount Allison. A long *Argosy* editorial in early 1882, prompted by the escape of Queen Victoria from an assassination attempt, had reflected on the benefits brought to all mankind by modern achievements in agriculture and in industry: 'the world is slowly, very slowly perhaps, approaching the millennium.' Even Sackville, reflected an editorial in the following year, was no longer 'an apparently slow-paced village,' but seemed to have 'caught a spirit of enterprise and progress. ...' And as for Mount Allison, remarked the magazine in the fall of 1890, it was 'moving forward to greater things. Within the past five years improvement after improvement has been made, but yet there is room for more.'[155]

The confidence expressed by the *Argosy* was widely shared by those associated with Mount Allison. In 1881, the institutions had faced a serious crisis which had threatened the very foundations on which they were based. Now, the foundations had been restored, and there was every reason to hope for continuing growth. 'As the sons and daughters of Mount Allison acquire wealth,' predicted the *Wesleyan*, 'they will be sure to enrich their Alma Mater and lead her on to a magnificent future.'[156] In early 1890 came an opportunity to reflect upon the distance that had been travelled since the beginnings of the college, with the death of Humphrey Pickard in Sackville on 28 February, at the age of seventy-seven. During the period of over twenty years since he had resigned as president, Pickard had retained an active association with Mount Allison, and was still a member of the board of governors at the time of his death. Paying him tribute at their meeting in May 1890, the board recalled the zeal and dedication with which he had headed the institutions. In later years he had offered the counsel of experience, and had assisted the board to find 'that golden mean between the past attainments and present anticipations which not only merits but ensures future success. ... While cautious he was in sympathy with that progressive spirit which has so marked the educational movements of the present day.'[157] It was a fair assessment, for Pickard had been known as principal and president to rejoice in the progress of the institutions. Yet his caution was real too, and had been hard-won through the many setbacks of a time when the kind of prosperity that was now apparent in 1890 had been inconceivable. Pickard may have had his doubts about the avid pursuit of expansion which had become characteristic of Mount Allison; it was a very different climate from that which had prevailed when the college had self-consciously rejected the notion of unrestrained growth. What was certain was that his funeral in Lingley Hall marked the severance of an important link with the past. Among the pallbearers were his two successors as president, David Allison and J.R. Inch, and students and faculty joined with Methodist and Baptist ministers and other mourners to make up a large congregation. The closing address, delivered by Charles Stewart, reviewed Pickard's 'busy and devoted life'; not since the death of Charles Allison in 1858 had the institutions mourned the passing of such a pre-eminent contributor to their development.[158]

The Mount Allison report of the general conference of 1890, held in Montreal, paid further tribute to Pickard and advanced the possibility of erecting a permanent memorial to him on the campus. The report went on to deal with plans to celebrate Mount Allison's approaching fiftieth anniversary, but then closed with a carefully phrased reference to a possible threat to Mount Allison's future prosperity. For several years, controversy had continued in Ontario over the question of whether Victoria University should enter into the federated University of Toronto. The general conference of 1886, following a long and heated debate, had resolved in favour of such a union, but opponents had been able to prompt the reopening of the question in 1890. In 1886, the notion of a Dominion-wide Methodist university had been seriously canvassed as an alternative: centred in Toronto, Montreal, or Ottawa, it would have comprehended the existing Methodist institutions, including Mount Allison, as affiliated colleges. The concept had been defeated, but was once again being discussed 1890. There was also the possibility that the inclusion of Victoria in the University of Toronto might bring about church pressure upon Mount Allison to enter into a similar federation in the Maritimes on terms not of its own choosing. Accordingly, the Mount Allison report expressed anxiety and alarm at the possible adverse effects upon Methodist education in the eastern provinces, and gave a veiled warning to the general conference:

> [The governors] respectfully but urgently ask that, whatever action may be decided upon by the General Conference in relation to other educational instititions, nothing may be done, or left undone, by which the independence of the Mount Allison University shall be compromised; or through which the bond of fraternal sympathy which has up to the present hour bound us in closest union to the Methodism of the Dominion, shall in the slightest degree be weakened.[159]

In the event, the warning was effective. The decision that Victoria should federate with the University of Toronto was reaffirmed, but with the proviso 'that the principle of Federation shall have no application to the Mount Allison University of the Maritime Provinces.' Inch, a delegate to the conference, must have taken satisfaction in this clause, even though he would have preferred to see Victoria remain as an independent institution, and unsuccessfully seconded a motion to that effect.[160] The episode was further evidence of the importance now attached to Mount Allison's own independent status.

With the successful negotiation of the general conference in September 1890, the ensuing academic year could be started with optimism. It saw yet more efforts to expand Mount Allison's activities. At the beginning of 1891, for example, a series of public lectures was started on the law. Beginning with an introduction to the principles of law by A.D. Smith, the seven lectures covered such topics as property law, contracts, torts, and legal tribunals. The lecturers were primarily judges and lawyers who were also former Mount Allison students. In his opening address on 31 January, Smith stressed that every citizen should have at least an elementary knowledge of the law. A few days later another of the lecturers, A.A. Stockton, wrote in the *Wesleyan* that the course was a continuation of the long-standing Mount Allison tradition which had begun with David Allison's courses in constitutional history, international law, and political economy.[161] Both of their statements were true; but the lecture course was also a prelude to the introduction of professional courses in law later in the 1890s.

The boldest proposal of 1891, however, was undoubtedly that of W.W. Andrews. In April and May, Andrews published a series of articles in the *Wesleyan* in which he called for the establishment of an engineering school at Mount Allison, together with related schools of manual training in the academy and domestic science in the ladies' college. He started from the assumption that 'a good engineering college' in the Maritime provinces was essential if the region were to prosper in the future, and suggested that Mount Allison's central location made it the ideal site. It was, he pointed out, close to the oil and natural gas fields of Albert County, New Brunswick, on one side; and as close on the other side to the ship railway, the new experimental farm at Nappan, Nova Scotia, and the coalfields elsewhere in Cumberland County. The project would be costly – he suggested that an endowment of over $150,000 would be needed – but less so than starting the engineering school elsewhere than at an established university; in any case the fine record of Mount Allison would be a reassurance for potential donors. He argued too that engineers would attain a broader outlook by studying at an arts college, and that their education should take place 'under the very noblest moral influences,' rather than at a purely secular institution. Successful adoption of the proposal would, Andrews believed, make Mount Allison 'the leading educational institution of the province for the next 50 years.'[162] This prospect, and the title which Andrews had given to his articles – 'Mount Allison's Possible Forward Movement' – quickly caught the imagination of many. On

1 June, Andrews addressed the alumnae, and obtained their strong support for 'a Scientific Cooking School in connection with the projected technological Institute.' Two days later he addressed the board of governors. The governors were less immediately forthcoming, but they did decide on the raising of a fund to mark the fiftieth anniversary in 1893, and appointed Andrews as one of those who were to go to the two Maritime conferences to seek support. Along with Inch and the new principal of the male academy, C.W. Harrison, he succeeded in obtaining the conferences' approval; the 'forward movement' was under way.[163]

The board of governors could afford to be in an expansive mood in the summer of 1891. The ladies' college was in its usual prosperous state; the debt of the university had been reduced to just under $5000, less than one-third of what it had been five years earlier; the academy's financing remained a problem, but the division of its debt between the institutions helped to avoid any insurmountable difficulty. One result of the favourable situation was the provision of a standard salary for long-serving professors: henceforth all professors were to be entitled to a salary of $1250 after seven years' service.[164] This did not necessarily represent an increase – Smith and Stewart were already making $1250, while Inch was receiving $1500[165] – but the introduction of a standard entitlement was a new departure. The governors did, however, have one major problem at this time. It was the resignation of Inch as president, in order to accept the position of superintendent of education for New Brunswick. At first, when presented with the resignation on 4 June, the board refused to accept it. Giving Inch much of the credit for the 'unprecedented prosperity of the University of Mt. Allison,' it deemed him 'all but indispensible' and offered an increase in salary of $500 to induce him to stay. Even so, as he informed an adjourned meeting in Windsor, Nova Scotia, just over two weeks later, he was unwilling to change his mind.[166] Inch had served Mount Allison long and well. It was nearly forty years since he had first arrived as a young teacher in the academy. Never an outstanding scholar, and without an obviously forceful personality, he had none the less led both the ladies' academy and the university through perilous times, had prompted important changes – including the admission of women to the degree programmes – and had brought the university to a position where the standards of its teaching and the scholarship of its faculty stood higher than ever before. He now went on to be a reforming superintendent; but asked by a Sackville friend why he had resigned the presidency, he gave a simple reply: 'when everybody wants one to stay, it is the best time to go.'[167]

One of Inch's last actions while still president was to take a hand in the selection of his successor. It was on Inch's nomination, seconded by Charles

Stewart, that the presidency was offered to Alexander Sutherland, a fifty-seven-year-old Ontario-born minister and currently missionary secretary of the Methodist Church. The selection of Sutherland was especially significant since he had taken a leading role in the unsuccessful movement to have Victoria University maintain its independence rather than join the University of Toronto. Inch and the board no doubt considered that he would be an effective defender of Mount Allison's independence in any future battles that might have to be fought.[168] On 22 July, however, the board met again to receive the news that Sutherland had declined the offer; some four years before, he had also declined to be nominated for the presidency of Victoria.[169] The next choice came closer to home: the board unanimously invited David Allison to return to his old position as president. Allison could not immediately relinquish his duties as Nova Scotia superintendent of education, but he accepted the offer nevertheless. On 10 November, he arrived at Sackville station to be met by the assembled professors and students, who escorted him to the university. Now fifty-five years old, Allison was not the youthful president he had been when he first attained the office in 1869, but he retained the same ebullient character. The *Argosy*, welcoming his appointment, predicted 'an administration of the most satisfactory nature.'[170]

6

An Age of Improvement: 1891–1904

'These are great days in the history of Mt. Allison institutions,' commented the Saint John *Sun* in 1894: 'no previous period has seen so much activity and so many signs of growth and progress.'[1] The last decade of the nineteenth century, and the first few years of the twentieth, saw the fulfilment of many of the ambitions which had emerged from Mount Allison's prosperity during the 1880s. New buildings were constructed by the university and the ladies' college, while student numbers rose in all three institutions: the academy, after years of difficulty and decline, began now to recover its stability. New directions were explored in the courses offered, with the university in particular expanding its activities in professional education of various kinds. Anniversary celebrations – the fiftieth anniversary of the academy in 1893, and that of the ladies' college in 1904 – gave occasions for expression of the prevailing optimism. The setbacks that did occur seemed minor when compared with what was being achieved. Suffused with the confidence of the high Victorian age, and supported by the continued status of the Maritimes as a major industrial region of Canada, Mount Allison moved forward. It was a time for boldness, for innovation; it was an age of improvement.

At the university, the most determined advocate of new and progressive policies was undoubtedly W.W. Andrews. Andrews had quickly gained a reputation on his arrival at Mount Allison for his commitment to original research as the major characteristic of scientific enquiry, whether by undergraduates or by more senior scientists, and this principle was evident in the revised science curriculum which he introduced in the fall of 1891. The introduction of biology as a discrete subject, a virtually complete change in the prescribed textbooks in all branches of science – including modern works by such authors as Darwin's collaborator A.R. Wallace – and a heavy emphasis upon laboratory work in each of the four years: all were characteristics of the new curriculum. The honours course, concentrating upon physics, chemistry, and geology, went further in prescribing that in each class the students would carry out 'independent work on the Seminar Plan, choosing some approved line of research and embodying the results in a thesis to be read and discussed before the class.'[2] Andrews himself was active in the field of chemistry, and had success in developing new pieces of chemical apparatus – such as a self-regulating gas generator subsequently manufactured in Germany, and an improved blow-pipe burner manufactured in the United States – as well as publishing research results based on blow-pipe work in papers during the 1890s in the journals of the American Chemical Society and the British Association for the Advancement of Science. He also experimented with the vegetable-growing potential of the Sackville marshland, and for several years supplied the Canadian Pacific Railway with celery from among the 12,000 plants he maintained.[3]

Andrews's interest in scientific technology – as applied both to chemical apparatus and to agriculture – was closely linked with his advocacy of the establishment of a school of applied science at Mount Allison, a project which was formally adopted by the board of governors in June 1892.[4] The same meeting of the board also heard an address from Andrews on another proposal: the commencement of an extension programme. The concept of university extension was not new, having originated in Great Britain some twenty years previously. In North America, however, it had a shorter history, and in late 1891 the *Educational Review* cited the University of New Brunswick, the University of Toronto, and Mount Allison as three Canadian universities which had begun extension work. The University of New Brunswick's extension programme in Saint John, begun in November 1891, envisaged courses of eight lectures each in ten different subjects, and in the same month Andrews travelled to Moncton to explore the possibility of a similar scheme to be instituted there by Mount Allison. 'The clerk, the mechanic and the laborer,' suggested the Moncton *Times* in announcing the meeting held by Andrews, 'can secure a higher education at their own firesides, at a trifling cost.'[5] In the event, the meeting was less successful than had been hoped. The audience, observed the *Times*, was regrettably small. Nevertheless, local officers were elected for a university extension society, and a three-month series of weekly lectures announced, to be delivered in a variety of disciplines according to the wishes of those attending. A further meeting was held in January 1892, and on 12 February Andrews formed his class for a lecture course in biology.[6] Mount Allison's extension movement also reached to

Prince Edward Island in this year, with a course of twelve lectures on botany being delivered in Charlottetown by a lecturer recruited for the purpose, Francis Bain.[7]

At the same time as he worked for the establishment of an extension programme in Moncton, Andrews also argued in general terms the case in favour of extension work, in a series of articles in the *Wesleyan*: 'in University Extension,' he suggested, 'we have the Methodist itinerant system applied to higher education.' Andrews went so far as to recommend that university standing should be given for courses conducted on the basis of twelve weekly lectures, with a professor travelling to a different location each day of the week, so as to cover six centres within a day's travel of Sackville. Once again, as he had done in making the case for the school of applied science, Andrews cited Mount Allison's central situation in the region and inferred ways in which this could be turned to the advantage both of the university and of those it served.[8] Thus, when he addressed the board of governors in June he did so on the strength of both practical experience and his published arguments, as well as with the strong editorial support of the *Argosy*.[9] The results were not conclusive, as the board referred the matter of extension to the faculty, and apparently no action was taken to implement a permanent programme.[10] Andrews did continue, however, to promote adult education activities at Mount Allison, including the holding of a summer school of science in 1893. The summer school was not a project originated by Mount Allison, but had been founded in 1887 as a voluntary organization of teachers throughout the Maritime provinces for the purpose of sponsoring such a school each year. Two weeks long, the summer school attracted over 100 participants who studied, as Andrews pointed out in the *Wesleyan*, a curriculum not confined to science: the subjects taught included elocution, English literature, psychology, and tonic sol-fa, as well as botany, chemistry, geology, mineralogy, physics, physiology, and zoology. Especially popular was the field trip to the Joggins fossil cliffs. The role played by Andrews in the organization of the 1893 summer school led to his election as president of the next year's session in Charlottetown, and he retained his association with the school in the ensuing years.[11] Thus, although Andrews's ambitious extension scheme of 1892 was not implemented, he was able to ensure, through such means as the summer school of science and the public lectures which he periodically gave in Sackville and elsewhere, that the vigour of Mount Allison's science teaching was felt beyond the confines of the regular classroom.

One curriculum innovation that soon became permanent was the introduction of courses in law. Presaged by the public lecture series of early 1891, formal legal education at Mount Allison was begun in 1895 with the addition of H.A. Powell to the faculty as part-time lecturer in contract law. Powell, a Mount Allison graduate of 1875 and a Sackville lawyer, had recently been elected Member of Parliament for Westmorland in a by-election, after serving for five years as a Conservative in the provincial legislature. The *Argosy*, welcoming his appointment to the faculty, noted that students proceeding from Mount Allison to the faculty of law at Dalhousie would now be able to reduce their period of study after graduation from three to two years, by studying law under Powell and David Allison in their final year at Mount Allison. In 1896, this was confirmed in the university calendar, with Allison's courses in constitutional law and international law being specified along with Powell's course in contracts.[12] Also reorganized during the mid-1890s was Mount Allison's own approach to post-graduate study. In 1895, the PHD degree programme was quietly omitted from the calendar – as had also been the fate in 1894 of the PHB course, which had not had a graduate for seven years – in what was clearly a recognition of its failure to attract students during any of the previous eleven years. The MA degree remained, however, and was redefined in 1897. Instead of being offered only to those who were honours graduates of three years' standing, the degree was now to be available to honours graduates only one year after graduation, on presentation of a thesis, or to non-honours graduates on satisfactory completion of a year's post-graduate work 'in some special line of study' in addition to the thesis. This was a further step in the direction of making the Master's degree an award purely for post-graduate achievement, and diminished the extent to which it was an honorary recognition of work already completed at the undergraduate level.[13]

How far Mount Allison could continue at this time to adapt its educational approaches to modern needs depended, as in other eras, upon its material prosperity. The anniversary of January 1893 – marking fifty years since the opening of the Wesleyan Academy – was an opportunity to combine celebration with an appeal for funds. Due attention was given to the past at a banquet for former students of the academy on the 18th, and at the official jubilee celebration in Lingley Hall on the following morning. As well as David Allison, the speakers included Albert Carman, former bishop of the Methodist Episcopal Church and now General Superintendent of the Methodist Church in Canada, Thomas Pickard, the former academy teacher and college professor, and W.H. Tuck, justice of the New Brunswick supreme court. As Tuck recalled in his speech, he had been one of the boys sent to gaol forty-four years before for non-payment of highway taxes; it was, he assured his audience, a pleasant memory.[14] In the evening, however, at a reception for alumni held at the ladies' college, the emphasis was upon the future and the major speech was delivered by Josiah Wood, treasurer of the institutions. 'The improvements to be seen on every hand,' he declared, as reported in the Saint John *Sun*, 'afforded him great pleasure and gratification.' Yet there was more to be done. Better residential accommodation, further improvement of science instruction, and additions to the faculty were, Wood suggested, necessities if Mount Allison were to continue to send its graduates well qualified into what was now a 'different world ... as compared with that into which the graduates of many years ago began their battle of life.' Repeating the role which he had played in the past, Wood thereupon promised a donation of $5000 to the semi-centennial fund, and by the end of the evening a further $8000 had been added by others. There was also a rumour that 'a wealthy capitalist and manufacturer of Sackville' was considering making 'a gift worthy of his means which may take the form of a students' residence called by his name.'[15]

This rumour, reported by the *Sun*'s correspondent, was apparently unduly optimistic, for no such donation was made. It soon emerged, in fact, that to appeal for funds from a basis of prosperity was more difficult than had been true of past campaigns which had aimed at rescuing Mount Allison from dangerous crises. As the university admitted several years later to the Methodist general conference, 'the receipts from the Semi-Centennial Fund ... fell far short of what was hoped and expected.'[16] Even before the jubilee celebration itself, the campaign had had an unsteady beginning, owing to a well-publicized argument between Albert Carman and Judge Tuck in early January 1893. Preaching in Saint John on the 8th, Carman had launched an attack upon the prime minister of Canada, Sir John Thompson, on religious grounds. Thompson, a Nova Scotian and a Conservative, had been converted as a young man from Methodism to Roman Catholicism; since his appointment as prime minister just over a month previously, on 6 December 1892, he had been publicly denounced by George Douglas, principal of the Wesleyan Theological College in Montreal, as a creature of the Jesuits.[17] This accusation was sustained by Carman in his sermon; on the following evening, still in Saint John, he shared the platform at a Mount Allison campaign meeting with two staunch Conservatives – although both prevented by their occupations from being openly partisan – in the persons of Tuck and David Allison. Following initial speeches byAllison and the theological professor Charles Stewart, Tuck lost no time in taking outspoken exception to the 'sectarian narrowness' of the views expressed by Carman and Douglas, which contrasted in his view with the 'liberality of thought' characteristic of Mount Allison. After Carman had heatedly defended himself, Allison closed the meeting with an impromptu speech in which he praised both Douglas's long church career and the character of Sir John Thompson, but with more obvious warmth of feeling for the latter: Thompson's political acts and principles, he believed, must be judged on their merits and not according to the prime minister's religious convictions.[18] It was a curious scene, played out under the chairmanship of Sir Leonard Tilley, another prominent Conservative and now lieutenant-governor of New Brunswick. If there had been any hopes of restricting public knowledge of what had taken place, they were soon dispelled by the editorial of the following day in the *Sun*. Under the editorship of S.D. Scott, the *Sun* was a consistent supporter both of Mount Allison and of the Conservative party. On this occasion, it interpreted the 'little passage of arms between Judge Tuck and Dr. Carman' as reflecting credit upon David Allison for the moderation of his concluding speech, but none at all upon Carman. He, as 'a westerner' – he came from Ontario – must have failed to understand, the *Sun* reflected, that Mount Allison, perhaps unlike Douglas's theological college in Montreal, prided itself upon its non-sectarian principle.[19]

Such an incident, even when couched in terms favourable to Mount Allison, could not but damage the financial campaign before it had properly started. Other newspapers soon took up the story, the Moncton *Times* giving it front-page prominence under the headline, 'An Interesting Episode at the Mount Allison Celebration in St. John.'[20] Also revealed, and made explicit by the *Sun*'s reference to Carman's Ontario background, had been the continuance of those tensions over Mount Allison's position within the Methodist church which had been so evident at the general conference of 1890. Carman had not, in fact, been the university's first choice as a visiting speaker from church headquarters, as the invitation had originally been extended to John Potts, General Secretary of Education. Potts had refused on the ground that he had commitments elsewhere, and had indicated that Carman already planned to travel east on other church business that winter and so would be an appropriate substitute. Potts, however, may well have had additional reasons for not being closely associated with the Mount Allison appeal. On the day before he wrote to decline the Mount Allison invitation, he had written to the editor of the *Wesleyan*, John Lathern, to complain that little money was being raised in Nova Scotia for the central educational society of the church, and to ask for more attention to the matter in the *Wesleyan*. 'This will not, in any way,' he assured Lathern, 'interfere with your Sackville Jubilee efforts.'[21] Yet a few months later, in the educational society annual report, Potts specifically blamed competing appeals from individual institutions for a reduction in the society's revenues, and warned sternly that 'the sober judgment of the Methodist Church in Canada, and the world over, is in favor of connexionalism in all our operations, a principle which is the constitutional strength of our polity.'[22]

Connexionalism – the centralizing principle – certainly did have a long history within Methodist churches in Canada and elsewhere, although it had also occasioned many serious disputes. For Mount Allison, there was reason to suspect that connexionalism was a convenient means of asserting the primacy of Victoria University within the church. Attempting to persuade Lathern in 1892 to print in the *Wesleyan* an appeal for funds from Victoria, Potts had described that university as 'the great central educational institution of our Church.'[23] Furthermore, of the funds disbursed each year to the four Methodist colleges by the educational society, Victoria's share at this time was a full 50 per cent. The Montreal theological college and Wesley College, Winnipeg, received 18 per cent each; Mount Allison received only 14 per cent, which amounted during the 1890s to an average of $1550. The figure itself gave no cause for complaint, as the average annual total of contributions to educational funds from the Maritime conferences was slightly less, at $1482.[24] Yet the assumption of primacy by Victoria could have results well beyond the confines of financial affairs. In 1897, for example, Potts made a private approach to W.W. Andrews to invite him to be a candidate for the presidency of a proposed Methodist college in British Columbia. The plan did not in fact materialize at this time, but Potts's closing injunction to Andrews was a revealing one: 'you must be very careful not to mention this at Sackville until your own mind is made up and the position is offered you. Chancellor Burwash [of Victoria] is of opinion that a man for your position at Sackville could be easily found, but it is not so easy to get a man fitted for the principalship.'[25] That such covert deliberations should take place on the staffing of Mount Allison was an indication of the extent to which the union of 1884 had shifted power westward, and gave point to the complaint of the editor of the *Wesleyan* some years later, in a letter to Carman, that 'it is felt in the East that some of our leaders are centering everything in Toronto.'[26] Certainly in the context of the Mount Allison appeal of 1893, Carman's intervention had shown that the importation to the Maritimes of issues that were supposedly connexional in importance was not necessarily beneficial.

No exact goal had been set for the semi-centennial fund, but the board of governors had decided in June 1892 that the funds raised would be used to build a new university residence, develop technical and applied science training at both the university and the academy, upgrade the facilities for art education at the ladies' college, expand the theological faculty, and augment the endowment. With the fund eventually amounting to only some $25,000, this ambitious programme clearly could not be carried out in full. Yet it was an indication of confidence when the board decided, in June 1893, at least to make a beginning by constructing a new residence and an art gallery, both to be built in brick or stone. The residence was to be designed to accommodate at least 100 students, with provision made for future expansion.[27] By August, the university had acquired a four-acre field on the opposite side of York Street from the existing campus, and the beginning of construction was imminent.[28] A year later it was complete. Panelled in hardwood, lighted by electricity, heated by hot air circulation from eleven furnaces, and with running water throughout, it presented a marked contrast with the rigours of the old college building. For the students, commented the *Sun*, there would be 'no more hewing of wood and drawing of water.'[29] It was the exterior of the new residence, however, that was most striking. Constructed of brick, with stone facings, it stood four storeys high above the basement, and was two hundred feet in length; its mansard roof was surmounted by a tower above the main door, flanked by turrets on either side and at the two front corners. At the rear, a large ell projected ninety feet, housing the kitchens and dining hall: for the first time since the college had opened, the students would have their own dining facilities, rather than sharing those of the academy. The building was large and impressive even by urban standards. Seen in the rural surroundings of Sackville, against the background of fields and woods, it rose dramatically from the small eminence on which it stood. It was a solidly Victorian symbol of progress, or as the *Wesleyan* remarked, a sign of 'large and generous faith in the future.'[30]

The residence was also an expensive venture, the cost of construction and furnishing being reckoned finally at almost $70,000, of which just over $10,000 was offset by appropriations from the semi-centennial fund. The resulting large increase in debt was funded chiefly by the issuance of debenture bonds to the amount of $50,000, specially authorized by New Brunswick legislation of 1894.[31] Thus the level of debt was higher, and substantially higher, than it had ever been before. Yet so too was the amount of the assets against which the bonds had been issued. In 1898, the land and buildings of the university alone – not counting those of the other institutions – were valued at $115,000, while endowment funds stood at over $120,000.[32] Student numbers rose steadily throughout the early 1890s, with undergraduate enrolment totalling 94 in the year 1895–6, more than half as many again as five years before.[33] To be sure, there were some limitations that had to be recognized, at least for the time being. The board of governors listened sympathetically in May 1894, for example, to Andrews's proposal to convert the old college building for scientific uses, but no action was possible in the existing financial climate: for now, the notion of an applied science school at Mount Allison necessarily went unrealized.[34] None the less, temporary limitations could not depress the mood of the time. The *Argosy*, welcoming in October 1894 the opening of the residence and the arrival of the largest freshman class in the university's history, looked forward with unbounded optimism. Making a claim that would not have gone uncontested in some quarters, its editorial set out an ambitious goal for Mount Allison: 'having been recognized for some years as the leading University of the Maritime Provinces, she now aspires to a higher dignity – a universal recognition as the leading University of Canada.'[35]

A similar spirit characterized the ladies' college throughout the 1890s, and was seen particularly in the rapid development of the fine arts. The success of the conservatory of music inevitably led to thoughts of a similar expansion of the existing course in drawing and painting, and in June 1892 the *Wesleyan* carried an editorial which made the parallel explicit, and predicted success; 'Principal Borden,' it revealed, had already begun 'to plead for the erection of an Art Hall.'[36] The editor of the *Wesleyan*, John Lathern, was well aware – for he was also chairman of the Mount Allison board of governors – that Borden had in fact been quite specific in the proposal he had presented in the privacy of the governors' meeting of 1 June. He had been in contact with Robert Reed, chief trustee of the Owens Art Gallery in Saint John, concerning the possibility of transferring the Owens collection to Mount Allison. The board was receptive, and expressed a general willingness to enter into negotiations. By the following January, it had approved the purchase in principle, and gave final confirmation on 31 May 1893. The collection would be moved to Sackville at Mount Allison's expense. Mount Allison would also undertake to contribute $800 towards renovation of the existing gallery in Saint John so that it could be used as a church, and would pay off the debts of the Owens trust to the amount of $500. Exclusive of the costs of constructing a new gallery in Sackville, Mount Allison thus acquired for a total expenditure of only $1593 a collection which was shortly afterwards valued at $40,000.[37]

The acquisition, of course, was not a commercial purchase, but rather the assumption of a charitable trust. John Owens, who had died in 1867 at the age of seventy-seven, had been a wealthy shipbuilder and merchant of Saint John. Nine years before his death, he had resigned his membership of the Portland Methodist Church to protest against the installation of an organ in the church – instrumental music in church apparently contravened his religious convictions – and founded the Zion Church elsewhere in Saint John. In his will, Owens provided a fund for the church and its pastors, and also left a further bequest for the purposes of giving instruction in art and music to children and founding an orphanage. It soon became apparent, however, that the proceeds of the estate were insufficient for the fulfilment of these intentions, and by the early 1880s even the Zion Church was unable to find a pastor to serve in return for the limited stipend permitted by the will. Accordingly, the trustees of the estate, led by Reed, had obtained an act of the New Brunswick legislature to merge the various provisions by authorizing the conversion of the church to house an art gallery and a school of art.[38] A Montreal artist, John Hammond, was engaged as principal of the school, and during frequent travels in Europe and North America during the ensuing years he built up a teaching collection of both original works and facsimiles of well-known originals. As described in 1889 by the art critic of the *Montreal Gazette*, S.E. Dawson, the Owens collection was especially strong in sketches and watercolours by nineteenth-century British artists, with smaller representations of modern French, Italian, and Canadian artists – the last including Hammond himself – and copies of the old masters. Dawson praised the school's 'excellent work among the young people of St. John' and predicted great achievements in the future.[39] His optimism was understandable, for within a year of its opening the school had attracted over 100 pupils and had employed several assistant teachers. Once again, however, funds had run short, and the discussions between Reed and Borden had resulted. For a short time in early 1893 it seemed that an effort would be made to acquire the gallery for the city of Saint John, and this possibility was specifically recognized in the provincial legislation which allowed the Owens trustees to negotiate a transfer of the collection; but the act also permitted the trustees to dispose of it to any educational institution in New Brunswick where it would be used 'for the purpose of Art culture.' Mount Allison's proposal, eventually, was the only one to be made.[40]

Along with the Owens collection came the principal of the school, John Hammond, now to be the first professor of fine arts in the ladies' college since John Warren Gray. In his earlier years, Hammond had fought the invading Fenians in 1866, had spent two and a half years panning for gold in New Zealand, and had travelled in the Canadian west with the first Transcontinental Survey in 1870. Only then, in his late twenties, had he devoted himself to painting. In recent years, his career had flourished. After spending several months in Europe during 1885 and 1886, painting with J.M. Whistler in the Netherlands and with Jean François Millet in France, he exhibited works at the Paris Salon Exhibition, at the Royal Academy in London, and at the National Gallery in New York. Elected an associate of the Royal Canadian Academy in 1890, he became a full member in 1893 and exhibited regularly at the Academy's exhibitions for the next forty years. His style was often compared with that of J.M.W. Turner by contemporary critics, and the influence of Whistler was also evident in his subtle use of tone and colour in his several portrayals of Saint John harbour. In later years he also painted in Japan and China – in 1900 he narrowly escaped death in the Boxer rebellion – and in western Canada, where he travelled widely to paint landscapes at the behest of his friend and patron Sir William Van Horne. By virtue of acquiring the services of Hammond, even more than by securing the Owens collection, Mount Allison became an important centre of the fine arts in the Maritimes and in Canada as a whole, a status which it was to retain long after the ladies' college had ceased to exist as such.[41]

An immediate question in 1893 was that of where the new art school was to be housed while Mount Allison was in the process of fulfilling its commitment to build a suitable gallery as a permanent location. The problem was solved by the temporary conversion of Lingley Hall, which was promptly stripped of its seats to make room for sculptures, and hung with paintings. Renamed 'Victoria Hall' for the duration of its transformation, it also accommodated Hammond's own studio.[42] By early 1894, a competition had been held for a design for the new building, and had been won by the Toronto architect Edmund Burke, in competition with six other entries.[43] By May, the contract had been awarded to J.F. Teed of Dorchester – already the builder of the academy, Centennial Hall, and the residence – and in January 1895 the Owens Museum of Fine Arts was first used by Hammond, his two associate teachers Bessie Alcorn and Ethel Ogden, and their students, who numbered 45 in that year.[44] Constructed of light olive sandstone from nearby Rockport, the gallery stood between the main ladies' college and the university residence – one ladies' college student noted with approval that it blocked the view between those two buildings[45] – and was long and low, with skylights at either end, and decorated by terracotta friezes on each exterior wall. The interior was divided into display galleries and students' workrooms. On the walls of the galleries, hung closely together, were the 338 pictures which comprised the Owens collection. The *Argosy* suggested in January 1895 that this was probably 'the finest art building in the Dominion of Canada,' and this view would have found no dissenters at the official opening on 28 May 1895. John J. Fraser, lieutenant-governor of New Brunswick, looked forward in his speech to the achievements of the young Maritime artists who would receive their training at the Owens Museum in the future, and paid a general tribute to Mount Allison's progress: 'the institutions here,' he declared, 'had not only a maritime province reputation but were well known from one end of the Dominion to the other.'[46]

Lieutenant-Governor Fraser also praised Mount Allison's role in the provision of higher education for women, and noted that women were now competing effectively with men not only in university classes but also in their later working careers. This was in fact an especially appropriate day for such a reflection, for in the evening Mary Mellish Archibald was able to report to the alumnae association that women would henceforth have representation on the board of governors. The alumnae had initiated their campaign two years before, but much discussion and an act of the provincial legislature had been necessary before the change could take place. At its annual meeting in May 1894, the board had considered the alumnae request for parity with the four seats held by the alumni and had eventually decided upon a compromise by which two alumnae seats would be added along with two more for the alumni. Thus, when the consent of the general conference had been obtained and the necessary legislation enacted in March 1895, 24 of the 32 board members were to be appointed by the church, six by the alumni, and two by the alumnae.[47] On 29 May the first two alumnae representatives were formally added to the board. One, not surprisingly, was Archibald. The other was Jane Heartz, a minister's daughter from Amherst who had obtained the MLA diploma in 1888, had gone on to study at the Women's Medical College in New York, and was now a doctor in Chicago.[48] She was one of three who had gone on to become medical doctors, out of the 32 MLA graduates of the 1880s.[49]

As well as being the first women on the board of governors, therefore, both Heartz and Archibald were examples of the opportunities now open to women in the 1890s. Not that this had gone unrecognized before. In May 1894, for example, the anonymous 'Ladies' College Notes' in the *Argosy* had declared that 'politically, intellectually, socially, the position of woman today is a commanding one', and that '"Home is Woman's Sphere" is a wrong principle if it must shut her out from all other avenues of usefulness.'[50] The small numbers of women who in fact broke through the barriers of the more prestigious male-dominated professions would later show the writer's comments to have been over-optimistic. Yet the careers followed by women BA graduates from the university confirmed that this was a decade of greater opportunity than before. Although 15 of the 31 women graduates between 1891 and 1900 were listed in 1903 as having no formal employment, the majority had taken some form of paid work. Eleven had become teachers, while one was a missionary, one a doctor, one a stenographer, and one a governess. Three had entered journalism, although by 1903 only one was still active in that field. Thus, more than half of the women graduates had clearly attained at least for the time being a position of independence in society based upon the education they had received at Mount Allison.[51]

For all that, at the ladies' college, there remained questions as to how serious in intent was the education offered. That Principal Borden felt the need, in his report given at the closing exercises in May 1895, to express publicly his disapproval of the term 'finishing school' was an indication that the phrase was being used more often than he liked. Over a period of years, recalled Borden, the lower grades of education had been surrendered almost entirely to the public schools: 'while we are prepared to take pupils in all grades,' he went on, 'this college is especially strong (I will not say as a 'finishing school' as I do not like the expression) but as a school where advanced pupils in literary courses, as well as in music and the fine arts, may enjoy exceptional advantages.'[52] Similarly, the *Wesleyan* went out of its way in an editorial of 1898 to declare that 'in literary work, which after all is the main work of the College – for education is the main thing, and accomplishments, however graceful, must be secondary – in literary work the College is holding to its good record.'[53] The fact was, however, that of the ladies' college's annual enrolment of about 180 throughout the 1890s, a substantial proportion were attending with the aim of developing ladylike accomplishments rather than intellectual prowess for its own sake. An anonymous visitor to the institution in 1894, for example, reserved highest praise for the topic receptions: 'not the least valuable part of an education is the restoration of an almost lost art, that of sensible drawing room talk.' The same correspondent also observed that the reception had clearly shown that Mount Allison 'must have the patronage of the first families of the provinces.'[54] Here again was a sensitive issue, for on 27 June 1895 the editor of the *Chignecto Post* reported comments made by a farmer attending a recent ladies' college reception that the extravagant dresses worn by the students were enough to exclude those from families of limited means; the editorial cautiously concluded that 'it is just possible that those who govern Mount Allison might in this repect hold the reins a little tighter.'[55] The editorial was answered two weeks later by 'a resident of Sackville' – identified by a contemporary as Nellie Greenwood Andrews, wife of W.W. Andrews – who denied that dress at Mount Allison was luxurious by comparison with standards elsewhere. A father 'in moderate circumstances,' she suggested, need have no hesitation on that ground in sending his daughter to Mount Allison, where morality and scholarship were the prime concerns. Yet the letter also emphasized the social advantages of a Mount Allison education:

> If we speak of the matter of style, let us not forget that the beautiful and suitable in dress have an educative effect and it is one of the acknowledged advantages of a ladies' school, that there, girls from quiet country homes may gain a knowledge of what is customary in dress and deportment in the great world outside.[56]

Clearly, there was a discrepancy between the stated aims of the school and the purposes for which many of the pupils attended, and there was little that could be done to remove the ambivalence. The catalogue for 1895–6 contained a new admonition to parents that muslin or cashmere dresses should be worn by students at festive occasions, and that silk was both unnecessary and unsuitable.[57] More fundamentally, efforts could be made to ensure that the MLA curriculum – which was completed by only a small proportion of the students, as less than five MLA's were awarded per year on average during the 1890s – retained its intellectual vigour under the leadership of Mary Mellish Archibald. The 1894–5 year, for example, saw the introduction of practical laboratory work in chemistry for MLA students, while two years later social science was included in the form of political economy, with 'lectures on the Canadian Banking Law, Sociology, and the various modern problems of applied economics.'[58] Music and the fine arts, similarly, could be offered at high enough levels that they need not be taught merely as social accomplishments. The recruitment of an artist of the quality of Hammond was one step in this direction. In the conservatory, even after the departure of Mack in 1893, increasing emphasis was put upon the teaching of musical theory by a succession of professors throughout the ensuing decade. One, John J. Wootton, argued strongly in the *Argosy* in 1897 that the prejudice that music was of no intellectual value was held by all too many individuals who, 'musically considered, cannot tell a hawk from a handsaw.'[59] Music, for Wootton, was a demanding discipline and an important professional occupation, and this view was reflected in the diploma courses of the conservatory – both a 'teacher's diploma' and an 'artist's diploma' could be obtained – which prescribed both practical and theoretical work. 'The performer who does not understand these sciences,' admonished the catalogue with reference to the study of harmony and theory, 'is much like a person reciting a poem in a foreign language, while not understanding a word of what he is speaking.'[60]

Such developments prevented the ladies' college from being merely a finishing school, although Borden's disclaimer of 1895 did not alter the fact that it remained a finishing school among its other purposes. That it should do so was inevitable given the demand for such education, and given also the intense competition which had developed within the region between the institutions which sought to satisfy that demand. In late 1896, Borden fought a bitter battle in the columns of the *Chignecto Post* with W.C. Vincent, Baptist minister in Sackville, who maintained that the Acadia Seminary could give as good training as the Mount Allison ladies' college at a cost of $50 less per year. Degenerating to personal abuse, and to aspersions upon the competence of the respective teaching staffs, the encounter ended inconclusively and led the editor of the newpaper to reflect that such arguments 'can do no good and may create a great deal of hard feeling.'[61] The truth was that the education of young women in the 1890s was sufficiently competitive, and important enough to the financial welfare of the institutions, that hard feelings were seldom far from the surface. Yet the Mount Allison ladies' college had much of which it could legitimately boast. The conservatory and the Owens gallery were visible symbols of growth. It was true that the gallery, built at a cost of over $25,000, had left a debt of almost four-fifths of that sum; but with annual surpluses averaging about $1500 in the middle years of the decade, that was cause for only mild concern. In addition to Borden and Archibald, the staff of teachers had grown by 1896 to 15: five in literary subjects, one in shorthand and typewriting, three in fine arts, and six in the conservatory.[62] For both teachers and students, there was a vigorous quality to life in the ladies' college, and a cosmopolitanism that left an especially deep impression upon Maude Pettit, a university student of the late 1890s from Simcoe, Ontario. Pettit, who resided, as did all female university students at Mount Allison, in the ladies' college, recalled her experiences romantically but evocatively in 1904:

Your room-mate is perhaps the daughter of a sea-captain; she has spent two years at sea in her father's ship. She is familiar with the ports of South Africa, South America and the West Indies. She spreads on the floor the skin of some wild beast slain in Africa. She drapes the mantel with some dainty fabric which she purchased in Buenos Ayres. Your next door neighbour proves to be the daughter of a seal-merchant from Newfoundland. She, too, has had her quota of strange experiences. Across the hall in No. 90 is a sweet, blue-eyed maid from 'the land of Evangeline.' She has been reared in sight of the old historic willows in the meadow of Grand Pre. Her room-mate later tells you of her home in 'the garden of the Gulf,' as they call Prince Edward Island. Down the corridor a little Creole girl from the West Indies is unpacking a commodious trunk, and a few of the denizens of Quebec, Ontario and the Eastern States have just arrived. At the Y.M.C.A. reception, the first social event of the season, you meet a 'theologue' who relates to you something of his experience as a probationer among the fisherfolk and the ice-floes of Newfoundland and 'the Labrador.' Your next number is taken up by a homesick Academy lad from the Bermudas. You begin to wish you were in some way connected with the literary profession, so fertile a field does Mt. Allison offer the pen of a ready writer.[63]

Also sharing in the general optimism of the 1890s, although at times the subject of controversy, was the academy. C.W. Harrison, a graduate of Victoria University and an experienced high school teacher and principal in

Ontario, was appointed academy principal in 1890, and declared to the Nova Scotia Conference in the following year that he was 'tired of having the Academy apologized for, and would put new life into it.'[64] In financial terms he succeeded, for the academy's operations showed a small surplus during his four-year term as principal.[65] The basis of Harrison's ambitions for the academy was the commercial college, which he successfully revived. During the years since the abolition of the first commercial college in 1879, the academy had continued to offer instruction on a limited basis in such subjects as bookkeeping and shorthand. When Harrison became principal, the full-time teaching staff of the academy was only three including himself, with one teacher in shorthand and typewriting shared between the academy and ladies' college, and with music teaching also available from members of the ladies' college staff. By the autumn of 1892, however, this situation had been considerably altered. Although certain appointments were still shared with the ladies' college, the academy now had a staff of six teachers, including a graduate of the Ontario Business College, A.W. Young, who was styled chief of the commercial college staff. Along with two other instructors, he supervised the teaching of a newly elaborated commercial programme, including not only the basic subjects which had been continued since 1879 but also an 'actual business department' – in which, as under Whiston during the 1870s, students conducted imaginary business transactions using Mount Allison currency and tokens representing merchandise – and a 'Telegraph Department,' equipped with suitable electrical apparatus. The academy thus offered two distinct options to students: the matriculation course, and the commercial course.[66]

The new arrangements quickly proved attractive enough to raise attendance at the academy from 79 in 1891–2 to 99 two years later.[67] In the summer of 1894, however, a crisis suddenly developed, as rumours spread in Sackville that the commercial college was to be closed and that Harrison would resign in protest. A letter to the *Chignecto Post* from an anonymous local businessman urged the board of governors to retain the commercial college on the ground that it was of great practical benefit for students; 'which cannot be said,' he went on, 'of some other studies that are perhaps placed more prominently.' This last sally was rejected as 'uncharitable and ill-natured' by the editor of the newspaper, but the case for retention of the commercial college was strongly endorsed. Yet the same edition carried the news that Harrison had indeed resigned, maintaining that 'the academy cannot be self-supporting under the restrictions placed by the board of regents.'[68] What had provoked the conflict? Harrison expressed surprise that there should be dissatisfaction with the work of the commercial college, and the minutes of the board did give some evidence of concern that the diplomas conferred might represent lower attainments than at other commercial schools in the region.[69] It is likely, however, that the real cause was entirely different. For over thirty years the academy had supplied meals to the students of the university, and it had become customary for the university to pay for this service at such a high rate as to be equivalent to an annual subsidy from university to academy. In 1893–4, for example, the university's payment of over $6300 had been more than enough to pay the entire cost of running the dining hall.[70] With the opening of the university residence, which had its own dining facilities, the academy would no longer enjoy this revenue. The obvious way of compensating for the change was to cut down the recently expanded academy staff, and the interests of the university dictated that retrenchments should come in the commercial course rather than in the matriculation course which was useful for the recruiting of students. Accordingly, after accepting Harrison's resignation, the board of governors proceeded to define the academy's future role:

> That while the Acad. should be conducted so as to afford every opportunity for a general English, Commercial and Classical training for stud. not intending to pursue their studies further, its primary object should be to act as a preparat. School for the College, and that the Course of study should naturally lead up to matriculation.[71]

Although, therefore, the functions of the commercial college had not been abolished entirely – the rumours had been exaggerated in that respect – the primacy of the university over the academy had decisively been reaffirmed. Perhaps anticipating that the circumstances of Harrison's departure would make it difficult to find a successor, the board also voted that an increased salary should be given to the new principal if this was necessary in order to secure 'a thoroughly competent man.'[72] The choice fell upon James Marshall Palmer, thirty-three-year-old teacher of French and classics at the Collegiate School in Fredericton. A native of Gagetown, a river port near Fredericton, he had graduated with high honours from the University of New Brunswick in 1880 and had subsequently taught in Campbellton and Chatham before returning to Fredericton.[73] Slight in appearance and reserved by nature, Palmer stood in marked contrast with the ebullience of David Allison and the brisk geniality of Borden. Yet if he was sometimes underestimated by colleagues and students, he was seldom underestimated for long, for over his thirty-six years as principal he achieved distinction as a teacher, as a strict disciplinarian, and as a tireless advocate of the best interests of the academy.

An early example of his determination was seen in his retention of the greater part of the commercial course which he had inherited from Harrison, and of the term 'commercial college.' Although the academy teaching staff was cut to four, with one other appointment shared with the university and one with the ladies' college, the restrictions of the curriculum were minimal. Even in the negotiation of joint appointments, Palmer was vigilant for the interests of the academy: disputes over whether he or Borden should select the teacher of shorthand and typewriting, who taught at both the academy and the ladies' college, and as to which institution female students of these subjects should belong, led over the years to outright rivalry between the two. When the matter was finally brought before the board of regents in 1906, Palmer was vindicated and was given exclusive control, on behalf of the commercial college, over secretarial training. 'There was a good deal of feeling over the matter,' he recalled many years later, 'and yet much satisfaction on the campus over our victory.'[74]

In the short term, Palmer's task was well defined, although difficult: to steer the academy through the financial strains brought about by the loss of revenue from the university and the more subtle crisis of confidence provoked by Harrison's resignation. The retention of the commercial college was an effective start towards solving the latter difficulty and although student attendance fell noticeably in Palmer's first year, it soon recovered and regularly approached 100. During his initial eight years, Palmer reported to the church general conference in 1902, the average attendance had been 93, with an average of 41 boarding students, and he was inclined to attribute this success largely to the commercial college: 'the increasing efficiency of the public schools of the Province limits more and more the number of those seeking a purely academic education away from home, and any material increase in the number of such students can hardly be expected. But there is a greater demand for a preparation for a commercial life, and the excellent course of study pursued in our business college has attracted such students to our institution in increasing numbers. ...'[75] As the high proportion of non-resident students revealed, the academy now depended in large measure upon the attendance of local students, and the remarks of the *Post* in 1895 as to the importance of the commercial college as a link with the Sackville community were well justified as increasing numbers of local men and women took the one-year diploma course in commercial and secretarial subjects. At the same time, as Palmer was well aware, the role of the academy as a complement to the other Mount Allison institutions depended upon its continuing to function also as an academic high school, specializing in matriculation courses for university entrance. Palmer's success lay in his ability to balance the institution's two major purposes. Financially, he was able to report a small surplus by the summer of 1897, much earlier than had been expected.[76] As for the matter of confidence, the *Wesleyan* commented in September 1895 that 'the Male Academy was for some years the weak point in the Institutions. It is so no longer. At the head of it is an experienced and successful teacher, a good scholar, a Christian gentleman.'[77] This verdict did less than justice to Harrison, who had laid the foundations of the academy's recovery, but it accurately conveyed the sense of renewal. The prosperity of the time was shared by all three institutions, the academy no longer excluded.

Also common to all the institutions, and contributing in its own way to the expansive mood of the time, was an enthusiasm which Mount Allison shared with other Canadian universities: the rise of rugby football to pre-eminence as a collegiate sport. Several years had now passed since the famous series of matches between McGill and Harvard during the 1870s, and in the meantime Canadian football had begun to emerge in Quebec and Ontario from the originally haphazard varieties of local rules which had governed the several distinct combinations of soccer and rugby played at the colleges.[78] A different tradition developed in the Maritimes, where rugby union rules were followed, but the excitement generated was just as evident. Football – the term was originally applied to all varieties of football, and continued in the Maritimes to be applied to rugby until the importation of Canadian football into the region in the 1940s – had been played intermittently at Mount Allison at least since 1875, when the *Argosy* commented briefly that 'foot-ball is the favorite game of the Academy Students this year.'[79] It was apparently not until 1890, however, that the first organized team represented Mount Allison, when a college side travelled to Saint John and recorded a convincing 8–0 win over the home club. In the following season, five matches were played and won, all against city rather than college clubs: Saint John was defeated twice, Fredericton, Moncton, and Amherst once.[80] The beginning of intercollegiate football at Mount Allison came a year later, on 4 November 1892, described by the *Argosy*, as 'a day long to be remembered.'[81] So it was, not least because Sackville was visited on that Friday not only the by the team from UNB but also, on their way back to Halifax from a fixture in Moncton the previous day, by that of Dalhousie. In the morning, Mount Allison convincingly accounted for the Fredericton side by 17 points to none. After only a short rest, they then lined up at three o'clock against the reputedly more powerful team from Dalhousie. The *Chignecto Post* noted that even the friends of Mount Allison could scarcely hope for a victory, and Dalhousie duly prevailed, although only by virtue of a hotly disputed try which was converted to give a final score of 5–0.[82] The *Post* remarked on the sportsmanlike feeling between the two teams during and after the contest, but the *Argosy* was not above pointing out that the referee was from Dalhousie; nor, a month after, did it hesitate to reprove the *Dalhousie Gazette* for a patronizing report of the game.[83]

The rivalries characteristic of intercollegiate rugby, sometimes friendly, sometimes not, were to persist for more than sixty years from that beginning. Nor was the enthusiasm confined to the university. The academy had its own team, which was capable on occasion of surprising the university's second fifteen, as well as playing against clubs from such local communities as Amherst and Dorchester.[84] The ladies' college, by November of 1894, was described in the *Argosy* as being 'thrown into a perfect furor of excitement' over the prowess of the university team; a suggestion that a ladies' college team should be organized was apparently soon abandoned, but it was reported that 'many a one wished to be a boy if it were only for the pleasure of joining in the fray.'[85] Even faculty members were not immune. The normally equable S.W. Hunton broke his gold-headed cane in the excitement of the encounter with Dalhousie in 1892 – rumours that he had broken it over the head or shoulders of a particularly brash supporter of the visiting team were probably mistaken – while at a match with Acadia some years later David Allison increased his fame by joining loudly in the crowd's chant of 'give them hell, boys, give them hell.'[86]

The 1894 season brought to a peak the first wave of excitement over football at Mount Allison, as it saw an attempt to launch a New Brunswick league composed of Mount Allison and UNB sides and club teams from Saint John and Moncton. It soon became clear that the championship would be won either by Mount Allison or by Saint John, each of the two having inflicted upon the other its only defeat. Accordingly, on 30 November they played off on a frozen and snow-covered ground in Moncton. The match was marred by the broken leg suffered by one of the Mount Allison half-backs, Percy Butler, by arguments over the referee's timing of the game – which allowed Saint John to win by virtue of a try scored, according to Mount Allison observers, five minutes after full time – and most of all by subsequent allegations that the Saint John players had used illegal metal spikes on their boots. While the resulting protest was dismissed, the bitterness aroused was reflected in a sharp skirmish between the *Argosy* and the Saint John *Telegraph*, and was enough to destroy the league.[87] It also cooled the ardour of the Mount Allison students. 'Of course we like to see our team come out ahead,' commented a magazine produced at the ladies' college, 'but we do not like to see our players mangled as if they had just come off a battle field.'[88] The following season, as the *Argosy* noticed with regret, saw a conspicuous waning of interest: only three matches were played, defeats by Dalhousie and Acadia being compensated by the 51–0 drubbing of an unfortunate village side from nearby Dorchester.[89] When interest in the game recovered, as it soon did, Mount Allison's opponents tended to be college rather than town teams, and from Nova Scotia rather than from New Brunswick. Fixtures with UNB continued, but the greatest enthusiasm was now aroused by contests with Dalhousie and, increasingly becoming the major rivalry, with Acadia. 'To college men,' remarked the *Argosy* in 1897, 'inter-collegiate games are far more interesting than college and town, or town and town games. ...'[90]

Intercollegiate competition was not confined to football. In the spring, cricket and baseball continued into the early years of the twentieth century to compete for adherents. Cricket, which had its last major revival in 1903, was not an intercollegiate sport, but occasional contests with the Collège St-Joseph were held in baseball.[91] The only sport in any way comparable in popularity to football, however, was hockey. Mount Allison was late in adopting hockey as a major sport, partly, as the *Argosy* frequently complained, because of the lack of a Mount Allison rink. The first university team to be organized, in 1896 – some twenty years after the sport had been taken up by McGill – had to be content with only one hour of practice per week on the privately owned Sackville rink.[92] Even so, they managed to defeat a Sackville team by 4 to 2. A year later, after an inter-class league had been launched in order to provide for more competitive practice, Mount Allison made its first venture into intercollegiate competition in hockey, only to be defeated by a more experienced visiting side from Dalhousie. The reverse was avenged, however, in Halifax in March 1898, and hockey was henceforth a major preoccupation at Mount Allison during the winter months.[93] So much so, in fact, that within a few years the rivalries fostered by the inter-class league had become intense enough to cause dissension within the university side. 'Mount Allison first,' admonished the *Argosy* in January 1904, 'then when you have done your best for the garnet and old gold it will be time enough to think of [the classes of] noughty this and that.' Evidently in that year there was little to worry about, for Acadia was roundly beaten 11–1 in the only intercollegiate match of the season, but the warning itself was evidence of heightened class loyalties.[94]

The same warning was applied at this time to the field of debating. When the first suggestion was made for intercollegiate debates, in a letter to the *Argosy* in 1899 from an anonymous alumnus, the idea had been dismissed in an editorial which argued that the Eurhetorian debates would be overshadowed and much of the educational value of debating lost.[95] On 14 March 1902, however, a competitive debate was held in Sackville with the University of New Brunswick: it was won by the visitors, who opposed the motion – topical at a time when antitrust laws were under discussion in the United States – 'that trusts are beneficial to the community.' Despite the defeat for the Mount Allison team, the event was clearly a success.[96] A return engagement in Fredericton the following year was won by Mount Allison, arguing in favour of Canadian support for an imperial defence fund, and it was in looking forward to the selection of the team for the corresponding debate in 1904 that the *Argosy* suggested that class rivalry might threaten its success as it did that of the hockey team.[97] As in the case of hockey, however, this fear was apparently unjustified. The Mount Allison debaters were sufficiently eloquent in their opposition to nationalization of Canadian railways to prevail in front of a large audience in the Sackville music hall.[98] The interest aroused by debating in these years was reflected also in the health of the Eurhetorian Society, which met weekly to discuss such issues as the justification or otherwise of the Boer war, the future of capital punishment, votes for women, the question of whether Christian missionaries were responsible for the Boxer revolt in China, and whether 'natural ability is a more potent factor in the formation of character than environment.'[99] The Eurhetorian Society also issued, in 1903, a handbook for prospective students. The book had high praise for every aspect of Mount Allison, and clearly came in response to the frequent contention of the *Argosy* that the university did not advertise itself adequately: 'the amount of advertising done for our college,' the magazine commented in 1902, 'is about as extensive as the famous chapter on snakes in the Natural History of Iceland.'[100] Naturally, the handbook gave some prominence to the Eurhetorian Society itself and to intercollegiate debating, which it described as a 'war of words.'[101] This was a competitive era – 'the strenuous life' was the ideal put forward by Theodore Roosevelt – and intercollegiate debate, along with athletic contests, had become established as an important means of maintaining the honour of Mount Allison.

One observer who was not convinced of the merits of the competitive spirit was the theological professor, Charles Stewart. Reporting to the board of regents in June 1903 that the attendance of students had fallen at religious services and prayer meetings, Stewart suggested that 'the eagerness for Athletic superiority' might be a major reason for the decline.[102] Yet over the preceding decade there had been a variety of changes in the religious life of Mount Allison, often in response to more general developments in Canadian Methodism. When Albert Carman had visited the Maritimes in the summer of 1892, he had won praise from the *Wesleyan* for a sermon before the New Brunswick and Prince Edward Island Conference in which he had attacked the 'so-called Higher Criticism.' Carman's views were certainly in harmony with those of Stewart, who himself declared to the Nova Scotia Conference two years later that he held to traditional methods of biblical study and, as reported in the *Wesleyan*, 'advised them to get some one else if they were anxious to propagate modern criticism, etc.'[103] Both Carman and Stewart were thus avowing their adherence to one side in a dispute which was gathering increasing force within the Methodist church as in other major Protestant denominations. The approach to biblical study known as the 'lower criticism' – the examination and comparison of various texts in order to decide which was the authentic version and therefore the genuinely inspired word of God – was not in question. Carman, for example, had specifically exempted such researches from his criticism in 1892, while Stewart had long expounded techniques of textual analysis to his students at Mount Allison; he had also lectured in this vein to the Mount Allison YMCA in the spring of 1892, on 'some misread and unread portions of the Old Testament.'[104] The 'higher criticism,' however, was the product of more modern approaches to literary study, as applied to the Bible. When W.M. Tweedie had stressed, in his inaugural address, the need to study the evolution of language, and the desirability of placing literary study in the wider context of the study of man in society, he identified insights that had become crucial to the more radical forms of biblical criticism. He himself dealt on occasion with scriptural topics, but within his own field of English literature rather than in terms of the original biblical languages: his contribution to the YMCA lecture series of 1892 concerned 'the Bible in England before the Authorized Version.'[105] The higher criticism as such concentrated upon analysing the sources and methods used by the authors of biblical books in order to determine such questions as the authorship, the date, the historical background, and the cultural context of each. The implication was that while the scriptures did represent the word of God, they had been set down in writing by people who had not only the limitations shared by all human beings, but also those imposed by their own personal characteristics and the culture of their times. It was therefore necessary to interpret accordingly, and some parts of the Bible might well be found to be less important than others, some to be taken literally and others allegorically. Among other insights, the biblical account of creation might be seen as the attempt of a relatively unscientific culture to express a truth which in modern times could be better rendered by exploring the mysteries of God's work through evolution; the new interpretations of the words of Jesus could also lead, together with other intellectual currents of the times, to a social interpretation of Christianity.[106]

Clearly, for an older generation of Methodists, there was much in the higher criticism that challenged the traditional Protestant concept of Christian faith, which had been based upon literal interpretation of scripture and the winning of individual souls. Charles Stewart, wrote a former Mount Allison theological student, 'like Elijah ... was very jealous for the honor of God and very desirous of defending the "young brethren" from the leaven of modern thought, which, much to his dismay, he felt was beginning to vitiate the purity and power of the Christian faith.'[107] Modernist approaches, therefore, were not taught in the faculty of theology at this time. In addition to Stewart, the teaching members included David Allison (an *ex-officio* member as president and also professor of logic and biblical literature), Ralph Brecken (professor of homiletics until 1901), and C.H. Paisley (professor of New Testament exegesis and church history from 1896 and Stewart's successor as dean in 1903). Each of the ordained members was a veteran – Stewart had become a probationary minister in 1852, Paisley in 1866, and Brecken in 1869 – and none had received any part of his training in the strongly liberal faculty of theology at Victoria University.[108] This did not imply that teaching at Mount Allison had a closed or authoritarian character. Paisley in particular was well known for inviting dissent from the arguments he presented in class: 'nothing pleased him more,' recalled one of his students, 'than to have [the students] ... give intelligent reasons for disagreement.'[109] Yet there is no evidence of any fundamental disagreement within the faculty. Reports made quadrennially to the general conference identified certain problems during the 1890s, but they were practical difficulties concerning the need to persuade financially hard-pressed theological students to invest five years in college training, including a four-year arts course, rather than taking the minimum of two years followed by a longer probationary period. 'The cause of the Redeemer demands the best trained intellects for the salvation of men,' declared the report presented by Stewart in 1902. Of the commitment of the theological faculty to intellectual quality there was no doubt; but as yet the framework was that of traditional evangelistic Methodism.[110]

Outside of the theological faculty, however, the modern strains of thought had greater currency at Mount Allison. During the early 1890s, the *Argosy* expressed concern on several occasions at the small attendances at Sunday morning Bible classes: attendance at a short chapel service each morning was compulsory, as was attendance each week at a church of the student's choice, but other religious meetings were held on a voluntary basis. 'It is well known,' declared an editorial in November 1891, 'that those who are anxious to study the bible are for the most part dissatisfied with the present system.' The solution, it suggested, lay in a more systematic curriculum, preferably laid out over four years and integrated into the general university course: students might thus acquire 'a fair knowledge of that Book which more than any other influences the destinies of men and nations.'[111] Six months later, in an editorial praising the lectures given by Brecken, Stewart, Tweedie, and Borden in the YMCA series, the magazine repeated its suggestion, adding that the Bible study course should be made compulsory for all students. Whether that proposal would have been supported by the student body as a whole is doubtful, and the suggested radical reform of Bible study was never implemented; yet the success of the lecture series, which caused the *Argosy* to hope 'that this is but the thin end of the wedge in the matter of Bible study at Mount Allison,' showed the interest that existed.[112] By 1897, another problem had been identified. In the otherwise adequate university library, the *Argosy* suggested, there was one 'woeful lack': there were few modern theological works, and 'nothing whatever bearing on the great questions which are agitating the whole realm of theology.'[113] That questions, and fundamental ones, should be characteristic of theological enquiry was a principle that the higher criticism fostered, and the 1890s at Mount Allison saw an increasing tolerance of the resulting complexities. The admonition to freshmen delivered by the *Argosy* in October 1900 recognized that there might be wide variations among students in their personal responses to such questions, while still affirming the basic importance of spiritual life:

> We are as anxious as you are that you should develop yourself mentally and physically. 'Mens sana in corpore sano,' you know. But we would also urge upon your consideration the fact that man is a tripartite being, and would suggest that you take special pains while at Mount Allison to develop the spiritual side of your nature. Attend the meetings of the Y.M.C.A. You are a Christian? Then do not fail to become an Active member. You are *not* a Christian? Then you may at least enrol yourself as an Associate member, and just as the members of the Association throw themselves into your sports and games, so you may aid them in their efforts – feeble ones perhaps, but still efforts – to ensure that every graduate of their *Alma Mater* shall be a complete well-rounded, manly man.[114]

Also evident in student publications was a profound concern for the moral implications of Christianity. The Eurhetorian handbook of 1903, in fact, had little to say about church attendance or other forms of religious observance in its general comments on student life, but instead stressed moral qualities: 'professors, teachers and students all unite in discouraging profanity, the use of tobacco, and intemperance. ...'[115] It was an emphasis that agreed well with the views of Howard Sprague, member of Mount Allison's first graduate class, Methodist minister in Sackville from 1899 to 1901, and a future dean of theology, who had declared in a Sackville sermon in early 1901 that at the judgment day he would rather be a Unitarian – and thus a non-believer in the miracles and the resurrection – who had striven to live a Christ-like life than an orthodox Methodist who had not.[116] As Sprague and the students were well aware, morality had a social as well as a personal aspect, and the doctrines of the social gospel were much in evidence at Mount Allison at the turn of the century. Leadership was provided by the two ministers on the arts faculty who were not members of the faculty of theology: W.W. Andrews and B.C. Borden. An historian has observed that 'the social gospel movement viewed social problems with an air of crisis,' with especial attention to the evils produced by unbridled *laissez-faire* capitalism.[117] This description was certainly borne out by Andrews and Borden in their public statements. Borden clearly showed his position when he preached in Sackville Methodist Church on 19 March 1899:

> We propose considering the school as the representative of knowledge and the church as the repository of that higher wisdom which has the fear of the Lord as its beginning. If our world is to be saved from the forces which threaten its destruction, from the economic and social evils which are gnawing at its heart, these are the twin powers which are to effect its regeneration.[118]

Andrews, for his part, served in 1902 as chairman of the Methodist connexional committee on sociological questions. This committee, first struck in 1894, was one of the major driving forces behind the social gospel movement in the Methodist church. Under the chairmanship of Andrews, its quadrennial report to the general conference in 1902 was forthright in its condemnation of economic evils, and had especially severe words for those who accumulated wealth for its own sake and those who indulged in financial speculation. The report did not adopt a socialist solution – 'there is no necessary antagonism between capital and labour' – but instead advocated Christian integrity and stewardship and 'the gospel of unselfishness.' Only through the social teachings of the church, the report argued, could salvation be found for a world preparing for 'a new industrial order' and undergoing 'the birth-throes of such a revolution.'[119]

In its strictures upon industrial evils, the social gospel clearly had greater significance in urban than in rural areas. Within the Maritime Methodist conferences – representing a region still predominantly rural despite the disproportionately great economic effects of industrial activity during the last two decades of the nineteenth century – there were divided feelings. Many conference committees balanced their advocacy of social reform with calls for personal evangelism of the traditional kind, and where social gospel measures were endorsed it was often in the hope that an ethical revival might lead to the ultimate goal of a spiritual revival.[120] By preaching the need for salvation from an impending economic crisis, therefore, Borden and Andrews were participating in a national movement but were not entirely in the mainstream of Methodist thought in their own region. One issue upon which there was substantial agreement, however, was that of the prohibition of liquor. Borden in particular was an active campaigner in this field – which he frequently linked with another major concern of the social gospel, that of electoral corruption – and won high praise from the *Wesleyan* in late 1899 for his strenuous efforts on behalf of renewal of the Canada Temperance Act, better known as the Scott Act.[121]

One member of Mount Allison who had incurred a quite different press reaction, however, in an incident of 1898, was David Allison. Under pressure from prohibitionists, the government of Sir Wilfrid Laurier had tardily fulfilled an earlier election promise to call a Dominion-wide plebiscite on the question of national prohibition. Speaking in the Sackville Methodist Church on 24 July 1898, just over two months before the vote, Allison made a number of impromptu remarks on the extent to which prohibition was likely to be effective in checking the liquor trade. As reported in the Halifax *Mail* – a report which he angrily contested a few days later – he had predicted that such a measure 'would become a useless statute on our law books' and had declared himself unable to support it. The reaction was swift and vehement, with published denunciations ranging from a reference by an anonymous Methodist clergyman, quoted in the *Chronicle*, to Allison's 'betrayal of confidence' to the Sackville *Post*'s description of his remarks as 'exceedingly inopportune and ill-advised.' Allison's disclaimer, published in the Halifax press on 30 July, admitted that he had doubts, but contended that he had been misquoted and stressed that he intended to vote in favour of prohibition when the plebiscite was held. Yet the fact that *Wesleyan* editorials were devoted to his defence on both 3 and 10 August suggests that the storm did not easily abate.[122] The damage done to the cause was probably not great, as prohibition was overwhelmingly endorsed by the three Maritime provinces, although a heavily adverse vote in Quebec was enough to reduce the national majority to a narrow one, and thus comprised the justification given by the government for not acting upon the result.[123] Nevertheless, the harshness of the condemnations visited upon Allison revealed that he had gone against strong currents of opinion in expressing his reservations on the matter. His was an older generation which had placed less faith in the legislation of social reform than did younger churchmen; as he had recalled during his controversial speech, he could remember the disastrous attempts to legislate prohibition in New

Brunswick in 1853 and 1856. Another veteran of that era was Charles Stewart, who as a young minister had clashed with the 'Ultra temperance men' and had reflected in his diary in 1856 that 'much evil ... in our own church' would result from prohibition.[124] If Stewart still had his doubts, however, he was evidently wise enough to keep them to himself. In this as in other respects, this was the age of progress, and the cause of prohibition was a matter of faith which was unlikely to be denied by scepticism rooted in experiences forty years before.

Charles Stewart, in fact, was approaching the end of his long period of service as dean of the faculty of theology. Seventy-six years old, he was succeeded by Paisley in 1903, although continuing to serve on a part-time basis as professor of homiletics until his death in 1910. The teaching faculty in theology had been reduced to two in 1901 when Brecken had resigned on grounds of ill-health, and financial difficulties had prevented his replacement.[125] In 1903, following an appeal for endowment funds, a third member was added in the person of William G. Watson.[126] With the arrival of Watson as professor of Old Testament exegesis and systematic theology, the theological faculty at Mount Allison gained its first committed advocate of modernist theology. Thirty-five years old at the time of his appointment, Watson was a native of Ontario and had obtained his BD degree from Victoria University in 1898. His inaugural address on 5 October 1903 made quite clear where he stood on his chosen subject, biblical study. While rejecting the notion that the historical method was new in the nineteenth century – it had been applied, he believed, by scholars of the early church and by the great reformers of the sixteenth century – Watson maintained that each book of the Bible 'arose in some particular historical situation, and the more we know of the times and conditions, of prevailing modes of thought, of the surrounding history, of the personal characteristics of the author, his habitual temper, whether gloomy or sanguine, his station in life, the better will we be able to understand and appreciate his work.' The scriptures contained crudities and imperfections, he went on, but to understand these was to be able to discern the true word of God underneath. The book of Genesis , for example, was not an exact scientific statement but 'a noble song of creation, in which the fact that *God created the world* stands out in blazing letters of light.' The new light shed by modern criticism, in short, had made the essential truth of the scriptures more clear than ever before.[127]

A theological student of the time, J.W. O'Brien, later recalled that Watson's views had initially seemed 'to many students brought up in the traditional school, ... somewhat radical.'[128] Charles Stewart's retirement as dean had coincided with the appointment of a faculty member whose theological standpoint was quite different from his own. Yet the transition was made without conflict: the vote of thanks for Watson's inaugural address, for example, was moved by Paisley and seconded by Stewart.[129] Stewart had long been known as a theological conservative, and he had never pretended to be otherwise. During the years since he had landed in Nova Scotia as a young circuit rider in 1852, and during his thirty-three years as professor of theology, his overriding ambition had been to serve God by saving individual souls. As a teacher, he had concentrated upon the practical preparation of young ministers for this same task. While new approaches had grown up in the meantime, challenging aspects of his beliefs, the integrity of his faith and his unyielding commitment to the religious purpose of Mount Allison had never been challenged. The *Argosy*, commenting on his retirement, refused to offer any fulsome panegyric, on the ground that Stewart had never sought nor desired such a tribute. Briefly, however, it recorded on behalf of the students, 'our cordial appreciation of the genuine manliness of Dr. Stewart's character, the ungrudging devotion of all his powers of thought and work to the interests of the students, his resolute, unswerving adherence to what is right, his sincere and unaffected piety, his accuracy and enthusiasm as a teacher, his mastery of all the subjects taught by him, above all his incomparable knowledge of the Scriptures.'[130] At the time of his retirement, Stewart's professoriate was the longest in the history of the university, and his ministerial career went back to the time when the Wesleyan Academy had been the only Mount Allison institution. Since that time, he had consistently spent himself in the interests of an able and vigorous Methodist ministry in Eastern British America.

The turn of the twentieth century came at a time of intellectual exhilaration and creativity not just at Mount Allison but throughout the western world. This was a period of discovery both in science and the arts, when outstanding names emerged in many fields. Curie, Einstein, Weber, Freud, Zola, Joyce, Sibelius, Picasso: these were but a few of those who contributed to an extraordinary flowering of knowledge and of aesthetic experience. Yet in other respects it was a time of profound discouragement and fear of the future. The attack on traditional concepts of rationality implied by modern developments in psychology, the growth of anarchism and the resulting series of assassinations of heads of state, including President William McKinley of the United States, and the growing recognition of the social problems brought about by urbanization: such were some of the elements of the uncertainty which in North America paralleled the 'fin-de-siècle pessimism' of many European thinkers. Faith in progress, therefore, had its paradoxical aspects.

The progressive optimism of the social gospel was inseparable from the profound sense of crisis which gave the movement its urgency. The strenuous life and the high value put on athletic achievement had its counterpart in the perception, gained from Freud and others, that the human being had sinister depths hitherto unsuspected. The higher criticism of the Bible, while frequently cited, as by Watson, as a joyful reaffirmation of religious truth, was none the less built upon a rejection of more traditional beliefs in the light of modern scientific and humanistic discoveries. Mount Allison, as well as feeling reverberations from these wider disturbances, also encountered at the turn of the century a brief interruption in the hitherto invincible optimism of the two previous decades. The ideals of the university were called into question, and the result was a temporary loss of confidence, a revelation of ambivalent feelings which was soon lost in a further surge of expansion but which deserved to be remembered for the future.

Among the most acute and consistent critics, to judge by the columns of the *Argosy*, were the students. When David Allison remarked in a speech in Halifax during the spring of 1895 that modern students 'demanded to know the reasons of things,' he no doubt had in mind not only recent conflicts between students and administration at the University of Toronto, but also a strongly worded editorial of support for the Toronto students in the *Argosy*. A university had obligations towards those who agreed to pay to take its courses, the *Argosy* suggested, and the student magazine itself had an important role in ensuring that those obligations were fulfilled:

> At the annual discussion of University affairs representatives of the students are not usually called on to give their views of the general condition and management of the University. If this were the case it could no longer be said that it would be right for them to point out defects in the government of the University through the college paper – but as long as they have no other opportunity to explain their views on such subjects the pages of the college journal must be left open to publish honest convictions and good suggestions from any students or body of students.[131]

The *Argosy* practised what it preached. A few months before, it had published a strong attack on examinations as a means of evaluation. Targets in the ensuing years included senior orations – 'the system is a farce and ought to be abolished,' declared an editorial in 1899 – and inadequate sports facilities.[132] In 1902, a new campaign began with an editorial lamenting the lack of growth in student numbers over a ten-year period, and suggesting that many students were now drawn from families which had a long association with Mount Allison:

In other words, while other institutions are enlarging their borders, Mt. Allison is living, so to speak, in the past, with but a feeble attempt to build up a new class of patrons. ... There is no reason in the world why the Ladies' College across the way should be filled to overflowing, while our superb Residence has a dozen or so vacant rooms. These are prosperous times for the Maritime Provinces, and prosperity should be felt in the University as well as in the busy mart.[133]

The *Argosy*'s comments on student numbers were incontestable. In the decade between 1891 and 1901, the number of undergraduates had grown by only eleven, from 62 to 73. Within that period, there had been growth up until the 1895–6 year, when a peak enrolment of 94 was reached, and then decline until 1900–1. The following year of 1901–2 saw a renewed rise to an enrolment of 86, but there was no doubt that in an age which valued progress the growth during the overall period was unimpressive.[134] The *Argosy* was inclined to attribute the difficulty to a lack of advertising, and this was obviously potentially easy to correct, despite David Allison's statement to the board of regents in 1899 that he considered deliberate advertising to be less appropriate for the university than for the other two institutions.[135] What might be more damaging was the increasing tendency in the late 1890s for Mount Allison students to attend because of family connections. Clearly the building up of family traditions at the university was not harmful in itself; but the *Argosy* was well justified in commenting that 'no one should be attending Mt. Allison *simply* because his father or uncle, or some other relative attended before him.'[136] Worst of all was the possibility that the university would come to be seen as an exclusive club. At a time when higher education was attained only by a small proportion of society, any institution which drew its clientele overwhelmingly from families whose older members had been to university was serving only a small elite. Mount Allison had purported from the beginning, and had earnestly striven, to make education available to all who sought it and could profit by it. A special educational number of the *Wesleyan* in 1896 had praised the increasing availability of bursaries, and had stressed that Mount Allison was not only for the rich.[137] It was true that prize and scholarship funds had grown. It was also true that individual professors had been known to assist hard-pressed students by guaranteeing loans.[138] But by the turn of the century there was reason to fear that this crucial element of what Mount Allison had always stood for was in serious jeopardy. Furthermore, there was still a strong tendency for Mount Allison graduates to enter certain professions. Although the proportion of graduates of the 1890s entering the clergy and the law had fallen somewhat by comparison with the three previous decades, this had been compensated by a larger proportion entering teaching and medicine. What had remained constant since the college began was that just over 80 per cent (80.6 per cent in the 1890s) of those known to have entered a formal career after graduation had entered one of the four professions.[139] Thus, if the Mount Allison student body was not growing and was made up substantially of members of Mount Allison families, the university would be open to the observation that it was not only serving an elite but was perpetuating it by producing graduates in their parents' image.

There was also another respect in which Mount Allison's fulfilment of its professed ideals was questionable at the turn of the century. One of the principles on which the college had been founded was that it would help to keep trained and talented Maritimers within their own region. In the 1890s, for the first time in four decades, less than half of the Mount Allison bachelor's degree graduates (48 per cent) stayed in the Maritime provinces, as measured by their locations in 1903. It was true that a further 4.6 per cent were located in Newfoundland and 2.0 per cent in Bermuda, both of which comprised parts of Mount Allison's traditional constituency; but there were now very substantial minorities moving either elsewhere in Canada (19.1 per cent) or to the United States (21.7 per cent).[140] It would, of course, be foolish to blame Mount Allison for the personal choices made by its graduates in later life. Out-migration from the Maritimes in the late nineteenth century was characteristic of all parts of the region and all sections of society. 'The exodus,' one historian has written, 'had taken on the characteristics of a mass migration. ...'[141] Similarly, the lack of growth of the student population must be seen in the context of the stagnation of overall population growth which had been caused by out-migration and more specifically in that of the related lack of growth in the membership of the Methodist church in the region. Between 1891 and 1921, in fact, membership grew from 102,368 to 105,349, a rise of only 2.9 per cent in thirty years.[142] Yet even allowing for these circumstances, a university which was serving a narrowing clientele within the Maritime provinces, and was increasingly training students who would soon take their talents elsewhere, had little justification for claiming to itself the ideals that Mount Allison did. New developments after the turn of the century would help to restore the balance, but in this respect the late 1890s had been a dangerous time.

Also at this time, Mount Allison faced serious criticism in the local community. In late 1895, 'a suffering tax-payer' wrote to the *Chignecto Post* to protest against the tax-free status of the institutions. The writer did not question the status of the educational buildings, but pointed out that the university also owned certain pieces of property adjoining the campus which were rented for profit. 'They should pay taxes on that property in the same proportion as it has always been taxed,' the letter concluded, 'as all can readily see that if they got clear of taxes the moment they purchased property, with their immense means it is only a question of time when they will own the principal part of the town.' The point was apparently well taken, despite an anonymous letter in defence of the institutions the next week, for when tax assessments were published in April 1896 Mount Allison was included with an assessment of $7000: a small amount that clearly did not represent the campus itself but rather the off-campus lands.[143] Two years later, the institutions were suspected of self-seeking motives of a different kind, when S.W. Hunton resigned from the local school board to protest allegations – presumably based on the assumption that the academy was being protected from competition – that Mount Allison was using its influence to prevent the building of a public high school.[144] The year of 1898, in fact, was not a good one for the local reputation of the institutions, for in the late summer a pamphlet was circulated by C.L. Chisholm, dismissed in July from his position of violin teacher in the conservatory for alleged drunkenness. In lurid detail, Chisholm described episodes of 'gluttony, hard drinking and sensualism' at the ladies' college. The nature of his revelations made them difficult to refute, although the later comment of another teacher that 'Chisholm had the most fertile imagination, almost, of anyone I have ever known' was probably accurate enough.[145] On this or on more substantial issues, Mount Allison did not lack supporters in the town of Sackville. The *Post* reminded its readers in late 1901 that each student spent about $260 per year in the local district, and suggested that the economic, cultural, and educational benefits to the town had ensured in recent years 'that the appreciation of the Mt. Allison colleges on the part of the average citizen has been steadily increasing. ...'[146] It remained true, however, that the growth of the institutions, which had made them more and more conspicuous in the life of Sackville, had increased the scope for friction between town and gown.

A measure of the extent to which faith in progress was shaken at Mount Allison by the uncertainties of the late 1890s was the appearance of statements which, by implication at least, challenged the very desirability of growth. The *Argosy*, in March 1896, was willing to accept that there were limits to what Mount Allison should seek to accomplish:

Probably very few ever expect to see a law or medical faculty added to our arts faculty for the simple reason that Sackville is but a country town and has no supreme court or general hospital. A country town may be an ideal place for an arts college, but it seems imperative that the university that embraces law and medicine should have its seat in some large city where students in law can have the privilege of visiting the courts, and students in medicine, the hospitals.[147]

In themselves, these arguments were unremarkable. Twenty years before, they would have seemed so obviously true as to be trite. Yet ten years before they would have been hotly disputed. The acceptance of limits upon Mount Allison's growth was not characteristic of the 1880s or of the early 1890s, nor would it be of the first decade of the twentieth century; but the ideal of the small college, which was never entirely lost at Mount Allison even in the expansionist years, re-emerged strongly in the period at the turn of the century.[148] The ambivalence as to the essential nature of Mount Allison, presaged at this time, was to become a major issue as the institutions struggled to cope with the changed conditions which followed the First World War.

Mount Allison's turn-of-the-century crisis of confidence was resolved by a further phase of expansion. The roots of this development, however, lay in a more tangible misfortune. Early in the morning of 11 June 1899, fire was discovered in the university residence and by seven o'clock the building had been reduced to a ruin. As the building was empty of students at the time, there was no danger of loss of life, but almost nothing was saved from the furniture or other contents. Among the items lost were most of the personal possessions of W.M. Tweedie, at the time dean of the residence, including his library; and the contents of David Allison's office, also located in the building. The *Post*, reporting that the fire had probably originated accidentally in the furnace room, rightly pointed out that matters could have been worse: the Owens museum was saved only by the action of John Hammond and some others in continuously pouring water on the roof to extinguish sparks; and a stronger wind could have started a major conflagration in the centre of Sackville.[149] As it was, the damage was serious enough. The residence – the great symbol of prosperity at the university – had cost nearly $70,000 to build and was insured for only $45,000.[150] Yet there was little evidence of dismay. On the contrary, when the board of regents met in special session in Saint John on 20 June, it quickly resolved to use the foundation of the burned residence to build a new one as good or better: 'there should be no retrogression in any respect.'[151]

In part, the board's boldness no doubt stemmed from anticipation of the payment of a bequest of $100,000 from the estate of the wealthy Ontario manufacturer of agricultural implements Hart A. Massey. When the bequest

– one of several to Methodist institutions in various parts of Canada – was announced shortly after Massey's death in early 1896, the board had hailed it as a 'princely benefaction,' and one showing the 'unselfish and broadminded spirit of connectionalism.'[152] Connexionalism was evidently a palatable principle when it brought about the largest donation in the history of Mount Allison. It was over four years, however, before the first half of the bequest was paid, and thus the expectation of it was able to soften the blow of the residence fire. In the meantime, in 1898, a further bequest had been received from a Sackville landowner, George T. Bowser, by which a quantity of land adjoining the residence had been conveyed to the university; this provided an additional reason for rebuilding on the old site.[153] Also in prospect was the Twentieth Century Thanksgiving Fund, a national church campaign from which Mount Allison eventually drew almost $15,000. The report of 1902 to general conference expressed the 'poignant regret' of the board of regents that this sum should have had to be devoted 'to repairing loss rather than to inaugurating new agencies and appliances,' but it was none the less appropriated entirely to the rebuilding of the residence.[154]

The new residence was eventually built for just under $80,000. With creditable optimism, David Allison had predicted that it could be open by January 1900, but the blowing down of the partly completed walls by a wind and rain storm the preceding October had ended any such hope.[155] It was, in fact, September 1900 when the new building opened to the students. Constructed of brown stone, it was closely comparable to its predecessor in size, although the substitution of a 'hip-roof' for the mansard roof of the old building made the new residence a few feet higher. The *Argosy* reported mixed feelings among the students. The new residence was, it reported, undoubtedly more comfortable than the old one, and was a more substantial building. Yet it was less pleasing aesthetically – a fair point – because of the lack of a tower at the south end to balance those in the centre and to the north; and the interior suffered from a lack of ventilation.[156] The university calendar was more laudatory, as it enumerated the many modern amenities of the building. Understandably, it stressed that the danger of fire had been carefully guarded against in the building's design, with brick fire walls and a sophisticated system of water-hoses throughout. The residence, in short, 'may challenge comparison with any students' residence in Canada.'[157] The surmounting of such a disastrous fire as that of 1899 was an invigorating experience. A pessimist might have been tempted to point out that the costly rebuilding had ensured that, even after the first $50,000 of the Massey bequest had been added to the university's balance sheet in 1902, a debt of $51,184.71 remained outstanding. A more common reaction, however, was that of A.D. Morton, a graduate of 1864 and a member of the Nova Scotia conference visiting committee to Mount Allison. Inspecting the campus in late 1899, while the new residence was under construction, Morton was profoundly affected by what he saw:

> The first half century in the history of these Institutions has witnessed great progress, but they are only as yet in their initial stages of development. Fifty years from now! But my mind staggers. My pen is inadequate to the portrayal of what will be.[158]

The prospect of future expansion did not stagger the mind of W.W. Andrews. Since his first proposal in 1891, Andrews had never given up the notion of a school of applied science at Mount Allison. From time to time he had reminded the board of governors of this possibility, and during the 1890s he had introduced certain elements of engineering work into his science curriculum: all freshmen science students, for example, studied 'the Dynamo, the Motor, the Transformer, the Telegraph and Microphone' as part of their course in physics.[159] In early 1901, Andrews started a serious effort on behalf of engineering at Mount Allison by approaching the faculty of applied science at McGill University for a definition of the conditions under which Mount Allison students might enter the advanced years of engineering at McGill.[160] Receiving an encouraging reply, he set about the difficult task of raising funds. By May, he had enlisted the assistance of the retiring lieutenant-governor of New Brunswick, A.R. McClelan. McClelan, an academy student of the 1840s, was a former member of the board of governors and a former president of the alumni association. His political career as a Liberal had been a long one, beginning with his election to the New Brunswick legislature in 1854 and including almost thirty years in the Canadian Senate prior to his appointment as lieutenant-governor in 1896.[161] McClelan's agreement to donate $5000 enabled Andrews to go before the board of governors with a specific proposal for a 'McClelan Institute.' Discussing the matter on 28 May, the board was sympathetic. Andrews, with the assistance of J.M. Palmer, was authorized to inspect the 'Old Lodge' – the original college building, which now stood empty – to ascertain whether it was in a suitable condition to be adapted as an applied science building. If the verdict were favourable, work could start on renovations as soon as a total of $10,000 had been raised for the purpose.[162]

By March 1903, after a winter of campaigning, Andrews was reported to be near completion of the $10,000 fund, including the contribution from McClelan. During the summer, the old lodge was raised five feet to accommodate a basement, and the interior fitted with facilities not only for engineering, but also for physics, chemistry, biology, and geology. In September, the university was able to issue a special bulletin announcing that Mount Allison students would henceforth be able to complete 'the first two years in Architecture and Civil, Electrical, Mining and Mechanical Engineering, as they are given at the chief technical universities.' The McClelan School, as now instituted, differed from the full-scale engineering school envisaged by Andrews in 1891, in offering only two years of the applied science degrees. The advantages of this arrangement were obvious, however, in that costly purchases of equipment were avoided. Students could also be advised, as in the bulletin of 1903, to take the full BA course at Mount Allison, including engineering options, and then to go on to McGill for completion of professional training: not only would engineering graduates thus acquire a broader humanistic education, but the engineering and arts programmes at Mount Allison would be complementary rather than competitive. Students were informed that living expenses and tuition fees at Mount Allison were lower than at McGill, and reminded of the advantages of Sackville's location. 'Great use will be made,' the bulletin promised, 'of the foundries of Sackville, the fine engineering shops of Amherst and the railway shops of Moncton which will be visited by the students in company with their instructors.'[163] The McClelan School also enabled the academy to extend its curriculum, by providing courses in 'manual training,' which could be a means of entry into a variety of skilled trades, or could be used as the basis of a university training in applied science. In this field, the academy was thus able to keep pace with recent developments in the public schools of New Brunswick, which had been encouraged by government grants.[164]

The original faculty of the McClelan School had four teaching members, including Tweedie and Hunton, who were to teach English and mathematics respectively. Andrews was professor of chemistry and physics, and in 1905 would be designated dean of the school, while the professorship of mechanical arts and engineering was held by a graduate of the Massachusetts Institute of Technology, W.J. Sweetser.[165] Sweetser's arrival was delayed by illness until December, and the renovated science building was also late in opening in the fall of 1903. It was not until early 1904, therefore, that instruction was seriously begun. The *Argosy* was enthusiastic over what it described as 'the most spacious scientific building in this part of Canada,' and used its editorial welcome for Sweetser to call for the expansion of the two-year course into a full degree programme.[166] Four months later, at the official opening on 19 April 1904, McClelan himself endorsed this hope in his speech before the large assembled crowd. In the meantime, however, the affiliation with McGill had successfully been negotiated, so that holders of Mount Allison's two-year certificate of applied science were entitled to admission to the third year of the McGill applied science programme. Even as operated on a two-year basis, the

McClelan School was the only one of its kind in Canada at a Methodist institution, as the *Wesleyan* pointed out with satisfaction. There was satisfaction too for veterans of Mount Allison to see the original college building put to good use once again; David Allison recalled in his speech at the opening that he had taught the first class to be held there forty-two years before.[167]

Although the affiliated engineering course was new in 1904, Mount Allison graduates had enrolled in the McGill applied science programme in the past, on the basis of the science courses they had taken from Andrews. They had gained a high reputation. Assuring Andrews in late 1903 that the Mount Allison request for affiliation would be granted without difficulty, the dean of the McGill applied science faculty had based this assessment on 'my experience of the students you have already sent us, who are amongst the very best we have ever had in the Faculty.'[168] As an unsolicited testimonial this was clearly a compliment not only to Andrews but also to the general academic standards of Mount Allison. That Andrews and Tweedie may have been the most demanding of the professors is suggested by the results of a survey of matriculation standards at Maritime universities, conducted by the *Educational Review* in 1897, which found that Mount Allison's requirements were especially rigorous in science and English.[169] Yet there was evidence too of academic success in other fields. From the honours mathematics course taught by Hunton, ten graduates went on to post-graduate study between 1893 and 1904, including seven who subsequently gained degrees from Harvard University; four of the ten ultimately gained PHD degrees and took academic appointments.[170] A.D. Smith, who was affectionately described by a student of the 1890s as teaching 'rather in the manner of a genial host entertaining his guests,' had also won praise from an earlier student, J.C. Webster, for his 'masterly grasp of his subject.' From Webster, who at the time of writing was much more inclined to see the bad than the good in Mount Allison, this was an exceptional tribute.[171] In its curriculum, the university was introducing extensions in various directions. History, for example, emerged as a subject in its own right with the introduction of a course on medieval Europe in 1897. The emphasis on professional subjects was shown not only in applied science, but also in the preparatory work available in law and medicine – the exemption from the first year of legal study at Dalhousie, granted in 1896, was matched in 1904 by a similar exemption in medicine granted by McGill to honours science graduates from Mount Allison – and in the introduction in 1903 of a two-year diploma course in 'Finance and Commerce' for graduates of the academy's commercial programme who wished to continue their studies at a higher level.[172] Enjoying academic success and seeking to extend its clientele through increased attention to professional education, Mount Allison University in the early years of the twentieth century experienced a renewal of confidence.

At the same time, student numbers rose substantially. From the attendance of 73 in the 1900–1 year, there was steady growth even before the engineering students began to swell the numbers further. In the autumn of 1904, enrolment in the regular arts programme surpassed one hundred for the first time, and the 15 engineers made up a total of 116.[173] Expansion and optimism were evident once again, and one sign of the mood of the time was the curt rejection given in 1902 by Mount Allison to an effort initiated by Dalhousie University to reopen the question of university federation. 'Under present circumstances,' loftily declared the board of governors, 'the Board does not feel itself at liberty to respond favorably to the request for a Committee such as the communication [from Dalhousie] desires.'[174] The *Argosy* was not so sure, wondering why the Maritime provinces could not 'form a "Trust" and do away with the "wastes of competition,"' but it was a solitary voice. The university senate was prepared to co-operate with Dalhousie on such a matter as mounting a joint campaign for Rhodes Scholarships for the Maritimes, but on the question of federation Mount Allison now took the same view as did Acadia: that there was no point in discussing a dead issue.[175] By October 1903, the *Argosy* had regained its assurance that Mount Allison could and should stand alone. The editors' exhortation to the freshman class had a militaristic tone as it looked forward to future advances:

> You have come to us in an eventful year, the yar of the birth of the greater Mount Allison. New professors, new departments, new laboratories and halls of teaching have come all at once. Now as never before we can advocate Mount Allison. Good men in the ranks of her students were worthy of the former days. Let your class set a new pace and be worthy of the new days. One, two, catch the step. Quick march![176]

The sense of a new era was characteristic too of the largest of the Mount Allison institutions, the ladies' college. Yet the twentieth century had begun tragically for the ladies' college, with the unexpected death of Mary Mellish Archibald, of pneumonia, while on a visit to New York in January 1901. For fifteen years, she had taken a leading part not only in teaching and administration but also, with Borden, in promoting the great expansion of the early 1890s. 'Although a genuine woman,' recalled an article in her memory in the *Argosy*, 'with all the gracious and benign experiences of a wife and mother, she was no insipid sentimentalist, but as resolute in the right as Luther himself, and quite capable at times, when occasion called for it, of using the steel hand under the velvet glove.'[177] The importance of Archibald's role at the ladies' college had been recognized in 1897 when her title had been changed from the traditional one of chief preceptress to vice-principal. A further tribute was the appointment of an experienced administrator and highly qualified academic as her successor in that position. Emma S. Baker had held positions as preceptress for a total of thirteen years in women's colleges in Ontario and Pennsylvania. In 1899, she had graduated from the University of Toronto, and she had then spent two years in post-graduate study at Toronto in psychology – working on the aesthetics of light and colour – before her appointment at Mount Allison. In 1903, she attained the distinction of receiving the first PHD degree in philosophy granted by the University of Toronto, and one of the first two such degrees in any discipline granted by that university to women.[178] That a candidate as strong as Baker should become vice-principal showed clearly that after Mary Mellish Archibald there could be no question of a return to the previous custom of relying upon an inexperienced teacher as the chief female administrative officer of the ladies' college.

The graduation of Baker in 1903 also brought to two the number of ladies' college faculty members who held the PHD. The university, by comparison, had none. The other was Raymond C. Archibald, the son of the deceased vice-principal. Since graduating from Mount Allison with honours in mathematics in 1894, Archibald had studied in the United States and Germany, taking his MA degree from Harvard and his PHD from the University of Strasburg.[179] A talented violinist as well as a mathematician, he had returned to the ladies' college as teacher of geometry in the literary department, and teacher of violin and harmony in the conservatory. Profoundly affected by the death of his mother, Archibald decided to remain at the ladies' college for a number of years beyond what he had originally intended to be a short stay, in order to build up a library in her memory. It was a project in which he had the support of the alumnae association – 'for many years,' the association had commented in May 1901, Mary Mellish Archibald had been 'the central personality in our Society' – and resulted in the permanent inclusion of the Mary Mellish Archibald Memorial Library as a distinct part of the library first of the ladies' college and then of the university.[180]

Mary Mellish Archibald also left an important legacy to the ladies' college in the form of the plan for expansion upon which she and Borden had been working at the time of her death. In late 1900 Borden had begun to consult architects on a possible new north wing, to replace Lingley Hall. The ultimate goal, which Borden later attributed to Archibald's 'grand faith and wise provision,' was to replace all the existing wooden buildings by structures in stone or brick.[181] By May 1901, he was ready to put the proposed new wing before the board of governors; with an attendance of 168 students in 1900–1, and considerable growth foreseen, he was able to present a strong case.[182] Nevertheless, the board's consent was not easily obtained. While a resolution was passed approving a new building when financial conditions might permit, the scheme was deferred for the time being. The postponement represented the growing concern of some members of the board, and notably the treasurer of the institutions, Josiah Wood, over the growing burden of debt: quite apart from the large amount owed by the university, the ladies' college still had an amount of almost $20,000 outstanding on the Owens Museum. Wood's personal friendliness towards the ladies' college was shown later in the year, when he arranged for the excavation of a small lake on the college grounds which was thenceforward an adornment of the campus. Yet when the board met again in May 1902, he still opposed the proposed extension. This time Borden was ready. The Massey bequest, he argued, had been given to the institutions as a whole and not solely to the university, and the ladies' college was entitled to share in the benefits. Borden won his point, at least in that the matter was referred to the board's executive committee, which reported back to a special meeting in January 1903. The recommendation was not for a north wing, but rather for a brick annex to be built out from the back of the central ladies' college building; it would supply residential accommodation for forty students, as well as a new dining hall and kitchen. On the basis of this compromise proposal, approval was given, and the addition was complete by the end of 1903.[183]

When the annual profits of the ladies' college were added to the $10,000 allocated from the Massey bequest and over $14,500 raised during 1903 specifically for the new building, Borden was able to meet construction expenses without adding to the debt. There was an anxious moment in early 1904 when contractors' bills were presented before funds were available to meet them, but for the most part optimism prevailed. The *Wesleyan* looked forward to further expansion, while the newly started ladies' college magazine, *Allisonia*, noted that Borden had declined a student request that the new annex should be named in his honour. 'He wishes,' the report continued, 'to immortalise the name of the man (or woman) who will put a new Stone Ladies' College in front of the addition which has just been completed.'[184] The institution's next venture, in fact, was not a new stone college, but it did bear the name of a woman whose donation had made possible its development: the Lillian Massey-Treble School of Household Science. When W.W. Andrews had first proposed the establishment of a school of applied science at the university, he had envisaged the inclusion of a programme in 'Domestic Chemistry.'[185] This concept had been endorsed by the alumnae association, and it was natural that the beginning of the McClelan School should prompt its revival. Accordingly, the bulletin announcing the engineering programme in September 1903 also announced that a course in domestic science would be offered as a training for teachers, with special emphasis on the study of food products and home hygiene. The original intent had been to accommodate the laboratories in the basement of the new ladies' college annex, but on the prompting of Lillian Massey-Treble a more ambitious scheme was adopted of refitting the original ladies' college gymnasium – a small building first opened in 1855 – which had been moved in 1892 to a site behind the main building to serve as a dining hall, and would be replaced by the new dining facilities in the annex. Massey-Treble, the daughter of Hart Massey, had already begun the flourishing Lillian Massey School of Household Science and Art in Toronto and her offer in early 1904 to finance the conversion of the old gynmasium carried the condition that graduates of that school would have preference as teachers of household science at Mount Allison; her proposal was quickly accepted.[186]

Work on the household science hall got off to a slow start when the contractor, C.J. Silliker, was distracted by an unsuccessful campaign to become mayor of Amherst. Writing his regular column of Sackville news in the Saint John *Globe*, A.D. Smith predicted that Silliker would now 'doubtless hasten to drown his disappointment by concentrating his energies on this job, which Dr. Borden is anxious to get done as soon as possible.'[187] His optimism was apparently justified, for by May the Sackville *Tribune* – a new local newspaper begun in 1902 by a young Mount Allison graduate, C.C. Avard – was greeting the new facilities with the expectation that 'girls will go out from this school fully equipped to grapple with domestic difficulties and as veritable household angels, to comfort and bless.' More prosaic, but just as welcome, was the verdict of the New Brunswick department of education: J.R. Inch, still superintendent, informed Borden that the ladies' college diploma would henceforth be accepted as a sufficient qualification in domestic science for teachers in the public schools of the province.[188] The two-year normal course remained the principal programme in household science, although in 1905 a one-year course was added for those who were already teaching, and also a 'housekeeper's course' for non-teachers.[189] Along with music and the fine arts, household science – or 'home economics' as it was later known – would be one of the three ladies' college departments to survive the demise of that institution. It would continue to be taught at the university until suspended in 1971.

The inclusion of domestic science was not the only development in the ladies' college curriculum in the early years of the twentieth century. Instruction in elocution had been offered for many years, but in 1902 it was formalized in a three-year diploma course, designed to enable the student 'to give forcible and graceful expression to her ... thoughts,' as well as being a training for potential teachers of the subject. Two years later, the course was elaborated, retitled 'Oratory,' and affiliated with the Emerson College of Oratory in Boston.[190] There was also talk of offering degrees in music, given by the university on the basis of instruction in the conservatory: the proposal was not acted upon for the time being, but was studied by a committee of the university senate in 1903.[191] What was clear was that the ladies' college was now able to offer to its students a great variety of choices. Whether a student came simply to finish her education in social skills, or whether she looked towards a working career, suitable instruction could be offered in several fields. It was this diversity which provided the basis for much of the rejoicing and congratulation which marked the institution's fiftieth anniversary, celebrated by a series of gatherings on 4 and 5 October 1904. One of the highlights was the speech on the evening of the 4th, in Beethoven Hall, by the only living former principal, J.R. Inch. Recalling the 'dilapidated building, badly equipped in every way' which he had found on taking office in 1864, he contrasted the uncertainties of that time with the solid prosperity of the present. The ladies' college, he declared, 'provides courses to meet the demands of the most exacting advocate of the educational needs of women'; it was, indeed, in his opinion, 'the leading Ladies' College in the Dominion of Canada.'[192]

Inch's own achievements in the interests of women's education gave him a right to that opinion. He was voicing a faith in progressive improvement which not only fitted with the mood of that particular evening but was also characteristic of his own approach to reform in the public schools as he endeavoured to make education more widely available throughout New Brunswick society.[193] Inch further represented a common sentiment, among those celebrating the ladies' college jubilee, when he affirmed that 'for the many progressive steps that have been taken for the high reputation which the Ladies' College enjoys ... we are indebted to the present energetic principal and those associated with him.' Borden himself, in his immediately following speech, modestly gave much of the credit to former principals, and to Mary Mellish Archibald.[194] Yet just over a year before, Borden had spoken of the expansionist years in a different vein. His report at the closing exercises of 1903 had been delivered at a time when work was beginning on the new brick annex:

> While rejoicing in our prospects for growth, our outlook has some gloom and discouragement. We are undertaking an expenditure of $40,000 with less than nothing. Some tell me this means embarrassment and perhaps ruin for an institution that

has perhaps done more towards refining the homes and beautifying the life of the Maritime Provinces than any other single institution in the past 50 years. I myself should despair of working my way out from under this burden if I had not faith in God and the people of these provinces. This enterprise has not been undertaken recklessly or in a fool-hardy spirit. We have been forced to it by necessity. It was a question of going ahead and meeting the demands of the age and holding our place as the premier ladies' school in this part of Canada, or else dropping back and handing over the work to more worthy hands.[195]

Borden was an expansionist. He was also a realist, for he knew that expansion carried risks as well as opportunities. He knew that expansion could be dictated not by outrightly idealistic motives but by the more worldly necessity to compete with other institutions, and he did not shrink from that knowledge. Another whose expansionist ideals were tinged with a hard realism was W.W. Andrews. Familiar as he was with the characteristics of heavy industry – its economic demands, its social costs, its technological needs – he knew that the prosperity of Mount Allison depended upon the prosperity of the region it served. As enunciated by him, the school of applied science was not merely an aggrandizement of Mount Allison, but also a contribution to maintaining the industrial health of the Maritimes. Together the university and the regional economy could, and must, grow. Andrews, more so than Borden, was an expansionist through basic conviction. It is hard to imagine him sharing the doubts that Borden expressed in 1903. Yet he was not an expansionist for narrowly institutional reasons: he knew that the blast furnaces of Amherst, or indeed the farms of Point de Bute, were just as important to the overall community as was Mount Allison University, and he believed with the passion of the social gospel that all should serve one another. Both Andrews and Borden – and they, with Archibald, had been the major architects of growth at Mount Allison during the 1890s and the early twentieth century – had a sense of the responsibilities that were implied by expansion. The lighthearted assumption of a bright future that had been characteristic of the 1880s, understandable as it was in those for whom a growing Mount Allison had been a novelty, was not open to them. The period from 1891 to 1904 was an age of improvement, a satisfying time for Mount Allison in many or most respects. As in so much of the intellectual, social, political, or economic life of the turn-of-the-century period, however, the issues were complex. There was a sense that underneath many an expression of faith in progress there was an anxious prayer that that faith should not be misplaced.

7

Strains of the Twentieth Century: 1904–1914

In August 1958 an alumni luncheon at Mount Allison was addressed by Judge Ivan C. Rand of the Supreme Court of Canada, a graduate of 1909. 'The golden age of Mount Allison,' he maintained, 'was between 1905 and 1909. ...'[1] It was a claim that might have been made by many nostalgic alumni of different generations. Yet Rand's assertion was different, in that it was not based entirely on hindsight: he was expressing a point of view which had been widely held even during the years of which he spoke. The president and secretary of the New Brunswick and Prince Edward Island Conference remarked in their pastoral address of 1906 upon the 'unprecedented success' of Mount Allison; the Sackville *Tribune*, in the same year, was confident of 'unexampled progress and prosperity for our institutions.'[2] There was much evidence to support these conclusions. Student attendance was rising rapidly: all three institutions increased their enrolments substantially during the first decade of the twentieth century, with the total attendance of 678 in 1910–11 representing an increase of almost 80 per cent from that of 1900–1. The university had more than doubled the number of its undergraduates during this period, with the years from 1905 to 1909 in themselves witnessing an increase from 118 to 150 students.[3] The teaching staff grew also, and by 1909 there were 13 professors among the three faculties of the university. The teaching careers of the generation of professors represented by Andrews, Borden, Hunton, and Tweedie were now reaching their zenith, and it was not surprising that high academic achievements were attained. In the single year of 1905, for example, shortly after Rhodes scholarships had been opened to candidates in the Maritimes and Bermuda, Mount Allison graduates took two of these awards: Frank Parker Day the scholarship for New Brunswick, and Arthur J. Motyer for Bermuda.[4] Day and Motyer inaugurated a tradition by which 29 Rhodes scholarships would come to Mount Allison candidates over the first sixty years of the awards.

The McClelan School of Applied Science had also become well established. Writing to Frank Parker Day shortly after Day had arrived at Christ Church, Oxford, to take up his Rhodes scholarship, David Allison was in characteristically expansive mood: 'Everything has been going on well here. A hundred boarders in Residence. The new Engineering students taken as a whole are a splendid lot and embrace some of the finest young men we have ever had. ...' The *Wesleyan* looked forward to even greater things, predicting that 'in a short time we are destined to see at Mount Allison one of the largest and best engineering schools in the Dominion.'[5] Such was certainly the hope of the school's dean, W.W. Andrews, who called in April 1907 for the development of a large technical institution to serve the two provinces of New Brunswick and Nova Scotia and argued that it must be located near the interprovincial border, a description which naturally applied neatly to the McClelan School.[6] This ambition, however, was not to be fulfilled. The timing of Andrews's proposal had been no accident, for in that very month the Nova Scotia legislature had been discussing a bill to establish a technical college which all engineering students in the province could attend for their final two years, having already taken two years at one of the other colleges. In late March, the provincial government had threatened to abandon the project because of disputes over the location of the proposed college, Mount Allison presumably being one of the claimants, but the bill was ultimately passed, and the college established in Halifax under the direction of F.H. Sexton, until then professor of mining and metallurgy at Dalhousie. It opened in 1909.[7] For Mount Allison's own ambitions, the location of the Nova Scotia Technical College was a setback, despite the naming of Andrews to the governing board.[8] Yet for the continuation of the McClelan School's activities along the lines already successfully established, the foundation of the technical college in Halifax did no harm, and provided an alternative to McGill for students who had completed two years at Mount Allison. The new venture was certainly a rare effort at practical co-operation between Maritime universities.

For Andrews, the failure to have the McClelan School transformed into an interprovincial technical school acted as a spur to further advocacy of the expansion of Mount Allison. Later in 1907, he wrote in the *Argosy* of the need for new facilities at all three institutions, including the construction of a new science building for the university. 'To have a check put upon our natural expansion at this time,' he believed, 'would be a calamity which all friends of Mt. Allison may well hope to see prevented.' As a means of avoiding the limitations he feared, Andrews turned to a notion which he believed essential to the solution of the manifold social problems of the age, that of Christian stewardship.

Our help must come from those with great wealth who, since the public is the silent partner in every business, seek, by investing in our future, to pay something of the natural debt they owe to the community in which their wealth has been produced. A college is an undying institution, and he who invests life or funds in such an enterprise assures for himself an influence also undying – a place among the immortals – and makes an investment which, on account of the rich elements the colleges pour into a nation's life, must yield in perpetuity the largest and most precious returns to him who wishes his country well.[9]

As examples of what might be achieved by philanthropic donations, Andrews cited the contributions to Mount Allison of Charles Allison, Hart Massey, and Jairus Hart. The second half of the Massey bequest had recently been received and invested largely in the endowment of a chair in psychology and logic, held for the time being by David Allison. The bequest of Jairus Hart, a wealthy Methodist merchant of Halifax, had become known in late October 1906 and was expected ultimately to amount to over $100,000 after life rent had been paid to certain other legatees. A sum of $20,000 was to be made immediately available to be used for a new ladies' college building.[10]

Encouraged by the magnitude of these bequests and no doubt with the prompting of Andrews, David Allison now began a more active search for large-scale funding, although unsuccessfully. In the summer of 1907 he wrote to Andrew Carnegie to solicit funds for a new library, stressing the lack of sectarian bias at Mount Allison, as Carnegie was known to avoid donations to institutions affiliated to any particular religious body. No reply has survived on record, but in the spring of 1908 Allison wrote again to Carnegie in similar vein. This time a quick and firm refusal was received from Carnegie's secretary, James Bertram. The composition of the board of regents, Bertram wrote, showed clearly the Methodist character of Mount Allison, and even had this not been so a more careful justification of the proposed library and of the financial management of the university would have been required.[11] For the time being, this rebuff was sufficient to prevent any further appeal to potential donors outside of the Methodist community. It did not discourage Andrews, however, who now concentrated his efforts in a series of sermons and Sunday school visits throughout the Maritimes in which he spoke on Mount Allison's behalf. 'The creation of an enthusiasm for higher education,' he wrote in April 1909 to J.W. Graham of the Methodist Board of Education, 'is one of your and our great problems.' That Andrews's own dedication had not gone unnoticed had been shown a few weeks before when a correspondent of the *Wesleyan* had attributed the high student attendance at Mount Allison largely to the efforts of 'one enthusiastic man.' The strenuous efforts of Andrews during this period were in themselves arguments in favour of his contention of 1907 that 'heretofore if Mt. Allison has been convicted of folly by the passing years it has been not for the largeness but for the littleness of her plans.'[12]

At the ladies' college, growth was facilitated both by the large rise in student attendance – from 188 in 1900–1 to 322 in 1910–11 – and by the provisions of the Hart bequest. Giving his annual report at the closing exercises of 1908, Principal Borden spoke of his vision for the future of the institution: a reconstructed and enlarged Lingley Hall should be moved to a new site away from the ladies' college itself, so as to allow the erection of a new stone building on its existing site; the conservatory should be developed so as to become 'the musical centre of the maritime provinces'; and the art school should be enlarged by the beginning of a programme in 'arts and crafts,' to be regarded both as an artistic training and as a branch of technical education. By these means, Borden believed, the ladies' college would be able to maintain indefinitely its position as 'the premier ladies' college of Canada.'[13] For the realization of the more tangible elements of his plan, Borden did not have long to wait. On the basis of the Hart bequest, and with prompting from Borden, the board of regents decided on 3 June 1909 to go ahead with the stone addition, and shortly afterwards the tender was let for just over $44,000.[14] The same board meeting discussed a letter received from Charles W. Fawcett – owner of the Fawcett iron foundry in Sackville – and his sister Mabel Ryan, both former Mount Allison students, who offered to contribute $6000 for a building to replace Lingley Hall and to be named in honour of their father, Charles Fawcett. The offer was accepted, and the new Fawcett Hall planned for a site between York Street and the ladies' college lake, several hundred yards north-east of the site on which Lingley Hall was soon to be replaced by Hart Hall.[15]

Hart Hall, although not completely finished, was opened with little ceremony in early 1910 to relieve severe overcrowding arising from accommodation of the increased student population in the existing buildings. Constructed of red sandstone, it was connected to the main ladies' college by a small wooden passage, and provided rooms for some 50 students along with a new gymnasium, apartments for the college principal, and several classrooms.[16] Much more elaborate were the celebrations that accompanied the opening of Fawcett Hall on 26 May. The new building's wooden construction and white Doric pillars recalled the appearance of Lingley Hall, which it replaced, but it was a much larger structure, with a stage capable of seating 300 people, and space in the body of the hall for some 1200 more. It was presented formally to the institutions by J.R. Inch, on behalf of the donors, and received by David Allison: in speeches by those two old colleagues, and by Josiah Wood as chairman for the evening, the building was praised as a symbol of the mutual contributions of business and education. It was then inaugurated by the holding of a series of concerts – four in three days – by students of Mount Allison's own conservatory and by members of the Boston Festival Orchestra. According to the local *Tribune* the entire celebration was a notable success: not only did the concert performers bring forth 'storms of applause,' but Fawcett Hall would stand henceforth as 'an effective memorial to one of Eastern Canada's most successful men.'[17]

To be sure, the building of Hart Hall and Fawcett Hall was not without its difficulties. One problem was a short but spirited dispute between Borden and the Sackville town council over the water supply to Hart Hall. 'I do not think,' wrote Borden in a private letter in November 1909, 'that they are specially anxious to accommodate us.' The matter was settled in the following month when Borden agreed to guarantee an annual payment of $25 towards interest payments on a new water pipe; but it had shown once again that the provision of town services to the tax-exempt buildings of Mount Allison was a sensitive issue.[18] Not so quickly solved was the question of what was to be done with the displaced Lingley Hall. Consideration had originally been given to the breaking up of the fifty-five-year-old building to provide construction materials for Fawcett Hall, but this notion had been rejected eventually, and instead Lingley Hall was removed from its foundations and shifted a short distance down the hill towards the lake. There it stayed for some two and a half years, its condition deteriorating. In better days, Lingley Hall had been a graceful adjunct to the ladies' college and for many years it had housed the various ceremonial occasions of the institutions. That it should now lie derelict was the cause of much disquiet among older alumni, including the Halifax poet Matthew Richey Knight, who allowed the building to speak for itself:

> Sons, daughters mine, behold my shame,
>   Torn from mine ancient place.
> Sharers are ye in all my fame,
>   Sharers in my disgrace.
>
> Torn from the spot where once I stood
>   Since I am old and gray,

And fit not with the finer mood
   And fashion of to-day.

Another occupies my throne,
   And lords it from the hill;
But winged hosts of memories grown
   Thro' long years haunt it still.[19]

To some, the plight of Lingley Hall was a standing joke, but for others it was a serious and contentious issue: J.M. Palmer later recalled that it grew into 'the greatest snarl and biggest or knottiest question for solution I ever knew at Mt. A.'[20] Eventually, Lingley was taken apart in early 1912 and reconstructed as a gymnasium on a site near the university residence. Painted entirely in white, the new gymnasium was described by A.D. Smith as 'a ghostly and pathetic reproduction' of one of Mount Allison's earliest buildings. Its indignity, however, did not last long, as it was destroyed by fire just nine years later.[21]

Whatever the animosities aroused by the fate of Lingley Hall, the raising of Hart Hall and Fawcett Hall as its successors could not but be seen as evidence of the prosperity of the institutions, and of the ladies' college in particular. Another of Borden's ambitions was achieved in late 1909 with the completion of a new workroom in the basement of the Owens Museum for metalworking classes, which permitted the addition of further applied art courses to those in leather work, wood carving, and copper etching, which had been introduced in 1908.[22] A further area of development was the ladies' college library, which expanded from 6000 volumes in 1906 to some 10,000 in 1910, partly through the fund-raising efforts of Raymond Archibald for the specialized library of 'English and American poetical and dramatic works of the past four centuries' established by him in his mother's memory. Archibald continued to build up this collection even after his departure in 1907 to become professor of mathematics at Acadia University, and later at Brown University in Providence, Rhode Island.[23] There was also scope for optimism at the academy, where the efforts of Palmer had resulted by 1910 in physical improvements – the academy building was now lighted completely by electricity, and the fourth floor converted from an unfinished attic into boarding accommodation for 36 students – made possible by rising enrolments and annual surpluses. The academic quality of the institution was reflected in the increasing numbers of students receiving matriculation certificates for entry to the university: the 21 such graduates in 1910 represented the largest matriculating class in the academy's history.[24] As for the university, an outsider's verdict was published in November 1908, after a visit to Mount Allison by the editor of the

Educational Review. Praising the high ideals and progressive spirit of the institutions, the editor remarked upon the large classes being taught by Hunton and Tweedie. Especially warm was his description of David Allison: 'still vigorous for his years, and with his splendid teaching abilities apparently unimpaired, he is a fine example of what a scholarly and simple life may do to prolong a man's years and usefulness.'[25] Steadily growing, and under a president whose association with Mount Allison went back more than fifty years, the university had found, it seemed, an ideal balance of continuity and change.

Yet, in reality, the balance was more precarious than was immediately obvious. As early as 1907 the *Wesleyan* had given a clue, buried among its customary congratulations on the successful conclusion of the academic year, that all was not well. 'These schools,' it declared of the three institutions, 'are experiencing the embarrassment of success. In some departments more room is needed, in some more professors, and in all more money.'[26] The 'embarrassment of success' argument was frequently advanced in the interests of fund-raising in the ensuing years: the institutions, according to this interpretation, were hard-pressed to satisfy the demands created by their educational excellence, and needed further financial assistance in order to accommodate growing numbers of students and give them the best of instruction. It was an attractive and simple proposition, but it was too simple to express adequately the perilous financial predicament into which Mount Allison was drifting. First of all, the problem was not common to all three institutions. The ladies' college, admittedly fortunate in being named the chief Mount Allison beneficiary of the Jairus Hart bequest, had greatly expanded its facilities and yet by 1910 had an accumulated surplus of $5700. The debt incurred through the building of the Owens Museum in 1895 and of the annex in 1903, almost $20,000, had been paid off partly by the balance of the Hart bequest which had remained after the building of Hart Hall – about $7000 – but largely from the healthy annual profits of the institution. Even the academy, which had long been burdened by debt, was able to make improvements during these years and still reduce its encumbrance from almost $8000 in 1904 to less than $5200 in 1910.[27] These two institutions were clearly capable of enjoying success without embarrassment.

Not so the university. The debt which had first attained large proportions with the building of the university residence in 1893, and had then steadily increased, had been reduced to just over $51,000 when most of the first half of the Massey bequest had been applied to it in 1902. The extent to which debt was now assumed to be a permanent, or at least a long-lasting, condition was shown in 1904, when provincial legislation raised Mount Allison's legal maximum borrowing power by bonds or debentures from $50,000 to $100,000. Annual deficits thenceforward raised the university's debt to well over $75,000 by 1910.[28] It was possible to put a good face on the situation, as the 'embarrassment of success' argument attempted to do. After all, the debt was still relatively small when compared with the university's assets in terms of land and buildings – estimated at $397,000 in 1910 – or even with its approximately $236,000 of endowment. Furthermore, in most years – 1903–4, 1904–5, and 1907–8 were exceptions – the university had a deficit only because of the interest payments on the accumulated debt, and would have shown a small operating profit had it not been for that encumbrance.[29] Yet the fact was that the period between 1902 and 1910 had been one of rapidly growing student enrolment and one when no major capital projects had been charged to the university, since the conversion of the science building and the construction of Fawcett Hall had been separately funded by private donations; and yet serious financial losses had been incurred. That in itself was alarming, and it was all the more so for two contributing circumstances, one specific to Mount Allison and the other more general.

The specific matter was the question of whether the university's finances were being properly managed. Although the position of treasurer continued to be held by Josiah Wood, the days when the volume of the institutions' business had been small enough to be conducted by one part-time officer were long past. Wood continued to concern himself intimately with the management of the endowment fund, and his influence over general financial policies remained strong; but the day-to-day running of financial affairs inevitably took place within each institution. This situation had been recognized formally in 1904 when the board of regents had adopted new financial by-laws authorizing the heads of the institutions to open and operate bank accounts with any chartered bank and to arrange loans and overdrafts within certain limits.[30] At the university, therefore, the operating revenues and expenses, amounting by 1910 to almost $50,000 annually, were the responsibility of David Allison as president. That this responsibility was being exercised without even the aid of a bookkeeper suggested in itself that the methods used would have been more appropriate to the tiny budget which had existed during Allison's first term as president in the 1870s than to modern conditions. That few accurate financial records of any kind were being kept became apparent only after Allison's retirement in 1911, when a chartered accountant was employed to put the accounts in an orderly enough state that they could be taken over by a trained bookkeeper.[31] Allison himself took the lead in putting the matter to rights, for it was he who proposed to the board of regents in November 1911 that it should appoint a committee to enquire into his financial stewardship.[32] Nevertheless, there was much confusion. Payments due on bank loans and payments to annuitants of the university were among the items Allison had paid at times without any written record. Likewise, he had received payments and had included them in the general funds of the university without entry in the books. Thus, for example, it was difficult to assess the extent of debts that might be due to the university, as Allison's successor found out in 1911 and 1912 when trying to collect the accounts owed by former students. As late as 1944, a query in regard to the payment of a gift to Mount Allison during the early years of the century had to go unanswered because of the lack of financial records for the period.[33] The claim that the university's financial troubles were due to its success in attracting students was obviously, in this context, open to challenge.

Yet the claim, while oversimplified, was not altogether without foundation. The more general factor aggravating the university's difficulties was one which was certainly beyond its control: the incipient decline of the Maritimes as a region within the Canadian confederation. The expansion of Mount Allison had always implied an expression of confidence in the future. David Allison had appreciated this and had remained firmly optimistic; Andrews had appreciated it and had drawn the conclusion that the university must contribute directly to maintaining the prosperity of the region through its programmes in applied science; Borden had appreciated it and had occasionally had agonizing doubts. Mount Allison had always depended upon the region it served, and if the region should fall into decline while Mount Allison was expanding on borrowed money, then no amount of financial expertise would prevent a crisis: it was in this sense that the university's predicament was indeed related to the success of its deliberate growth over the previous three decades.

The industrially based prosperity which had resulted in certain areas of the Maritime provinces from the inauguration of the National Policy and the coming of the railroad had not solved all of the region's economic problems. The wealth generated had not been distributed evenly, and as some towns had experienced rapid industrial growth others had failed to recover from the decline of trade and the collapse of the shipbuilding industry which had occurred during the 1870s. The persistently high rate of out-migration from the region was evidence of the plight of these communities and of many rural areas. Nor had prosperity been uninterrupted even in the industrialized towns. During the early 1890s, primacy in the manufacturing sector of the Maritime economy passed from the secondary industries which had initially flourished, particularly in New Brunswick, such as cotton, sugar, rope, and glass, to those more directly based on the region's own resources, such as the coal, iron, and steel industries of Nova Scotia. Yet despite these problems, this era had raised the real possibility of a new industrial order for the Maritimes, and had created an optimism reflected in developments in many aspects of life in the region, as at Mount Allison. A crucial deficiency, however, and one which soon jeopardized whatever prosperity had been achieved, was the failure to develop a strong metropolitan financial centre within the region. Halifax might have fulfilled this role, but it was only at a late stage that its financiers began to show a serious interest in applying their investments to Maritime industries rather than to banks and railroads. In the absence of such a centre, Maritime firms were increasingly vulnerable to the control of interests based in Toronto or, more commonly, in Montreal. During the early years of the twentieth century, and especially in a series of consolidation movements beginning in 1909, control even of the coal, iron and steel, and related heavy industries slipped away from Maritime entrepreneurs. 'By 1914,' one historian has remarked, 'the Maritimes had become a branch-plant economy.'[34]

Thus, forces were already at work which would ultimately result in the de-industrialization of the Maritimes. By their nature, these were long-term trends, and their results did not become fully apparent until the time of the depression which followed the First World War. At that time also, a heavy blow was struck to the region by measures taken by the federal government to consolidate railway ownership, resulting in the removal of the headquarters of the Intercolonial Railway from Moncton to Toronto and the abandonment in 1920 of the differential freight rate structure which had hitherto operated with the intent of enabling Maritime products to compete on equal terms on the continental market with the products of central Canada. The 1920s, despite the strenuous political exertions of those who argued for Maritime rights, would see the region reduced to a condition not only of commercial dependence upon outside interests but also of chronic economic depression.[35] The extent of that calamity, so often in hindsight wrongly assumed to have been inevitable, could not be foreseen in the years prior to the First World War. Yet just as economic decline was already foreshadowed at that time, so too was the decline in political influence which would later ensure that even the best efforts of the region's representatives would be insufficient to safeguard Maritime interests. Crucially important in this respect was the flow of population to the west, which resulted in a reduction of Maritime representation in the federal House of Commons after each successive census. Protests brought some concessions, but by 1914 the Maritimes held only 13 per cent of the seats in the House, as compared with 24 per cent for the west; twenty years earlier the respective proportions had been 18 and 8 per cent.[36] Even more damaging in an immediate sense were the large awards of land and subsidies to the western provinces by the federal government, particularly after the establishment of Alberta and Saskatchewan in 1905.[37] Had these arrangements been accompanied by compensating monetary payments to older and smaller provinces, as had been the practice in the United States, they could have met no serious objection from the Maritimes. As it was, they ensured that the Maritime provinces would be at a further disadvantage within a Confederation which their prosperity and self-confidence had originally made them reluctant to enter.

Disparities between the Maritimes and the west were soon manifested at Mount Allison. The tendency for increasing numbers of graduates to find employment in the west was not new. 'Many of those whom Mount Allison counts among its alumni,' commented the *Argosy* in December 1903, 'are to be found in the west.'[38] Although the draining away of educated young people did not bode well for the future of the region, the trend was not immediately harmful to Mount Allison, especially if western alumni would take the *Argosy*'s advice and send generous donations back to their *alma mater*. What was unquestionably damaging was the growing inability of Mount Allison to recruit and hold faculty members of high calibre in the face of competition from the greater opportunities available in the west. In the fall of 1909, for example, two of the younger faculty members – A.D. Miller and R.K. McClung – departed for the west after only two years of service at Mount Allison. In the case of Miller, a Victoria graduate who had been professor of English Bible in the faculty of theology and professor of ethics in the faculty of arts, there were several reasons for his removal to Edmonton to become dean of theology at Alberta College. His appointment at Mount Allison had been on a temporary basis, while F.W.W. DesBarres, a minister designated to an appointment in the theological faculty, had been studying in Great Britain. Also, according to W.G. Watson, Miller had had disagreements with several of his colleagues in the faculty of arts. None the less, as Watson also pointed out, Miller was 'a strong teacher and ... respected by the students,' and his loss to Mount Allison was regrettable.[39] The departure of McClung, a DSC graduate of McGill who in 1907 had been appointed to a new chair in physics in the McClelan School, was evidently a more straightforward case of the greater attractions of the University of Manitoba for a young faculty member praised by the *Argosy* (along with Miller) for 'high scholarship and eminent professional ability.'[40]

Most shocking of all was the unexpected loss of W.W. Andrews to Regina College, Saskatchewan, in late 1910. Andrews's appointment as president of that institution came as no surprise at the headquarters of the Methodist Church, since it had already been discussed in correspondence of the board of education and had been advocated by Chancellor Burwash of Victoria.[41] Nor was it a complete surprise at Mount Allison, since Andrews had left for consultations in Regina in October, to the regret of the local *Tribune*:

Dr. Andrews is a man whom Mount Allison can ill afford to lose. It is much to be hoped that the authorities of the University will see to it that no possible step which might lead him to remain here is left untaken. Already this University has lost several strong men to the west, much to the regret of many friends of the institutions and especially to the regret of many of the younger alumni of the University.[42]

The newspaper's sentiments were undoubtedly widely shared, for Andrews's contribution to Mount Allison over a twenty-year period had been prodigious. Just a few days later, however, he cabled his resignation to David Allison, and asked to be released by Christmas; by January he was gone.[43] In the event, his career at Regina College was not long: less than two years later, he resigned the presidency of the college, after disagreements with his board of governors over plans for future development, and thenceforth devoted himself to private scientific research in Regina.[44] Mount Allison had lost not only a gifted teacher and scientist, but also a perceptive and eloquent exponent of the university's role in the region, and one who had carried the university's message into the wider community through his membership of such bodies as church conferences and the Sackville board of trade, of which he had been president. Andrews's departure was evidence in itself that the expansionist era at Mount Allison was coming to an end.

The *Argosy* gave Andrews a warm send-off in a valedictory editorial wishing him success in Regina. Recalling the recent departures of Miller and McClung, however, it also delivered a blunt warning:

We do not wish to appear selfish, but we feel it is a great pity that we should lose such men. The west is advancing by leaps and bounds, and if we must give them so liberally of our best, we will soon find ourselves placed at a hopeless disadvantage. ... If it requires increased salaries to keep able professors Mt. Allison must give them. At any price she cannot afford either to allow her educational standard to deteriorate, or her faculties to become demoralized through such frequent changes in her professoriate.[45]

It is true that salaries, as well as the opportunity for rapid advancement in new institutions, were more attractive in the west. Mount Allison's standard professorial salary remained at $1250, and one alumnus from Calgary, paying off his student account at Mount Allison, wrote in 1912 of the much higher sums available in Alberta: 'things do not seem just right with the principal here [at Mount Royal College, a newly opened Methodist college in Calgary] getting $3600 and a free house while some of you men at Mount Allison with so much more to look after toil for love and loyalty to Mount Allison.'[46] Certainly there were those who preferred to live and work in the Maritimes regardless of salary, as in the case of Frank E. Wheelock, a graduate of Acadia who had taken his PHD from Yale and had then taught at the University of Missouri, and who accepted the chair of physics at Mount Allison in 1912 as a means of returning to 'the Provinces,' despite the substantial reduction in salary which the move entailed.[47] More often, though, low salaries would inevitably be discouraging to potential faculty members. Also in 1912, a serious effort was made to induce W.M. Tweedie to accept appointment to the faculty of the University of British Columbia, expected to open shortly afterwards. Tweedie declined; but the very possibility that another of Mount Allison's senior professors might have followed Andrews to the west was an indication of the difficulty that the university now had to expect in endeavouring to maintain its academic standards.[48]

The maintenance of standards at Mount Allison was also an issue in a more general sense, particularly in 1910 and 1911, as applied to student behaviour. The growing numbers of students at the university had continued to weaken the cohesiveness of the student community, and to make more difficult the disciplinary tasks of Tweedie as residence dean. Residence regulations had been liberalized in some respects. In 1904, for example, the time at which the residence door was locked was changed from 10:00 p.m. to 11:30. Also, Tweedie had experimented in 1908 with the election of a 'student-body president' to participate in disciplinary enforcement: the *Argosy* supported him, in calling for 'total reformation in our college life' and diagnosing selfishness as 'the efficient cause of all our social and our moral ills.'[49] Yet, according to complaints which began to arrive at the university from a number of quarters, matters did not improve. During the 1910–11 year, rumours of disorder were widespread. Some reports stressed that freshmen had been subjected to a brutal initiation and year-long hazing. Others concerned alleged drinking and gambling. Some blamed the sophomore class, others the football team, others yet were not sure whom to blame. What all the reports had in common was the sense that the university residence had become, in the words of one worried father from Yarmouth, 'a veritable den of iniquity.'[50]

In part, the rumours were no doubt exaggerated: such was found to be true, for example, of a report that some Mount Allison students had been seen 'passing round a black bottle' at a football game in Truro.[51] In part, they clearly represented too the fact that older Methodist standards of personal conduct no longer necessarily prevailed among young people in the second decade of the twentieth century. Yet two damaging facts were clear. First, the rumours – which J.M. Palmer described as having spread 'throughout the Provinces' – had a basis in fact, especially as they related to the degrading treatment experienced by first-year students. Palmer, who had sent a considerable number of academy graduates to the university in 1910, wrote of 'conduct that would be regarded by many as atrocious.'[52] Secondly, no matter how much the rumours had been exaggerated in some respects, they were widely believed to be true. 'It it not encouraging' wrote A.M. Bell of Halifax, a member of the board of regents, privately to J.R. Inch, 'to have parents expressing regret that they allowed their sons to go to Sackville, and more than one has stated this to me.' Similarly, it was reported from Yarmouth in September 1911 that Mount Allison had acquired 'a pretty tough name' and that several parents intended to send their children elsewhere.[53] This prediction was certainly borne out in the enrolment that autumn, which dropped to 132 after having risen steadily for a decade and having reached 155 in the previous year. Palmer attributed the reduction squarely to the loss of public confidence which had resulted from the troubles at the university residence, and there is little doubt that his verdict was correct.[54] At a time when the university was already struggling to cope with financial and academic difficulties, it could ill afford such a substantial reduction in student numbers.

Despite the apparent prosperity of Mount Allison in the early years of the twentieth century, therefore, there were grave underlying difficulties, and by 1911 these problems were beginning to be visible for all to see. Some, such as the inability to pay competitive salaries to faculty members, were related to general trends beyond the control of the institutions. Others, such as financial laxity and disorders among the students, were more clearly the result of causes within the university. Inevitably, David Allison had to take much of the blame. Yet the responsibility could not be foisted exclusively on him. Almost seventy-five years old, Allison was a great servant of the university who was nearing the end of his active career, although still far from the end of his long life. The question was raised, therefore, as to whether the board of regents should not have taken a more active role, at least in the area of finance. 'The pity is,' wrote A.M. Bell to B.C. Borden in 1912, presumably including himself among those he criticized, 'that the Board did not insist on properly audited accounts years ago.'[55] Both Borden and Bell's son Winthrop, a graduate of 1904 and now studying in Germany, were inclined in fact to be more forthright in their opinions of the board, at least in private. Borden wrote scathingly to Raymond Archibald in April 1911 of the board's habit of '[allowing] things to drift on in their usual shilly-shally way,' while Winthrop Bell had written to Archibald in 1909 of 'indifference and absenteeism.' Bell had gone on to suggest that few if any of the board members had any realistic idea of what a university was about. 'I am afraid,' he had concluded, 'that so long as the board remains so preponderantly a Church-appointment, it will exemplify the hymn that goes: "And must I then forever live at this poor dying rate."'[56]

Bell's opinion was based on certain solid facts. The Mount Allison board at this time was constituted of 24 members appointed by the quadrennial general conference of the Methodist Church – half of whom were, by convention, ministers and half lay nominees – along with six alumni representatives elected for staggered three-year terms and two alumnae elected annually. It was, therefore, church-dominated in that the majority were church appointments. It was also, in practice, dominated by clergymen. Both because the lay church appointees tended to be infrequent attenders and because alumni representatives were sometimes ministers, there was normally throughout the quadrennium during which Bell had written his comments (1906–10) a majority of clergymen present at meetings. The only exception was the meeting of 29 May 1907, when the numbers were even at 12 attenders each of clerical and lay members.[57] Not that this in itself justified Bell's verdict – it would be foolish to assume that clergymen were by nature less competent than lay members, especially when their number included such full-time faculty members as Andrews, Borden, and Howard Sprague, dean of theology from 1908. For the board to operate successfully as planned, however, the ministerial influence had to be complemented by that of lay members. The 12 laymen nominated by general conference supposedly provided for representation of a wide variety of geographical and occupational background on the board, to reflect the varied constituency served by Mount Allison. Within limits, they did so. Of the 12, all were Methodists. Six were from New Brunswick (including three from Sackville), four from Nova Scotia (three from Halifax, and one from Bridgewater), and one each was from Prince Edward Island and Newfoundland. Their occupations were predominantly those of the wealthier strata of the middle class: five were owners or senior managers of industrial firms (including two who had also been active politicians, Josiah Wood and J.S. Pitts); three were retail merchants; two were administrators in higher education (David Allison, and Frank Woodbury, dean of the Dalhousie Dental School); one was a building contractor, and one a lawyer.[58]

What made it difficult for these men to function effectively as board members was, however, exactly what Bell had complained of: that they were often absent from meetings. Of the 12 ministers nominated by general conference, six attended all five board meetings during the quadrennium, and a further three attended the majority of the meetings. The only consistent non-attender was Reverend Levi Curtis of the distant Newfoundland conference; the remaining two seats changed occupants during the quadrennium owing to the deaths of the incumbents, but still produced five attendances between them. The alumni representatives were not quite such regular attenders – they averaged an attendance of three out of a possible six, the attenders often being residents of the Sackville area – although the two alumnae representatives were invariably present, except for one absence at a special meeting on 4 March 1908. The church-appointed laymen were the least regular attenders. Only two of them – David Allison and Josiah Wood, both Sackville residents and officers of the institutions – were present at every meeting. F.B. Black, Sackville merchant and son of the recently deceased J.L. Black, attended four times; H.A. Powell, now of Saint John, and the Charlottetown merchant James Paton, attended thrice. Five others attended only once: Woodbury, A.M. Bell, the Halifax contractor S.M. Brookfield, lumber manufacturer Frank Davison of Bridgewater, NS, and industrial manager Alfred Rowley of Marysville, NB. Two other industrialists, J.S. Pitts of Newfoundland and J.D. Chipman of St Stephen, did not attend at all. With the majority of the lay appointees thus taking only a limited interest in Mount Allison, there was an evident lack of balanced guidance of the institutions by the board of regents. When David Allison announced his resignation as president on the evening of 1 June 1910, to take effect a year later, the possibility was created that a serious crisis of leadership would be added to the university's other troubles.[59]

The designation of Allison's successor took several months. On 3 November 1910, a special meeting of the board of regents formed a committee which immediately considered several names but was unable to make any firm recommendation.[60] According to a rumour reported by the local *Tribune* some weeks before, a leading candidate had been an unnamed 'Upper Canadian gentleman,' although the newspaper had been uncertain whether he would accept the position if offered. At least one Sackville resident and graduate of the university was unconvinced that such a candidate would be suitable in any case: 'I do hope,' wrote Harriet Starr Stewart to her brother on 9 November, 'it will be a Mar. Prov. man and a Mt. A. graduate.' W.G. Watson, himself an Ontarian, had remarked in 1908, in the context of the departure of A.D. Miller, that 'there is prejudice here against Ontario men'; whether the feeling was expressed positively, as by Stewart, or negatively, as by Watson, it was probable that the new president, like all his predecessors, would be a Maritimer.[61] It was likely too that, again in common with the three previous presidents, the new president would already have strong connections with Mount Allison. There were several possible candidates who fitted this description, but one of the strongest was B.C. Borden, whose successful and profitable management of the ladies' college was a particular recommendation at this time of financial exigency. By January 1911, Borden was hinting in private correspondence that a move to the university was in prospect. 'I would be quite content,' he wrote to R.C. Archibald on the 11th, 'if they would leave me alone and let me do the work that I feel able to manage with more or less of confidence.' Content or not, Borden was the sole nominee when the board of regents met on 19 April to select a president, and his appointment was quickly confirmed.[62]

Borden accepted the position with few illusions. 'You will notice by the papers,' he remarked in a letter to Archibald the following day, 'that I have acted the fool once more and have consented to go over to the University.' Archibald's reply was apparently quick and to the point, for Borden reflected to him half-apologetically in a further letter six days later that 'I supposed you would call me all sorts of a fool for attempting to lift the University out of the hole it is in at my time of life. However some of us never learn wisdom.'[63] The new president-designate was already critical of the board of regents on two counts. The first concerned the board's failure to find a successor to him as principal of the ladies' college, when by this time of year it would already be difficult to find a suitable candidate to serve at short notice. 'The poor institution,' observed Borden, 'is now begging for a head.'[64] Several names were in fact being considered, including those of J.M. Palmer and George J. Trueman, a Mount Allison graduate of 1902 who was now principal of Stanstead College, a Methodist institution in the Eastern Townships of Quebec. The eventual appointee, however, was not initially selected to head the ladies' college, but was instead recruited to assist Borden in fund-raising. G.M. Campbell was a veteran minister of the New Brunswick and Prince Edward Island conference, an honorary DD graduate of Mount Allison in 1908, and currently an alumni representative on the board of regents. On 31 May 1911 he was appointed to a professorship in the faculty of theology, but with the understanding that his chief duties would concern the raising of endowment funds. At the time, there was no mention of the ladies' college, but shortly afterwards Campbell was designated as acting principal and a year later the appointment was made permanent.[65] Campbell was no stranger to the ladies' college. In the earliest days of the regime of Borden and Mary Mellish Archibald, for example, he had canvassed actively for students while minister in St Stephen. That his view of women's education had a different emphasis from those of previous principals was suggested, however, by the predominance of his concern that the ladies' college should prepare its students for domestic life. In his first annual report in 1912 he said, '"Women for Homes is the consistent and the peculiar motto of Mount Allison. ...'[66]

The other matter which caused Borden to be critical of the board of regents at the time of his appointment was the fund-raising campaign itself. The need for such a campaign was evident from the financial straits of the university, and had been broached to the board in the spring of 1910 in a resolution of the alumni society. At that time the board had endorsed in principle the idea of a campaign for $200,000, and had delegated to its executive committee the task of implementing the alumni society's suggestion that a full-time agent should be employed. By the time of Borden's appointment in the following April, no agent had been found, and the board voted instead that Borden should supervise the campaign personally and should submit his plans for so doing to the annual board meeting in the following month. It was this instruction which caused Borden to remark upon 'the complacent way in which the Board raises $200,000 for an Endowment Fund by passing a resolution authorizing the new President to collect it.'[67] Pressure from Borden no doubt played a part in prompting the recruitment of Campbell, although Campbell's subsequent appointment at the ladies' college would obviously diminish his usefulness as a fund-raising agent. Borden, writing to Archibald in June, took a philosophical view. 'I am beginning to understand a little more fully,' he admitted, 'the size of the contract I have undertaken in attempting the University. We will, however, have to do the best we can.'[68]

Before Borden formally took over the duties of president on 1 August 1911 there were ceremonies to be duly completed. In particular, the retirement of David Allison was a milestone in the history of the institutions that called for the commemoration of a long and distinguished career. In later years it had become evident that Allison's grip upon the affairs of the university was less sure than it once had been. Yet the vigour of his personality, which like the resonance of his great voice would remain with him throughout the years of his retirement, was still memorable for those he met or worked with. There were many ways of illustrating the length of his service to the institutions. The board of regents recalled in a lengthy tribute to Allison's career that he had come to Mount Allison 'in its early history, first as a student and then as a teacher,' while the address presented to him by the students pointed out that of the fifty-eight years since he had first arrived at Mount Allison he had spent no less than twenty-nine as president of the university.[69] Allison himself made the point strikingly in a speech on 30 May 1911, at his last convocation as president, when he recalled that of the 626 arts degrees given by Mount Allison up to that time, he himself had conferred 493.[70] Ultimately, it was for his personal qualities that Allison was best remembered: his zest for teaching, his impulsive generosity, his unembarrassed affection for the students of the university. These traits had marked his career from beginning to end, and they accounted now for the warmth of the good wishes which accompanied him into retirement.

With Allison on the platform of Fawcett Hall at the 1911 convocation was J.R. Inch, who in 1909 had retired as superintendent of education, had returned to live in Sackville, and had then rejoined the Mount Allison board of regents as a church nominee in 1910. Absent was Charles Stewart, who had died in August 1910 at the age of eighty-three, having remained as part-time member of the faculty of theology and member of the board of regents until the time of his death. These three were the last of those who had been active at Mount Allison before it had been a college – Allison and Inch as teachers at the academy, Stewart as a member of educational committees of the conference of Eastern British America – and had then participated in its development through a period of profound social, political, and economic change. After the death of Inch in late 1912, Allison would write in the *Argosy* of episodes in the earlier history of Mount Allison 'most of which there is no one left now to remember but myself.'[71] Theirs had been a generation which had founded the college as a small rural institution serving the provinces of Eastern British America, and had seen it become a prosperous university in a rapidly industrializing region of a great continental dominion. That achievement entitled their generation – and its last member in particular – to an honourable retirement. Their successors' task was to steer Mount Allison through another period of profound change, during which the role of Mount Allison might again have to be reappraised as conditions altered around it.

Borden, as a preacher of the social gospel, was no stranger to the notion of reform, although his appointment was locally welcomed rather because of his administrative record at the ladies' college. 'As an executive head,' commented the *Tribune*, 'Dr. Borden has premier qualifications.'[72] The *Argosy*, while recognizing Borden's reputation as a shrewd administrator, made more of his progressive bent. A biographical article in the issue of May 1911 recalled the baccalaureate sermon he had preached at the closing exercises two years before, in which he had denounced materialism as a basis for social relations, as an example of his 'power in the pulpit.' An editorial in the same issue – presumably written by Fletcher Peacock, the editor-in-chief and himself no mean educational reformer in later years – praised Borden's 'largeness of vision, and general progressiveness' and predicted great advances for the university. 'No man,' it concluded, 'better knows Mount Allison's existing conditions, and appreciates more keenly her crying needs than does Dr. Borden, and so it is with the expectation of big results that we contemplate his term of office.'[73]

When Borden himself spoke of his hopes for Mount Allison, as he did in a speech at the 1911 convocation, his emphasis was rather different from that which many may have expected. Although he was not yet president, his speech inevitably took on much of the flavour of an inaugural address, and it began with two suitably radical questions. 'First,' he asked, 'has Mount Allison any reason for existence and secondly if that reason for existence can be fairly established what means are necessary to perpetuate and extend her inflence?'[74] Borden's answer to the first question offered a fresh perspective, for it did not assume that the university should aspire to constant growth. Instead, Mount Allison could offer its students the advantages of a small, residential institution, where they could develop close friendships both with their professors and with their fellow students. Borden's attitude towards expansion, even while at the ladies' college, had been complex: while he had pursued expansion with determination, he had professed to do so out of necessity rather than on the basis of any fixed principle, as a means of meeting competition from other institutions. Now, at the university, his view was still complex, and did not imply any absolute conversion. Especially in the heat of campaigning for funds, he was occasionally prone to rely on expansionist rhetoric, as in a speech of June 1913 to the New Brunswick and Prince Edward Island Conference in which he declared, as reported in the *Tribune*, that 'the campaign is only the beginning of bigger things for Mount Allison.'[75] Nor was he free of the shadow of competition with the old rival Acadia College – 'it will require a lot of hard work on our part to get an endowment which will enable us to keep pace with them,' he wrote in September 1911 – although supporting the concept of co-operation between Maritime colleges by attending a conference of presidents in Truro later in 1911.[76] Borden's address of May 1911 did not mean the end of expansionism at Mount Allison, but it did imply a renewed appreciation of the possibility that Mount Allison's worth did not depend upon some great manifest destiny.

The benefits of the small college, however, comprised for Borden only part of the reason for Mount Allison's existence, and were ancillary to a greater cause: the propagation of sound moral and religious values. In elaborating on this theme, Borden showed not only his social gospel background, but even more clearly the nationalistic fervour which was characteristic of Canadian

Methodism at this time. The 'national gospel' was more deeply rooted in Ontario than in the Maritimes, and such issues as the effect of immigration upon the British character of the dominion had more obvious relevance in areas where non-British immigration had occurred on a large scale. Yet for Borden national concerns were the key to an important role which the old-established educational institutions of the Maritimes might fulfil: the Maritimes should be the repository of all that was highest and best in Canadian life, and should spread those virtues far and wide.

Canada [he declared] with her broad acres, her fertile prairies, her untamed water powers, her undiscovered mines, her unsolved problems, her alien un-Canadianized millions is calling for just such forces as ... small colleges with their hand-picked men are able to supply; and she can only find men of that type in colleges where moral values are emphasized. In the fact that we claim to be a Christian college is found the great, supreme, outstanding reason for our existence. Material wealth is increasing at a phenomenal rate in Canada, and our country does not need men to tell her how to turn the silica of her prairies into golden wheat so much as she needs cultured, Christian men and women to refine, sweeten, purify and elevate the moral and political life of the country. We cannot overestimate the value of the work that is being done in our Eastern colleges in preparing men of this type who are to-day helping to redeem and Canadianize our great West.[77]

This argument, coming from the first ordained minister to be president of Mount Allison since 1869, represented an effort to place the university in the mainstream of Canadian Methodism, although in a way which still allowed a distinctive and honourable role to the Maritime region. Connexionalism, it implied, should be a support for Mount Allison's particular aspirations rather than a vehicle for unwelcomed intrusions from outside. It also suggestd an approach to answering Borden's second question, as to what practical means were necessary to ensure a secure future for the university. Given the existing financial crisis – which must, Borden suggested, lead to bankruptcy if not soon brought to an end – new funding was needed to raise faculty salaries from their current inadequate levels, to add new faculty members in certain fields, and to create new space for laboratories and classrooms. He was confident that the supporters of Mount Allison in the Maritimes would once again contribute generously, but he appealed also to those Allisonians now participating in the wealth of the west. This was, he believed, 'the strategic moment and every loyal son and daughter of dear old Mount Allison should come to her rescue.'[78] Mount Allison, like the Maritime region as a whole, had much to contribute, in Borden's view, to the future well-being of Canada;

but only with the aid of those whom it had already sent westward could it continue to fulfil its high calling.

In due course, Borden would personally take his message to the Canadian west. First of all, though, there were immediate difficulties to be confronted, of which the first concerned the quality of student life on the campus. It was all very well to preach the virtues of Mount Allison graduates and their ability to purify the social mores of the dominion. But when potential students were being kept away by parents who feared that they would be harassed and eventually corrupted by their older colleagues in the university residence, such idealism had a decidedly empty ring. Already, in its issue of May 1911, the *Argosy* had called for reform, and during the summer several students wrote to Borden to promise their support: W.T. Ruggles, for example, a senior student from Bear River, Nova Scotia, called for 'a radical change' in the rules governing the residence.[79] The first change was in the regulations for class attendance. Although attendance had always been assumed to be compulsory in theory, there had been few efforts at enforcement in recent years; now, a small number of absences from each class was specified as permissible, while any further unexcused absence would result in reduced marks or failure in the course concerned. The rule was evidently successful, as Borden commented in November that 'the neglect of classes has been practically cured.'[80] Compulsion in this sense, and a strict interpretation of rules, was clearly inevitable as an element of the new disciplinary regime, although there also existed the possibility that the effort to tighten standards would lead to harshness in individual cases. One female student was refused permission to return in the fall of 1911 after evidence had been found that during the summer she had spent a night in a cottage on the Northumberland Strait with two other students who had just been secretly married, and a male friend of the bridegroom. Exaggerated reports of the episode had apparently spread on the campus, but no impropriety had been seriously alleged beyond the simple fact that the four had been in the same cottage. Among several protesters at the severity of the verdict was a member of the board of regents, H.A. Powell, who remarked that '99 people out of 100 would look upon the matter as a joke.' After the decision had been reviewed by a general meeting of faculty, however, Borden informed Powell that it would not be reversed despite personal sympathy for the student involved, and defended it on the ground that 'the reputation of an institution like this is its life. ...' The student thus paid a high price for the university's good name.[81]

To be fair, the coercive aspect was not the only part, or even the predominant part, of the disciplinary reform at this time. There were unpopular measures in certain areas, as in the case of the ban jointly imposed on intercollegiate hockey by Mount Allison, Acadia, and the University of New Brunswick in late 1911, on the ground that it had interfered unduly with class attendance. The *Argosy* protested that the students had not been consulted, but the ban stood for the time being and only inter-class games were sanctioned until it was reversed in early 1913.[82] Also criticized by the students was compulsory attendance at morning chapel, another regulation which had lain dormant and was revived in September 1912. By early 1913 the *Argosy* was strongly opposed not only to 'compulsory religion,' but also to the practice of deducting class marks for absence at chapel: the system, it argued, was 'decidedly unfair, and almost bordering on the childish.' There had, in fact, been reservations among the faculty as to the desirability of this regulation, as S.W. Hunton had informed a correspondent: 'at our first Faculty meeting we passed a resolution to establish compulsory prayers each morning at 8.20! I don't think B.C.B. [Borden] bargained for the early hour, but Bigelow pressed it very hard and said that it would help matters so much in the Residence that his view prevailed.'[83] Yet the cornerstone of the new disciplinary approach, as implemented in particular by the residence dean whom Hunton mentioned – H.E. Bigelow – was not the imposition of authoritarian rules, but the devolution of responsibility for most disciplinary matters to the students themselves.

'Student self-government' was not altogether a new principle in Canada, nor was it unprecedented at Mount Allison. In late 1908 and early 1909, at the suggestion of Tweedie as dean, a series of general meetings of the students in the men's residence had resulted in the election of a student president and a small committee, but the movement had apparently gone little further. The *Argosy*, while supporting the measure, had noted in May 1909 that it had not gained universal support among the students themselves, having been 'viewed by certain individuals with suspicion, – by others with slight disparagement.'[84] In October 1911, however, the magazine announced that a more serious attempt was to be made: 'the Faculty have granted to the students absolute and unqualified control of purely Residence matters and in doing so we believe they have acted wisely. The students have accepted the offer and are therefore bound to the responsibilities which accompany it.' On the faculty side, Bigelow as 'Residence Professor' would now have primarily an advisory function, although the general faculty could still overrule student decisions on his recommendation. On the student side, authority was put in the hands of an elected council, the composition of which reflected faithfully the hierarchy of the student body: four members were to be drawn from the senior class, two each from the junior and sophomore classes, and in the second term a single member from the freshman class. 'All that is now needed,' the *Argosy* commented, 'is the heartiest support of each and every student and there can be no doubt as to the results.'[85]

By the end of the academic year, in May 1912, the *Argosy* saw no reason to change its optimistic tone, declaring that the system had proved that 'student control of student matters is far in advance of any other system yet devised.'[86] To be sure, the year had not gone by without its troubles, but in general these had been resolved jointly by faculty and students. Two students, for example, were 'rusticated' from the residence by the student council in January 1912 for taking part in a theft of food from the residence kitchen; one of them was expelled from the university a month later amid suspicions that he had gained his revenge by systematically taking cards from the library card catalogue and strewing them around the university grounds.[87] In the wider community, popular suspicions of the unruliness of Mount Allison students had not entirely abated, as was shown on 29 March, when the Moncton *Times* declared in front-page headlines that the students had burned down the university gymnasium to celebrate a debating victory over Acadia. The building referred to – which was the old gymnasium, a small wooden structure newly replaced by Lingley Hall – had indeed burned down during the celebrations, which had included a bonfire and had been marked by some disputes between students and youths from the town. But, as S.W. Hunton reported privately to Borden after he and Bigelow had conducted an investigation, there was no evidence that students had started the fire, and the *Times* subsequently retracted its story.[88] Despite these difficulties, therefore, Borden felt able at the end of the year to echo the *Argosy*'s opinion by reporting to the board of regents that 'the institution of Student Government had worked very successfully and the atmosphere of the Residence was to-day healthy.'[89]

The success of the experiment, which resulted in the permanent establishment of student self-government at Mount Allison, was obviously due primarily to the attitude of the students themselves. As J.M. Palmer wrote in early 1912, 'the students of the University as a body have been making a great effort to weed out undesirable conditions. ...'[90] Palmer was especially impressed by the lack of harassment of freshmen by sophomores, and although that custom was revived to some extent later in 1912 – one freshman of the fall of that year later recalled that he was 'hazed ... unmercifully' – the reputation of the residence certainly improved, and a rising enrolment showed that tales of indiscipline were no longer a serious obstacle to student attendance.[91] The *Argosy* was inclined to give much of the credit to Bigelow, 'the man who by his tact and courtesy has most materially aided the work of the Council during the year.'[92] Bigelow was a Mount Allison graduate of 1903, and it was thus not many years since he had himself lived in the men's residence. So young did he appear, in fact, when he arrived at Mount Allison in 1911, that one sophomore student greeted him as a freshman and offered to sell him his old textbooks.[93] In reality, Bigelow had just completed five years of work in organic chemistry at Harvard University and had gained his PH D shortly before returning to take over the chair in chemistry at Mount Allison vacated by his former teacher W.W. Andrews. As a successful scientist as well as a young former student of Mount Allison, he was well qualified for his duties both in the laboratory and in the university residence.[94]

Student self-government did not extend to all the students of the university during the 1911–12 year. However, on 7 October 1912 the first women's student council held its inaugural meeting. With 45 women now enrolled in the BA programme of the university – comprising 31.3 per cent of the overall enrolment, and 41.3 per cent of those registered in arts – there was obviously no reason for denying to these students the rights acquired by their male colleagues.[95] In recent years, in fact, women had even made their appearance in the faculty of theology, although only in small numbers and studying as special students in preparation for missionary work.[96] Yet in the matter of student government there were difficulties faced by the women students which did not parallel those of the men, and which illustrated the different behaviour expected of the two sexes. The ladies' college, in which the majority of the women students boarded – the only exceptions were those living at home or boarding in town – was no den of iniquity. On the contrary, its rules were sufficiently strict that it was known to its inmates as 'the penitentiary.'[97] A long list of instructions and prohibitions enjoined, for example, that residents must take at least one hour of exercise in the open air each day, but must not attract attention from their windows; the first rule of all, moreover, was that students must 'respond promptly to all bell calls.' Apart from being permitted to retain their lights until 11:00 each evening except Sunday, the only concession made to the university women was that once past their first year they were allowed to go out more often unaccompanied by a teacher than were the ladies' college students: 'University students (except freshmen) ... can receive permission from the Principal to go out one evening each week to a party or other entertainment, and once in three weeks to spend Sunday.' They were warned, though, not to go to the station or the wharf without permission.[98]

That university students should be regulated to this extent, especially when their male counterparts were allowed out until 11:30 each night and had few restrictions on their freedom within the residence, had been a source of annoyance for some years before 1912. A serious effort had been made in

1906, in a petition presented to the board of regents by the four female graduates of that year, to prompt the establishment of a separate university women's residence. The petition had been supported by an article in the *Argosy* by 'Samara' – probably one of the four petitioners – which argued that it was regrettable, given Mount Allison's distinguished record in women's education, that 'our Alma Mater ... has been unreasonably backward in making suitable provision for the accommodation of those young women steadily increasing in number, who wish to take up university work in Sackville.' Construction of a new residence, the author went on, would not only release space for the ladies' college but would forestall the increasing trend by which potential women students were deciding against enrolling at Mount Allison because of the 'absurd' restrictions to which they would be subjected. 'The Board of Regents,' the article warned, 'should not defer consideration of this matter.' That, however, was exactly what the board did: on 30 May, the women graduates' petition was tabled indefinitely.[99] By 1912, with financial resources in short supply, the construction of a new residence was no longer a possibility, and in this situation the devolution of discipline to the student council represented an attempt to find the best available remedy as well as to reduce the inequities between male and female students. Under the general supervision of Emma Baker, the ladies' college vice-principal, who stood in the same advisory relationship to the women's council as did Bigelow to that of the men, the university women could at least have some influence in the writing and the enforcement of their own rules, even if the physical fact of their presence in the ladies' college prevented any radical departure from the existing regime. It would become clear within a few years that even this limited special status for the university women would create tensions arising from the perception by other residents that they had become a privileged class. For the time being, however, as the local *Tribune* reported in October 1912, 'the student government has worked very satisfactorily and the expectation is that it will continue to do so.'[100]

With some success attained in the devolution of disciplinary powers to student councils, the regulation of student life became for the time being a less pressing question at Mount Allison. The recruitment of well-qualified faculty members still presented difficulties, made even more immediate by the renewed tendency for student enrolment to increase. Although there were eleven professors in the faculty of arts in 1911–12, two – Borden and Palmer – were also heads of institutions, and another three taught primarily in the faculty of theology. Of the remaining six, three – Smith, Hunton, and Tweedie – were long-standing members, but the fact that the other three were in their first year at Mount Allison was evidence of the problems experienced in inducing young professors to stay.[101] As a means of filling immediate vacancies, Borden resorted to dealing with teacher agencies in the United States, such as the Fisk agency of Chicago and Boston and the American and Foreign Teachers' Agency of New York. In the short term this strategy was justified, as when a professor of physics was finally located through the Fisk agency on 18 September 1911 for the term beginning three days later.[102] As a means of building a permanent faculty it was obviously not promising, especially as Mount Allison was offering salaries much lower than those of competing institutions in the United States. The ideal solution was to raise salaries, and thus reduce the turnover of staff, but that required money that Mount Allison would not have until fund-raising efforts had borne fruit. In the meantime, the best that could be done was to persevere with short-term appointments, while also looking for well-qualified candidates who were themselves Maritimers, and so might be induced to let their personal ties to the region compensate for a low salary.

In science, such candidates were found: Bigelow, arriving in 1911, and Wheelock, who took over the chair in physics in the fall of 1912. Also in 1912, Borden believed he had found an ideal recruit for the chair in psychology and logic – in effect it was an appointment in philosophy – which had been temporarily filled in the previous year by a Harvard graduate student, P.L. Given.[103] Borden's candidate was Winthrop Bell, Mount Allison graduate of 1904 and now a graduate student in philosophy at the German university of Göttingen. Another temporary appointment had been made for the 1912–13 year, and in any case Bell was not yet near the end of his post-graduate study. Thus it was an appointment in September 1913 that Borden offered him in a letter written during the summer of 1912. 'Dr. Bigelow is doing splendid work,' Borden wrote, 'and I am satisfied that if I could gather around me more of you brilliant young men we could make things go at Mount Allison.' Yet Borden's hopes were not to be fulfilled, for Bell refused the offer. His response had been influenced by a phrase in Borden's letter, in which Borden had indicated a contributory reason for his desire to have the university's own graduates on the faculty: since Bell was already familiar with 'the views that are held among our patrons and governors upon the religious and philosophical questions,' he would be able to avoid causing conflict through some 'unguarded utterance or ventilation of doubts.' Bell's reaction, despite the affection he professed for his old university, was indignant: 'to have any institution devoted to higher learning or scientific research under the control of a body with rigid dogmas and preconceived beliefs is enough of an anomaly. To try and prosecute philosophical investigations under such circumstances is almost farcical.' A further approach from Borden caused Bell to relent in October to the extent of agreeing to consider taking a position if his academic freedom could be convincingly guaranteed; but he was never in fact appointed.[104]

This incident clearly had implications far beyond the matter of who was to take the professorship in philosophy, for it raised basic questions as to the academic integrity of Mount Allison. It was, in one sense, an ironic turn of events. Borden's appointment as president had been a final confirmation of the ascendancy of liberal theology at Mount Allison, and this had taken place without the bitter public disputes with more fundamentalist theologians which had shaken Victoria University from time to time. At Mount Allison, the transition had been gradual. It had begun not in the theological faculty but in the faculty of arts, where the influence of Andrews and Borden during the 1890s had led to a firm meeting of the challenges posed by new scientific discoveries and by the application of evolutionary concepts to social development. That unrestrained scientific enquiry was the best way to uncover the divine scheme for the universe and that the Christian message was aimed at the redemption of society as well as that of individuals were principles that had long been familiar to Mount Allison undergraduates. Borden's particular concern in recent years had been the outlawing of electoral corruption, and articles in the *Argosy* on this and other social issues – such as the relationship of capital and labour, the abuse of child labour, and the rise of socialism – showed that the social gospel had retained currency among the students of the university.[105]

In the faculty of theology, the introduction of modernist influences had been later, and the appointment of Watson in 1903 marked the beginning of a heavier emphasis upon new techniques of biblical criticism. Under the tolerant supervision of C.H. Paisley as dean, whose daughter he married in 1906, Watson became a well-established member of the faculty. Paisley's sudden death at the age of sixty-four in early 1908 was, as Watson commented to J.W. Graham of the Methodist Board of Education, 'quite a blow to the College': it deprived Mount Allison of a professor who had served for twelve years, in addition to his earlier period as principal of the academy from 1879 to 1883, and who was described in the *Argosy* as 'an accomplished scholar, an exceedingly painstaking and efficient teacher, and a most amiable and godly man.'[106] As dean, Paisley was succeeded by Howard Sprague, one of the first graduates of Mount Allison, and the same who had declined the presidency of the university in 1878 and the deanship of theology when first offered it in 1903.[107] Sprague, who now became professor of systematic theology and New Testament exegesis as well as dean, was known as a liberal theologian, and yet his long association with Mount Allison and with Methodism in the region ensured that his teachings were supported by substantial personal prestige. By late 1908, as Watson informed Graham, the theological faculty was prospering once again:

Dr. Sprague is taking hold of his work well, and his appointment to our staff is a decided advantage. He stands high in the estimation of the Church, and it is necessary for us to keep en rapport with the ministers in the Conferences. His theology is decidedly liberal, but no one will dare to object to Dr. Sprague's teaching, because he stands so high in their esteem. We expect Mr. DesBarres back from England next year, and I think his presence on our Faculty will strengthen our position in the Nova Scotia Conference.[108]

DesBarres, who took up his appointment as professor of English Bible and apologetics in the fall of 1909, was another graduate of Mount Allison, and he now began a long career at the university during which he taught both theology and history. As Watson implied, he had served the Nova Scotia conference for most of the period from his entry into the ministry in 1890 until his departure for study leave in Great Britain in 1907. During that time, he had joined other preachers of the social gospel in calling for a revival of public morality as well as for more traditional forms of evangelization aimed at individual conversion. At a time when committees of both of the Maritime conferences were calling for attention to social goals, the addition of DesBarres to the theological faculty was timely.[109] Sprague, Watson, and BesBarres would comprise the full-time theological faculty for the next seven years, until the death of Sprague in 1916: they were able to a remarkable degree to combine modern teachings with a harmonious relationship to the conferences, and the appointment of Borden as university president in 1911 added to their ability to do so.

Yet harmony did not entirely prevail, and in 1912 the teachings of Watson brought complaints to Borden. If any of the theological professors was to arouse controversy, it was likely to be Watson, for he was the youngest and the only one whose personal roots were not in Maritime Methodism; he was also the most acute exponent of the higher criticism. In January 1912, a prominent Methodist layman of Yarmouth, A.J. Fuller, informed Borden that he had discussed Watson's teaching of evidences of Christianity with a number of students who had been in Yarmouth for the Christmas break, and had concluded that they amounted to Unitarianism.[110] The matter was eventually resolved, but not before considerable argument had been generated: it was apparently this which prompted Borden to comment to Winthrop Bell that one of the Mount Allison professors had recently 'set three conferences by the ears,' and was the direct cause of the admonition to which Bell objected so strongly. The Maritime conferences were ambivalent in their attitudes to the liberal theological principles which had now become strongly rooted at Mount Allison. While some conference committees were strongly sympathetic, there remained a large body of opinion committed to the more traditional evangelistic Methodism. Through the general respect which had been enjoyed in the conferences by such long-established ministerial members of Mount Allison's faculties as Andrews, Borden, and Sprague, as well as through the tolerance within the theological faculty which had allowed, for example, Watson and Stewart to work together harmoniously despite their widely differing views, damaging conflict had been avoided. That achievement, however, remained fragile. Any dispute resembling that over the teachings of George Jackson, which had racked Victoria University in 1910, could only weaken Mount Allison's support among Maritime Methodists, upon which it had traditionally relied. Such a prospect was dismaying for any supporter of the university, but especially so for Borden, whose concept of Mount Allison was so squarely based on its role as a denominational college.[111]

As Borden was forced to realize, however, Bell's questioning of academic freedom at Mount Allison also demanded attention. The only circumstance in which Bell would consent to come to Mount Allison, he informed Borden in October 1912, would be if it were understood by the board of regents 'that it was engaging one who regarded as open all the questions which the Church dogmas treat as settled,' and he summarized the guarantees he would require:

> The great thing would be ... that no one outside the University should have the right or power of interfering with my position because any of my professional utterances disagreed with any belief of his or with any creed of any church; and that the only grounds on which anyone, either outside the University or within it, could demand or obtain my dismissal, would be neglect of my work on my part, or such incompetence in the subject taught as would be ground of dismissal in *any* university. In asking for this understanding I am merely asking for one of the privileges of the men in the larger universities – taken for granted there, in fact, and necessary as a condition of good work anywhere.[112]

Coming from an alumnus who otherwise professed a strong sympathy for Mount Allison, and admiration for the intellectual quality of work performed there in less sensitive areas than philosophy – citing Tweedie's teaching of English as an example – Bell's remarks raised with stark clarity the dilemma of the denominational institution. In Mount Allison's earliest years, the distinction between denominationalism and sectarianism had been easy enough to sustain: the denominational character of the institutions would ensure that all students would receive a Christian education, but their particular beliefs would not be challenged. By the twentieth century, however, much had changed. The assumption which had originally prevailed at Mount Allison – influenced particularly by the natural theology of William Paley – had been that empirical and revealed knowledge could not conflict. When scientific discoveries had challenged that assumption, modernist theologians had responded by recasting the notion of revealed knowledge so as to allow for scientific developments, and had also adopted scientific techniques in efforts to arrive at a more sophisticated version of religious truth. At Mount Allison, such approaches now predominated, to the chagrin of some church members. What remained unanswered was the problem posed by the potential faculty member who responded to the tension between scientific and religious truth by going even further than the modernist theologians and insisting that every proposition, including the very existence of God, must be regarded as questionable. If such teaching was acceptable at Mount Allison, could the university any longer claim to have a denominational character? If it was unacceptable, could the university any longer claim to be committed to intellectual enquiry? The issue that Bell had raised was whether Mount Allison was in fact attempting to serve two masters.

Bell himself had suggested certain principles which, along with guarantees of academic freedom to individual faculty members, might reduce the severity of the dilemma even if not solving it altogether. He hoped in particular that the board of regents might be reconstituted to allow for greater alumni representation as compared with that of the church; and that a distinction should be kept between the theological faculty, which might reasonably be expected to conform to Methodist requirements, and other faculties, which should be free of such restrictions. It is hard to avoid seeing these proposals, together with the increase in alumni influence which was natural in view of the appeal to alumni in the financial campaign of the time, as being the major force behind the revision of the university's statutes which was embodied in provincial legislation enacted on 20 March 1913.[113] The new act was the first complete consolidation of Mount Allison's constitution since the original act of incorporation of the academy, and it finally repealed that statute of 1849.

As well as remodelling certain more minor administrative arrangements, the act added four members to the board, two to be elected by the alumni, two by the alumnae. The general conference would continue to name 24 members, but a full third of the board – eight alumni, four alumnae – would not be church appointments. The role of the reconstituted board was emphasized by the designation of 'The Regents of Mount Allison' as the corporate title: 'the Mount Allison University,' 'the Mount Allison Ladies' College,' and 'the Mount Allison Academy' were defined as the three institutions to be operated by the regents. The title 'the University of Mount Allison College' had thus disappeared. As regards academic freedom, however, the most important element of the act was not what it said but what it did not say. The original act of 1849 had contained a clause prescribing that nothing should be taught in the academy that contravened the doctrines of John Wesley. This restriction had never been repeated in any further legislation, and had never specifically been confirmed as applying to the faculty of the college as well as that of the academy. None the less, it had remained technically in force. Now, it was repealed, and the act of 1913 contained no statement on the teachings that might or might not be promulgated at Mount Allison. Furthermore, the senate, which had hitherto consisted of all regents and all faculty members, thus ensuring a majority of church appointees, was now to consist of the university faculty, the principals of the academy and the ladies' college, and only twelve regents. Since the senate was to enjoy, as it already did, exclusive authority in the prescription of the university's courses of study, that power would now rest with a body consisting primarily of members not directly appointed by the church, given that the number of faculty members would not decline. To be sure, the two-thirds majority of church appointees on the board ensured a continuing church influence on many important matters, including the appointment of faculty. In May 1913, in the context of a suggestion that dancing and other such unedifying entertainments had been condoned at the ladies' college, the board declared that all heads of institutions must aim 'to secure the services of Methodist Teachers consistent with obtaining the specialized talent that is needed for the work to be done.' Nevertheless, the denominational affiliation of Mount Allison undoubtedly had a less restrictive character after the legislation of 1913 than before.[114] Winthrop Bell would never become a faculty member of Mount Allison, although in later life he would serve on the board of regents; yet he had significantly influenced the character of the university.

The character of both the university and the ladies' college was also being influenced at this time by important curriculum changes. Two major innovations were the introduction of a three-year programme, given jointly by the ladies' college and the university, leading to the degree of Bachelor of Music, and the introduction at the university of a four-year degree of Bachelor of Science. This latter programme was designed to overcome certain difficulties that had become clear in recent years: the general anomaly that arts degrees were regularly being given for work done, at least in the junior and senior years, primarily in science; and the fact that the Latin language requirement was seen as an unnecessary burden by many science students, and was dissuading students in the McClelan School from enrolling in a degree course at the same time as working towards their engineering certificate. The BSC was therefore offered '(a) for those who wish to take up advanced work in Science, (b) for those who wish to take work similar to that of the course in Arts without Latin, and (c) for those who wish to take this latter work while obtaining a certificate in the two years engineering course.' A common curriculum was provided for the initial two years, including courses in English literature and modern languages as well as introductory science and mathematics. The final two years were structured according to which of the three categories the student chose: honours work in science, a general programme including languages and social sciences as well as science, or the engineering certificate course.[115]

In adopting a genuinely scientific BSC course – as opposed to the less demanding BS which had been awarded during the early years of the college – Mount Allison was following a trend already established at a number of Canadian universities, although the numbers of such degrees granted at English-language universities had remained small. When Mount Allison granted its first BSC in 1918 to G.F. Palfrey of Lawrencetown, Nova Scotia, it was one of only ten given at English-language institutions in that year.[116] After this slow beginning, at Mount Allison and elsewhere, the BSC became a more popular programme, and during the 1920s graduating classes numbered as many as twelve at Mount Allison alone. The adoption of the BSC degree was an effort to bring the arts and engineering faculties closer by encouraging students to study in both. It also gave added substance to the arguments of Bigelow, as dean of the McClelan School and professor of chemistry in the faculty of arts, when he urged the board of regents in November 1913 to authorize the construction of 'a small Science building' to relieve congestion in the existing science building. No fewer than 55 students had enrolled in engineering in that autumn – more than a third of the entire undergraduate enrolment – and it seemed clear that Mount Allison's prosperity as a centre of science education was assured.[117]

The Bachelor of Music programme, also introduced in 1912, made Mount Allison one of a small number of Canadian institutions which granted such degrees. The University of Toronto regularly granted degrees to candidates from the Toronto Conservatory, the Hamilton Conservatory, and the Toronto School of Music, while Bishop's University and McGill had awarded music degrees in small numbers. In the Maritimes, the Halifax Conservatory had been affiliated with Dalhousie since 1898, but the first degrees were not given until 1915. Mount Allison was thus the second university in the region to adopt a Bachelor of Music programme, with Acadia following suit in 1917, the year in which Mount Allison's first music degree was awarded to Mary Elsinore Tait of St John's, Newfoundland.[118] First mooted at Mount Allison in late 1911, the Bachelor of Music course was quickly organized on the basis that the university would provide courses in English and French (to be taken in the first year) and physics and German (to be taken in the third year), while all professional instruction would be provided by the ladies' college. Harmony, counterpoint, and the history of music were particularly emphasized, although competence in composition was also required of all potential graduates, and in performance on piano, organ, or violin.[119]

For the conservatory, the introduction of the degree programme was not a radical departure in terms of curriculum content, since the diploma courses in music had been growing steadily more complex and demanding, with an increasing stress upon musical theory as well as performance. None the less, the degree course implied an even stronger claim to offer instruction of an academic and professional nature rather than for the sake of drawing-room accomplishment. The implementation of this approach fell to the newly appointed director of the conservatory, J. Noel Brunton. Brunton, who arrived in the fall of 1911, was a Scot who had studied at the Stern Conservatory in Berlin and then had taught and performed in London for several years before coming to Mount Allison. Among his innovations – apart from beginning the new degree programme, in connection with which he returned to London in the summer of 1912 to recruit faculty members in organ and choral work – was the introduction of 'local examinations,' including the assessment of promising music pupils in their home communities or nearby towns by travelling members of the conservatory. Such a scheme had already been operated successfully by the University of Toronto; and the board of regents was informed in November 1913 that the McGill Conservatory had expressed interest in making the Mount Allison scheme a joint venture, aimed at attracting students to both Montreal and Sackville. At first, the board baulked at the expense involved, and the proposed partnership with McGill was not brought about, but Brunton's local examinations eventually became an important aspect of the conservatory's activity throughout the Maritime provinces.[120]

Brunton also put heavy emphasis upon regularity and quality of musical performance. Weekly recitals were now held, at which students played or sang before an audience of teachers and other students, while public concerts were given each month. Brunton himself lost no time in making his concert debut in Sackville: his performance at a recital on 3 November 1911 showed him to be, the *Tribune* commented, 'a pianist of great brilliance, well trained, faithful and strong.'[121] He also arranged for concerts by eminent visiting artists, as when the closing exercises of 1912 were preceded by a series of three concerts, advertised as a 'Grand Musical Festival,' featuring the well-known cellist Boris Hambourg of Toronto, and his brother Jan on violin. The series was adjudged by the *Tribune* to have been 'one of the very best musical festivals ever held at Mount Allison,' and it began a long tradition of such events.[122] Yet these innovations were not unanimously welcomed. They raised, in fact, certain long-standing tensions within the ladies' college that had never entirely been resolved. Even the *Wesleyan*, normally a faithful propagandist of Mount Allison, tempered its praise of the 1912 closing exercises by commenting that 'if we would hazard a criticism, we would say that we think the musical programs presented by the Institution are sufficiently attractive without importing expensive performers, whose concert fees make a large drain upon the slender purses of many students just called on to pay their term bills and to purchase homeward tickets.'[123] The Shediac minister George Steel went much further in a letter to the board of regents in the following year, in which he condemned 'the many entertainments of various character that pupils are expected to support by their presence and their pocket.' Such functions – by which he apparently also meant receptions and sports events such as skating parties – were harmful in his view both to the academic work of the students and to their moral welfare, especially when combined with 'foolish and extravagant display in dress.' Steel also hinted at 'games of a doubtful nature' among the students, which came perilously close to gambling.[124]

Steel's letter was, necessarily, taken seriously by the board when read at its meeting of 29 May 1913, and a committee was struck, including the three heads of institutions and four other regents, to report the same day. It recommended that 'the simple life' should be encouraged at Mount Allison and, more specifically, 'that gifts of flowers at recitals and graduation exercises be prohibited, and that steps be taken by the Heads of the Institutions to reduce the expenses of the students in connection with the Senior Receptions, Sports, Skating Parties and similar functions.' To reinforce the point, the regents then elected Steel to a vacant seat on the board. Principal Campbell, moreover, had another uncomfortable session at the board's next meeting in November, when he denied that dancing had taken place in the ladies' college but then went on to rekindle suspicions by revealing 'that in fact Beethoven Hall had been refused to the students in order that such should not be carried on.'[125] Campbell was in a difficult position. When such criticisms of the ladies' college had arisen in the past, particularly during the regime of Borden and Archibald before the turn of the century, they had been met by a determination to balance the 'ornamental' aspects of the institution's teaching by the continuation of a rigorous literary programme, and by sustaining high academic and professional standards in fine arts, music, and later in household science. For Campbell, however, given his emphasis upon 'women for homes,' such an approach was not easy. Furthermore, the literary programme had fallen upon bad times even before his arrival as principal, no doubt largely because so many women were now choosing to attend the university. During the decade from 1905 to 1914, only 16 MLA diplomas were awarded, as compared with 54 between 1895 and 1904, and 44 between 1885 and 1894.[126]

Now, too, the professional and normal schools of the ladies' college were taking on a life of their own, in ways which were capable of creating new dilemmas. The conservatory provided an excellent example. To teach music purely as an ornamental subject was, as Mary Mellish Archibald had clearly seen, to risk demeaning the academic quality of the institution, and was likely also to bring allegations of elitism. Yet to aspire to have a first-rate conservatory, run by a vigorous and well-travelled professional musician such as Brunton, brought its own tensions and renewed fears on the Methodist circuits that Mount Allison was becoming far removed from its rural roots. Once again, as at the university, the years of expansion were giving place to a serious questioning of the purposes for which Mount Allison existed. One sign of the times was the emergence of conflict between Campbell and the staff of the conservatory, which led to Brunton's resignation as director in 1914; he also resigned as professor of piano in 1915, although he returned a year later, and became director once again in 1918.[127] To be sure, the ladies' college was still flourishing – although there was a worrying financial loss of over $7000 in the 1913–14 year – with over 300 students regularly in attendance.[128] Nevertheless, it had serious unresolved questions to face.

As for the academy, it stood by 1914 in the unaccustomed position of being the least troubled of the three institutions. Its expansion during the previous two decades had been modest, but real. In recent years, partly because of the successful outcome of the battle fought by Palmer against Borden in 1905 for control of the courses in shorthand and typing, increases in enrolment had been especially marked in the commercial college, but the academic department was also prospering. In the 1913–14 year, the total enrolment was reported by Palmer to be 180, including 74 boarding students.[129] Financially, the academy was profitable despite charging fees that were described by the principal of Stanstead College, G.J. Trueman, as the lowest charged by any school he knew of. During the period from 1910 to 1914, despite a number of renovations to the academy building, a debt of $5197 was paid off in full, and a small surplus accumulated. In part, this reflected the practice of employing university students as part-time teachers in return for board, thus reducing the outlay on salaries in a way which was only possible because the university happened to be nearby. However achieved, it was a healthy state of affairs, and one that allowed pupils to attend without great expense at the same time as each year it gave several university students the opportunity to work their way to a degree. Trueman, during his own university days, had been one of them.[130]

The academy had thus successfully met the challenge posed by the growth of public schools, which had threatened at one time to destroy it. The commercial college comprised one essential reason for that success. Another was the tendency, under Palmer, for the academy to return to the principles with which it had begun some seventy years before. As well as the low fees, Palmer was accustomed to stress the variety of pupils whom the academy served. 'We always have,' he wrote, for example, to a correspondent in the summer of 1912, 'a number of older boys and young men, some 25 and 26 years old, taking elementary work, so that no one, however backward he may be, need feel that he is further behind than his class-mates.'[131] That individual attention could be given to each student, so as to overcome any particular difficulties he might have, was described in the calendar as one of the major advantages of the academy as opposed to public schools. Yet lest the school should become a haven for negligent students, the calendar also insisted that a high moral standard would prevail, and that 'those seeking admission to the Academy as students must present certificates of character, signed by the minister of their church, or by the teacher of the school last attended.'[132] Teachers also had strict rules with which to conform. In 1912, for example, Palmer had a brisk response for one potential appointee: 'in the event of your wishing to be regarded as an applicant please inform me as to whether you are a member of any church, also whether you use tobacco in any form, and whether you are a total abstainer from the use of intoxicants.' To another correspondent some two years later, Palmer wrote that 'about a dozen of our lads last year decided for Christ and went home with better conceptions of what life means and their obligations to their God.'[133] At the academy of 1914, much more than at the university, Humphrey Pickard would have felt very much at home.

Whether or not the university's latest president would himelf come to feel at home there depended in large part, when he first took office, upon the success of the financial campaign. 'I think I shall really enjoy my work at the College,' wrote Borden to Archibald in November 1911, 'if I can only raise money enough to run it without a debt and improve the staff.'[134] By that time the campaign was already under way, having been launched with a printed appeal on 15 June. The extent to which the campaign was personally identified with Borden was reflected in the drawing of the major points of the appeal from the speech he had made at convocation at the end of May. 'Mount Allison,' declared the pamphlet, 'is supplying the Great West with teachers, clergymen and intelligent citizens.' That it should continue to do so was essential if 'the incoming millions' of immigrants were to be 'educated and Canadianized.' Mount Allison deserved support, therefore, from all patriotic Canadians, but especially from 'her prosperous sons whose lives have been enriched by the culture and brain power she has given them' and by 'her children everywhere.' The sum of $250,000 was described as sufficient to ensure the university's future: $200,000 of additional endowment would provide for augmentation of faculty salaries and other ongoing needs, while a further $50,000 would be spent on a new science building. The board of regents had already subscribed $38,000, and, the appeal concluded, all donors would 'send their name down to the latest posterity fragrant with the gratitude of successive generations of earnest students.'[135]

Campaign rhetoric aside, collecting funds was slow work. And, as with other aspects of the reforms at Mount Allison which characterized Borden's early years as president, there was a more negative, restrictive aspect which went along with the positive measures. In this case, an effort was made to tighten the levying and collection of students' accounts. To collect accounts that were in many cases long overdue was a difficult task and one that risked creating more animosity than it was worth. None the less, Borden wrote numerous letters in early 1912, appealing for payment rather than demanding it. 'You will see by the enclosed financial statement,' went a typical letter, 'that the institution needs at least everything that is due it.' Alumni in the west who had outstanding accounts received an additional admonition: 'I hope you are sharing in the general prosperity of the West and will feel disposed not only to square the old balance but to contribute something to our endowment fund.'[136] Existing students were discouraged from allowing their bills to accumulate by a ruling of the board of regents that only those whose board and tuition fees were fully paid would be eligible to receive examination marks. According to Palmer, the three heads of the institutions refused to enforce this as a rigid rule, but it was certainly cited at times as a means of pressing for payment of overdue accounts.[137] Where one group of students felt the severity of the financial climate more immediately was in the faculty of theology. Theological students paid no fees, and had been accustomed to have a church grant of $25 credited to each of their accounts for board and lodging. Now, according to a new interpretation by Borden of the conditions of the grant, the $25 was retained by the university as compensation for free tuition. Aggrieved students had the president of the Nova Scotia Conference, the Mount Allison alumnus G.J. Bond, intercede on their behalf to the Board of Education in Toronto, but to no avail.[138] A further retrenchment of church-related privileges came in May 1913, when the 20 per cent discount on board and tuition fees hitherto given by the university to the children of clergymen was redefined to apply only to tuition.[139]

Clearly, however, such economies could only bring small returns, and were ancillary to the greater task of raising funds in much larger amounts. The financial campaign started in 1911 was conducted vigorously and using innovative methods. The closing exercises of 1912, for example, were filmed by a camera crew borrowed from the Gaumont company, and during the ensuing summer two theological students travelled throughout the region showing the film along with others relating to missionary work in China. According to the *Tribune*, Mount Allison was the first university in Canada to adopt this means of publicizing itself.[140] Modern technology was invoked in a different way in a series of three letters sent to alumni at intervals of a few days in the spring of 1913, which took the form of imaginary telephone conversations between Borden and the recipient, who was eventually asked in the third letter to contribute to the fund and to participate in local canvassing.[141] A further campaign strategy which depended upon recent developments – in this case, the establishment of large-scale philanthropic foundations – was also pursued, but with little success. In an appeal to Chester Massey for a further donation from his father's estate, Borden commented that 'we have no wealthy men in the East though our people are prepared to give to the limit of their means; in fact the constant drain that is going on from the East to the West is depriving us largely of the support we should have at such a time as this.' Massey was unable to help, Mount Allison already having received $100,000 from the otherwise fully committed estate, but he suggested approaching Andrew Carnegie. This Borden did, and he also wrote to John D. Rockefeller, but to no avail. Rockefeller, already giving large sums to Acadia University, declined Mount Allison's request, while Carnegie's secretary simply referred Borden to the previous refusal of 1908 on the grounds that Mount Allison was a denominational institution. The refusals were probably inevitable, although Borden can hardly have advanced the cause by misspelling in his letters the names of both 'Carnagie' and 'Rockerfeller.'[142]

The campaign's success depended in practice upon the cooperation of three groups with a more immediate interest in Mount Allison: the Methodists of the region; the local community; the students and alumni. In each case, there was good reason to hope for generous support, as indicated by the strong endorsements given. In June 1911 Borden addressed both the Nova Scotia Conference in Yarmouth and that of New Brunswick and Prince Edward Island in Saint John, and was welcomed at both with assurances of cooperation. Through efforts of ministers and church members on the various circuits, backed by frequent *Wesleyan* editorials, the needs of Mount Allison were kept prominently before the congregations, and the campaign culminated with coordinated appeals from pulpits in May 1913.[143] Support for Mount Allison in the Sackville district had been promoted in recent years by contacts between the university and the local board of trade, of which W.W. Andrews had been elected president in early 1910. Three years before, Borden himself had addressed the board of trade on the interdependence of town and university.[144] The Mount Allison campaign was not received entirely uncritically in Sackville, and it occasioned renewed comments on the tax-free status of the campus. The local press, however, gave strong support, and in March 1913 the *Tribune* printed a leading article describing Mount Allison as 'a civic asset of the highest value.' The article pointed out, rightly, that there had been suggestions in the Halifax press that all the Maritime colleges should be centralized in the Nova Scotian capital, and hinted that there were other New Brunswick towns which would be happy to provide lands and funding if Mount Allison would relocate. 'Mount Allison,' it concluded, 'may be starved out or frozen out of Sackville. The time is approaching for Sackville to say in a practical way how much she values her educational institutions.'[145] The *Argosy* was no less forthcoming, and again its consistent support for the campaign culminated in the spring of 1913, when a special 'endowment number' was published in April. 'The prospects point towards a Great Mount Allison of the future,' the *Argosy* editors urged: 'the critical moment is *Now*.'[146]

In depending upon the church and the local community, with the moral support of the students of the institutions, the campaign reflected the traditional pattern of Mount Allison's support. To that extent, little had changed since the earliest days of the academy. What was missing, by comparison with that era, was government funding, and from that stemmed the crucial importance now of endowment funds and consequently, given the large amounts sought between 1911 and 1913, of the generosity of the alumni. It had been the alumni association which had first called for an endowment campaign at its meeting in May 1910, and so its support was committed from the start.[147]

Whether that support would be effective in practice depended upon the extent to which it could be translated into action in local areas. In early 1912, an effort was made to promote the foundation of alumni associations, first in the major cities of the Maritimes and then further west. In Saint John, an alumni association had existed during the 1890s, while S.D. Scott had been the editor of the *Sun*, and it was now revived under the leadership of E.R. Machum, a former academy student of the 1880s and now a Saint John insurance agent.[148] In Halifax, the lead was taken by a more recent alumnus: Ralph Pickard Bell, younger brother of Winthrop and a graduate of 1907. Now working in his father's hardware business, Bell set about the task of alumni organization briskly, and – in the same style as was to characterize his term as chancellor of the university half a century later – was not slow in administering a rebuke to Borden when the president tried to excuse himself from attending an inaugural banquet of the Halifax association in late February: 'the Executive thinks that it would be well for you to reconsider your decision and put yourself out to some extent in order to be present.'[149] One reason for Borden's reluctance to travel to Halifax was undoubtedly the imminence of his departure for the west. On 14 March, he attended the founding meeting of an alumni chapter in Montreal, and similar events followed later in the month in Winnipeg, Regina, Saskatoon, Calgary, and Edmonton. By the beginning of April, Borden had reached Vancouver, where he attended an inaugural banquet for the local association, under the presidency of S.D. Scott, and spent several days before returning eastward, stopping in Toronto on 15 April to receive a 'hearty response' from over 50 alumni and guests.[150] As a means of encouraging western alumni, Borden's long journey had undoubtedly been successful.

Whether that success was enough to ensure the overall success of the campaign, however, was still in doubt. Borden reported to the annual meeting of the alumni association in May 1912 that subscriptions of some $94,000 had been given, although only a small proportion had as yet been paid. The target figure was still far distant. Furthermore, later in 1912, the results of the audit which had been in progress for over a year were finally announced to the board of regents. They showed an accumulated debt which was much higher than had been expected: it amounted to no less than $113,775.89, including over $39,000 in debentures, $15,000 owed to the Royal Bank, and a long list of smaller amounts owed to individuals or due to be returned to the endowment funds.[151] One result of this discouraging news was the decision to consult with a professional fund-raiser, R.A. Cassidy of New York, on whose advice it was determined that the campaign would close with a concentrated effort in the spring of 1913.[152] This plan was duly carried into effect, and the result was to bring the amount subscribed up to $215,000. It was a substantial amount, but not as much as had been hoped for. 'We have not finished our Campaign,' confided Borden to Archibald in June, 'and I suppose never will.' As was made clear in the Mount Allison report of 1914 to the general conference, only some $65,000 of the amount suscribed had as yet been paid in cash, and the income from that sum had already been offset by modest increases in professorial salaries and certain other expenses.[153] Nor had the salary increases had the desired effect of stabilizing the faculty, at least to judge by the departure of H.E. Bigelow to take up a position at Brown University in Rhode Island in the summer of 1914. It had been R.C. Archibald who had drawn Bigelow's attention to the opportunity, and when Borden became aware in late March that he was about to lose the services of one of the most successful young faculty members at Mount Allison, his reaction was one of resentment, directed not against Bigelow but against Brown University. 'It seems to me,' he informed his old friend Archibald, 'that there might be plenty of men found to fill such a position ... without robbing the weak to stengthen the strong.'[154]

By the spring of 1914, therefore, the financial campaign had not resolved the difficulties confronting Mount Allison during the early years of Borden's presidency, although it had certainly mitigated them to some extent. The truth was that the university's most fundamental problems were not financial, but rather concerned its very character and role. In its early years, the Mount Allison college had sought to serve its constituency – Eastern British America – as a small and unpretentious institution. Until 1881, it had earnestly sought to function as part of a greater federated university in either New Brunswick or Nova Scotia. By the second decade of the twentieth century, some things had changed but little since those days. Mount Allison University still primarily served the same geographical area: in the year 1910–11, 87.7 per cent of the students came from the three Maritime provinces, and a further 6.5 per cent from Newfoundland. The Maritime students continued to some in large part from rural areas and small towns – 39.0 per cent from small communities in 1910–11 and 14.7 per cent from incorporated centres with a population of between 1001 and 2500 – with a substantial minority from larger centres, including 19.9 per cent in 1910–11 from the larger towns and cities of over 10,000 people.[155] But if the proportions had not changed radically, the numbers had, and so had the physical environment of the campus. The ending of government grants in 1881 had launched Mount Allison on a period of rapid expansion, fuelled by industrial developments in the Maritime region. New programmes and new buildings had followed one another, each entrenching yet more firmly the vision of a greater Mount Allison, and student attendance in the 1910–11 year stood at 155, more than six times the enrolment as it had been in 1881.

Exhilarating as the expansionist era had been, it was now at an end. Borden's vision of a glorious national role for Mount Allison as Canada consolidated its control of the west represented a serious effort to come to grips with the reality of the crisis which had become clear in 1911: never an expansionist for its own sake, he had admitted the possibility that Mount Allison's future role might not be that of a large university. Whether its mission as a Methodist institution would be as he had envisaged in 1911 still remained to be seen in 1914. What also remained to be seen was the overall role which would be played within the dominion by the Maritime region. The suggestion that it might come to be recognized, like New England in the United States, as a region where rural and industrial pursuits flourished together and where old-established institutions provided university education of high quality, was not a foolish one. Yet just as there were already signs of economic decline and consequent social disruption in the region, so at Mount Allison the pace of the university's recovery from the crisis of 1911 had been frustratingly slow. The campaign had shown that donations from Maritime industrialists could no longer, as they had during the 1880s, rescue the university from its financial straits, and even the appeal to western alumni had not done so entirely. Not that all was gloom. Even after the departure of Bigelow, there was still talk of a new science building, for some $35,000 of the funds subscribed during the campaign had been directed towards this goal.[156] According to Borden, there was much encouragement to be had also from the high academic standards of the students of the university: 'educationally everything is going splendidly,' he commented to Archibald in March 1914. 'I do not despair,' he concluded, 'of the working out of all our difficulties and am satisfied that there is a future, even if a modest one, for our little College.'[157]

Borden's assessment was as moderate as its tone was serene. Given the right circumstances, the current uncertainties might be favourably resolved. In the world at large, however, there were greater uncertainties in the year of 1914. During the early summer would begin the Balkan crisis that would transform the already growing military preparedness and international tension into outright conflict. Even at Mount Allison, military matters were already under discussion. An approach from the Department of Militia and Defence in 1911 regarding the formation of an officers' training corps had produced no response from the university. When renewed in 1913, it was received more enthusiastically: Lingley Hall, although established on its new site, had not yet been fitted out as a gymnasium, and it was hoped that the military authorities might furnish it at their expense so as to use it as a drill hall.[158] Negotiations were still in progress when, on 4 August 1914, Canada went to war. The Allisonians most immediately affected were those in Europe at the time. George Trueman, coming towards the end of a year's study leave from his duties as principal of Stanstead College, was at the University of Berlin during the summer of 1914, but was already on his way to Paris when war was declared. Winthrop Bell was not so lucky, and spent the next four years in an internment camp.[159] For those safely in Canada, the *Wesleyan* had a reassuring message, and a familiar one in the early months of the war: 'business as usual.'[160] It would not be long before it was clear at Mount Allison, as elsewhere, just how empty that reassurance was.

ABBREVIATIONS

NOTES

TABLES

INDEX

Abbreviations

CCA	Carnegie Corporation of New York, Archives
DCB	Dictionary of Canadian Biography
DUA	Dalhousie University Archives, Halifax, NS
MAA	Mount Allison University Archives, Sackville, NB
MCA	Maritime Conference Archives, United Church of Canada, Halifax, NS
NBM	New Brunswick Museum, Saint John, NB
PAC	Public Archives of Canada, Ottawa, Ontario
PANB	Provincial Archives of New Brunswick, Fredericton, NB
PANS	Public Archives of Nova Scotia, Halifax, NS
UCA	United Church Archives, Toronto, Ontario
WMMS	Wesleyan Methodist Missionary Society Archives, University of London, School of Oriental and African Studies

Notes

CHAPTER 1

1 United Church of Canada, Maritime Conference Archives, Halifax [hereafter MCA], minutes of the New Brunswick District, 1826–49, pp. 218–19. C.F. Allison to W. Temple, 4 June 1839, University of London, School of Oriental and African Studies, Wesleyan Methodist Missionary Society Archives [hereafter WMMS], box 101, file 11b, no. 14. When the New Brunswick District had been detached from that of Nova Scotia in 1826, it had been defined to include the Annapolis Valley region of Nova Scotia, while the new Nova Scotia District also included Prince Edward Island. Thus, the two districts included all three Maritime provinces. See Goldwin French, *Parsons and Politics: The Role of the Wesleyan Methodists in Upper Canada and the Maritimes from 1780 to 1855* (Toronto, 1962), 86.

2 Letter of Enoch Wood to the *Wesleyan* (Halifax), 19 May 1882. On other Methodist schools in non-urban locations, see Mary Godfrey Evans, 'Mount Allison Wesleyan Academy and College' (M ED thesis, Bishop's University, 1978), 14, 70ff.; Carl F. Price, *Wesleyan's First Century: With an Account of the Centennial Celebration* (Middletown, Conn., 1932), 15–18.

3 MCA, minutes of New Brunswick District, 1826–49, p. 218.

4 *Religious and Literary Journal* (Saint John, NB), vol. 1, no. 30 (15 August 1829), 236.

5 William Croscombe to Richard Watson, 31 December 1832, WMMS, box 97, file 7a, no. 94; article by 'S.L.S', in the *Wesleyan*, 5 June 1890; see also T. Watson Smith, *History of the Methodist Church within the Territories Embraced in the Late Conference of Eastern British America, including Nova Scotia, New Brunswick, Prince Edward Island and Bermuda*, 2 vols. (Halifax, 1877–90), II, 389.

6 *Religious and Literary Journal*, 1, no. 30 (15 August 1829), 236. On Wesley's

concept of education, see Maldwyn Edwards, 'John Wesley,' in Rupert Davies and Gordon Rupp, eds., *A History of the Methodist Church in Great Britain, Volume I* (London, 1965), 45, 67; and Evans, 'Mount Allison,' 19–20. On Methodist tolerance in matters of church polity, see John Lawson, 'The People Called Methodists: 2. "Our Discipline,"' in Davies and Rupp, *Methodist Church in Great Britain*, I, 189–90.

7 William Croscombe to Richard Watson, 31 December 1832, WMMS, box 97, file 7a, no. 94; MCA, minutes of New Brunswick District, 1826–49, p. 107; MCA, minutes of Nova Scotia District, 1827–40, pp. 174–6, 186–7, 194–5; Smith, *Methodist Church in Eastern British America*, II, 389–90; H.H. Walsh, *The Christian Church in Canada* (Toronto, 1956), 164. The failure of fund-raising in Nova Scotia was blamed in part on the economic depression of 1834; see also W.S. MacNutt, *The Atlantic Provinces: The Emergence of Colonial Society, 1712–1857* (Toronto, 1965), 199.

8 John Beecham to the chairman, Nova Scotia District, 27 February 1834, WMMS, box 24, letterbook, 1820–36, pp. 427–8. Beecham also addressed a similar, though shorter, letter to the New Brunswick District on 5 March 1834, ibid., p. 431.

9 Pickard to Alder, 4 March 1837, WMMS, box 100, file 10b, no. 4; G.G. Findlay and W.W. Holdsworth, *The History of the Wesleyan Methodist Missionary Society*, 5 vols. (London, 1921), I, 333–4. On the early organizational history of Methodism in the Maritimes, see ibid., ch. 5; French, *Parsons and Politics*, chs. 2–4; E. Arthur Betts, *Bishop Black and His Preachers* (Halifax, 1976), part I; Smith, *Methodist Church in Eastern British America*, I, chs. 12, 14, 15; II, chs. 1, 4, 5.

10 Betts, *Black and His Preachers*, 88–91; French, *Parsons and Politics*, 92–3; Smith, *Methodist Church in Eastern British America*, II, 407–10. The *Religious and Literary Journal*, published in Saint John in 1829–30, had been edited by the Methodist preacher Alexander McLeod, but had not been an avowedly Methodist publication.

11 E.P. Thompson, *The Making of the English Working Class*, 2nd ed. (London, 1968), 46–8. The Methodist doctrines which are briefly sketched in this paragraph are discussed in great detail in many published works on Wesleyan theology. I have drawn in particular upon Davies and Rupp, *Methodist Church in Great Britain*, I; and Bernard Semmel, *The Methodist Revolution* (New York, 1973).

12 On the internal conflicts within British Methodism in the early nineteenth century, see in particular W.R. Ward, *Religion and Society in England, 1790–1850* (London, 1972), esp. pp. 135–76.

13 See Semmel, *Methodist Revolution*, 146–69; but see also the critique of certain

aspects of Semmel's argument in Stuart Piggin, 'Halévy Revisited: the origins of the Wesleyan Methodist Missionary Society: An examination of Semmel's Thesis,' *Journal of Imperial and Commonwealth History*, 9(1980–1), 17–37.

14 Beecham to chairman, Nova Scotia District, 27 February 1834, WMMS, box 24, letterbook, 1820–36, pp. 427–8.

15 French, *Parsons and Politics*, 87.

16 Among the major works on Alline and his movement are J.M. Bumsted, *Henry Alline* (Toronto, 1971); and Gordon Stewart and George A. Rawlyk, *A People Highly Favoured of God: The Nova Scotia Yankees and the American Revolution* (Toronto, 1972). On the strained relationship between Black and Alline, see Betts, *Black and His Preachers*, 6–8; Bumsted, *Alline*, 59–60; French, *Parsons and Politics*, 32–3; and Walsh, *Christian Church in Canada*, 125.

17 For general treatments of the religious history of the Maritimes in the late eighteenth and early nineteenth centuries, see MacNutt, *The Atlantic Provinces*, 104–7, 159–65; and Walsh, *Christian Church in Canada*, chs. 9 and 10. On the role of Bishop Inglis, see Judith Fingard, *The Anglican Design in Loyalist Nova Scotia, 1783–1816* (London, 1972), passim.

18 Betts, *Black and His Preachers*, 70; French, *Parsons and Politics*, 90; MacNutt, *The Atlantic Provinces*, 159. In addition to the Wesleyan Methodists, there was also a small number of Bible Christian Methodists in Prince Edward Island, a movement which had originated in the west of England by seceding from the main Wesleyan connection. See William Howard Brooks, 'The Changing Character of Maritime Wesleyan Methodism, 1855–1883' (MA thesis, Mount Allison University, 1965), 37–40.

19 Quoted in French, *Parsons and Politics*, 64. See also Brooks, 'Maritime Wesleyan Methodism,' 32–3.

20 See Walsh, *Christian Church in Canada*, 128; MacNutt, *The Atlantic Provinces*, 161–2; and C.M. Wallace, 'Lemuel Allan Wilmot,' in *Dictionary of Canadian Biography* (hereafter DCB), ed. George Brown *et al.* (7 vols to date, Toronto, 1966–), IX, 709–10.

21 Petition of Point de Bute Circuit, Westmorland County, to Sir William Colebrooke, 1 February 1842, appendix, Provincial Archives of New Brunswick [hereafter PANB], RG2, RS8, group 1, 1/4. Similar petitions from other circuits are also filed here. For discussion of the social and political concerns of Methodists in the Maritimes, and comparisons with Upper Canada, see French, *Parsons and Politics*, chs. 3–5.

22 See French, *Parsons and Politics*, 91.

23 On Allison's conversion, see Smith, *Methodist Church in Eastern British America*, II, 285–7; a description of the revival meetings in Sackville can be found in letter of J.B. Strong, 12 April 1836, WMMS, box 99, file 9b, no. 22.

24 See Leonard Allison Morrison, *The History of the Alison or Allison Family in Europe and America* (Boston, 1893), 181–6, 194–5; W.C. Milner, *History of Sackville, New Brunswick* (Sackville, 1934), 114; John G. Reid, 'Charles Frederick Allison,' DCB, VIII. On the family tradition which holds that Joseph Allison, grandfather of Charles, left his home in Limavady, Northern Ireland, because of an altercation with a rent-collector who felt that Allison could afford to pay more rent because he possessed a set of new silver spoons, see Harold Garnet Black, 'Hinges of Fate: The Remarkable Story of the Founding of Mount Allison University, Sackville,' *Atlantic Advocate*, 56, no. 9 (May 1966), 48.

25 Milner, *History of Sackville*, 142–3; Dale E. Alward, 'Down Sackville Ways: Shipbuilding in a Nineteenth Century New Brunswick Outport' (BA thesis, Mount Allison University, 1978), 7–8. For evidence of the operations of Crane and Allison, see New Brunswick Museum [hereafter NBM], New Brunswick Historical Society papers, packets 24, 25, 26; see also Graeme Wynn, 'Industrialism, Entrepreneurship, and Opportunity in the New Brunswick Timber Trade,' in Lewis R. Fischer and Eric W. Sager, eds., *The Enterprising Canadians: Entrepreneurs and Economic Development in Eastern Canada, 1820–1914* (St John's, Nfld., 1979), esp. pp. 12–16; and Wynn, *Timber Colony: A Historical Geography of Early Nineteenth Century New Brunswick* (Toronto, 1981), 71, 76, 124.

26 Alward, 'Down Sackville Ways,' 136–7. On the development of Sackville in its earliest years, see James D. Snowdon, 'Footprints in the Marsh Mud: Politics and Land Settlement in the Township of Sackville, 1760–1800' (MA thesis, University of New Brunswick, 1974).

27 Milner, *Sackville*, 142–5; W.S. MacNutt, *New Brunswick: A History, 1784–1867* (Toronto, 1963), 247. Crane served briefly in the Legislative Council after being defeated in the provincial election of 1842.

28 'The Old Sackville Academy,' article by 'An Old Boy,' in the *Argosy* (Mount Allison student magazine), February 1913, p. 264; E.B. Chandler to C.F. Allison, 20 February 1849,Mount Allison University Archives [hereafter MAA], C.F. Allison papers, 7946/6, p. 7; Allison to Chandler (draft), 1 March1849, ibid.

29 MAA, Sackville United Church records, 7933/1/39.

30 Gerald T. Rimmington, 'English Educational Ideas and Forms in a New Brunswick Parish: Sackville 1818–1837,' *History of Education Society Bulletin*, no. 27 (Spring 1981), 46–8; Katherine F.C. MacNaughton, *The Development of the Theory and Practice of Education in New Brunswick, 1784–1900* (Fredericton, 1947), 65–9.

31 Proposal of W. Botsford, W. Crane, and Edward Dixon, 3 January 1820, MAA, Archibald papers, 5501/13/8, p. 24.

32 Rimmington, 'English Educational Ideas and Forms,' 49.

33 On the operations of the Westmorland Grammar School up until 1836, see MAA, Westmorland Grammar School papers, 7603; NBM, Milner documents, packet 9, no. 1; Rimmington, 'English Educational Ideas and Forms,' 49–50. On the county grammar schools in general, see MacNaughton, *Education in New Brunswick*, 62–3, 107–9. There is no further evidence of the Westmorland Grammar School in Sackville after 1837: the last known teacher, Hugh Allen, was granted £50 by the New Brunswick assembly in 1839 as compensation for his teaching in the yars 1836 and 1837. *Journals of New Brunswick House of Assembly*, 1839, p. 327. The school was apparently revived in Shediac in the 1850s, and in the 1870s was attended by the future historian J.C. Webster. Rimmington, 'English Educational Ideas and Forms,' 49; John Clarence Webster, *Those Crowded Years, 1863–1944: An Octogenarian's Record of Work* (Shediac, 1944), 3.

34 William B. Hamilton, 'Society and Schools in Nova Scotia,' in J.D. Wilson, R.M. Stamp, and L.-P. Audet, eds., *Canadian Education: A History* (Toronto, 1970), 92–9; W.S. MacNutt, 'The Universities of the Maritimes: A Glance Backwards,' *Dalhousie Review*, 53 (1973–4), 431–8; Gerald T. Rimmington, 'The Founding of Universities in Nova Scotia,' *Dalhousie Review*, 46(1966–7), 320–7. The political struggles through which the accessibilityof the Pictou Academy to members of all denominations became intimately linked with the reform movement in Nova Scotia, and the influence of this issue on the Baptist decision to found the Horton Academy, are fully discussed in William B. Hamilton, 'Education, Politics and Reform in Nova Scotia, 1800–1848' (PHD thesis, University of Western Ontario, 1970), 102–3, 128, 136–7, 150–1, 174–9; and Barry M. Moody, 'The Founding of Acadia College' (paper presented to Atlantic Canada Studies Conference, Halifax, NS, April 1980), 3–5. On the general question of changes in Baptist attitudes towards education, see Barry M. Moody, 'The Maritime Baptists and Higher Education in the Early Nineteenth Century,' in Moody, ed., *Repent and Believe: The Baptist Experience in Maritime Canada* (Hantsport, NS, 1980), 88–102.

35 Quoted in D. MacMurray Young, 'The Politics of Higher Education in the Maritimes in the 1820s: The New Brunswick Experience' (paper presented to Atlantic Canada Studies Conference, Halifax, NS, April 1980), 4–5. On the more general aspects of the development of the College of New Brunswick, see Alfred G. Bailey, 'Early Foundations, 1783–1829,' in Alfred G. Bailey, ed., *The University of New Brunswick Memorial Volume* (Fredericton, 1950) 15–21.

36 Quoted in Frances A. Firth, 'History of Higher Education in New Brunswick to 1864' (MA thesis, University of New Brunswick, 1951), 181; on the background to the granting of the charter, see Young, 'Politics of Higher Education,' passim.

37 Firth, 'Higher Education in New Brunswick,' 229; Frances A. Firth, 'King's College, Fredericton, 1829–1859,' in Bailey, *Memorial Volume*, 23–7.

38 See *N.B. Assembly Journal*, 1837–38, pp. 23, 76, 152, 200, 220, 223, 228, and appendix 10; also MacNutt, *New Brunswick*, ch. 10; Firth, 'King's College,' 23–4; and Allison A. Trites, 'The New Brunswick Baptist Seminary, 1833–1895,' in Moody, *Repent and Believe*, 103–8.

39 D.C. Harvey, *An Introduction to the History of Dalhousie University* (Halifax, 1938), 15–61; Hamilton, 'Education, Politics, and Reform,' 260–4; Hamilton, 'Society and Schools in Nova Scotia,' 96–98; MacNutt, 'Universities of the Maritimes,' 433–6; Rimmington, 'Universities of Nova Scotia,' 324–9; Laurence K. Shook, *Catholic Post-Secondary Education in English-Speaking Canada: A History* (Toronto, 1971), 58–9; Moody, 'Founding of Acadia College,' passim. St Mary's College had a 'pre-history' of attempts dating from 1802, but its 'real story' began in 1838. Shook, 57–8.

40 William B. Hamilton, 'Society and Schools in New Brunswick and Prince Edward Island,' in Wilson, Stamp, and Audet, *Canadian Education*, 120.

41 The Wesleyan Day School which began in 1839 in the basement of Brunswick Street Church in Halifax started with a different aim – to give basic instruction to poor children – although by 1850 it too claimed the title of academy.Petition of the trustees of the Methodist Church in Halifax to the House of Representatives of Nova Scotia [1839], Public Archives of Nova Scotia [hereafter PANS], MG17, vol. 17, no. 65; Judith Fingard, 'Attitudes Towards the Education of the Poor in Colonial Halifax,' *Acadiensis*, 2 (Spring 1973), 23.

42 For comment on Methodist attitudes to education, see Price, *Wesleyan's First Century*, 15–16.

43 See French, *Parsons and Politics*, 152–3, 158; C.B. Sissons, *A History of Victoria University* (Toronto, 1952), chs. 1 and 2. Richey's career as principal was shortened by the conflicts which led in 1840 to an outright breach in Upper Canada between the politically conservative supporters of the Missionary Society and the more reform-minded Methodists led by the Ryerson brothers, Egerton, John, and William.

44 *Wesleyan*, 9 April 1838. On Shenstone, see Smith, *Methodism in Eastern British America*, II, 228.

45 *Wesleyan*, 6 May 1838.

46 *Wesleyan*, 19 May 1882.

47 MCA, minutes of New Brunswick District, 1826–49, pp. 231–2.

48 Archives of the United Church of Canada, [hereafter UCA], Wesleyan Methodist Missionary Society Committee minutes, 1837–51 (microfilm), 118–20.

49 Enoch Wood to secretaries of Wesleyan missions, 24 January 1840, WMMS, box 101, file 11b, no. 42; D.W. Johnson, *History of Methodism in Eastern British America* (Sackville, [1925]), 365; Milner, *Sackville*, 15–32.

50 Wood to secretaries of Wesleyan missions, 24 January 1840, WMMS, box 101, file

11b, no. 42; summary of expenditure on academy to 31 December 1840, MAA, C.F. Allison papers, 7946/3, p. 1.

51 *British North American Wesleyan Methodist Magazine* (Saint John, NB), October 1840, p. 80.

52 Wood to secretaries of Wesleyan missions, 24 January 1840, WMMS, box 101, file 11b, no. 42; see also the *British North American Wesleyan Methodist Magazine*, October 1840, p. 80; and Wood's article in the *Wesleyan*, 19 May 1882.

53 Address of Richard Knight and William Temple, *British North American Wesleyan Methodist Magazine*, October 1841, p. 558.

54 Enoch Wood to secretaries of Wesleyan missions, 29 December 1840, WMMS, box 101, file 11b, no. 67; receipt of J.C. Bugbee, 31 December 1840, MAA, C.F. Allison papers, 7946/3, p. 3. Bugbee's daily fee was 15 shillings.

55 Address of Knight and Temple, *British North American Wesleyan Methodist Magazine*, October 1841, p. 558; Enoch Wood to Robert Alder, 30 June 1841, WMMS, box 102, file 12b, no. 9.

56 *British North American Wesleyan Methodist Magazine*, July 1842, p. 274; W.M. Leggett to 'Mr. McCausland,' 26 July 1842, MAA, 8123.

57 Temple to Alder, 27 January 1842, WMMS, box 102, file 12b, no. 16.

58 James Ross to C.F. Allison, 11 October 1842, MAA, C.F. Allison papers, 7946/3, p. 30. Some years before, Ross had taught at the Westmorland Grammar School in Sackville, and so had long been acquainted with Allison and with the town. He would end his career as president of Dalhousie College, a position he held from 1863 to 1885. See Allan C. Dunlop, 'James Ross,' DCB, XI, 772–3; Harvey, *Introduction to History of Dalhousie*, 85–109; Rimmington, 'English Educational Ideas and Forms,' 49–50. On the *Presbyterian Banner*, see Gertrude E.N. Tratt, *A Survey and Listing of Nova Scotia Newspapers, 1752–1957* (Halifax, 1979), 85–6, 169.

59 These figures are contained in a statement sent by William Temple and Sampson Busby, trustees of the Wesleyan Academy, to the Lieutenant-Governor, Legislative Council and Assembly of New Brunswick, 16 February 1843, PANB, RG2, RS8, group I, 1/4.

60 Rice to Allison, 2 August 1842, MAA, C.F. Allison papers, 7946/3, p. 30.

61 McNutt to Allison, 25 August 1842, ibid., p. 26; Rice to Allison, 27 October 1842, ibid., p. 30.

62 *British North American Wesleyan Methodist Magazine*, February 1842, pp. 72–3; MCA, minutes of New Brunswick District, 1826–49, p. 288.

63 Wood to Alder, 30 March 1842, WMMS, box 102, file 12b, no. 22; *N.B. Assembly Journal*, 1842, p. 176. On the same day, a grant of £250 was awarded to the Baptist school in Fredericton.

64 Petitions, January and February 1842, PANB, RG2, RS8, group I, 1/4; and RG4,

RS/24/842/pe/1–12. See also *N.B. Assembly Journal*, pp. 18, 59, 62, 69, 73, 76, 80, 85, 88, 91–2, 93, 101.

65 MCA, minutes of Nova Scotia District, 1841–52, p. 44; petitions, 1843, PANS, RG5, series P, vols. 71, 74; *Journals of the Nova Scotia Assembly*, 1843, pp. 371–9, 459, 474, 488.

66 *N.B. Assembly Journal*, 1843, pp. 90, 205.

67 Quoted in Ward, *Religion and Society in England*, 240.

68 Wood to Alder, 30 June 1841, WMMS, box 102, file 12b, no. 9; Temple to secretaries of Wesleyan missions, 15 December 1841, ibid., no. 15.

69 Temple to secretaries of Wesleyan missions, 15 December 1841, ibid., no. 15; Temple to Alder, 27 January 1842, ibid., no. 16.

70 Richey to Wood, 7 February 1842, ibid., no. 20. On Richey's career, see G. S. French, 'Matthew Richey,' DCB, XI, 733–5.

71 Wood to Allison, 20 August 1842, MAA, 8329; Wood to Allison, 6 September 1842, ibid.

72 Wood to Allison, 7 October 1842, ibid.

73 McNutt to Allison, 25 August 1842, MAA, C.F. Allison papers, 7946/3, p.26; Wood to Alder, 15 October 1842, WMMS, box 102, file 12b, no. 38.

74 Wood to Alder, 15 October 1842, ibid. Examples of the wording of the petitions may be found in Petitions of the Wesleyan Congregations and Others in Point de Bute Circuit, 1 February 1842, PANB, RG2, RS8, group I, 1/4; and Petitions of the Wesleyan Congregations and Others on the Lunenburg Circuit, [2 February 1843], PANS, RG5, series P, vol. 71, no. 94. On the career of Enoch Wood, see Calvin Glenn Lucas, 'Enoch Wood,' DCB, XI, 935–6.

75 Wood to Allison, 24 October 1842, MAA, 8329.

76 MCA, minutes of New Brunswick District, 1826–49, pp. 305–6.

77 On DesBrisay, see Smith, *Methodism in Eastern BritishAmerica*, II, 267; Betts, *Black and His Preachers*, 135; and MCA, minutes of New Brunswick District,1826–49, p. 160.

78 Ibid., p. 289.

79 MAA, journal of Humphrey Pickard, 8203, p.61.

80 Biographical accounts of Pickard can be found in G.S. French,'Humphrey Pickard,' DCB, XI, 687–8; Winthrop Bell, *A Genealogical Study* (Sackville, NB, 1962), 178–80; and Smith, *Methodism in Eastern British America*, II, 269–71. Details of his early career can also be gathered from the letters and other writings of his first wife, in Edward Otheman, ed., *Memoir and Writings of Mrs. Hannah Maynard Pickard* (Boston, 1845). On the rather complex processes by which a candidate proceeded towards the Wesleyan ministry, see Betts, *Black and His Preachers*, 71–5.

81 Petition of William Temple, Sampson Busby, and Enoch Wood, 27 December 1842, PANB, RG2, RS8, group I, 1/4.
82 Ibid.; inaugural address of Humphrey Pickard, *British North American Wesleyan Methodist Magazine*, August 1843, p. 289.
83 Letter of Hannah Maynard Pickard, 14 February 1843, in Otheman, ed., *Memoir and Writings of Hannah Maynard Pickard*, 199–201; see also MAA, journal of Humphrey Pickard, 8203, p. 62.

CHAPTER 2

1 'An Inaugural Address, Delivered at the Opening of the Wesleyan Academy, Mount Allison, Sackville, New Brunswick, by the Principal, the Rev. H. Pickard, A.M.' *British North American Wesleyan Methodist Magazine*, August 1843, p. 281.
2 *British North American Wesleyan Methodist Magazine*, August 1843, pp. 317–19.
3 Ibid, May 1843, pp. 198–9; letter of Hannah Maynard Pickard, 14 February 1843, in Otheman, *Memoir and Writings*, 201.
4 Inaugural address, p. 290.
5 Ibid., p. 282.
6 Temple to Alder, 29 March 1843, WMMS, box 103, file 13b, no. 3.
7 Inaugural address, p. 282.
8 Ibid. Fisk had also stressed the timeliness of educational development, in the context of contemporary efforts to ameliorate the human condition on an international scale, in his inaugural address at Wesleyan University on 21 September 1831. See Price, *Wesleyan's First Century*, 33–5.
9 Inaugural address, p. 284. On Ryerson's address and on the views of other contemporary British North American educators, see A.B. McKillop, *A Disciplined Intelligence: Critical Inquiry and Canadian Thought in the Victorian Era* (Montreal, 1979), 9–21.
10 Inaugural address, p. 289.
11 Inaugural address, p. 285. Pickard's discussion of capital outlay was clearly based on the statement which had been submitted to the New Brunswick legislature by William Temple and Sampson Busby, as trustees of the academy, on 16 February 1843, PANB, RG2, RS8, group I, 1/4.
12 Inaugural address, p. 289.
13 *Catalogues* of Wesleyan Academy, 1843–52, and *Mount Allison Academic Gazette*, 1853–7; report of James Brown, 26 November 1844, *N.B. Assembly Journal*, 1845, appendix, pp. ciii–civ.

14 MAA, financial statements of Wesleyan Academy, 8243/7, pp. 24–9; the figure of £411 for provincial grants is calculated exclusive of the special grant of £500 voted by the province of New Brunswick for the furnishing of the academy, which was entered in the 1843–4 financial statement.
15 Inaugural address, pp. 285–6.
16 See the obituary of Hea published anonymously in the Saint John *Globe* of 25 January 1905 by Professor A.D. Smith of Mount Allison, in MAA, Archibald papers, 5501/15, vol. 1, p. 83; also Kenneth A. MacKirdy, 'The Formation of a Modern University, 1859–1906,' in Bailey, *Memorial Volume*, 34.
17 Inaugural address, p. 286; C.F. Allison to Richard Knight, 1 April 1843, MAA, C.F. Allison papers, 7946/3, p. 36; Johnson, *History of Methodism in Eastern British America*, 366.
18 Inaugural address, p. 286.
19 Ibid., pp. 287–8.
20 See McKillop, *A Disciplined Intelligence*, 62–4.
21 *A Catalogue of the Officers and Students of the Wesleyan Academy, Mount Allison, Sackville, New-Brunswick, for the Year Commencing 19th January, 1843*, 9.
22 *Catalogue*, for year commencing 1 February 1844, p. 11.
23 *Catalogue* for year commencing 19 January 1843, p. 9; *Catalogue*, for year commencing 1 February 1844, pp. 11–12. The curriculum of the Wesleyan Academy bore clearly the signs of its close relationship with that of Wesleyan University, in Connecticut, from which Humphrey Pickard had graduated in 1839. The kinship of the mathematical, philosophical, and scientific subjects to those taught at Wesleyan University was especially striking and, although the academy catalogue did not specify the textbooks to be used, it is likely that they too were selected at least in part from among those with which Pickard had become familiar at Middletown. See *Catalogue*, Wesleyan University, 1838–9, pp. 15–18.
24 *Catalogues*, 1843–52.
25 *Wesleyan*, 5 October 1850.
26 Quoted in Smith, *Methodist Church in Eastern British America*, II, 397. For a general interpretation of the evolution of 'bourgeois colleges' in the Maritimes – institutions offering education to students from the middle strata of society so as to facilitate their entry into positions of authority hitherto dominated by an old-established Anglican elite – see Richard Tulloss Darville, 'Political Economy and Higher Education in the Nineteenth Century Maritime Provinces,' (PH D thesis, University of British Columbia, 1977), esp. pp. 344–7, 368–9.
27 *Wesleyan*, 14 July 1849.

28 Wood to Alder, 28 October 1843, WMMS, box 103, file 13b, no. 20.
29 *British North American Wesleyan-Methodist Magazine*, August 1843, pp. 317–19.
30 Pickard to Alder, 29 December 1848, WMMS, box 104, file 14b, no. 60.
31 Richard Shepherd to C.F. Allison, 5 October 1843, MAA, C.F. Allison papers, 7946/3, p. 46; *Catalogues*, 1843–7.
32 *New Brunswick Courier*, 27 January 1844.
33 William Croscombe to Humphrey Pickard, 17 November 1843, MAA, C.F. Allison papers, 7946/3, p. 38.
34 See Tables 1 and 2.
35 *Catalogue*, 1844–5.
36 Wood to Alder, 28 October 1843, WMMS, box 103, file 13b, no. 20.
37 *Catalogue*, 1843–4, p. 12.
38 NBM, journal of James Brown, section A, 1844–6, p. 136. On Thompson Trueman and his farm at Point de Bute, see Howard Trueman, *The Chignecto Isthmus and its First Settlers* (Toronto, 1902), 131–40.
39 Report of James Brown, 26 November 1844, *N.B. Assembly Journal*, 1845, appendix, pp. ciii–civ.
40 Wood to Alder, 12 October 1844, WMMS, box 103, file 13b, no. 36.
41 *New Brunswick Courier*, 27 April 1844; see also W.A. Spray, 'Joseph Cunard,' DCB, IX, 170–2. Cunard's comment on the paucity of students at King's College was substantiated by the college's report to the legislature, dated 3 February 1844, which listed only 13 resident students for the year 1843. *N.B. Assembly Journal*, 1844, appendix, p. cxlv. Yet, as a defender of King's College pointed out in 1845, to compare King's unfavourably with the Sackville academy on the basis of this figure was not entirely fair, for if the students of the collegiate school in Fredericton were added to those of King's itself, the total was much more nearly equal to the Sackville enrolment. See the letter of 'An Old Student,' in *Loyalist and Conservative Advocate*, 15 May 1845.
42 *New Brunswick Courier*, 10 August 1844.
43 *Loyalist and Consrvative Advocate*, 12 September 1844. Homunculus was referring to a passage in Pickard's inaugural address, p. 292, in which he had compared the minds of academy students to books to be written on earth and afterwards 'elevated to the library of Heaven.'
44 See Wood to Alder, 15 July 1843, WMMS, box 103, file 13b, no. 16. On the controversies in Nova Scotia, see French, *Parsons and Politics*, 206–7; Hamilton, 'Education, Politics, and Reform,' 287–96; MacNutt, *The Atlantic Provinces*, 219–22; and MacNutt, 'Universities of the Maritimes,' 434–7.
45 Wood to Alder, 29 May 1844, WMMS, box 103, file 13b, no. 30.

46 *Loyalist and Conservative Advocate*, 13 March 1845.
47 Ibid.; *British North American Wesleyan Methodist Magazine*, August 1843, p. 317.
48 *Loyalist and Conservative Advocate*, 13 March 1845.
49 E.B. Chandler to [Hugh Johnston], 22 March 1845, NBM, Chandler papers, box 1, no. 51.
50 Ibid.
51 *N.B. Assembly Journal*, 1845, p. 160; *Loyalist and Conservative Advocate*, 3 April 1845.
52 *New Brunswick Courier*, 22 March 1845.
53 Wood to Alder, 29 March 1845, WMMS, box 103, file 13b, no. 50.
54 Report of A. DesBrisay, May 1845, *British North American Wesleyan Methodist Magazine*, July 1845, pp. 62–3.
55 See Joseph Holdich, *The Life of Willbur Fisk, D.D., First President of Wesleyan University* (New York, 1842), 168–70, 181–3; Frederick Rudolph, *The American College and University: A History* (New York, 1968), 68–85; George P. Schmidt, *The Liberal Arts College, A Chapter in American Cultural History* (New Brunswick, NJ, 1957), 88–9.
56 Letter of Humphrey Pickard, 18 March 1845, in *New Brunswick Courier*, 29 March 1845.
57 *New Brunswick Courier*, 12 April 1845.
58 J.J. Coulter, obituary of J.R. Inch, *Wesleyan*, 27 November 1912; MAA, journal of Humphrey Pickard, 8203, pp. 111–12.
59 Wood to Alder, 31 January 1846, WMMS, box 104, file 14b, no. 4; Allison to Hon. A. Campbell, 27 March 1845, MAA, 8329.
60 Letter of Pickard, 18 March 1845, in *New Brunswick Courier*, 29 March 1845; letter of 'Observer,' *New Brunswick Courier*, 24 May 1845.
61 Letter of A.E. Botsford, 4 April 1845, *New Brunswick Courier*, 12 April 1845.
62 *N.B. Legislative Council Journal*, 1845, p. 304; *Acts of the New Brunswick Legislature*, 8 Victoria C111; Firth, 'Higher Education in New Brunswick,' 237–83; Firth, 'King's College,' 24–5; MacNutt, *New Brunswick*, 305–6.
63 Colebrooke to Stanley, 24 April 1844, Great Britain, Public Record Office [hereafter PRO], CO188/86, pp. 261–2; Colebrooke to Stanley, 26 September 1845, PRO, CO188/92, pp. 49–51; Colebrooke to Earl Grey, 20 October 1846, NB Executive Council, Education, Colleges, Correspondence, 1803–57, Public Archives of Canada, MG9, A1, vol. 110.
64 Wood to Alder, 27 March 1846, WMMS, box 104, file 14b, no. 7.
65 Wood to Alder, 26 February 1847, ibid., no. 25.
66 Ibid. The first three from the Sackville academy to enrol as non-resident students

of King's College were members of the teaching staff: J.R. Hea, George Milligan, and T.W. Wood. *N.B. Assembly Journal*, 1847, appendix, p. lxxxvi.

67 *Catalogue*, 1846, p. 13.

68 *Catalogue*, 1852, p. 3; Johnson, *Methodism in Eastern British America*, 366. Also added to the staff at this time was Arthur McNutt Patterson as tutor in English, who was remembered by one student for his efforts to teach singing as well as English. See Milner, 'Mount Allison: Its Earlier Years,' p. 3, NBM, Mount Allison University papers, packet 1. On Hea see Smith's obituary, in MAA, Archibald papers, 5501/15, vol. 1, p. 83. Smith gives the date of Hea's departure as 1851, but the true date of 1852 is established by a letter written by Hea to William Crane, 12 March 1852, NBM, New Brunswick Historical Society papers, packet 3, no. 104. Since the purpose of this letter was to enquire as to the possibility of Hea's appointment as a school inspector, it raises questions as to the reason for Hea's resignation, since it was clearly not his initial intention to open his own school. Furthermore, an undated letter to Hea from 35 students paid tribute to his teaching, expressed their regret at the 'unavoidably, abrupt termination of your labours amongst us,' and hinted at 'misrepresentation' and 'calumny' against him. MAA, Wesleyan Academy papers, 8243/1. Surviving evidence sheds no further light on the episode, which is made all the more intriguing because of Hea's abrupt – and well-documented – departure as president of the University of New Brunswick eight years later. See Firth, 'Higher Education in New Brunswick,' 474–84; on the founding by Hea of the school at Lower Horton later known as the Acacia Villa School, see M.V. Marshall, *A Short History of Acacia Villa School* (Wolfville, NS, 1963), 11–15.

69 *Catalogue*, 1852, p. 12.

70 Ibid., pp. 4–8.

71 *Wesleyan*, 21 February 1852.

72 Amos Purdy to David Purdy, 14 November 1846, MAA, 0105.

73 Allen Otty to George Otty, 24 July 1844, NBM, Earle-Otty family papers, packet 3.

74 Amos Purdy to David Purdy, [c. January 1847], MAA 0105. The date actually written on this letter is January 1846, but this was added by Purdy apparently at the same time as he wrote a lengthy postscript on 12 March. The letter was clearly written within a short time of another dated Thursday, 11 February 1846. In this latter case, the date seems to be an error for 1847, as it was in 1847 that 11 February fell on a Thursday. Also, the contents of a letter dated 14 November 1846 appear to establish that Purdy had first arrived at the academy in the fall of that year. It thus seems safe to date the two letters of [c. January] and 11 February to the year 1847, though why the date was originally written as 1846 remains unclear.

75 Amos Purdy to David Purdy, 17 September 1847, MAA, 0105.
76 Amos Purdy to David Purdy, [22 January 1847], MAA, 0105.
77 Amos Purdy to David Purdy, [11 February 1847], MAA, 0105.
78 'The Old Sackville Academy, By an Old Boy,' *Argosy*, February 1913, p. 262.
79 Amos Purdy to David Purdy, [11 February 1847], MAA, 0105. Handball was another popular sport, though not in the winter season. On this sport and Humphrey Pickard's prowess at it, see [J.R. Inch], 'Reminiscences of Mount Allison, By a Former Teacher,' *Allisonia*, May 1904, p. 106.
80 Amos Purdy to David Purdy, [c. January 1847], postscript of 12 March [1847], MAA, 0105.
81 Ibid.
82 *Wesleyan*, 10 February 1853.
83 *New Brunswick Courier*, 12 October 1844; see also the letter written on the same day by Enoch Wood, in similar words which suggest that he may just have finished reading the newspaper at the time, to Alder, 12 October 1844, WMMS, box 103, file 13b, no. 36.
84 'Sackville Academy in Old Times, By an Old Student,' undated clipping from the *Daily Times* (Moncton), in MAA, Trueman papers, 7837–1. See also Milner, 'Mount Allison: Its Earlier Years,' p. 2; and 'The Old Sackville Academy, By an Old Boy,' *Argosy*, February 1913, p. 263.
85 Inaugural address, pp. 288–9.
86 Amos Purdy to David Purdy, 23 October 1847, MAA, 0105.
87 *Wesleyan*, 26 January 1893; see also Milner, 'Mount Allison: Its Earlier Years,' 2.
88 Milner, 'Mount Allison: Its Earlier Years,' 2.
89 'Sackville Academy In Old Times, By an Old Student,' MAA, Trueman papers, 7837–1. The Mechanics' Institute was awarded a provincial grant of £30 in 1848. See *N.B. Assembly Journal*, 1848, pp. 163, 225.
90 *Catalogue*, 1843–4, p. 12.
91 *Wesleyan*, 31 January 1852.
92 *Catalogue*, 1844–5, p. 15.
93 MAA, financial statements of Wesleyan Academy, 8243/7, p. 26.
94 *British North American Wesleyan Methodist Magazine*, June 1846, pp. 38–9; Enoch Wood to Robert Alder, 30 June 1846, WMMS, box 104, file 14b, no. 12. DeWolfe's address rejected the possibility that there could be any discrepancy between 'the testimony of nature and revelation,' though his view of biblical revelation was not entirely a literalist one: he was prepared to accept, for example, that geological evidence might show the earth to have been 'a veteran in years' before the planting of the Garden of Eden, and considered this no contradiction of the book of Genesis. Charles De Wolfe, 'Science and Religion,' *British North American Wesleyan Methodist Magazine*, July 1846, pp. 53–60.

95 [Inch], 'Reminiscences of Mount Allison,' *Allisonia*, March 1904, pp. 71–2.

96 MCA, minutes of New Brunswick District, 3 July 1847, pp. 425–6.

97 MCA, minutes of New Brunswick District, 18 May 1848, p. 463; Knight to secretaries of Wesleyan Missionary Society, 18 August 1848, WMMS, box 104, file 14b, no. 57. The details of the purchase of the land for the female academy are unclear, though it is possible that this was the land already purchased by the academy in 1846 for £700 and mentioned in Enoch Wood to Robert Alder, 28 February 1846, ibid., no. 5. Later in 1846, however, the academy's management committee contemplated the purchase of a further lot of land 'on the opposite side of the Road, owned by Mr. Joseph Bowser,' and from this description it would seem more likely that this was the land on which the female academy was ultimately built in the early 1850s. Minutes of the managing committee of the Wesleyan Academy, 23 June 1846, WMMS, box 104, file 14b, no. 11. On Joseph Bowser and his landholdings, see Reginald Burton Bowser, *A Genealogical Review of the Bowser Family* ([Sackville, NB], 1981), 5, 55–6.

98 The Cobourg Ladies' Seminary was moved in 1845 to Hamilton, Canada West, where it was known as the Burlington Ladies' Academy until its closure in 1851; the founders of the other Cobourg school, the Cobourg Ladies' Academy, removed to Toronto in 1847 to found the Adelaide Academy, which also later moved to Hamilton. See Marion Royce, 'Methodism and the Education of women in Nineteenth Century Ontario,' *Atlantis*, 3, no. 2 (Spring 1978), 130–43; Sissons, *History of Victoria University*, 23, 30–1, 47, 76.

99 On the addition to the academy building in 1846, see *British North American Wesleyan Methodist Magazine*, June 1846, p. 39. Its financing had been assisted by a special grant from the province of New Brunswick: *N.B. Assembly Journal*, 1846, p. 244. A further special grant of £200 was voted in 1847 for the same purpose. *N.B. Assembly Journal*, 1847, p. 216.

100 See MacNutt, *The Atlantic Provinces*, 234–7; MacNutt, *New Brunswick*, 315–25.

101 Pickard to Alder, 29 December 1848, WMMS, box 104, file 14b, no. 60.

102 Ephraim Evans and A.W. McLeod to Hon. Joseph Howe, Provincial Secretary, 2 February 1850, PANS, MG17, vol. 17, no. 72.

103 Wood to Alder, 28 June 1845, WMMS, box 103, file 13b, no. 62. The earlier history of Allison's trust deed is summarized in the act of incorporation finally passed by the New Brunswick legislature in 1849, *New Brunswick Acts*, 12 Victoria c65.

104 Wood to Alder, 31 January 1846, WMMS, box 104, file 14b, no. 4; minutes of managing committee, 23 June 1846, ibid., no. 11.

105 Knight to general secretaries of Missionary Society, 18 August 1848, ibid., no. 57. See also the expression of anxiety for a settlement, in MCA, minutes of New Brunswick District, 18 May 1848, p. 458.

106 UCA, Wesleyan Methodist Missionary Society minutes, 1837–51, pp. 401–4; MCA, minutes of New Brunswick District, 31 May 1849, pp. 474–5; Pickard to Alder, 29 December 1848, WMMS, box 104, file 14b, no. 60.
107 *N.B. Assembly Journal*, 1849, pp. 82–3, 113–15, 347; *N.B. Legislative Council Journal*, 1849, pp. 410–13, 521.
108 See MCA, minutes of New Brunswick District, 12 July 1839, pp. 231–2.
109 *New Brunswick Acts*, 12 Victoria c65.
110 Evans to Alder, 7 February 1849, WMMS, box 105, file 15a, no. 2; Harvey, *Introduction to History of Dalhousie*, 63–7; *Nova Scotia Statutes*, 8 Victoria c26; petition of Wesleyans and others, [February] 1849, PANS, RG5, series P, vol. 75, no. 90; *Nova Scotia Legislative Council Journal*, 1849, p. 37.
111 Petition of Evans and McLeod, 3 February 1849, PANS, RG5, series P, vol. 75; *N.S. Assembly Journal*, 1849, p. 241.
112 Evans to Alder, 7 February 1849, WMMS, box 105, file 15a, no. 2; Hamilton, 'Education, Politics, and Reform,' 301–2; Ronald Stewart Longley, *Acadia University, 1838–1938* (Wolfville, NS, 1939), 58; French, *Parsons and Politics*, 207–8.
113 *Wesleyan*, 29 September 1849, 20 October 1849, 26 January 1850, 9 February 1850, 2, 9, 30 March 1850.
114 *N.B. Assembly Journal*, 1851, pp. 257–8.
115 *Wesleyan*, 14 February 1852.
116 See table 2. On the subsequent rapid decline of the proportion of students from the cities, see also table 4.
117 *Provincial Wesleyan*, 9 September 1852.
118 Letter of Charles Allison, 18 March 1853, in the *Provincial Wesleyan*, 24 March 1853; see also Raymond Clare Archibald, *Historical Notes on the Education of Women at Mount Allison, 1854–1954* (Sackville, NB, 1954), 1.
119 The actual debit balance was £1749/8/5, but this was offset by £608/17/6 in payments due from students. MAA, Accounts of Wesleyan Academy, 8243/7, pp. 46–7. In at least one community, Barrington, Nova Scotia, the academy agent found out that economic prosperity was not uniform throughout the region and that out-migration was already having its effects in some localities, for the number of potential donors in Barrington had been greatly reduced 'by the stern hand of death, and by emigration to the United States and to Australia.' *Wesleyan*, 10 November 1853. On out-migration, which was to become a general characteristic of Maritime social history from the 1860s onward, see Alan A. Brookes, 'Out-Migration from the Maritime Provinces, 1860–1900: Some Preliminary Considerations,' *Acadiensis*, 5 (Spring 1976), 26–55.
120 *Mount Allison Academic Gazette* (Sackville), December 1853, p. 7.
121 Pickard to Rev. George Osborn, 12 October 1852, WMMS, box 106, file 16b, no.

13; MCA, minutes of New Brunswick District, 1850–5, May 1852, pp. 44–5; Richard Knight to Wesleyan Methodist Missionary Society committee, 18 July 1853, WMMS, box 106, file 16b, no. 27.

122 Knight to Wesleyan Methodist Missionary Society committee, 18 October 1853, ibid., no. 31; *Mount Allison Academic Gazette*, June 1854, p. 3.

123 *Provincial Wesleyan*, 10 August 1854. See also Geoffrey Bilson, 'The Cholera Epidemic in Saint John, N.B., 1854,' *Acadiensis*, 4 (Autumn 1974), 85–99.

124 *Mount Allison Academic Gazette*, December 1854, pp. 2–4.

125 Ibid., June 1854, p. 7.

126 Charlotte Dixon, 'Mt. Allison in 1854,' 8. This written manuscript is in the possession of Charlotte Dixon's niece, Mrs W.S. Godfrey, with a copy in MAA. Most of the students could attend the New Year's reunion, as few at this time made the long winter journey to go home for Christmas. For a number of years, begining in 1855–6, the academic year in fact ran continuously from August to June, the *Mount Allison Academic Gazette* announcing in June 1855, p. 6, that 'there is to be but one vacation in the year, which will be in the summer season, when the necessary travelling to and from the Institution may be performed with so much greater ease, comfort, and safety than it could be in the winter.'

127 Mrs C. Christie to R.C. Archibald, 22 April 1904, MAA, Archibald papers, 5501/13/9, p. 40.

128 The years between 1849 and 1852 saw an exceptionally large number of students attending from Prince Edward Island. In part, this may reflect the greater ability of the island's agricultural economy to resist the economic pressures of these years, especially as crop failures were avoided, and in part may have resulted from anticipation of a greater demand for teachers in view of the public education plans then in prospect on the Island. Also a possible influence was the example set by the enrolment in the literary and scientific course in 1848 of George Campbell, sone of the island's lieutenant-governor, Sir Donald Campbell. See Pickard to Alder, 29 December 1848, WMMS, box 104, file 14b, no. 60; W.S. MacNutt, 'Political Advance and Social Reform, 1842–1861,' in Francis W.P. Bolger, ed., *Canada's Smallest Province: A History of P.E.I.* ([Charlottetown], 1973) 125–8.

129 See Fingard, 'Attitudes Towards Education of the Poor in Colonial Halifax,' 23; *N.B. Assembly Journal*, 1855, pp. 106, 337.

130 See tables 2, 3, and 4.

131 Rudolph, *American College and University*, 311–12. The first college to be opened specifically for women was the Georgia Female College at Macon, chartered in 1836 and opened in 1839, which in 1843 came under Methodist control. See Evans, 'Mount Allison,' 94.

132 George Edward Levy, *The Baptists of the Maritime Provinces, 1753–1946* (Saint

John, NB, 1946), 119–22; Edward Manning Saunders, *History of the Baptists of the Maritime Provinces* (Halifax, 1902), 234; Trites, 'The New Brunswick Baptist Seminary,' 106–9. The female department of the Fredericton seminary would be reopened in 1857. Also in the late 1850s, the private schools which would be the forerunners of the Acadia Seminary – the chief rival of the Mount Allison ladies' academy in the later yars of the nineteenth century – were established in Wolfville. See *Memorials of Acadia College and Horton Academy for the Half-Century 1828–1878* (Montreal, 1881), 107–8; and James Doyle Davison, *Alice of Grand Pré: Alice T. Shaw and Her Grand Pré Seminary: Female Education in Nova Scotia and New Brunswick* (Wolfville, NS, 1981), passim. For general discussion of the contribution of evangelical Christianity to women's education and to the feminist movement, see Olive Banks, *Faces of Feminism: A Study of Feminism as a Social Movement* (New York, 1981), 185–6.

133 *Wesleyan*, 12 August 1839, 12 January 1850. Early girls' schools in the Maritimes are discussed in Davison, *Alice of Grand Pré*, 33–42.

134 *Mount Allison Academic Gazette*, June 1854, p. 7.

135 Elsie Pomeroy, 'Mary Electa Adams: A Pioneer Educator,' *Ontario History*, 41 (1949), 107–10; Dixon, 'Mt. Allison in 1854,' 1–2.

136 *N.B. Assembly Journal*, 1854, pp. 93,223. The committee appointed to consider the request reported favourably on 25 March 1854 and recommended a grant of £200, but it was apparently too late to implement this recommendation before the end of the session. A similarly favourable report was made in the following year and the £300 grant approved on 27 March 1855. *N.B. Assembly Journal*, 1854–5, pp. 108, 189–90, 261.

137 *Mount Allison Academic Gazette*, June 1854, p. 7.

138 Ibid., December 1855, p. 7.

139 Ibid., p. 6.

140 Ibid., pp. 5–7. For further discussion of the role of the female academy, see John G. Reid, 'The Education of Women at Mount Allison, 1854–1914,' *Acadiensis*, 12 (spring 1983), pp.3–33.

141 *Mount Allison Academic Gazette*, December 1855, p. 6.

142 See [Inch], 'Reminiscences of Mount Allison,' *Allisonia*, May 1904, p. 105.

143 *Provincial Wesleyan*, 15 February 1855.

144 Ibid.

145 Ibid.

146 Saint John *Globe*, 9 November 1896, clipping in MAA, Archibald papers, 5501/13/3, p. 9.

147 On the staff of the two academies in 1854–5, see *Mount Allison Academic Gazette*, December 1854, p. 1.

148 David Allison, 'A Personal Appreciation and Tribute,' *Argosy*, January 1913, p. 211.

149 MAA, accounts of Wesleyan Academy, 8243/7, pp. 41–61.
150 *Provincial Wesleyan*, 15 February 1855.
151 See Otheman, ed., *Memoir and Writings of Hannah Maynard Pickard*, 233–50; Bell, *Genealogical Study*, 181–2.
152 'Sackville Academy in Old Times By an Old Student,' MAA, 7837–1; Milner, 'Mount Allison: Its Earlier Years,' p. 3.
153 Benjamin Russell, *Autobiography of Benjamin Russell* (Halifax, 1932), 50–3.
154 [Inch], 'Reminiscences of Mount Allison,' *Allisonia*, May 1904, p. 106; David Allison, 'Humphrey Pickard, 1812–1890,' *Christian Guardian* (Toronto), 9 March 1904.
155 Wood to Alder, 31 January 1846, WMMS, box 104, file 14b, no. 4.
156 See Brooks, 'Maritime Wesleyan Methodism,' 45–53; French, *Parsons and Politics*, 196–200.
157 Betts, *Black and His Preachers*, 99–104; Brooks, 'Maritime Wesleyan Methodism,' 54–68; French, *Parsons and Politics*, 200–2.
158 *Minutes of Several Conversations between the Ministers of the Wesleyan Connexion, or Church, of Eastern British America at their first Conference, Begun in Halifax, Nova Scotia, on July 17th, 1855* (Halifax, 1855), 15–17.
159 Knight to Osborn, 6 April 1854, WMMS, box 106, file 16b, no. 35; see also MCA, journals of New Brunswick District, 1843–55, 5 June 1854.
160 *Provincial Wesleyan*, 11 October 1855.
161 Ibid., 13 September 1855.
162 See Elijah Hoole, 'Memoir of John Beecham, D.D.,' *Wesleyan Methodist Magazine*, 5th ser., II (1856), 472–3; and *Mount Allison Academic Gazette*, June 1857, pp. 6–7; MAA, minutes of the Mount Allison board of trustees, 1858–1899, p. 13.

CHAPTER 3

1 *New Brunswick Acts*, 19 Victoria c65.
2 Ibid.; Alward, 'Down Sackville Ways', 77–81; K.G. Pryke, 'Stephen Fulton,' DCB, IX, 294–5; George MacLean Rose, ed., *A Cyclopaedia of Canadian Biography: Being Chiefly Men of the Time* (Toronto, 1888), 18–19.
3 *New Brunswick Acts*, 12 Victoria c65.
4 *New Brunswick Acts*, 19 Victoria c65.
5 Allison, 'A Personal Appreciation and Tribute,' *Argosy*, January 1913, p. 210.
6 Morrison, *History of the Allison Family*, 197; see also Milner, 'Mount Allison: Its Earlier Years,' NBM, Mount Allison University papers, packet 1.
7 Ladies' academy *Catalogue*, 1859; see also MAA, Archibald papers, 5501/13/9, p. 2.
8 *Mount Allison Academic Gazette*, June 1857, p. 1; December 1860, p. 1; June

1863, p. 2. A.S. Reid in 1859 became principal of the new Wesleyan Academy in St John's, Newfoundland, while Patterson in 1860 took over the Acacia Villa school in Lower Horton, previously operated by J.R. Hea. See Marshall, *Acacia Villa School*, 12, 15.

9 *Provincial Wesleyan*, 8, 22 October 1857.

10 Letter to Rebecca Trueman, 1 April 1858, PANB, Wood papers, MC218/8/19.

11 Ibid.

12 *Catalogue*, 1857–8, pp. 18–19; see also Beth Light and Alison Prentice, eds., *Pioneer and Gentlewomen of British North America, 1713–1867*, (Toronto, 1980), 63–7, 82–4.

13 Ladies' academy *Catalogue*, 1859, p. 18.

14 See John Allison to Chickering and Co., 17 July 1859, MAA, 7737.

15 See the *Provincial Wesleyan*, 2 July 1857; and Charles A. Holsted to [Albert Trueman], 14 January 1856, MAA, Trueman scrapbook, 0102/4/9.

16 Ladies' academy *Catalogue*, 1859, p. 19.

17 Ibid., p. 13.

18 Ibid., p. 12.

19 *Provincial Wesleyan*, 1 April 1858.

20 *The Parish School Advocate and Family Instructor: For Nova Scotia, New Brunswick and Prince Edward Island*, 1, no. 4 (April 1858), 57. On Monro, see also Gerald T. Rimmington, 'Alexander Monro and the Development of Education in New Brunswick,' (unpublished manuscript). See also MacNaughton, *Education in New Brunswick*, 164–70; and J.E. Picot, *A Brief History of Teacher Training in New Brunswick, 1848–1973* (Fredericton, 1974), 19–21.

21 Allison to Tilley, 26 December 1860, PANB, RG4, RS24/861/re/1.

22 PANB, board of education minutes, RG11, RS113/RED/BE/1/2, 12 April 1860. The request from Sackville academy was made in conjunction with a similar one from an academy in St Stephen.

23 PANB, board of education minutes, RG11, RS113/RED/BE/1/2, 13 July 1860; see also Alison Prentice, 'The Feminization of Teaching in British North America and Canada, 1845–1875,' in Susan Mann Trofimenkoff and Prentice, eds., *The Neglected Majority: Essays in Canadian Women's History* (Toronto, 1977), 49–65.

24 Ladies' academy *Catalogues*, 1859 and 1860; Allison to Tilley, 26 December 1860, PANB, RG4, RS24/861/re/1.

25 *Provincial Wesleyan*, 4 April 1860; MAA, minutes of board of trustees, 1858–99, pp. 26–7.

26 Allison to Tilley, 26 December 1860, PANB, RG4, RS24/861/re/1; see also Allison to Howe, 6 January 1862, PANS, MG17, vol. 17, no. 97. On Howe's granddaughter, who attended the ladies' academy in 1871–2, see Howe to J.R. Inch, 15 May 1872, MAA, Archibald papers, 5501/13/1, p. 46; and J.R. Inch to R.C. Archibald, 3 November 1902, MAA, Archibald papers, 5501/13/8, p. 40.

27 MAA, minutes of board of trustees, 1858–99, p. 29. On the adoption of decimal currency by New Brunswick and Nova Scotia in 1860, see R. Craig McIvor, *Canadian Monetary, Banking and Fiscal Development* (Toronto, 1958), 63.
28 *Minutes of Several Conversations between the Ministers of the Wesleyan Connexion, or Church, of Eastern British America at Their Third Conference Begun in Sackville New Brunswick on June 24th, 1857* (Halifax, 1857), 17–19.
29 *Provincial Wesleyan*, 11 June 1862; Longley, *Acadia University*, 70–1.
30 See table 5.
31 MacNutt, *New Brunswick*, 349.
32 Commission report, 28 December 1854, *N.B. Assembly Journal*, 1855, appendix pp. 183–99. See also MacNutt, *New Brunswick*, 349–50; Firth, 'King's College, Fredericton,' in Bailey, *Memorial Volume*, 30–1; D.G.G. Kerr, *Sir Edmund Head: A Scholarly Governor* (Toronto, 1954), 102–5; James A. Gibson, 'Sir Edmund Walker Head,' DCB, IX, 381–6; and Richard Wilbur, 'Edwin Jacob,' DCB, IX, 408–9.
33 *N.B. Assembly Journal*, 1857–8, pp. 95, 97, 114, 124; see also MacNutt, *New Brunswick*, 369.
34 *Provincial Wesleyan*, 8 April 1858.
35 *New Brunswick Acts*, 21 Victoria c57.
36 Firth, 'Higher Education in New Brunswick,' 445; *New Brunswick Acts*, 21 Victoria c35.
37 *Minutes of Several Conversations Between the Ministers of the Wesleyan Connexion, or Church, of Eastern British America at Their Fourth Conference, Begun in Halifax, Nova Scotia, on June 23rd, 1858* (Halifax, 1858), 17.
38 *Provincial Wesleyan*, 8 July 1858; MAA, accounts of Wesleyan Academy, 8243/7, pp. 68–9.
39 *New Brunswick Acts*, 22 Victoria c63.
40 John Allison to Charles Churchill, 27 November 1858, WMMS, box 108, file 18b, no. 7; *Provincial Wesleyan*, 25 November 1858.
41 Reprinted in *Mount Allison Academic Gazette*, December 1859, p. 13.
42 Ibid., pp. 8–10.
43 Ibid., pp. 13–14.
44 See Arthur R.M. Lower, *Great Britain's Woodyard: British America and the Timber Trade, 1763–1867* (Montreal, 1973), 120–1.
45 MAA, minutes of board of trustees, 1858–99, pp. 16–19.
46 Ibid., p. 23.
47 *Minutes of Several Conversations Between the Ministers of the Wesleyan Connexion, or Church, of Eastern British America at Their Fifth Conference Begun in Charlottetown, P.E. Island, on June 22nd, 1859* (Halifax, 1859), 19–21.
48 *Provincial Wesleyan*, 18 July 1860; *Minutes of Several Conversations Between the Ministers of the Wesleyan Connexion, or Church, of Eastern British America at*

Their Sixth Conference Begun in Fredericton, N.B., on June 27th 1860 (Halifax, 1860), 22–4.

49 DeWolfe to Alder, 21 December 1838, WMMS, box 100, file 10a, no. 77; Betts, *Black and His Preachers*, 135–6; *Minutes of Several Conversations Between the Ministers of the Wesleyan Connexion, or Church, of Eastern British America at Their Seventh Conference Begun in St. John, N.B., on June 26th 1861* (Halifax, 1861), 17–18.

50 DeWolfe to William Arthur, 31 August 1861, WMMS, box 108, file 18b, no. 23.

51 *Minutes of Sixth Conference*, 19–20.

52 *Provincial Wesleyan*, 8 February 1860; 22 February 1860; 4 April 1860.

53 MAA, minutes of board of trustees, 1858–99, p. 25.

54 *Provincial Wesleyan*, 21 November 1860.

55 See above, chapter 2, note 68.

56 Quoted in Firth, 'Higher Education in New Brunswick,' 494.

57 *Provincial Wesleyan*, 12 December 1860.

58 Ibid., 19 December 1860.

59 Quoted in Firth, 'Higher Education in New Brunswick,' 503–4.

60 Wood to Thompson and Rebecca Trueman, 8 February 1861, PANB, Wood papers, MC218/8/23; see also Firth, 'Higher Education in New Brunswick,' 507–8.

61 See the *Provincial Wesleyan*, 10 October 1860; and the *Mount Allison Academic Gazette*, December 1861, pp. 6–8.

62 *Provincial Wesleyan*, 16 January 1861.

63 Ibid., 23 January 1861.

64 Ibid., 30 January 1861.

65 Ibid., 6 February 1861; 20 February 1861.

66 Ibid., 20 February 1861.

67 MAA, minutes of the board of trustees, 1858–99, pp. 29–31.

68 Pickard to Tilley, 17 January 1862, PANB, RG2, RS8, group 1, 1/4. See also the emphatic statement of these views in an editorial in the *Mount Allison Academic Gazette*, December 1861, pp. 4–6.

69 See Gammon, 'The Strange Case of Dr. Joseph Hea,' typescript in UNB archives; Firth, 'Higher Education in New Brunswick,' 474–84; MacNutt, *New Brunswick*, 371–2.

70 *N.B. Assembly Journal*, 1862, p. 146.

71 MAA, minutes of board of trustees, 1858–99, pp. 32–6.

72 DeWolfe to W.B. Boyce, 20 May 1862, WMMS, box 108, file 18b, no. 25.

73 DeWolfe to Boyce, 27 February 1863, ibid., no. 53.

74 *Provincial Wesleyan*, 9 July 1862.

75 As recalled by 'A.W.N.' (undoubtedly A.W. Nicholson, in 1862 a young minis-

ter stationed at Cornwall, PEI), in the *Wesleyan*, 27 March 1901. See also Humphrey Pickard to W.B. Boyce, 16 August 1864, WMMS, box 109, file 19b, no. 28.

76 *Minutes of Several Conversations Between the Ministers of the Wesleyan Connexion, or Church, of Eastern British America at Their Eighth Conference, Begun in Halifax, N.S., on June 25th, 1862* (Halifax, 1862), 22–3.

77 This principle is also explored, chiefly in relation to the later history of Mount Allison, in John G. Reid, 'Mount Allison College: The Reluctant University,' *Acadiensis*, 10 (Autumn 1980), 35–66.

78 See the *Mount Allison Academic Gazette*, June 1863, p. 3; and *Provincial Wesleyan*, 28 January 1863.

79 *Provincial Wesleyan*, 24 September 1862; 1 October 1862.

80 *Provincial Wesleyan*, 28 January 1863.

81 MAA, minutes of board of trustees, 1858–99, p. 43; see also *Provincial Wesleyan*, 27 May 1863.

82 Morrison, *History of the Allison Family*, 197–8; Bell, *Genealogical Study*, 174–7, 179, 192; the *Argosy*, November 1912, p. 96; the *Argosy*, May 1902, p. 279.

83 Pickard to Boyce, 16 August 1864, WMMS, box 109, file 19b, no. 28.

84 *N.B. Assembly Journal*, 1863, appendix no. 5, pp. 44–7; ibid., 1864, appendix no. 5, pp. 53–5; *Mount Allison Academic Gazette*, June 1863, p. 6. It is unclear from surviving records what arrangements were made for the professors' living accommodation in the academy. If, as seems likely, board and lodging was available free of charge then this would of course add to the real value of the salaries paid. Humphrey Pickard, as president, certainly received the use of a furnished cottage and the services of one domestic servant, although this would not have made up for the discrepancy between his salary and that of Brydone Jack. See MAA, minutes of board of trustees, 1858–99, p. 94.

85 *Catalogue*, 1864–5, pp. 14–15.

86 *Catalogue*, 1867–8, pp. 9–11.

87 Ibid., p. 11; see also Russell, *Autobiography*, 81.

88 *Catalogue*, 1867–8, pp. 12–13.

89 *Catalogue*, 1869–70, p. 8.

90 Ibid. For further discussion of British North American college curricula at this time, and the principles that underlay them, see Robin S. Harris, *A History of Higher Education in Canada, 1663–1960* (Toronto, 1976), 38–54; and McKillop, *A Disciplined Intelligence*, 24–34.

91 *Catalogue*, 1864–5, p. 16.

92 [Ralph Brecken], 'Holidays and Sports of Yore,' *Argosy*, December 1901, pp. 79–83.

93 Eurhetorian Society minutes, printed in the *Argosy*, January 1901, pp. 10–11; letter of Josiah Wood, *Argosy*, October 1912, p. 81; Russell, *Autobiography*, 84;

Price, *Wesleyan's First Century*, 40. On the earlier history of student societies in the United States, see James McLachlan, 'The *Choice of Hercules*: American Student Societies in the Early 19th Century,' in Lawrence Stone, ed., *The University in Society*, 2 vols. (Princeton, 1974), II, 449–94.

94 *Catalogue*, 1864–5, p. 17; see also letter of Wood, *Argosy*, October 1912, p. 81.

95 *Provincial Wesleyan*, 2 September 1863; Russell, *Autobiography*, 84–6.

96 See table 6.

97 *Provincial Wesleyan*, 16 January 1861; 27 August 1862.

98 See table 6.

99 *N.B. Assembly Journal*, 1862, appendix no. 3, p. 56; ibid., 1865, appendix no. 5, p. 52.

100 *Catalogue*, 1864–5, p. 21; MAA, minutes of board of trustees, 1858–99, pp. 45–53; for Inch's recollection, see MAA, Archibald papers, 5501/13/10, p. 7.

101 George Butcher to W.L. Thornton, 14 February 1865, WMMS, box 109, file 19b, no. 39; *N.B. Assembly Journal*, 1866, appendix no. 5, p. 54.

102 Thomas Wood to Thompson and Rebecca Trueman, 8 February 1861, PANB, Wood papers, MC218/8/23; MAA, minutes of board of trustees, 1858–99, p. 45; John Allison to John A. Clark, 11 October 1862, MAA, 7412; David Allison to W.G. Watson, 4 March 1921, MAA, 0126/1.

103 MAA, minutes of board of trustees, 1858–99, p. 40; *Mount Allison Academic Gazette*, June 1863, p. 8; MAA, Archibald papers, 5501/13/10, p. 7; Archibald, *Women at Mount Allison*, 4.

104 Pickard and DeWolfe to Boyce, 30 September 1863; WMMS, box 108, file 18b, no. 50; DeWolfe to [?Boyce], 7 February 1866, ibid., box 109, file 19b, no. 63; Pickard to Boyce, 24 March 1866, ibid, no. 66; DeWolfe to Boyce, 3 December 1866, ibid., no. 79. On the social background of candidates for the ministry, see Brooks, 'Maritime Wesleyan Methodism,' 32–3.

105 Boyce to Pickard, 15 October 1864, WMMS, box 26, letterbook, 1864–7, pp. 75–6.

106 Male academy financial statement, 1861–2, PANB, RG2, RS8, group I, 1/4; *N.B. Assembly Journal*, 1866, appendix 5, p. 53.

107 Pickard to Boyce, 24 March 1866, WMMS, box 109, file 19b, no. 66.

108 *N.B. Assembly Journal*, 1866, appendix 5, p. 53.

109 *Minutes of Several Conversations Between the Ministers of the Wesleyan Methodist Church or Connexion of Eastern British America at their Eleventh Conference, Begun in Yarmouth, N.S., on June 28th, 1865* (Halifax, 1865), 23.

110 *N.S. Statutes*, 26 Victoria C24; see also Harvey, *Introduction to the History of Dalhousie University*, 72–5.

111 *Minutes of Several Conversations Between the Ministers of the Wesleyan Connexion, or Church, of Eastern British America at Their Tenth Conference Begun in*

Sackville, N.B., on June 22nd, 1864 (Halifax, 1864), 30–2; see also the editorials in the *Provincial Wesleyan*, 18 November 1863, 2 December 1863, 9 March 1864, 30 March 1864; and Harvey, *Introduction to the History of Dalhousie University*, 29, 77–87.

112 *Provincial Wesleyan*, 2 December 1863; 9 March 1864.

113 *N.S. Assembly Journal*, 1865, pp. 84, 87–8, appendix no. 58. The Mount Allison grant from Nova Scotia had been raised to £250, or $1000, from £150 in 1855. See *N.S. Assembly Journal*, 1855, pp. 717, 726.

114 DeWolfe and Stewart to general secretaries of the Wesleyan Methodist Missionary Society, [17 January 1866], WMMS, box 109, file 19b, no. 62; *Provincial Wesleyan*, 24 January 1866. Among the effects lost by David Allison was 'a very large and very valuable collection of pamphlets and memos relating to the early history of the Institutions ...'; this was the first, though not the last, loss of irreplaceable Mount Allison records by fire. David Allison to W.G. Watson, 4 March 1921, MAA, 0126/1.

115 *Provincial Wesleyan*, 14 February 1866; on the organization of the alumni society, see ibid., 27 January 1864.

116 *Provincial Wesleyan*, 24 January 1866.

117 MAA, minutes of the board of trustees, 1858–99, pp. 61–8.

118 Charles DeWolfe and Humphrey Pickard to Boyce, 30 September 1863, WMMS, box 108, file 18b, no. 50; Pickard to Boyce, 24 March 1866, ibid., box 109, file 19b, no. 66; Boyce to Pickard, 1 June 1866, ibid., box 26, letterbook, 1864–7, p. 305; *Minutes of Several Conversations Between the Ministers of the Wesleyan Methodist Church or Connexion of Eastern British America, at Their Twelfth Conference, Begun in Saint John, N.B., on June 27th, 1866* (Halifax, 1866), 22–6.

119 MAA, minutes of board of trustees, 1858–99, pp. 76–9.

120 *Provincial Wesleyan*, 21 August 1867; on the meetings held at Mount Allison on the confederation question, see the *Borderer and Westmorland and Cumberland Advertiser* (Sackville, NB), 13, 20, 27 January, 3 February 1865.

121 DeWolfe to Boyce, 3 December 1866, WMMS, box 109, file 19b, no. 79; *Catalogue*, 1866–7, p. 7; *Catalogue*, 1868–9, p. 7.

122 MAA, minutes of board of trustees, 1858–99, pp. 84–5, 88–90; *Provincial Wesleyan*, 17 June 1868.

123 Josiah Wood to C.H. Wood, 29 November 1868, PANB, Wood papers, MC218/11/68.

124 *Minutes of Several Conversations Between the Ministers of the Wesleyan Methodist Church or Connexion of Eastern British America, at Their Fourteenth Conference, Begun in Fredericton, N.B., on June 24th, 1868* (Halifax, 1868), 23–6.

125 See table 7.
126 *Provincial Wesleyan*, 31 January 1866; MAA, minutes of board of trustees, 1858–99, pp. 70–3; *Catalogue*, 1867–8, p. 20.
127 *Provincial Wesleyan*, 23 October 1867.
128 MAA, minutes of board of trustees, 1858–99, pp. 79–80, 87, 93.
129 See Russell, *Autobiography*, 55–64.
130 Reprinted in the *Provincial Wesleyan*, 15 August 1870.
131 DeWolfe apparently returned to his position on a temporary basis in 1869–70, pending the arrival of his successor. See *Minutes of Several Conversations Between the Ministers of the Wesleyan Methodist Church or Connexion of Eastern British America at their Fifteenth Conference, Begun in Charlottetown, P.E.I., on June 23rd, 1869* (Halifax, 1869), 24–5.
132 *Provincial Wesleyan*, 2 June 1869; see also Wallace, 'Lemuel Allan Wilmot,' DCB, X, 713–14.

CHAPTER 4

1 Typescript of F.W.W. DesBarres, Notes on Early Mount Allison, in MAA, Flemington papers 7102. See also Nathanael Burwash, *The History of Victoria College* (Toronto, 1927), 423; Sissons, *Victoria University*, 195.
2 John Burwash, 'A Sermon Preached Before the Theological Union of Mount Allison College,' in Theological Union of Mount Allison Wesleyan College, *Fifth Annual Lecture and Sermon, Delivered June 1883* (Saint John, 1884), 45. See also Trevor Levere, 'What is Canadian about Science in Canadian History?' in R.A. Jarrell and N.R. Ball, eds., *Science, Technology, and Canadian History* (Waterloo, Ont., 1980), 19–20; Levere and Jarrell, eds., *A Curious Field-book: Science and Society in Canadian History* (Toronto, 1974), 107–11; and McKillop, *A Disciplined Intelligence*, 125–34.
3 Burwash, 'Sermon,' 45–6; see also McKillop, *A Disciplined Intelligence*, 137–41, 181.
4 Charles Stewart, address to students, Christmas, 1878, MAA, Charles Stewart papers, 8039/5/24.
5 Stewart to Arthur D. Morton, 28 April 1870, MAA, Stewart papers 8039/2/24; see also the *Provincial Wesleyan*, 7 July 1869. Details of Stewart's recruitment to the ministry in Nova Scotia and of his earlier career can be found in MAA, Stewart papers.
6 Stewart to Morton, 20 September 1870, MAA, Stewart papers, 8039/2/25.
7 Stewart to Morton, 9 October 1865, MAA, Stewart papers, 8039/2/8.
8 H.A. Powell to Mrs C. Stewart, 2 September 1910, MAA, Stewart papers, 8039/2/37.

9 Quoted in John S. Astbury to L.E.G. Davies, 27 December 1952, MAA, biographical files, A.D. Smith. See also J.W. O'Brien, *A Parson Reminisces* (Sackville, NB, n.d.), 22–3; Clayton A. Munro, *A Methodist Epic: An Historical Record of the Methodist Church in Bermuda* (Bermuda, 1949), 12; Eurhetorian Society, *Hand Book of the Institutions of Mount Allison, the Central Institutions of the Maritime Provinces, Containing Information for the Benefit of Intending Students* (Sackville, NB, [c. 1904]), 8.

10 See Rose, *Cyclopaedia of Canadian Biography*, 661–2; John Willis, *A History of Dalhousie Law School* (Toronto, 1979), 25–7, 250–1. On the development and the importance of the PH D degree in the United States, see John Higham, 'The Matrix of Specialization,' in Alexandra Oleson and John Voss, eds., *The Organization of Knowledge in Modern America 1860–1920* (Baltimore, 1979), 5, 10–12; also Hugh Hawkins, 'University Identity: The Teaching and Research Functions,' ibid., pp. 290–1.

11 On the various early professors of music, see [R.C. Archibald], 'An Historical Note: Music at Mt. Allison,' *Argosy*, May 1895, p. 8; on the appointments of Mellish and Martens, see *Catalogue*, 1869–70, pp. 32, 38.

12 *The Borderer and Westmorland and Cumberland Advertiser*, (Sackville), 19 August 1869. See also Virgil Hammock, 'Art at Mount Allison,' *Arts Atlantic*, vol. 1, no. 3 (Summer/Fall 1978), 17; obituary of J.W. Gray, Saint John *Globe*, 2 March 1912, in MAA, Archibald papers, 5501/13/13, p. 100.

13 *Catalogue*, 1869–70, pp. 25, 38.

14 *Catalogue*, 1872–3, p. 39.

15 MAA, minutes of board of trustees, 1858–99, p. 120.

16 Ibid., p. 92.

17 *Minutes of General Conversations Between the Ministers of the Wesleyan Methodist Church of Eastern British America at Their Sixteenth Conference Begun at Yarmouth, Nova Scotia, on the twenty-second of June, 1870* (Halifax, 1870), 27–30; *Minutes of the Seventeenth Annual Conference of the Wesleyan Methodist Church of Eastern British America* (Saint John, NB, 1871), 28–31, 33.

18 Petition of the trustees and governors of Mount Allison academies and college, [1870], PANB, RG2, RS8, group 1, 1/4.

19 *New Brunswick Acts*, 34 Victoria c21. See also James Hannay, *History of New Brunswick*, 2 vols. (Saint John, 1909), II, 292–301; McNaughton, *Education in New Brunswick*, ch. 8; George F.G. Stanley, 'The Caraquet Riots of 1875,' *Acadiensis*, 2 (Autumn 1972), 21.

20 McNaughton, *Education in New Brunswick*, ch. 9; Stanley, 'Caraquet Riots,' 21–38; Peter M. Toner, 'The New Brunswick Separate Schools Issue, 1864–1876' (MA thesis, University of New Brunswick, 1967), passim.

21 Toner, 'Separate Schools Issue,' 38.

22 *N.B. Assembly Journal*, 1872, p. 112. Also cut off in 1872 was the $800 grant to the Roman Catholic Collège St-Joseph; see Martin S. Spigelman, 'The Acadian Renaissance and the Development of Acadien-Canadien Relations, 1864–1912: "des frères trop longtemps séparés"' (PH D thesis, Dalhousie University, 1975), 99–100.
23 MAA, minutes of board of trustees, 1858–99, pp. 113–14.
24 Ibid., p. 114; *N.B. Assembly Journal*, 1872, appendix no. 4, p. 60.
25 Inaugural address, p. 291.
26 *Provincial Wesleyan*, 5 June 1872.
27 MAA, minutes of board of trustees, 1858–99, p. 115; *Catalogue*, 1870–1, pp. 29, 40; *Catalogue*, 1872–3, pp. 29, 40.
28 MAA, minutes of board of trustees, 1858–99, pp. 115, 123; *Provincial Wesleyan*, 17 July 1872; *Minutes of the Eighteenth Annual Conference of the Wesleyan Methodist Church of Eastern British America* (Saint John, NB, 1872), 39–42.
29 MAA, minutes of board of trustees, 1858–99, p. 140.
30 Ibid., p.171.
31 Johnson, *Methodism in Eastern British America*, 12.
32 For general accounts of the union of 1874, see Johnson, *Methodism in Eastern British America*, 11–12; Smith, *Methodism in Eastern British America*, II, 478–82; Brooks, 'Maritime Wesleyan Methodism,' ch. 6.
33 *First Annual Report of the Educational Society of the Methodist Church of Canada* (Toronto, 1875), 10.
34 Ibid., p. 8; MAA, minutes of board of trustees, 1858–99, p. 171.
35 MAA, minutes of board of trustees, 1858–99, p. 179; *Journal of the Proceedings of the Second General Conference of the Methodist Church of Canada* (Toronto, 1878), 217–18.
36 *New Brunswick Acts*, 37 Victoria c78. The terms of the act did not exclude former students of the female branch of the academy, but the existence of a separate and active though non-incorporated Alumnae Association at this time makes it clear that the Alumni Society was indeed a male preserve.
37 MAA, minutes of board of trustees, 1858–99, p. 126. The composition of the board was redefined by a further act of 1875, in accordance with the terms of the church union of the previous year: sixteen of the eighteen members were to be appointed by the general conference, with the alumni society continuing to appoint two. This legislation also changed the corporate name to 'the Board of Governors of Mount Allison Wesleyan College and Academies,' although the board members continued to be referred to commonly as the trustees. *New Brunswick Acts*, 38 Victoria c74.
38 MAA, minutes of Alumnae Association, 8029/2/2, 23 May 1871, 28 May 1872; *Provincial Wesleyan*, 5 June 1872.

39 MAA, minutes of college board and senate, 1863–1941, pp. 44–5.
40 *Chignecto Post and Borderer* (Sackville), 3 June 1880. See also Russell, *Autobiography*, 89–90, for an account of an impromptu speech by Allison in which he made 'a heroic effort to exalt the merits of his own sex.'
41 Rudolph, *The American College and University*, 323.
42 *Provincial Wesleyan*, 5 June 1872; 12 June 1872.
43 See ch. 2 above.
44 *Provincial Wesleyan*, 5 June 1872; 12 June 1872.
45 *Provincial Wesleyan*, 5 June 1872.
46 *Catalogue*, 1872–3, p. 9.
47 Price, *Wesleyan's First Century*, 172.
48 *Provincial Wesleyan*, 22 November 1871; Rudolph, *American College and University*, 316–23.
49 Girton College, Cambridge, for example, was incorporated in 1874, but its students could not qualify for degrees, despite the strong arguments advanced by the Mistress of the college, Emily Davies. Even London University, well known for its liberal admission policies, had refused to allow women to matriculate, as Davies and her colleague Elizabeth Garrett had found out when they had attempted to gain admission in 1862. In Canada, McGill University came close to admitting women in 1870, but a favourable resolution of the institution's board of governors in that year was not implemented. See Mary Cathcart Borer, *Willingly to School: A History of Women's Education* (London, 1976), 273–6, 288–90; M.C. Bradbrook, *'That Infidel Place': A Short History of Girton College, 1869–1969* (London, 1969), chs. 1, 2; Stanley Brice Frost, *McGill University: For the Advancement of Learning, Vol. I, 1801–1895* (Montreal, 1980), 251–6; Margaret Gillett, *We Walked Very Warily: A History of Women at McGill* (Montreal, 1981), 51–8; Phylllis Stock, *Better Than Rubies: A History of Women's Education* (New York, 1978), pp. 179–83.
50 *Morning Herald* (Halifax), 26 May 1875.
51 *Eurhetorian Argosy*, June 1875, p. 60.
52 *Chignecto Post*, 3 June 1880. On the later career of Grace Annie Lockhart, see MAA, biographical files, G.A. Lockhart. On other early women graduates from universities in Great Britain and other parts of the British Empire, see Archibald, *Education of Women at Mount Allison*, 7. The publication of an item by Archibald on Lockhart's graduation, in *Notes and Queries*, yielded the information that the first woman to take a degree of any kind from a British university was apparently James Miranda Stuart Barry, a woman who normally dressed as a man and graduated with the degree of MD from Edinburgh University in 1812. See *Notes and Queries*, 198 (1953), 125, 222, 362; also John D. Comrie, *History of Scottish Medicine*, 2 vols.; 2nd ed. (London, 1932), II, 749.

53 See tables 9 and 10.
54 *Eurhetorian Argosy*, January 1875, p. 7; *Argosy*, February 1880, p. 54.
55 *Argosy*, December 1877, pp. 30–1.
56 *Argosy*, February 1878, pp. 54–7; March 1878, pp. 66–7.
57 *Catalogue*, 1873–4, p. 37. The regulation was first adopted in this year.
58 *Argosy*, November 1877, p. 22.
59 *Catalogue*, 1877, p. 43.
60 *Argosy*, November 1877, p. 19. The Latin phrase was adapted for the occasion from the works of Horace.
61 *Argosy*, May 1878, p. 93; December 1878, p. 34.
62 *Argosy*, October 1878, p. 10.
63 *Argosy*, December 1878, p. 31; January 1879, p. 45; February 1879, pp. 56–7.
64 *Argosy*, October 1875, p. 7.
65 *Argosy*, November 1884, p. 18; November 1885, p. 21.
66 *Chignecto Post*, 3 May 1877. See also ibid., 24 May 1877.
67 *Eurhetorian Argosy*, January 1875, pp. 4–5.
68 *Eurhetorian Argosy*, February 1875, pp. 15–16.
69 *Eurhetorian Argosy*, May 1875, pp. 48–9.
70 *Argosy*, March 1879, pp. 66–7.
71 On the reforms at Harvard and elsewhere, see Rudolph, *American College and University*, ch. 14.
72 *Argosy*, January 1880, pp. 44–5.
73 *Argosy*, December 1879, p. 34.
74 W.N. Forbes to W.T.R. Flemington, 11 February 1934, MAA, Flemington papers, 7835–14. On the other buildings, see Archibald, *Women at Mount Allison*, 4; and E.E. Hewson, 'Mount Allison of Earlier Years,' *Argosy Weekly*, 9 March 1940.
75 *Argosy*, November 1880, pp. 19–20.
76 *Argosy*, February 1880, pp. 54–5.
77 *Argosy*, May 1880, pp. 90–1.
78 *Argosy*, October 1879, pp. 2–3.
79 *Argosy*, November 1876, p. 43.
80 See tables 11, 12, 13. On the overall population of the Maritime provinces in 1880–1, see Canada, *Census of Canada, 1881*, vol. 1, table 1, pp. 2–25.
81 *Argosy*, April 1880, p. 78.
82 See tables 8 and 9.
83 *Eurhetorian Argosy*, February 1875, pp. 14–15.
84 *Provincial Wesleyan*, 23 November 1870.
85 *Provincial Wesleyan*, 26 July 1871.
86 *Provincial Wesleyan*, 14 December, 21 December, 28 December 1870, 11 October, 27 December 1871, 10 January, 14 February 1872.

87 See W. Stewart Wallace, *The Macmillan Dictionary of Canadian Biography*, 3rd ed. (Toronto, 1963), 319–20.

88 *Provincial Wesleyan*, 19 September 1874; MAA, minutes of board of trustees, 1858–99, pp. 129–30; Harvey, *History of Dalhousie*, 95.

89 *N.S. Statutes*, 38 Victoria c27.

90 Petition of Mount Allison board of governors to the Nova Scotia Assembly [22 February 1876], PANS, RG5, series P, vol. 78, no. 31. The petition was presented on 22 February 1876; *N.S. Assembly Journal*, 1876, p. 15.

91 *N.S. Statutes*, 39 Victoria c27, c28.

92 Nova Scotia Assembly, *Debates and Proceedings*, 1876, pp. 134–5.

93 MAA, minutes of college board, 1863–1941, pp. 54–5.

94 *Wesleyan*, 13 May 1876; *Memorials of Acadia College*, p. 99; Denis Healy, 'The University of Halifax, 1875–1881,' *Dalhousie Review*, vol. 53 (1973–4), 39–46; Gerald T. Rimmington, 'Mount Allison and the University of Halifax a Century Ago' (unpublished ms), 2–3.

95 *Wesleyan*, 1 July 1876.

96 Quoted in the *Provincial Wesleyan*, 14 June 1871.

97 *N.S. Assembly Journal*, 1876, appendix 7, pp. 56–62.

98 Russell, *Autobiography*, 81.

99 MAA, minutes of board of trustees, 1858–99, p. 182; *Argosy*, November 1878, p. 19; J.C. Webster to G.J. Trueman, 3 May 1926, Dalhousie University Archives (hereafter DUA), President's Correspondence, Mount Allison University: University Federation, DAL/MS/1/3.

100 *Catalogue*, 1881, p. 5; *Catalogue*, 1878, pp. 25, 31; MAA, minutes of board of trustees, 1858–99, p. 182. In 1853,the academy teacher Arthur McNutt Patterson had been named librarian for a short time, but this of course predated the establishment of the college. *Mount Allison Academic Gazette*, December 1853, p. 9. See also F.W.W. DesBarres and Winifred Snider, 'Early Mount Allison Libraries,' in the *Argosy Weekly*, 9 March 1940. For a comparative discussion of library size at other Canadian institutions, see Harris, *History of Higher Education in Canada*, 80–1.

101 MAA, minutes of board of trustees, 1858–99, p. 128; *N.B. Assembly Journal*, 1875, appendix no. 15, p. 5.

102 MAA, minutes of board of trustees, 1858–99, pp. 142, 155–6.

103 *N.S. Assembly Journal*, 1876, appendix 7, p. 61; *N.B. Assembly Journal*, 1876, appendix 13, pp. 23–5. No comparison is possible at this time with the Collège St-Joseph in Memramcook, which had not yet begun to exercise the degree-granting powers included in its charter of 1868, and would not do so until the 1880s. See *Annuaire du Collège Saint-Joseph*, 1883–4, p.6; *Annuaire du Collège Saint-Joseph*, 1887–8, p. 38; Clément Cormier, *L'Université de Moncton Historique* (Moncton, 1975), 8.

104 MAA, minutes of board of trustees, 1858–99, p. 171. The ladies' academy apparently made no such payment; it may be that the professors taught additional classes in the male academy, or simply that the payment was an administrative legacy of the previous close financial relationship of the college and the male academy.
105 *Proceedings of Second General Conference*, 215.
106 *Provincial Wesleyan*, 13 July 1874.
107 *Catalogue*, 1875, p. 19.
108 *First Annual Report of Educational Society of Methodist Church of Canada*, 10; Sissons, *History of Victoria University*, 143–4; see also *Journal of the Proceedings of the First General Conference of the Methodist Church of Canada* (Toronto, 1874), 81–2, 149–53.
109 Reprinted from the *Presbyterian Witness*, in the *Wesleyan*, 27 February 1880.
110 J.C. Webster to G.J. Trueman, 3 May 1926, DUA, president's corespondence, Mount Allison University: university federation, DAL/MS/1/3.
111 Webster, *Those Crowded Years*, 3–5; F.W. Nicolson to F.P. Keppel, 10 May 1926, Carnegie Corporation Archives (hereafter CCA), Mount Allison University files. On Webster's career, see G.F.G. Stanley, 'John Clarence Webster: The Laird of Shediac,' *Acadiensis*, 3 (Autumn 1973), 51–71.
112 Quoted in Harris, *History of Higher Education in Canada*, 79–80.
113 F.J. Toole, 'The Scientific Tradition,' in Bailey, ed., *Memorial Volume*, 71–3; see also Richard Jarrell, 'Science Education at the University of New Brunswick in the Nineteenth Century,' *Acadiensis*, 2 (Spring 1973), 55–79; and J.E. Kennedy, 'William Brydone Jack,' DCB, XI, 446–8.
114 *Argosy*, June 1875, pp. 54–5.
115 MAA, Charles Stewart papers, lectures, 1884, 8039/5/18.
116 *Provincial Wesleyan*, 19 September 1874.
117 *Catalogue*, 1878, p. 10. See also the more elaborate discussion of this subject by J.R. Inch, in *Canadian Methodist Magazine*, vol. IX (January-June 1879), 509–10.
118 *Wesleyan*, 15 April 1881.
119 *Catalogue*, 1876, p. 50; 1877, p. 47.
120 *Provincial Wesleyan*, 30 November 1870.
121 *N.S. Assembly Journal*, 1871, appendix 21, p. 46; *N.S. Assembly Journal*, 1878, appendix 5, p. T2.
122 *Catalogue*, 1876, p. 12; see also W.M. Tweedie, 'Early Days of Mount Allison and the University of Halifax,' *The Maritime Advocate and Busy East*, vol. 29, no. 4 (November 1938), 17–18. On the curriculum committee of the University of Halifax, see PANS, MG20, University of Halifax papers, senate minutes, vol. 347, pp. 12, 32–8.

123 *Catalogue*, 1876, pp. 10–12; 1877, pp. 11–13. The prescription of the curiously uneven number of 47 subjects is clearly implied by the explanation of optional subjects in the catalogue, although it would obviously have been more symmetrical to have required 46, on the pattern of 10 in the first year, 12 in the second, 12 in the third (instead of 13), and 12 in the fourth. The press comments were reprinted in the *Wesleyan*, 9 June 1877 and 3 November 1877.

124 PANS, MG20, general register, faculty of Arts, vol. 344; report, July 1880, examination correspondence, vol. 346.

125 *Argosy*, November 1879, pp. 21–2; Tweedie, 'Early Days of Mount Allison,' p. 18. The examinations had been scheduled in July in order to avoid conflicts with the colleges' own examinations.

126 *Argosy*, January 1881, p. 44.

127 *Catalogue*, 1878, p. 16.

128 *Wesleyan*, 27 February 1880.

129 *Morning Herald*, 14 November 1877; *Chignecto Post*, 15 November 1877; for indications of Allison's acting in a dual role, see letters of November 1877 in PANS, University of Halifax papers, letterbook, vol. 349, pp. 213, 224.

130 MAA, minutes of board of trustees, 1858–99, pp. 166–8; NBM, MacBeath papers, E.T.C. Knowles scrapbook, p. 37.

131 MAA, minutes of board of trustees, 1858–99, p. 173.

132 *Wesleyan*, 16, 23 March 1878.

133 *Argosy*, March 1878, p. 66.

134 On the life of J.R. Inch, see Wallace, *Macmillan Dictionary of Canadian Biography*, 338; Johnson, *Methodism in Eastern British America*, 381; MAA, biographical files, J.R. Inch; and [J.R. Inch], *The Inch Family of Ulster, Ireland, and New Brunswick, Canada* (Sackville, NB, 1912), pp. 24–8.

135 *New Brunswick Acts*, 38 Victoria c74. On the previous careers of Kennedy and Longley, see George H. Cornish, *Cyclopaedia of Methodism in Canada*, 2 vols. (Toronto, 1881–1903), I, 109, 114, 708, 778.

136 MAA, minutes of board of trustees, 1858–99, p. 179; ladies' academy *Catalogue*, 1878, pp. 6–8.

137 See *Memorials of Acadia College*, 107–8.

138 Ladies' academy *Catalogue*, 1879, pp. 6–8; 1880, pp.6–8; 1881, pp. 6–8.

139 See table 15.

140 Ladies' academy *Catalogue*, 1878, pp. 10–11; 1879, pp. 10–12.

141 See table 16.

142 *Catalogue*, 1874, p. 26.

143 *Catalogue*, 1875, p. 33; remarks of *Chignecto Post*, quoted in the *Wesleyan*, 25 July 1874.

144 MAA, minutes of board of trustees, 1858–99, p. 136; *Wesleyan*, 26 February 1876.

145 See table 16; also *Catalogue*, 1877, pp. 25–6; male academy *Catalogue*, 1878, pp. 14–16.
146 T.W. Wood to Thompson and Rebecca Trueman, 14 February 1879, PANB, Wood papers, MC218/8/60. The bills continued in use at the commercial college until late in the nineteenth century. See Ray Mabee, 'A Double Surprise and the History of College Banknotes,' *Coin Stamp Antique News*, vol. 8, no. 24 (1 May 1971), 8.
147 Annie R. Trueman to Albert Trueman, 23 April 1879, PANB, Wood papers, MC218/4/9.
148 Annie R. Trueman to Albert Trueman, 2 May 1879, PANB, Wood papers, MC218/4/11. The letter does not state directly that it is the principal, B. Longley, who is referred to rather than an assistant teacher, George Longley; but the devising of punishments would seem likely to have been a prerogative of the principal.
149 MAA, minutes of board of trustees, 1858–99, p. 192; academy *Catalogue*, 1880, p. 11.
150 Annie R. Trueman to Albert Trueman, 29 August 1879, PANB, Wood papers, MC218/4/17; academy *Catalogue*, 1880, pp. 14–15; 1881, pp. 15–16.
151 *Wesleyan*, 4 June 1880.
152 On the role of the examiners, see, for example, F.C. Sumichrast to John Burwash, 8 September 1879, PANS, MG20, University of Halifax, letterbook, vol. 350, p. 117.
153 *Morning Herald*, 7, 8 January 1880; PANS, MG20, vol. 347, senate minutes of University of Halifax, pp. 370–2.
154 John S.D. Thompson to F.C. Sumichrast, 8 May 1880, PANS, MG20, vol. 346, examination correspondence; Sumichrast to Inch, 5 July 1880 and 2 September 1880, PANS, MG20, vol. 350, University of Halifax,letterbook, pp. 436, 449; committee report, 28 December 1880, PANS, MG20, vol. 346, examination correspondence; PANS, MG20, vol. 347, senate minutes, p. 408.
155 PANS, MG20, vol. 347, senate minutes, p. 396. See also Healy, 'University of Halifax,' 46–9. The six colleges specifically designated as affiliates in the university act were King's, Acadia, Dalhousie, St Mary's, St Francis Xavier, and Mount Allison.
156 Sumichrast to Inch, 6 November 1878, PANS, MG20, vol. 349, letterbook, p. 417.
157 *Proceedings of Second General Conference*, 217–18.
158 MAA, minutes of college board, 1863–1941, p. 60.
159 College *Catalogue*, 1879, pp. 17–18; MAA, minutes of college board, 1863–1941, p. 62; Harris, *History of Higher Education in Canada*, 126; Price, *Wesleyan's First Century*, 121.

160 College *Catalogue*, 1879, p. 18; 1880, p. 18; MAA, minutes of board of trustees, 1858–99, pp. 192, 205–6.
161 *Morning Herald*, 26 January 1881.
162 *Morning Herald*, 4 April 1881.
163 Inch to Holmes, 2 March 1881, printed in the *Wesleyan*, 22 January 1885; see also the *Morning Herald*, 4 April 1881.
164 *Argosy*, April 1881, pp. 78–9. On the government bill and the Methodist petitions, see *N.S. Assembly Journal*, 1881, pp. 10, 27, 55, 58, 59; and the *Wesleyan*, 25 March 1881.
165 *N.S. Assembly Journal*, 1881, p. 59; *N.S. Legislative Council Journal*, 1881, pp. 53, 61–2; Healy, 'University of Halifax,' 42–3.
166 Sumichrast to A.G. Archibald, 11 May 1881, PANS, MG20, vol. 350, letterbook, pp. 478–9.
167 MAA, minutes of board of trustees, 1858–99, p. 211.

CHAPTER 5

1 *Wesleyan*, 8 July 1881.
2 On the effects of the National Policy on Maritime industry, see T.W. Acheson, 'The National Policy and the Industrialization of the Maritimes, 1880–1910,' *Acadiensis*, 1 (Spring 1972), 3–12; for a recent interpretation of the complexities of the decline of wooden shipbuilding and shipping, and a counterweight to more traditional interpretations, see Eric W. Sager and Lewis R. Fischer, 'Atlantic Canada and the Age of Sail Revisited,' *Canadian Historical Review*, 63(1982), 125–50. The commercial depression of the mid-1880s, and the more general question of the role of bankers in the economic developments of this era, are explored in James Douglas Frost, 'Principles of Interest: The Bank of Nova Scotia and the Industrialization of the Maritimes, 1880–1910' (MA thesis, Queen's University, 1978), esp. pp. 53–9, 67, 73–4. Other important discussions include Delphin Andrew Muise, 'Elections and Constituencies: Federal Politics in Nova Scotia, 1867–1878' (PHD thesis, University of Western Ontario, 1971), 359, 368–70; S.A. Saunders, *The Economic History of the Maritime Provinces: A Study Prepared for the Royal Commission on Dominion-Provincial Relations* (Ottawa, 1939), 8–22; and, on local developments in Sackville, Alward, 'Down Sackville Ways,' 109–19.
3 Figures calculated from accounts submitted by the board of governors in 1883 to the Methodist general conference. *Journal of Proceedings of the Third General Conference of the Methodist Church of Canada* (Toronto, 1882), 169–78.
4 MAA, minutes of board of governors, 1858–99, pp. 212–15.
5 Ibid., pp. 216–17.

6 T.W. Acheson, 'The Social Origins of the Canadian Industrial Elite, 1880–1885,' in David S. Macmillan, *Canadian Business History: Selected Studies, 1497–1971* (Toronto, 1972), 158–60. See also Michael Bliss, *A Canadian Millionaire: The Life and Business Times of Sir Joseph Flavelle, Bart., 1858–1939* (Toronto, 1978), 12–13.

7 *Proceedings of Third General Conference*, 163, 172; on G.H. Starr, see the *Morning Herald*, 9 June 1887.

8 *Wesleyan*, 24 June 1881; 8 July 1881.

9 MAA, minutes of board of governors, 1858–1899, pp. 235, 272–3; 'Mount Allison University,' anonymous ms, MAA, 7837–38; *Argosy*, November 1883, p. 18; *Argosy*, March 1918, p. 230. In 1882, Mount Allison reported to the church general conference that it had already received three donations of $10,000, but did not specify the names of the donors; since the Chipman bequest could not yet have been included, there was clearly another gift of equivalent amount to those of Wood and Gibson. *Proceedings of Third General Conference* (1882), 163.

10 Dean Wendell Jobb, 'Josiah Wood (1843–1927): "A cultured and honoured gentleman of the old school"' (BA thesis, Mount Allison University, 1980), 18–19, 32–41; Acheson, 'National Policy,' 8–9.

11 Acheson, 'National Policy,' 10–11.

12 Ibid., p. 9; Peter DeLottinville, 'Trouble in the Hives of Industry: The Cotton Industry Comes to Milltown, New Brunswick, 1879 – 1892,' *Historical Papers: Montreal 1980*, 103–4; Rose, *Cyclopaedia of Canadian Biography*, 221.

13 *Argosy*, January 1881, p. 42; *Proceedings of Third General Conference*, 163; *Wesleyan*, 13 January 1882.

14 *Argosy*, January 1881, p. 42.

15 *Wesleyan*, 13 January 1882.

16 MAA, minutes of board of governors, 1858–99, pp. 232–5; *Wesleyan*, 24 February 1882; *Transcript* (Sackville), 9 February 1882.

17 *Wesleyan*, 24 February 1882.

18 Laura S. Wood, 'Journal of Everyday Affairs' (manuscript in possession of Miss P.A. Black of Upper Cape, NB, and cited with her kind permission), p. 34; *Wesleyan*, 9 June 1882.

19 *Chignecto Post*, 28 December 1882; see also the *Argosy*, December 1882, p. 31.

20 MAA, minutes of board of governors, 1858–99, pp. 238–9. Black's ministry had actually begun in 1781, but his first venture into the area of the modern province of Nova Scotia had been in 1782. See Betts, *Black and His Preachers*, 9–18.

21 MAA, minutes of board of governors, 1858–99, pp. 244–6; *Chignecto Post*, 21 December 1882; *Wesleyan*, 8 June 1883. The original intention of building Centennial Hall on a new site was to avoid the necessity of moving the old college building; however, for reasons that are not entirely clear, the old building was

moved westward at this time, to a site near Centennial Hall. See R.C. Archibald to W.T.R. Flemington, 21 August 1949, MAA, Flemington papers, 7804–100; MAA, minutes of board of governors, 1858–99, p. 259.

22 *Wesleyan*, 6 June 1884; 16 October 1884.

23 Subscription books used by the fund-raiser, Rev. D.D. Currie, in Prince Edward Island and New Brunswick show a large number of gifts, the vast majority amounting to a dollar or less. MAA, Currie subscription books, 8328.

24 MAA, minutes of board of governors, 1858–99, pp. 270–3; *Journal of Proceedings of the Second General Conference of the Methodist Church* (Toronto, 1886), 225, 227–30.

25 *New Brunswick Acts*, 46 Victoria c67.

26 MAA, minutes of board of governors, 1858–99, p. 247.

27 See Brooks, 'Maritime Wesleyan Methodism,' 114.

28 Brooks, 'Maritime Wesleyan Methodism,' 107–15; Cornish, *Cyclopaedia of Methodism*, II, 15–16; Smith, *Methodism in Eastern British America*, II, 480–2. For consideration of the Methodist union of 1884 in the context of the earlier union of 1874, see J. Warren Caldwell, 'The Unification of Methodism in Canada, 1865–1884,' United Church Archives *Bulletin*, 19 (1967), 3–61.

29 *New Brunswick Acts*, 49 Victoria c41.

30 MAA, minutes of board of governors, 1858–99, p. 288.

31 Petition of board of governors, 25 February 1886, PANB, RG4, RS24/886/pe/1, no. 1; *N.B. Assembly Journal*, 1886, p. 17.

32 *Wesleyan*, 16 October 1884. On Victoria, see Sissons, *History of Victoria*, 168–9; Burwash, *History of Victoria*, 258–60; *Statutes of the Province of Ontario*, 47 Victoria c93. The notion of a Methodist university for the Dominion had been adopted in principle by the general conference of 1883, although the subsequent growth of support for the entry of Victoria University into the University of Toronto forestalled any serious negotiations on the matter. See Burwash, *History of Victoria*, 341.

33 Petition of board of governors, 25 February 1886, PANB, RG4, RS24/886/pe/1, no. 1.

34 *New Brunswick Acts*, 49 Victoria c41.

35 Quoted in the *Wesleyan*, 11 March 1886.

36 *Chignecto Post*, 2 June 1881.

37 *Chignecto Post*, 9 June 1881.

38 *Chignecto Post*, 30 June 1881; *Canada School Journal*, vol. VII, no. 57 (February 1882), 45–6; summary of university consolidation pamphlet, MAA, 7102, notes of F.W.W. DesBarres.

39 See Harvey, *History of Dalhousie*, 101–2; and Willis, *History of Dalhousie Law School*, 25–6.

40 *Wesleyan*, 2 July 1885.
41 See Harris, *Higher Education in Canada*, 109–10.
42 Quoted in the *Wesleyan*, 22 January 1885.
43 *Wesleyan*, 22 January 1885.
44 *Argosy*, October 1885, p. 2.
45 Quoted in the *Wesleyan*, 30 December 1886.
46 *Argosy*, October 1882, p. 4.
47 Harriet Starr Stewart's BA and MA diplomas are in MAA, H.S. Stewart papers, 7828. See also Jean Stewart, 'My Aunt Harriet,' typescript in MAA. A tradition later grew up at Mount Allison that Harriet Stewart had been disallowed, as a woman, from wearing academic dress at her graduation: see the *Mount Allison Record*, vol. 37, no. 3 (1954), 118. However, this is belied by the comment of a contemporary upon the unfamiliar sight of a woman in cap and gown at the graduation exercises. Wood, 'Journal of Everyday Affairs,' p. 35. On the women who had previously graduated with the BA degree at other institutions in the British Empire, see *Notes and Queries*, 198 (1953), 125, 222–3, 362; and Archibald, *Women at Mount Allison*, 7. When the college board had opened all degrees to women, Mount Allison did not yet give the Bachelor of Divinity, and no woman ever took this degree during the years it was offered, from 1875 to 1926; however, the regulations for the degree were phrased in such a way tht it too was theoretically open to women. The admission of women to the ministry, of course, was a separate matter and outside the jurisdiction of Mount Allison.
48 *Chignecto Post*, 5 June 1884.
49 MAA, minutes of board of governors, 1858–99, pp. 263, 315.
50 Ibid., pp. 265–6; 279–81.
51 Ibid., pp. 307, 370.
52 *Chignecto Post*, 2 July 1885; see also the *Wesleyan*, 9 July 1885. On enrolments under Kennedy see ladies' academy *Catalogues*, 1881–5; and on the profits, see *Proceedings of Third General Conference*, 1882, p. 178, and *Proceedings of Second General Conference*, 1886, p. 230.
53 See *Mount Allison Record*, vol. 13 (1929–30), 3–4. On Borden's appointment as principal, see MAA, minutes of board of governors, 1858–99, pp. 275–7.
54 See *Catalogues*, 1869–73; Archibald, *Women at Mount Allison*, 9–10.
55 Ladies' college *Catalogue*, 1887–8, p. 12.
56 *Wesleyan*, 24 January 1889.
57 See the *Wesleyan*, 2 June 1887; Bell, *Genealogical Study*, 193.
58 R.A. Borden to B.C. Borden, 28 November 1886, MAA, Borden papers, 7508, 1886–1910, p. 48; MAA, minutes of Alumnae Association, 8029/2/2, [27 May 1888].
59 *Wesleyan*, 13 June 1884. An editorial note added that comments in the same vein had been made to the editor by others.

60 E.E. Rice to B.C. Borden, 28 July 1886, MAA, Borden papers, 7508, 1886–1910, p. 69.
61 See, for example, ladies' college *Catalogue*, 1886–7, p. 17.
62 Borden to [P.C.L. Harris], [February 1887], MAA, Borden papers, 7508, 1886–1910, p. 35. See also Harris to Borden, 15 February 1887, 25 February 1887, ibid., pp. 59, 60.
63 James Taylor to B.C. Borden, 15 December 1887, ibid., p. 36.
64 Thomas D. Hart to B.C. Borden, 14 January 1887, ibid., p. 15.
65 Ladies' college *Catalogue*, 1886–7, p. 11.
66 *Wesleyan*, 9 June 1887.
67 *Daily Times* (Moncton), 3 June 1887.
68 *Wesleyan*, 9 June 1887.
69 Ladies' college *Catalogue*, 1887–8, pp. 18–19.
70 See, for example, the advertisements placed in the *Argosy* from 1877 onwards.
71 Archibald, *Women at Mount Allison*, 11.
72 See the *Argosy*, December 1891, p. 34.
73 *Daily Times*, 2 June 1887; ladies' college *Catalogue*, 1887–8, pp. 4, 17.
74 MAA, minutes of Alumnae Association, 8029/2/2, [27 May 1888], 4 June [1888]; MAA, minutes of board of governors, 1858–99, pp. 320–1.
75 *Wesleyan*, 16 August 1888, 27 February 1890; Archibald, *Women at Mount Allison*, 9; see also MAA, minutes of board of governors, 1858–99, pp. 333–4.
76 Ladies' college *Catalogue*, 1890–1, pp. 37–47; *Wesleyan*, 11 June 1891.
77 Ladies' college *Catalogue*, 1888–9, p. 15.
78 *Argosy*, November 1889, p. 20; Archibald, *Women at Mount Allison*, 4.
79 *Allisonia*, November 1904, p. 61. For more detailed discussion of the dilemmas faced by the ladies' college in this period, and of the careers being followed by its graduates, see Reid, 'Education of Women at Mount Allison,' 20–7.
80 *Catalogue*, 1881–2, pp. 14–16.
81 *Catalogue*, 1884–5, p. 17; 1885–6, p. 17; 1888–9, p. 19. The teaching of psychology had apparently begun at least two years before it was advertised in the calendar as a separate subject, as shown by examanation results for the 1886–7 year. It was apparently taught by Inch. See *Catalogue*, 1887–8, pp. 26, 28; *Wesleyan*, 3 May 1888.
82 *Wesleyan*, 7 June 1888; MAA, minutes of board of governors, 1858–99, p. 319. The local history prize was apparently given for one year only, and lapsed after it had been won by E.P. Carey in 1888. See *Catalogue*, 1889–90, p. 39.
83 Quoted in the *Wesleyan*, 30 December 1886.
84 *Argosy*, March 1884, p. 69.
85 MAA, minutes of college board, 1863–1941, p. 70.
86 Harris, *Higher Education in Canada*, 129–31.

87 *Catalogue*, 1883–4, p. 10; 1884–5, pp. 19–21. The courses promised in the earlier catalogue were not precisely the same as those actually introduced, the chief difference being that the honours course in English was originally proposed as a broader course in modern languages and literature.
88 *Catalogue*, 1884–5, pp. 19–22.
89 *Catalogue*, 1889–90, pp. 14–27. See also MAA, senate minutes, 1863–1941, p. 81.
90 *Journal of Proceedings of the Third General Conference of the Methodist Church* (Toronto, 1890), 218.
91 MAA, minutes of college board, 1863–1941, pp. 64–6.
92 See MAA, minutes of faculty, 2 June 1883.
93 *Catalogue*, 1884–5, p. 23.
94 See Harris, *Higher Education in Canada*, 187; Peter N. Ross, 'The Establishment of the PH. D. at Toronto: A case of American Influence,' in Michael B. Katz and Paul H. Mattingly, eds., *Education and Social Change: Themes from Ontario's Past* (New York, 1975), 194–200; Hilda Neatby, *Queen's University, Volume I* (Montreal, 1978), 185. Details of the PH. D. programme at the University of New Brunswick are contained in the senate minutes of 24 May 1867, and in the university calendars of 1869–70 and 1870–1; for help in obtaining this information, I am grateful to Ms Linda Hansen of the University of New Brunswick.
95 *Catalogue*, 1884–5, pp. 23–4.
96 Sir Robert Falconer, 'The Gilchrist Scholarships: An Episode in the Higher Education of Canada,' *Proceedings and Transactions of the Royal Society of Canada*, 3rd series, XXVII (1933), section II, pp. 5–13; Harris, *Higher Education in Canada*, 188–90.
97 *Argosy*, October 1882, pp. 4, 6–7.
98 Smith to Tweedie, 22 September 1882, MAA, Tweedie papers, 5201/3/23.
99 See the *Wesleyan*, 29 April 1886.
100 See table 9.
101 Falconer, 'Gilchrist Scholarships,' 5, 8–10.
102 *Argosy*, April 1890, p. 79; see also Harris, *Higher Education in Canada*, 188.
103 *Proceedings of Third General Conference* (1890), 218.
104 *Catalogue*, 1889–90, p. 49; 1891–92, pp. 43–4.
105 Ibid.; *Argosy*, October 1889, p. 2; *Wesleyan*, 3 October 1889; *Proceedings of Third General Conference* (1890), 218.
106 *Argosy*, October 1889, p. 2.
107 *Argosy*, November 1890, p. 18. When W.L. Goodwin had arrived to join the faculty in 1882, he had brought with him £100 worth of equipment, purchased in Great Britain by authority of the board of governors, and this had been placed in the new laboratories in Centennial Hall when it was opened. Since

Goodwin's departure for Queen's in 1883, however, the equipment had apparently been allowed to fall into disrepair. See MAA, minutes of board of governors, 1858–99, p. 228; *Argosy*, October 1882, p. 6.

108 *Catalogue*, 1889–90, p. 38; *Proceedings of Third General Conference* (1890), 218.

109 *Proceedings of Third General Conference* (1890), 218.

110 *Chignecto Post*, 31 August 1882.

111 *Chignecto Post*, 30 November, 7 December 1882; 11, 25 January, 1, 4, 15, 22 February, 8, 15, 29 March, 12 April 1883.

112 *Argosy*, December 1882, p. 30. On the Ontario Agricultural College, see Douglas Lawr, 'Agricultural Education in Nineteenth-Century Ontario: an Idea in Search of an Institution,' in Katz and Mattingly, *Education and Social Change*, 169–92; also Levere and Jarrell, *A Curious Field-book*, 159–77.

113 Neatby, *Queen's University*, 164–6; 217–20. According to the history of Queen's ,Goodwin had proceeded to his studies in Europe from 'the wilds of New Brunswick': the aptness of this description of Mount Allison is open to question. Neatby, *Queen's University*, 164. On Goodwin's unexpected resignation in 1883, see the *Argosy*, October 1883, p. 11.

114 *Wesleyan*, 24 June 1886.

115 See A.G. Bedford, *The University of Winnipeg: A History of the Founding Colleges* (Toronto, 1976), 28, 106.

116 See Falconer, 'Gilchrist Scholarships,' 12.

117 *Mount Allison Record*, November 1940, p. 10.

118 Annie Trueman to Laura Wood, 23 August 1883, PANB, Wood papers, MC218/5/75; *Chignecto Post*, 1 January 1885.

119 *Catalogue*, 1884–5, p. 20.

120 O'Brien, *A Parson Reminisces*, 23–4.

121 See, for example, the *Argosy*, March 1887, pp. 62–4; see also Falconer, 'Gilchrist Scholarships,' 12.

122 Inch to Tweedie, 6 July, 4, 12, 16 August 1887, MAA, Tweedie papers, 5201/3/9; *Argosy*, October 1887, p. 1; *Catalogue*, 1888–9, p. 5.

123 Inch to Tweedie, 16 August 1887, MAA, Tweedie papers, 5201/3/9.

124 The text of the address was printed in the *Daily Sun* (Saint John), 11, 12 September 1888.

125 *Catalogue*, 1888–9, pp. 22–3.

126 O'Brien, *A Parson Reminisces*, 24; *Eductional Review*, vol. VIII, no. 6 (November 1894), 113.

127 *Argosy*, October 1890, p. 15.

128 Winthrop Bell to B.C. Borden, 31 August 1912, MAA, Borden papers, 7508.

129 *Argosy*, October 1890, pp. 2–3.

130 *Argosy*, October 1890, p. 2; Sissons, *Victoria University*, 197.
131 *Argosy*, October 1890, p. 2.
132 *Educational Review*, vol. VIII, no. 7 (December 1894), 137.
133 'W.W.A,' 'The Poetic Element in Literature and Science,' *Argosy*, January 1894, pp. 10–12. On the development of Hegelian idealism at Canadian universities, see McKillop, *A Disciplined Intelligence*, ch. 6.
134 O'Brien, *A Parson Reminisces*, 26; H.E. Bigleow, 'Baccalaureate Address,' [1946], typescript in MAA, Flemington papers, 7804–7.
135 Quoted in the *Wesleyan*, 3 May 1888; see also table 11. On the Wood Chair, see MAA, miscellaneous files, endowed chairs.
136 *Wesleyan*, 7 June 1888; see also letter of E.F. Moore, in the *Wesleyan*, 13 December 1888, and the *Argosy*, December 1890, p. 39.
137 *Wesleyan*, 3 October 1889.
138 MAA, minutes of board of governors, 1858–99, p. 303.
139 *Argosy*, February 1888, p. 54.
140 Thomas Estabrooks to B.C. Borden, 23 February 1887, MAA, Borden papers, 7508, 1886–1910, p. 83.
141 MAA, minutes of faculty, 8, 15 January 1886.
142 *Argosy*, November 1883, p. 18.
143 *Argosy*, November 1887, p. 19; *Wesleyan*, 29 May 1890.
144 *Argosy*, November 1890, p. 19.
145 *Argosy*, April 1891, pp. 85–6.
146 *Argosy*, January 1891, p. 48.
147 *Argosy*, November 1887, p. 18.
148 *Argosy*, November 1888, p. 17. This editorial recalled the selection of the university colours 'about two yeas ago.'
149 *Argosy*, January 1891, pp. 51–2.
150 For a fuller discussion, see George N. Emery, 'The Origins of Canadian Methodist Involvement in the Social Gospel Movement, 1890–1914,' *Journal of the Canadian Church Historial Society*, 19 (1977), 104–19; see also French, *Parsons and Politics*, 287; Brooks, 'Maritime Wesleyan Methodism,' 92–4; Richard Allen, *The Social Passion: Religion and Social Reform in Canada, 1914–1928* (Toronto, 1971), ch. 1.
151 *Argosy*, March 1890, pp. 67–8. See also the *Wesleyan*, 6 March 1890; and Ernest R. Forbes, 'Prohibition and the Social Gospel in Nova Scotia,' *Acadiensis*, 1 (Spring 1971), 11–36.
152 *Argosy*, April 1886, pp. 73–6.
153 *Argosy*, January 1891, pp. 52–3.
154 *Argosy*, March 1891, p. 71.
155 *Argosy*, March 1882, pp. 66–8; October 1883, p. 6; October 1890, p. 6.

156 *Wesleyan*, 24 October 1889.
157 MAA, minutes of board of governors, 1858–99, pp. 347–8.
158 *Morning Herald*, 4 March 1890; *Chignecto Post*, 6 March 1890.
159 *Proceedings of Third General Conference* (1890), 57–60, 221. Burwash, *History of Victoria*, 337–51; Alexander Sutherland, 'Our "Traditional Policy" at the Coming General Conference,' *Canadian Methodist Magazine*, vol. XXIV (July-December 1886), 156–64.
160 Burwash, *History of Victoria*, 390–2.
161 *Chignecto Post*, 29 January, 6 February 1891; *Wesleyan*, 5 February 1891.
162 *Wesleyan*, 23 April; 7, 21, 28 May 1891.
163 MAA, minutes of board of governors, 1858–99, pp. 363, 368, 370–1; *Wesleyan*, 25 June, 9 July 1891; *Minutes of the Eighth Session of the New Brunswick and Prince Edward Island Conference of the Methodist Church* (Saint John, 1891), 92.
164 MAA, minutes of board of governors, 1858–99, pp. 354–5, 365, 367, 370.
165 MAA, minutes of board of governors, 1858–99, p. 351.
166 MAA, minutes of board of governors, 1858–99, pp. 360, 363–4, 365.
167 W.C. Milner, 'Mount Allison: Its Earlier Years,' p. 4.
168 MAA, minutes of board of governors, 1858–99, p. 365. See also Rose, *Cyclopaedia of Canadian Biography*, 86–8; and Burwash, *History of Victoria*, 370–3. Sutherland had been closely associated in 1886 with the notion of a Dominion-wide Methodist university, but more recently had favoured the independence of Victoria.
169 Burwash, *History of Victoria*, 397.
170 *Argosy*, November 1891, pp. 14, 19–20.

CHAPTER 6

1 Quoted in the *Chignecto Post*, 7 June 1894.
2 *Calendar*, 1891, pp. 21–2, 29.
3 See Eurhetorian Society, *Hand Book of the Institutions of Mount Allison*, 11–12; the *Argosy*, April 1897, pp. 5–8; and the *Wesleyan*, 2 September 1903. See also W.W. Andrews, 'A Cheap form of Self-Regulating Gas Generator,' *Journal of the American Chemical Society*, 17(1895), 304–6; Andrews, 'Some Extensions of the Plaster of Paris Method in Blowpipe Analysis,' ibid., 18(1896), 849–69; Andrews, 'Reform in the Teaching of Chemistry,' *Report of the Sixty-Seventh Meeting of the British Association for the Advancement of Science Held at Toronto in August 1897* (London, 1898), 601–8; Andrews, 'The Plaster of Paris Method in Blowpipe Analysis,' ibid., pp. 625–7. On the revitalization of the *Journal of the American Chemical Society* as a respectable periodical shortly

before the appearance of Andrews's articles, see Daniel Kevles, 'The Physics, Mathematics, and Chemistry Communities: A Comparative Analysis,' in Oleson and Voss, eds., *Organization of Knowledge*, 148–9, 156.

4 MAA, minutes of board of governors, 1858–99, pp. 382–4.

5 *Educational Review*, vol. v, no. 6 (November 1891), 117–18; *Daily Times*, 11 November 1891.

6 *Daily Times*, 14 November 1891, 29 January 1892, 13 February 1892.

7 See the *Guardian* (Charlottetown), 18 February 1892; also the *Argosy*, April 1892, pp. 74–5.

8 *Wesleyan*, 14, 28 January, 4, 11 February 1892.

9 *Argosy*, March 1892, pp. 66–8.

10 MAA, minutes of board of governors, 1858–99, p. 385. The faculty minutes for the 1890s have not survived, but there is no indication from other sources of a positive decision on the ambitious extension programme proposed by Andrews.

11 *Wesleyan*, 29 June, 13 July 1893; *Educational Review*, vol. VII, no. 2 (August 1893), 27–8; MacNaughton, *Education in New Brunswick*, 247–50. On the musical elements of the curriculum of the summer school of science, see Nancy Fraser Vogan, 'The History of Public School Music in the Province of New Brunswick, 1872–1939' (PHD thesis, University of Rochester, 1979), 34–6.

12 *Argosy*, October 1895, p. 17; *Calendar*, 1896, pp. 20, 28–9. On Powell's career, see H.J. Morgan, ed., *The Canadian Men and Women of the Time: A Handbook of Canadian Biography* (Toronto, 1898), 830. As MP for Westmorland, Powell replaced Josiah Wood, who had been appointed to the Senate. The *Argosy* commented, rightly, that both had 'always manifested personal interest in our College life.' *Argosy*, October 1895, p. 17.

13 *Calendar*, 1897, pp. 8–9.

14 *Daily Times*, 20 January 1893; *Wesleyan*, 26 January 1893.

15 Reprinted in the *Daily Times*, 21 January 1893.

16 *Journal of Proceedings of the Fifth General Conference of the Methodist Church* (Toronto, 1898), 163.

17 See J. Castell Hopkins, *Life and Work of the Rt. Hon. Sir John Thompson, K.C., K.C.M.G., Q.C., Prime Minister of Canada* (Toronto, 1895), 40–3, 290–300.

18 *Daily Times*, 11 January 1893.

19 *Daily Sun*, 10 January 1893.

20 *Daily Times*, 11 January 1893.

21 John Potts to David Allison, 26 November 1892, UCA, Methodist Church papers: committee on education/board of education, 1887–1925 [hereafter Methodist education papers], box 5, Potts letterbook, p. 450; Potts to John Lathern, 25 November 1892, ibid., p. 444.

22 *Ninth Annual Report of the Educational Society of the Methodist Church* (Toronto, 1893), 5.

23 Potts to Lathern, 13 September 1892, UCA, Methodist education papers, box 5, Potts letterbook, p. 278.
24 *Annual Reports* of educational society of the Methodist Church, 1891–1900. The granting formula was enunciated in the 1890–1 report, pp. 5–7; it was adjusted in 1893–4 (p. 3) to accommodate small grants to two other colleges, but the Mount Allison percentage remained unchanged.
25 Potts to Andrews, 15 March 1897, UCA, Methodist education papers, box 10, Potts letterbook, pp. 184–5.
26 John Maclean to Albert Carman, 4 April 1903, UCA, Carman papers, box 11, file 57.
27 MAA, minutes of board of governors, 1858–1899, pp. 382–4, 388–9. On the amount raised by the semi-centennial campaign, see *Journal of Proceedings of the Fourth General Conference of the Methodist Church* (Toronto, 1894), 157.
28 MAA, minutes of board of governors, 1858–99, pp. 405–6; *Wesleyan*, 31 August 1893.
29 Reprinted in the *Wesleyan*, 31 August 1893; see also the description in the *Sackville Post*, 13 June 1899.
30 *Wesleyan*, 7 September 1893.
31 *Proceedings of Fifth General Conference* (1898), 172; *New Brunswick Acts*, 57 Victoria c78; MAA, minutes of board of governors, 1858–99, pp. 406–7, 412; 1899–1920, p. 1.
32 *Proceedings of Fifth General Conference* (1898), 169.
33 *Calendar*, 1896, pp. 11–13; see also table 11.
34 MAA, minutes of board of governors, 1858–99, pp. 417–18.
35 *Argosy*, October 1894, p. 2.
36 *Wesleyan*, 9 June 1892.
37 MAA, minutes of board of governors, 1858–99, pp. 374–5, 387–91; Hammock, 'Art at Mount Allison,' 18–19. *Proceedings of Fourth General Conference* (1894), 162; *Proceedings of Fifth General Conference* (1898), 169.
38 *New Brunswick Acts*, 47 Victoria c50; see also Hammock, *Art at Mount Allison*, 18–19; and [New Brunswick Museum], 'John Owens,' in *Mount Allison Record*, Spring 1955, pp. 26–7.
39 Quoted in ladies' college *Catalogue*, 1893, pp. 29–31. See also Owens Art Institution, *Catalogue of Works of Art in the Owens Art Gallery* (Saint John, NB, 1886); and Helen J. Dow, 'A Look at Nineteenth Century Values,' *Canadian Art*, 21 (1964), 76–9.
40 *New Brunswick Acts*, 56 Victoria c86; [NB Museum], 'John Owens,' 26; see also MAA, minutes of board of governors, 1858–99, pp. 387–8.
41 On Hammond, see J. Russell Harper, *Painting in Canada: A History*, 2nd ed. (Toronto, 1977), 198, 226–8; J. Aird Nesbitt, *A Short Biography of Canada's Oldest Artist: John Hammond, R.C.A.* (Montreal, 1929); and [Luke Rombout],

'John Hammond, R.C.A., 1843–1939,' in Sackville Art Association, *John Hammond, R.C.A., 1843–1939: A Retrospective Exhibition* (Sackville, 1967), n.p.

42 *Argosy*, October 1893, pp. 11–12.

43 *Argosy*, February 1894, p. 17; *Wesleyan*, 7 June 1894.

44 *Argosy*, January 1895, p. 7; ladies' college *Catalogue*, 1895, pp. 28–38.

45 *Wesleyan*, 13 September 1894.

46 *Daily Times*, 29 May 1895; *Argosy*, January 1895, p. 7.

47 MAA, minutes of Alumnae Association, 8029/2/2 30 May 1893, 28 May 1895; MAA, minutes of board of governors, 1858–99, pp. 412–13; *New Brunswick Acts*, 58 Victoria c65.

48 MAA, minutes of board of governors, 1858–99, p. 420; *Argosy*, January 1891, p. 57, and May 1897, p. 16.

49 Ladies' college *Catalogue*, 1895, pp. 5–6. For a fuller discussion of the career patterns of ladies' college graduates, see Reid, 'Education of Women at Mount Allison,' 13–14, 26.

50 *Argosy*, May 1894, pp. 9–10. Pointed references to the successful enfranchisement of women in general elections in New Zealand also revealed an awareness of that issue. Ibid., May 1894, p. 9; March 1896, p. 9.

51 See table 10. The 31 women graduates of the period 1891–1900 represented some 20 per cent of the total number of graduates for the period. For general discussion of the role of women in Canadian society at this time, and for discussion of specific fields of women's employment, see Ramsay Cook and Wendy Mitchinson, eds., *The Proper Sphere: Women's Place in Canadian Society* (Toronto, 1976), 1–4, 119–20, 166–7; Linda Kealey, 'Introduction,' in Kealey, ed., *A Not Unreasonable Claim: Women and Reform in Canada, 1880s–1920s* (Toronto, 1979), 1–14; Wendy Mitchinson, 'Canadian Women and Church Missionary Societies in the Nineteenth Century,' *Atlantis*, 2, part 2 (Spring 1977), 57–75; Prentice, 'The Feminization of Teaching,' 49–65; Wayne Roberts, '"Rocking the Cradle for the World": The New Woman and Maternal Feminism, Toronto, 1877–1914,' in Kealey, ed., *A Not Unreasonable Claim*, 31–40; Veronica Strong-Boag, 'Canada's Women Doctors: Feminism Constrained,' in Kealey, ed., *A Not Unreasonable Claim*, 109–29.

52 *Daily Times*, 28 May 1895.

53 *Wesleyan*, 8 June 1898.

54 *Wesleyan*, 8 February 1894.

55 *Chignecto Post*, 27 June 1895.

56 Ibid., 11 July 1895. The writer of the letter was identified by R.C. Archibald, a teacher of mathematics at the ladies' college at this time; see MAA, Archibald papers, 5501/13/2, p. 9.

57 Ladies' college *Catalogue*, 1895, p. 19.

58 Ladies' college *Catalogue*, 1894, pp. 16–17; 1896, p. 18.
59 *Argosy*, April 1897, pp. 3–5.
60 Ladies' college *Catalogue*, 1897, pp. 42–55.
61 *Chignecto Post*, 3, 10, 17, 24 December 1896, MAA, Archibald papers, 5501/13/3, pp. 10–11.
62 Ladies' college *Catalogue*, 1896, pp. 6, 32, 39; on the financing of the ladies' college, see *Proceedings of Fifth General Conference* (1898), 172–3.
63 Maude Pettit, 'Twilight Memories of Mount Allison,' *Methodist Magazine and Review*, vol. LIX (January–June 1904), 197. For detailed discussion of the social backgrounds of ladies' college students of this era, see Reid, 'Education of Women at Mount Allison,' 23–6.
64 *Wesleyan*, 25 June 1891. On Harrison's background, see the *Argosy*, October 1890, pp. 3–4.
65 *Proceedings of Fourth General Conference* (1894), 162–3. During this period, the academy's debt was reduced from $8689.21 to $2032.91, but all but $56.30 of this reduction represented the $6600 received by the academy from the other two institutions in 1891, when the board of governors decided to apportion out the academy's debt at that time. See MAA, minutes of board of governers, 1858–99, p. 370.
66 Academy *Calendar*, 1892, pp. 4, 13–20.
67 Academy *Calendar*, 1892, pp. 5–7; 1894, pp. 5–7.
68 *Chignecto Post*, 7 June 1894.
69 *Chignecto Post*, 7 June 1894; MAA, minutes of board of governors, 1858–99, p. 415.
70 MAA, minutes of board of governors, 1858–99, pp. 413–14. See also *Proceedings of Fifth General Conference* (1898), 166–7.
71 MAA, minutes of board of governors, 1858–99, pp. 414–15.
72 Ibid., p. 415.
73 *Argosy*, December 1894, p. 15.
74 J.M. Palmer to W.T.R. Flemington, 18 May 1931, MAA, Flemington papers, 7835–5; MAA, minutes of board of regents, 1899–1920, pp. 70, 72. For a discussion of factors producing a growing demand for commercial education at this time, see Janice Weiss, 'Educating for Clerical Work: The Nineteenth Century Private Commercial School,' *Journal of Social History*, 14(1980–1), 407–23.
75 *Journal of Proceedings of the Sixth General Conference of the Methodist Church* (Toronto, 1902), 245.
76 *Proceedings of Fifth General Conference* (1898), 166–7, 173–4.
77 *Wesleyan*, 4 September 1895.
78 See Nancy Howell and Maxwell L. Howell, *Sports and Games in Canadian Life: 1700 to the Present* (Toronto, 1969), 77–82.

79 *Eurhetorian Argosy*, October 1875, p. 11.
80 *Argosy*, December 1890, pp. 32, 36; December 1891, p. 33; January 1898, p. 14. The return match against Saint John was played on the same day, 29 November 1891, as the match against Moncton: thus two separate Mount Allison teams were victorious on that day.
81 *Argosy*, December 1892, p. 26.
82 *Chignecto Post*, 10 November 1892.
83 *Argosy*, December 1892, pp. 26–7; January 1893, pp. 42–3.
84 Ibid., December 1892, p. 27; November 1894, p. 15.
85 Ibid., November 1894, p. 9.
86 ibid., December 1892, p. 27; *Mount Allison Record*, Summer 1954, p. 76; O'Brien, *A Parson Reminisces*, 22. Hunton's cane was promptly replaced by one presented to him by the students' athletic association.
87 *Argosy*, December 1894, p. 23; January 1895, pp. 13–16; February 1895, p. 1.
88 *The Hum of the College*, vol. 1, no. 5 [1894], MAA, Archibald papers, 5501/13/1, p. 23a. This magazine was published by the ladies' college rhetoric class, but only during the 1894–5 year.
89 *Argosy*, November 1895, p. 1; January 1898, p. 14.
90 Ibid., November 1897, p. 2. The popularity of intercollegiate football was further affirmed in 1900, with the inauguration of a permanent football field adjoining the university residence. Prior to that time, games had been played at the university farm, about a mile from the campus. On 3 November 1900, the future novelist and literary scholar Frank Parker Day had the distinction of scoring the first intercollegiate points on the new field, with a try that put Mount Allison on the way to a 9–0 victory over UNB. See MAA, minutes of board of governors, 1858–99, p. 458; *Argosy*, October 1900, p. 3; November 1900, p. 20.
91 Ibid., May 1903, pp. 258–9.
92 Ibid., February 1896, p. 13; see also Howell and Howell, *Sports and Games in Canadian Life*, 74–5.
93 *Argosy*, February 1897, pp. 17–18; March 1898, p. 13.
94 Ibid., January 1904, pp. 102–3; March 1904, pp. 178–80.
95 Ibid., May 1899, pp. 1–3.
96 Ibid., March 1902, pp. 179–81, 203–5.
97 Ibid., April 1903, pp. 218–19; January 1904, pp. 102–3.
98 Ibid., April 1904, pp. 206–8.
99 MAA, minutes of Eurhetorian Society, 8284/2, 1899–1904, pp. 7, 11, 34–5, 87–8, 124. The debates were decided by a judge rather than by vote, and so did not give any precise indication of the conclusions of those present. Since 1899 the Eurhetorian had been an incorporated body under provincial legislation; see *New Brunswick Acts*, 62 Victoria c93.

100 *Argosy*, March 1902, p. 180.
101 Eurhetorian Society, *Hand Book of the Institutions of Mount Allison*, 39–40.
102 MAA, minutes of board of regents, 1899–1920, p. 38.
103 *Wesleyan*, 7 July 1892; 5 July 1894.
104 See MAA, Stewart papers, lectures, [1871–2], 8039/5/8–17; and the *Argosy*, May 1892, p. 87.
105 *Argosy*, May 1892, p. 87.
106 On the origins of the higher criticism, see George Alfred Boyle, 'Higher Criticism and the Struggle for Academic Freedom in Canadian Methodism' (TH D thesis, Victoria University, 1965), 24–34.
107 O'Brien, *A Parson Reminisces*, 26.
108 On the Victoria theological faculty, see Emery, 'Canadian Methodist Involvement in the Social Gospel Movement,' 109; and Boyle, 'Higher Criticism and the Struggle for Academic Freedom,' 36.
109 O'Brien, *A Parson Reminisces*, 27.
110 *Proceedings of Fifth General Conference* (1898), 164–5; *Proceedings of Sixth General Conference* (1902), 243–4.
111 *Argosy*, November 1891, p. 16.
112 Ibid., May 1892, p. 87.
113 Ibid., February 1897, p. 2.
114 Ibid., October 1900, p. 4.
115 Eurhetorian Society, *Hand Book of the Institutions of Mount Allison*, 52.
116 See MAA, diary of G.J. Trueman, 1891–1939, 7940/1, pp. 146–7.
117 Emery, 'Canadian Methodist Involvement in the Social Gospel Movement,' 111.
118 Saint John *Sun*, 8 April 1899, in MAA, Archibald papers, 5501/13/4, p. 181.
119 *Proceedings of Sixth General Conference* (1902), 175–8. For general comment on the committee on sociological questions, see Allen, *The Social Passion*, 12–13.
120 Twila F. Buttimer, '"Great Expectations": The Maritime Methodist Church and Church Union, 1925' (MA thesis, University of New Brunswick, 1980), pp. 90–6. For detailed discussion of the shift from purely personal evangelism to social evangelism, see also Harry Manning, 'Changes in Evangelism within the Methodist Church in Canada during the Time of Carman and Chown, 1884–1925: A Study of the Causes for the Shifts in Evangelism' (TH M thesis, Emmanuel College of Victoria University, 1975), esp. ch. 2.
121 *Wesleyan*, 13 December 1899. The Scott Act, first passed by the Dominion parliament in 1878, provided that individual cities and counties could prohibit liquor within their boundaries on the basis of a majority vote of the electorate. On the growth of the temperance movement into a campaign for social, rather

than personal, reform, see Forbes, 'Prohibition and the Social Gospel in Nova Scotia,' 12–16.

122 Press clippings on this incident are in MAA, Archibald papers, 5501/13/4, pp. 78–80; *Wesleyan*, 3, 10 August 1898.

123 See John G. Woolley and William E. Johnson, *Temperance Progress in the Century* (Toronto, 1903), 265–8.

124 MAA, Stewart papers, diary of Charles Stewart, 1852–66, 8039/4/1, pp. 16–19, 54–5. On the legislation of 1853 and 1856, see MacNutt, *New Brunswick*, 350–62.

125 *Wesleyan*, 12 June 1901. Technically Brecken was replaced as a regular member of the faculty by Paisley, whose position had been funded by a private annual donation from George Starr of Halifax, which had been given originally for four years and had already been extended for one year. See MAA, minutes of board of trustees, 1858–99, pp. 429; 1899–1920, pp. 7, 9, 16.

126 MAA, minutes of board of regents, 1899–1920, pp. 46–7; on the appeal for funds, see *Minutes of the Eighteenth Session of the New Brunswick and Prince Edward Island Conference of the Methodist Church* (Saint John, 1901), 76–7. For a biography of Watson, see E. Arthur Betts, *Pine Hill Divinity Hall, 1820–1970: A History* (Halifax, 1970), 55.

127 *Argosy*, October 1903, pp. 8–14.

128 O'Brien, *A Parson Reminisces*, 28.

129 *Tribune* (Sackville), 8 October 1903.

130 *Argosy*, May 1903, pp. 247–8.

131 Ibid., March 1895, p. 2. Allison's remark was quoted in the *Wesleyan*, 9 May 1895.

132 *Argosy*, October 1894, pp. 7–8; January 1898, p. 2; April 1899, pp. 1–2.

133 Ibid., May 1902, pp. 251–2. See also the issue of November 1902, pp. 44–6.

134 See table 11; and *Calendars*, 1891–1902.

135 MAA, minutes of board of governors,, 1858–99, p. 457.

136 *Argosy*, May 1902, p. 251. Italics mine.

137 *Wesleyan*, 26 August 1896.

138 For an example, involving assistance given to a student by W.M. Tweedie, see Albert M. Sanford to G.J. Trueman, 14 May 1937, MAA, Trueman papers, 7837–63.

139 See table 9.

140 See table 8.

141 Brookes, 'Out-Migration from the Maritime Provinces, 1860–1900,' 31.

142 See Buttimer, 'Maritime Methodist Church and Church Union,' 103.

143 *Chignecto Post*, 26 December 1895, 2 January, 16 April 1896.

144 See press cuttings, in MAA, Archibald papers, 5501/13/4, pp. 68–9. Hunton's letter, in which he announced his resignation, denied with equal force that

Mount Allison had opposed the school and that he had acted as a Mount Allison representative on the school board.

145 C.L. Chisholm, *To the Board of Regents of Mount Allison, Sackville, N.B.* (New Glasgow, NS, 1898), 3. The comment by R.C. Archibald, who owned the copy of the pamphlet now preserved in MAA, was written and dated September 1940 on the envelope containing the pamphlet. Chisholm later went on to be a successful supervisor of music for the school board of North Sydney, NS; see MAA, Archibald papers, 5501/13/10, p. 15.

146 Reprinted in the *Wesleyan*, 1 January 1902.

147 *Argosy*, March 1896, pp. 1–2.

148 See also an article on the virtues of the small college, in the *Argosy*, October 1901, pp. 8–11; and the reference in Eurhetorian Society, *Hand Book of the Institutions of Mount Allison*, 27.

149 *Sackville Post*, 13 June 1899; see also the *Wesleyan*, 28 June 1899.

150 *Proceedings of Sixth General Conference* (1902), 249.

151 MAA, minutes of board of regents, 1899–1920, pp. 1–2.

152 Ibid., 1858–99, pp. 436–7.

153 Ibid., pp. 446–7; on the payment of the first $50,000 of the Massey bequest in 1900, see the *Wesleyan*, 10 October 1900. On the Bowser bequest, see deed summary, George T. Bowser et Ux. and University of Mount Allison, Mount Allison University, comptroller's office, property files; also Bowser, *Genealogical Review*, 5.

154 *Proceedings of Sixth General Conference* (1902), 242, 249.

155 *Sackville Post*, 10 October 1899, in MAA, Archibald papers, 5501/13/4, p. 115; MAA, minutes of board of regents, 1899–1920, p. 1. On the cost of the residence, see *Proceedings of Sixth General Conference* (1902), 249.

156 *Argosy*, October 1900, p. 2; *Wesleyan*, 6 December 1899.

157 *Calendar*, 1900, pp. 38–41.

158 *Wesleyan*, 27 December 1899; on the debt in 1902, see MAA, minutes of board of regents, 1899–1920, p. 21.

159 *Calendar*, 1897, p. 19.

160 Henry T. Bovey, dean of applied science, McGill University, to Andrews, 11 April 1901, MAA, McGill affiliation file, 8330.

161 Morgan, *Canadian Men and Women of the Time*, 722.

162 MAA, minutes of board of regents, 1899–1920, p. 27.

163 *Wesleyan*, 14 March 1903; *Globe* (Saint John), 5 August 1903, clipping in MAA, Archibald papers, 5501/15, vol. 1, p. 29; *University Bulletin: Professional Courses at Mt. Allison*, MAA, Mount Allison pamphlets, p. 1. The date of the bulletin can be ascertained from the *Wesleyan*, 23 September 1903.

164 Ibid.; academy *Calendar*, 1904, p. 13; *Educational Review*, vol. 17 (1903–4), 231.

165 *Calendar*, 1904, p. 35.
166 *Argosy*, November 1903, pp. 47–8; December 1903, pp. 69–70. The *Argosy* also commented upon the recent addition to the scientific museum of a valuable collection of 'Egyptian antiquities,' donated by the Egypt Explorations Fund of London. What subsequently happened to these exhibits is unclear, although it seems likely that they were destroyed in the Centennial Hall fire of 1933. Also included in the museum were several items from China and Japan, including a 250-year-old Japanese clock brought back to Sackville by the sea-captain T.R. Anderson.
167 *Sackville Post*, 22 April 1904, in MAA, Archibald papers, 5501/13/10, p. 12; *Calendar*, 1904, p. 8; *Wesleyan*, 21 March 1906.
168 Henry T. Bovey to Andrews, 7 November 1903, MAA, McGill affiliation file, 8330.
169 *Educational Review*, vol. X (1896–7), 157–60.
170 List of mathematics honours graduates, MAA, 8335.
171 Pettit, 'Twilight Memories of Mount Allison,' 200; Webster to G.J. Trueman, 3 May 1926, DUA, president's correspondence, Mount Allison University: university federation, DAL/MS/1/3.
172 *Calendar*, 1897, pp. 28–9; *Calendar*, 1903, p. 31; *Calendar*, 1904, pp. 8–9.
173 *Calendar*, 1905, pp. 70–3. Theological students are not included in these figures, except for those also registered in the arts course.
174 MAA, minutes of board of regents, 1899–1920, pp. 26–7.
175 *Argosy*, March 1902, pp. 180–1; MAA, senate minutes, 1863–1941, p. 107; *Wesleyan*, 3 September 1902.
176 *Argosy*, October 1903, p. 6.
177 Ibid., January 1901, p. 6. According to an endorsement made in his copy of the magazine by R.C. Archibald, Mary Mellish Archibald's son, the article was written by Professor A.D. Smith.
178 *Allisonia*, November 1903, pp. 3–4; May 1905, p. 183. The other PH D degree granted by the University of Toronto to a woman in 1903 was to Clara Benson in chemistry. See also University of Toronto, *The University of Toronto and its Colleges, 1827–1906* (Toronto, 1906), 256.
179 List of mathematics honours graduates, MAA, 8335.
180 Raymond C. Archibald, autobiographical note [5 February 1940], MAA, Archibald papers, 5501/3/1; MAA, minutes of Alumnae Association, 8029/2/3, 20 May 1901.
181 *Allisonia*, November 1904, p. 61; *Wesleyan*, 5 December 1900.
182 MAA, minutes of board of regents, 1899–1920, p. 18; see also table 11.
183 MAA, minutes of board of regents, 1899–1920, pp. 18, 28–9, 35–6; *Allisonia*,

January 1904, p. 33. On the artificial lake, see the *Wesleyan*, 2 April 1902; and on the ladies' college debt, see *Proceedings of Seventh General Conference* (1906), 338.

184 *Wesleyan*, 13 January, 24 February 1904; *Allisonia*, January 1904, pp. 61–2.

185 *Wesleyan*, 21 May 1891; see also Gillett, *We Walked Very Warily*, 347.

186 MAA, minutes of Alumnae Association, 8029/2/2, [1 June 1891]; *University Bulletin: Professional Courses at Mount Allison*, 3–4; *Allisonia*, January 1904, pp. 34–6.

187 MAA, Archibald papers, 5501/15, vol. 1, p. 52.

188 *Tribune* (Sackville), 19 May 1904; Inch to Borden, 10 May 1904, MAA, Archibald papers, 5501/13/9, p. 50.

189 Ladies' college *Catalogue*, 1905, pp. 37–41.

190 Ibid., 1902, pp. 21–2; 1904, pp. 27–32.

191 MAA, senate minutes, 1863–1941, p. 110.

192 *Allisonia*, November 1904, p. 59. Beethoven Hall was the large concert hall in the conservatory of music.

193 See MacNaughton, *Education in New Brunswick*, 256–8.

194 *Allisonia*, November 1904, pp. 59, 61–2.

195 *Tribune*, 4 June 1903.

CHAPTER 7

1 *Mount Allison Record*, Fall 1958, p. 127.

2 *Minutes of the Twenty-Third Session of the New Brunswick and Prince Edward Island Conference of the Methodist Church* (Saint John, 1906), 14; *Sackville Tribune*, 28 May 1906.

3 See tables 11 and 17.

4 See *Proceedings of Seventh General Conference* (1906), 331–2; *Register of Rhodes Scholars, 1903–1945* (Oxford, 1950), 7, 9. The winning of the New Brunswick scholarship at this time was not a matter of inter-university competition, since the nomination was given to each university by rotation; however the winning of two scholarships in a single year by candidates from the same university was rare, and was repeated by Mount Allison in 1912, when F.M. Smith took the award for New Brunswick and P.V. Curtis that for Newfoundland. *Register of Rhodes Scholars*, 148, 153.

5 Allison to Day, 30 November 1905, DUA, Frank Parker Day papers, DAL/MS/2/288, C, no. 2; *Wesleyan*, 29 March 1905.

6 *Wesleyan*, 24 April 1907.

7 *N.S. Assembly Journals*, 1907, 32, 137, 150, 152, 210, 224, 235; *N.S. Statutes*, 7 Edward VII C1; *Morning Herald*, 22 March 1907; J. Castell Hopkins, *The Cana-*

dian Annual Review of Public Affairs 1907 (Toronto, 1908), 618; MacNutt, 'Universities of the Maritimes,' 443–4. In 1980, the Nova Scotia Technical College received a university charter as the Technical University of Nova Scotia.

8 *Canadian Annual Review, 1907*, p. 618. In 1908 there were reports that Andrews would move to Halifax to accept a position in chemistry at the technical college, but this possibility was never fulfilled. See Saint John *Globe*, 29 June 1908, MAA, Archibald papers, 5501/13/12, p. 43.

9 *Argosy*, December 1907, pp. 123–4.

10 *Evening Mail*, 30 October 1906, clipping in MAA, Archibald papers, 5501/13/11, p. 45. On the second half of the Massey bequest, see *Proceedings of Seventh General Conference* (1906), 332.

11 David Allison to Andrew Carnegie, 3 August 1907 (draft), MAA, 8333; Bertram to Allison, 30 April 1908, ibid.

12 Andrews to Graham, 5 April 1909, UCA, Methodist education papers, box 17; *Wesleyan*, 24 February 1909; *Argosy*, December 1907, p. 125.

13 *Tribune*, 28 May 1908.

14 MAA, minutes of board of regents, 1899–1920, pp. 131–2, 142, 149–52. The decision to proceed was made on the basis only of the $20,000 specifically bequeathed by Hart for a new ladies' college building, but the death of Hart's sister-in-law in late 1909, who had been the holder of life rent on another portion of the bequest, released a further $40,000 and ensured that the new building could be paid off in full. See Saint John *Globe*, 1 January 1910, clipping in MAA, Archibald papers, 5501/15, vol. II, p. 94.

15 MAA, minutes of board of regents, 1899–1920, p. 145.

16 *Argosy*, March 1910, p. 240; *Proceedings of Eighth General Conference* (1910), 200.

17 *Tribune*, 30 May 1910.

18 Borden to R.C. Archibald, 2 November 1909, MAA, Archibald papers, 5501/5/6; town of Sackville, minutes, 1909–14, pp. 37–8. See also *Tribune*, 11 October 1909.

19 *Allisonia*, May 1910, p. 111. Three stanzas cited of fourteen.

20 Palmer to W.T.R. Flemington, 31 October 1932, MAA, Flemington papers, 7835-8.

21 *Globe*, 10 April 1912, clipping in MAA, Archibald papers, 5501/15, vol. III, p. 106; *Tribune*, 3 February 1921.

22 Borden to R.C. Archibald, 2 November 1909, MAA, Archibald papers, 5501/5/6; ladies' college *Catalogue*, 1908, p. 65; 1909, p. 69.

23 See agreement, R.C. Archibald–board of regents, 26 May 1908, MAA, Trueman papers, miscellaneous, 3. An example of Archibald's fund-raising is the series of three orchestral concerts given by the Mount Allison conservatory orchestra to

urge attendances in February and March 1907. See MAA, Archibald papers, 5501/13/12, pp. 23, 26, 28.

24 *Tribune*, 13 July 1908; *Proceedings of Eighth General Conference* (1910), 201, 205–6.

25 *Educational Review*, vol. XXII, no. 6 (November 1908), 123. The editorial did not make clear the identity of its writer: either G.U. Hay, editor for New Brunswick, or A. McKay, editor for Nova Scotia.

26 *Wesleyan*, 5 June 1907.

27 *Proceedings of Seventh General Conference* (1906), 338–9; *Proceedings of Eighth General Conference* (1910), 205–6.

28 *New Brunswick Acts*, 4 Edward VII c70; *Proceedings of Eighth General Conference* (1910), 204.

29 *Proceedings of Seventh General Conference* (1906), 336–8; *Proceedings of Eighth General Conference* (1910), 202–4.

30 MAA, minutes of board of regents, 1899–1920, pp. 53–6.

31 Ibid., pp. 205, 215–16.

32 Ibid., p. 204.

33 See G.J. Trueman to J.A. Wheeler, 19 May 1944, MAA, Trueman papers, 7837–197; for an example of difficulties in collecting student accounts, see J.R.F. Kinney to B.C. Borden, 26 February 1912, MAA, Borden papers, 7508; and on other aspects of the financial confusion of this time, see David Allison to Borden, 14 December 1911, and Rebecca V. Bowser to Borden, 8 December 1911, ibid.,

34 T.W. Acheson, 'The Maritimes and "Empire Canada,"' in David Jay Bercuson, ed., *Canada and the Burden of Unity* (Toronto, 1977), 95; see also Acheson, 'The National Policy and the Industrialization of the Maritimes,' 12–28, and Frost, 'Principles of Interest,' 83, 164–5, 179.

35 See Ernest R. Forbes, *The Maritime Rights Movement, 1919–1927: A Study in Canadian Regionalism* (Montreal, 1979); and Forbes, 'Misguided Symmetry: The Destruction of Regional Transportation Policy for the Maritimes,' in Bercuson, *Canada and the Burden of Unity*, 60–75.

36 Forbes, 'Destruction of Regional Transportation Policy,' 65.

37 See Forbes, *Maritime Rights*, 17–22.

38 *Argosy*, December 1903, p. 87.

39 *Argosy*, October 1909, pp. 27–8; *Proceedings of Eighth General Conference* (1910), p. 199; MAA, minutes of board of regents, 1899–1920, pp. 112–14; W.G. Watson to J.W. Graham, 17 October 1908, UCA, Methodist education papers, box 16.

40 *Argosy*, October 1909, pp. 27–8. At McGill, McClung had studied with Ernest Rutherford. See Saint John *Globe*, 22 June 1908, in MAA, Archibald papers, 5501/13/12, p. 43.

41 J.H. Oliver to J.W. Graham, 19 October 1910, UCA, Methodist education papers, box 18; W.W. Andrews to Nathanael Burwash, 9 November 1910, UCA, Burwash papers, box 5, file 61.
42 *Tribune*, 27 October 1910.
43 MAA, minutes of board of regents, 1899–1920, p. 170; *Argosy*, January 1911, p. 198.
44 Andrews to Borden, 12 September 1912, MAA, Borden papers, 7508.
45 *Argosy*, January 1911, pp. 198–9.
46 J.H. Beazley to Borden, 1 January 1912, MAA, Borden papers, 7508.
47 Wheelock to Borden, 6 March, 8 April 1912,, ibid.
48 S.D. Scott to Tweedie, 24 September [1912], MAA, Tweedie papers, 5201/3/18. Scott, who had been a year ahead of Tweedie at Mount Allison and at the University of Halifax, was now editor of the Vancouver *News Advertiser* and was to be a member of the inaugural board of governors at the University of British Columbia. See Harry T. Logan, *Tuum Est: A History of the University of British Columbia* (Vancouver, 1958), pp. 42–5.
49 *Calendar*, 1904, p. 53; *Argosy*, December 1908, p. 118.
50 A.J. Fuller to Borden, 22 September 1911, MAA, Borden papers, 7508.
51 D.W. Johnson to Borden, 21 November, 12 December 1911, ibid.
52 Palmer to J.H. Beazley, 27 February 1912, MAA, Palmer letterbooks, 8327/1, pp. 35–6.
53 A.M. Bell to J.R. Inch, [1911]; A.J. Fuller to Borden, 22 September 1911, MAA, Borden papers, 7508.
54 Palmer to Beazley, 27 February 1912, MAA, Palmer letterbooks, 8327/1, pp. 35–6.
55 A.M. Bell to Borden, 25 November 1912, MAA, Borden papers, 7508.
56 Borden to Archibald, 20 April 1911, MAA, Archibald papers, 5501/5/6; Winthrop Bell to Archibald, 30 August 1909, ibid., 5501/5/2.
57 MAA, minutes of board of regents, 1899–1920, pp. 96–7, 111, 119, 130–1, 147. The quadrennium ran from the general conference of 1906 to the general conference of 1910, and analysis of attendance at board meetings has therefore been carried out without including the meetings of 30 May 1906 and 3 November 1910, which fell outside that period.
58 Henry James Morgan, *The Canadian Men and Women of the Time: A Handbook of Canadian Biography of Living Characters* (Toronto, 1912); *Who's Who and Why: A Biographical Dictionary of Men and Women of Canada and Newfoundland, 1915–6* (Toronto, [1915]); *McAlpine's New Brunswick Directory for 1903* (Saint John, n.d.)
59 MAA, minutes of board of regents, 1899–1920, p. 163.
60 Ibid., pp. 166–70.

61 *Tribune*, 15 September 1910; H.S. Stewart to C.D. Stewart, 9 November 1910, MAA, Stewart papers 8039/2/38; W.G. Watson to J.W. Graham, 17 October 1908, UCA, Methodist education papers, box 16.
62 MAA, minutes of board of regents, 1899–1920, pp. 173–5.
63 Borden to Archibald, 20, 26 April 1911, MAA, Archibald papers, 5501/5/6.
64 Borden to Archibald, 20 April 1911, ibid.
65 Borden to Archibald, 20 April 1911, 11 June 1911, ibid.; MAA, minutes of board of regents, 1899–1920, pp. 177–8, 192, 196, 218–19; *Tribune*, 15 June 1911; G.M. Campbell to Borden, 27 July 1911, MAA, Borden papers, 7508.
66 Campbell to Borden, 18 November 1886, ibid., 1886–1910, p. 48; *Tribune*, 30 May 1912.
67 MAA, minutes of board of regents, 1899–1920, pp. 148–9, 160, 174–5; Borden to Archibald, 20 April 1911, MAA, Archibald papers, 5501/5/6.
68 Borden to Archibald, 11 June 1911, MAA, Archibald papers, ibid.
69 MAA, minutes of board of regents, 1899–1920, p. 188; *Argosy*, May 1911, p. 382.
70 *Wesleyan*, 7 June 1911. The figure of 626 included both MA and BA degrees.
71 *Argosy*, January 1913, p. 214.
72 *Tribune*, 24 April 1911.
73 *Argosy*, May 1911, pp. 370, 383–4. Borden's sermon of 1909 had been described at the time as 'a trenchant, inspiring address,' and as 'one of the most powerful sermons which has been delivered from a Sackville pulpit.' *Tribune*, 31 May 1909.
74 *Argosy*, May 1911, p. 377.
75 *Tribune*, 16 June 1913.
76 Borden to Archibald, 21 September 1911, MAA, Archibald papers, 5501/5/6; A.S. Mackenzie to Borden, 29 September 1911, MAA, Borden papers, 7508; Borden to A.S. Mackenzie, 24 October 1911, DUA, president's correspondence, conferences: Maritime colleges, 1911–21, DAL/MS/1/3; A.H. MacKay to S.W. Hunton, 18 November 1911, ibid.
77 *Argosy*, May 1911, pp. 378–9. See also Carl Berger, *The Sense of Power: Studies in the Ideas of Canadian Imperialism, 1867–1914* (Toronto, 1970), 147–52; William H. Magney, 'The Methodist Church and the National Gospel, 1884–1914,' United Church Archives *Bulletin*, 20 (1968), 87–9; and J.H. Riddell, *Methodism in the Middle West* (Toronto, 1964), 312.
78 *Argosy*, May 1911, pp. 380–1.
79 *Argosy*, May 1911, pp. 384–7; W.T. Ruggles to Borden, 28 August 1911, MAA, Borden papers, 7508; see also G.A. Colpitts to Borden, 7 September 1911, ibid.
80 *Calendar*, 1911, p. 15; Borden to Archibald, 23 November 1911, MAA, Archibald papers, 5501/5/6.
81 Powell to Borden, 13 October 1911; Borden to Powell, 17 October 1911, MAA,

Borden papers, 7508. Whether the verdict would have been the same if the student had been male is a matter for speculation. The unmarried friend of the bridegroom was also a student, but had completed his engineering programme and so could not be disciplined.

82 G.B. Cutten, president, Acadia University, to Borden, 6 December 1911, MAA, Borden papers, 7508; *Tribune*, 18 December 1911; *Argosy*, January 1912, p. 211.

83 *Argosy*, February 1913, p. 289; S.W. Hunton to R.C. Archibald, 29 September 1912, MAA, Archibald papers, 5501/5/19.

84 *Argosy*, May 1909, pp. 327–8.

85 *Argosy*, October 1911, pp. 40–1.

86 *Argosy*, May 1912, p. 402.

87 Student council to Borden, 15 January 1912, MAA, Borden papers, 7508; Alice Borden to R.C. Archibald, 9 February 1912, MAA, Archibald papers, 5501/5/7; MAA, minutes of faculty, 8 February 1912. Three others were also expelled on 8 February, although the nature of their offences was not recorded in the faculty minutes.

88 *Daily Times*, 29 March, 1 April 1912; S.W. Hunton to Borden, [5 April] 1912, MAA, Borden papers, 7508.

89 MAA, minutes of board of regents, 1899–1920, p. 212.

90 J.M. Palmer to J.H. Beazley, 27 February 1912, MAA, Palmer letterbooks, 8327/1, p. 36.

91 MAA, interview with W.J. West, 26 November 1979, p. 2; see also A.J. Fuller to Borden, 28 December 1912, MAA, Borden papers, 7508. On attendance figures, see table 17.

92 *Argosy*, May 1912, p. 402.

93 *Argosy*, October 1911, p. 69; MAA, interview with W.S. and C.M. Godfrey, 15 December 1978.

94 See *Argosy*, October 1911, pp. 5–6.

95 *Argosy*, October 1912, pp. 60–1; *Calendar*, 1913, pp. 99–103.

96 MAA, minutes of board of regents, 1899–1920, p. 99; W.G. Watson to J.W. Graham, 16 April 1908, UCA, Methodist education papers, box 16.

97 MAA, interview with May Wells Trueman, 23 April 1977, pp. 4–5.

98 Ladies' college rules and regulations, c. 1900, in MAA, Archibald papers, 5501/13/4, p. 183.

99 *Argosy*, May 1906, pp. 364–8; MAA, minutes of board of regents, 1899–1920, pp. 84, 94.

100 *Tribune*, 14 October 1912; Archibald, *Women at Mount Allison*, 8.

101 *Calendar*, 1911, p. 5.

102 Fisk Teachers' Agency to Borden, 18 September 1911, MAA, Borden papers, 7508; see also Fisk Teachers' Agency to Borden, 13 September 1911, ibid.; and

M.J. Fulton, American and Foreign Teachers Agency, to Borden, 15 September 1911, ibid. The appointee was Guy Becknell, a recent PHD graduate of Clark University in Massachusetts. See *Argosy*, November 1911, p. 86.

103 See *Argosy*, November 1911, p. 85.

104 Borden to Bell, 16 August 1912; Bell to Borden, 31 August, 16 October 1912, MAA, Borden papers, 7508.

105 F.A. McCully to Borden, 23 February 1911; E.T. Case to Borden, 30 December 1911, MAA, Borden papers, 7508. *Argosy*, March 1906, pp. 258–61; February 1908, pp. 207–9; May 1908, pp. 313–21; March 1912, pp. 285–90.

106 W.G. Watson to J.W. Graham, 25 January 1908, UCA, Methodist education papers, box 16; *Argosy*, January 1908, pp. 168–9.

107 MAA, minutes of board of regents, 1899–1920, pp. 46–7.

108 Watson to Graham, 17 October 1908, UCA, Methodist education papers, box 16.

109 *Argosy*, October 1909, p. 10; *Minutes of the Proceedings of the Seventeenth Session of the Nova Scotia Conference* (Truro, 1900), 10–15; *Minutes of the Twenty-Fifth Session of the New Brunswick and Prince Edward Island Conference* (Sackville, 1908), 75; *Minutes of the Twenty-Sixty Session of the Nova Scotia Conference* (Truro, 1909), 77; Buttimer, 'The Methodist Church and Church Union,' 93.

110 A.J. Fuller to Borden, 1 January 1912 [the date on the letter is 1 January 1911, but this is clearly an error], 5 January 1912, MAA, Borden papers, 7508.

111 On the ambivalent attitude within the conferences, see Buttimer, 'The Maritime Methodist Church and Church Union,' pp. 90–6; on the Jackson case, see Sissons, *Victoria University*, 233–40; and Boyle, 'Higher Criticism and the Struggle for Academic Freedom,' 325–442.

112 Bell to Borden, 16 October 1912, MAA, Borden papers, 7508.

113 Bell to Borden, 31 August 1912, ibid. Unfortunately, presidential papers have not survived for the year 1913, and so it is impossible to be certain of the influences which shaped the legislation of that year.

114 *New Brunswick Acts*, 3 George V c80; MAA, minutes of board of regents, 1899–1920, pp. 245–7, 251–2, 271. The accusation that there had been dancing at the ladies' college, made by a Shediac minister, was hotly denied by Principal Campbell.

115 *Calendar*, 1912, pp. 46–50.

116 Harris, *Higher Education in Canada*, 239, 614–15.

117 *Calendar*, 1914, pp. 104–7; MAA, minutes of board of regents, pp. 276–7.

118 Harris, *Higher Education in Canada*, 178–9, 301–2, 611, 616–17. Albert College in Belleville, Ontario, had had a degree programme in music before its absorption into Victoria University, but had granted only one degree.

119 Ladies' college *Catalogue*, 1912, pp. 115–17.
120 C.C. Avard, 'Dr. James Noel Brunton, A Great Teacher, A Notable Pianist and a Loyal Friend,' *Maritime Advocate and Busy East*, vol. 45, no. 4 (December 1954), 21–4; *Wesleyan*, 3 July 1912; MAA, minutes of board of regents, 1899–1920, pp. 272, 288; Harris, *Higher Education in Canada*, 301; MAA, interview with Marie Brunton, 11 May 1977, p. 12; Helmut Kallman, Gilles Potvin, and Kenneth Winters, eds., *Encyclopedia of Music in Canada* (Toronto, 1981), 574, 958.
121 *Tribune*, 6 November 1911.
121 *Tribune*, 13, 16, 27 May 1912.
123 *Wesleyan*, 5 June 1912.
124 MAA, minutes of board of regents, 1899–1920, pp. 245–7.
125 MAA, minutes of board of regents, 1899–1920, pp. 251–3, 254, 271.
126 Ladies' college *Catalogue*, 1915, pp. 9–10.
127 MAA, minutes of board of regents, 1899–1920, p. 291; S.W. Hunton to R.C. Archibald, 31 May 1914, MAA, Archibald papers, 5501/5/19.
128 See table 11. Claims that attendance was over 400, as in *Proceedings of Ninth General Conference* (1914), 158, were inflated by the inclusion of students living in the ladies' college building but attending either the university or the commercial college. On the deficit in 1913–14, see ibid., p. 161.
129 *Proceedings of Ninth General Conference* (1914), 162.
130 Ibid.; Palmer to Trueman, 4 March 1912, MAA, Palmer letterbooks, 8327/1, pp. 56–7.
131 Palmer to James McKinney, Jr, 26 June 1912, ibid., pp. 314–15.
132 Academy, *Calendar*, 1913, pp. 5–6.
133 Palmer to R.O. Nimmo, 22 April 1912, MAA, Palmer letterbooks, 8327/1, p. 155; Palmer to J.C. Carruthers, 31 August 1914, ibid., 8327/2, p. 415.
134 Borden to Archibald, 23 November 1911, MAA, Archibald papers, 5501/5/6.
135 *Mount Allison University: A Statement and an Appeal*, 15 June 1911, MAA, Borden papers, 7508.
136 Borden to H.F. Ball, Borden to H.R. Way, 17 February 1912, ibid.
137 MAA, minutes of board of regents, 1899–1920, pp. 164–5; Palmer to Mrs F.M. Southgate, 19 March 1912, MAA, Palmer letterbooks, 8327/1, pp. 77–8.
138 Borden to J.W. Graham, 28 November 1911; G.J. Bond to Graham, 19 December 1911, UCA, Methodist education papers, box 19; MAA, minutes of board of regents, 1899–1920, p. 219.
139 Ibid., p. 245.
140 *Tribune*, 3 June 1912.
141 Borden to Archibald, 14, 25 March, 7 April, MAA, Archibald papers, 5501/13/13, p. 140.

142 Borden to Chester Massey, 1 May, 21 July 1911; Massey to Borden, 26 July 1911; Borden to John D. Rockerfeller [*sic*], 21 September 1911; Borden to Andrew Carnegie, 1 February 1913, Mount Allison University, comptroller's office, professorships files. Borden to Andrew Carnagie [*sic*], 26 July 1911; Steve J. Humphrey, for Rockefeller Committee, to Borden, 5 October 1911; James Bertram to Borden [6 February 1913], MAA, Borden papers, 7508. Borden's original letter to Carnegie was said by Bertram not to have been received, and this may well have been the result of the misspelling of Carnegie's name. On Rockefeller's gifts to Acadia, see Longley, *Acadia*, 105, 118, 122–3.

143 *Wesleyan*, 28 June 1911, 22 January, 26 March, 16 April, 30 April 1913. An example of the assistance that could be rendered by a local minister is that of Rev. Arthur Hockin of Canning, Nova Scotia, who offered Borden his pulpit to deliver Mount Allison's appeal, but suggested waiting until Sir Frederick Borden (a former cabinet minister in the Laurier government, and second cousin of B.C. Borden) had returned from Ottawa. Informed by Hockin when Sir Frederick arrived, Borden was able to secure a donation of $5000. Hockin to Borden, 29 November, 4 December 1911, MAA, Borden papers, 7508; *Tribune*, 14 December 1911.

144 *Wesleyan*, 16 Janaury 1907, 12 January 1910. In 1912, Borden was appointed chairman of the board of trade's education committee. G.R. McCord to Borden, 3 February 1912, MAA, Borden papers, 7508.

145 *Tribune*, 13 March 1913.

146 *Argosy*, April 1913, p. 406.

147 MAA, minutes of Alumni Association, 8029/3/2, 31 May 1910.

148 E.R. Machum to Borden, 8 February 1912, MAA, Borden papers, 7508.

149 R.P. Bell to Borden, 26 February 1912, ibid.

150 *Tribune*, 18 March, 4 April, 25 April 1912; see also newspaper clippings in MAA, Borden papers, 7508. It was apparently as a result of the Toronto meeting that the term 'Mount Allisonian,' later shortened to 'Allisonian,' was first coined as a description of a former Mount Allison student, in a report of the meeting prepared for the *Tribune* of 25 April by Maude Pettit, a university graduate of 1900.

151 MAA, minutes of Alumni Association, 8029/3/2, 28 May 1912; MAA, minutes of board of regents, 1899–1920, pp. 224–5.

152 See A.M. Bell to Borden, 28 June 1912, Borden papers, 7508; MAA, minutes of board of regents, 1899–1920, p. 236; R.A. Cassidy to Borden, 29 November, 5 December, 23 December 1912, Borden papers, 7508.

153 Borden to Archibald, 6 June 1913, MAA, Archibald papers, 5501/5/6; *Proceedings of Ninth General Conference* (1914), 156.

154 Borden to Archibald, 23 March 1914, MAA, Archibald papers, 5501/5/6.

155 See tables 12, 14. I have used the convenient phrase 'small communities' to apply to unincorporated places or incorporated centres of 1000 people or less.
156 *Proceedings of Ninth General Conference* (1914), 156; see also MAA, minutes of board of regents, 1899–1920, p. 292.
157 Borden to Archibald, 31 March 1914, MAA, Archibald papers, 5501/5/6.
158 Proposal of department of militia and defence, 19 December 1911, MAA, miscellaneous files, COTC file; MAA, minutes of executive committee of board of regents, 1913–32, pp. 4–6. On all matters connected with the COTC at Mount Allison, I am indebted to Major W. Alex Morrison, of Canadian Forces Command and Staff College, Toronto, who generously shared with me the results of his extensive research on this subject, as contained in his manuscript 'History of the Mount Allison COTC' (copy in MAA).
159 See Saint John *Globe*, 12 August 1914, in MAA, Archibald papers, 5501/15, vol. 4, p. 31; *Tribune*, 31 August 1914; *Argosy*, October 1914, p. 52.
160 *Wesleyan*, 28 October 1914.

TABLE 1
Geographical origins of students at Wesleyan Academy, 1843–53

	New Brunswick	Nova Scotia	Prince Edward Island	Newfoundland	Other	Total
1843	58 (72.5%)	20 (25.0%)	1 (1.3%)	–	1 (1.3%)	80
1844	95 (72.5%)	29 (22.1%)	4 (3.1%)	–	3 (2.3%)	131
1845	82 (60.7%)	44 (32.6%)	5 (3.7%)	1 (0.7%)	3 (2.2%)	135
1846	84 (60.0%)	50 (35.7%)	2 (1.4%)	3 (2.1%)	1 (0.7%)	140
1847	103 (71.5%)	36 (25.0%)	1 (0.7%)	3 (2.1%)	1 (0.7%)	144
1848	70 (64.7%)	30 (27.8%)	5 (4.6%)	3 (2.8%)	–	108
1849–51[1]	91 (52.9%)	59 (34.3%)	17 (9.9%)	4 (2.3%)	1 (0.6%)	172
1852	72 (56.3%)	36 (28.1%)	16 (12.5%)	3 (2.3%)	1 (0.8%)	128
1853	99 (66.0%)	36 (24.0%)	11 (7.3%)	2 (1.3%)	2 (1.3%)	150

Source: *Catalogues* of Wesleyan Academy, 1843–53.[2]

1 No catalogue was published in 1849 or in 1850, and the 1851 catalogue contained a combined listing of all students for the years 1849–51. The total numbers of students for the years 1849, 1850, and 1851 were 97, 79, and 89 respectively, but no indication was given in the catalogue of which students attended in any given year.

2 The figures in this table represent the total number of students listed in the *Catalogues* for each given year; they did not necessarily all attend at any one time during the year.

TABLE 2
Geographical origins of selected groups of students at Wesleyan Academy, 1843–53

	Sackville	Westmorland Co., N.B. (including Sackville)	Cumberland Co., N.S.	Saint John[1]	Fredericton	Halifax	Charlottetown
1843	22 (27.5%)[2]	38 (47.5%)	8 (10.0%)	9 (11.3%)	–	6 (7.5%)	–
1844	27 (20.6%)	46 (35.1%)	7 (5.3%)	23 (17.6%)	1 (0.8%)	13 (9.9%)	2 (1.5%)
1845	14 (10.4%)	28 (20.7%)	11 (8.1%)	26 (19.3%)	3 (2.2%)	16 (11.9%)	2 (1.5%)
1846	18 (12.9%)	31 (22.1%)	15 (10.7%)	25 (17.9%)	5 (3.6%)	12 (8.6%)	1 (0.7%)
1847	19 (13.2%)	40 (27.8%)	6 (4.2%)	28 (19.4%)	7 (4.9%)	10 (6.9%)	1 (0.7%)
1848	14 (13.0%)	28 (25.9%)	7 (6.5%)	16 (14.8%)	4 (3.7%)	11 (10.2%)	5 (4.6%)
1849–51[3]	25 (14.5%)	38 (22.1%)	11 (6.4%)	24 (14.0%)	1 (0.6%)	19 (11.0%)	12 (7.0%)
1852	17 (13.3%)	31 (24.2%)	6 (4.7%)	30 (23.4%)	–	12 (9.4%)	12 (9.4%)
1853	25 (16.7%)	44 (29.3%)	11 (7.3%)	35 (22.3%)	–	9 (6.0%)	8 (5.3%)

Source: *Catalogues* of Wesleyan Academy, 1843–53[4]

1 This category includes students from Carleton, Indiantown, and Portland, as well as those from the city of Saint John.
2 All percentages are percentages of the total enrolment at the Wesleyan Academy in the given year.
3 See note 1 to table 1.
4 See note 2 to table 1.

TABLE 3
Geographical origins of students at Wesleyan Academy, 1854–7

	Male branch			Female branch			Total		
	1854–5	1855–6	1856–7	1854–5	1855–6	1856–7	1854–5	1855–6	1856–7
New Brunswick	94 (59.9%)	85 (59.0%)	84 (64.1%)	98 (69.0%)	90 (67.2%)	70 (68.0%)	192 (64.2%)	175 (62.9%)	154 (65.8%)
Nova Scotia	51 (32.5%)	51 (35.4%)	38 (29.0%)	34 (23.9%)	32 (23.9%)	26 (25.2%)	85 (28.4%)	83 (29.9%)	64 (27.4%)
Prince Edward Island	10 (6.4%)	6 (4.2%)	6 (4.6%)	7 (4.9%)	8 (6.0%)	–	17 (5.7%)	14 (5.0%)	6 (2.6%)
Newfoundland	2 (1.3%)	1 (0.7%)	3 (2.3%)	–	–	–	2 (0.7%)	1 (0.4%)	3 (1.3%)
Other	–	1 (0.7%)	–	3 (2.1%)	4 (3.0%)	7 (6.8%)	3 (1.0%)	5 (1.8%)	7 (3.0%)
Total	157	144	131	142	134	103	299	278	234

Source: *Mount Allison Academic Gazette*, 1854–7. The figures in this table represent the total number of students listed in the *Gazette* for the period from August of one year to June of the next. All the students did not necessarily attend at any one time within that period.

TABLE 4
Geographical origins of selected groups of students at Wesleyan Academy, 1854–7

	Male branch			Female branch			Total		
	1854–5	1855–6	1856–7	1854–5	1855–6	1856–7	1854–5	1855–6	1856–7
Sackville	25 (15.9%)[1]	18 (12.5%)	21 (16.0%)	45 (31.7%)	45 (33.6%)	36 (35.0%)	70 (23.4%)	63 (22.7%)	57 (24.4%)
Westmorland Co., N.B. (including Sackville)	44 (28.0%)	36 (25.0%)	36 (27.5%)	64 (45.1%)	65 (48.5%)	42 (40.8%)	108 (36.1%)	101 (36.3%)	78 (33.3%)
Cumberland Co., N.S.	14 (8.9%)	14 (9.7%)	7 (5.3%)	11 (7.7%)	3 (2.2%)	5 (4.9%)	25 (8.4%)	17 (6.1%)	12 (5.1%)
Saint John[2]	29 (18.5%)	25 (17.4%)	21 (16.0%)	17 (12.0%)	5 (3.7%)	10 (9.7%)	46 (15.4%)	30 (10.8%)	31 (13.2%)
Fredericton	1 (0.6%)	–	–	–	3 (2.2%)	6 (5.8%)	1 (0.3%)	3 (1.1%)	6 (2.6%)
Halifax	9 (5.7%)	4 (2.8%)	–	3 (2.1%)	3 (2.2%)	3 (2.9%)	12 (4.0%)	7 (2.5%)	3 (1.3%)
Charlottetown	7 (4.5%)	5 (3.5%)	4 (3.1%)	5 (3.5%)	7 (5.2%)	–	12 (4.0%)	12 (4.3%)	4 (1.7%)

Source: *Mount Allison Academic Gazette*, 1854–7[3]

1 All percentages are percentages of the total enrolment in the particular branch of the academy, or of the total enrolment, in the given year.
2 See note 1 to table 2.
3 See note to table 3.

TABLE 5
Age structure of Mount Allison student body, 1857–63

	Male academy					Female academy				
	12 &under[1]	12–15	15–18	18 & over	Total	12 & under	12–15	15–18	18 & over	Total
1857–8[2]	6 (4.7%)	28 (21.9%)	47 (36.7%)	47 (36.7%)	128	25 (15.9%)	45 (28.7%)	50 (31.8%)	37 (23.6%)	157
1858–9	6 (5.0%)	31 (26.1%)	39 (32.8%)	43 (36.1%)	119	No figures available				
1859–60	14 (9.2%)	41 (27.0%)	44 (28.9%)	53 (34.9%)	152	19 (11.6%)	50 (30.5%)	55 (33.5%)	40 (24.4%)	164
1860–1	19 (10.3%)	43 (23.4%)	56 (30.4%)	66 (35.9%)	184	23 (13.8%)	55 (32.9%)	53 (31.7%)	36 (21.6%)	167
1861–2	10 (6.3%)	37 (23.3%)	57 (35.8%)	55 (34.6%)	159	–	16 (11.0%)	34 (23.3%)	96 (65.8%)	146[3]
1862–3[4]	12 (7.9%)	34 (22.4%)	59 (38.8%)	47 (30.9%)	152	6 (5.7%)	30 (28.6%)	50 (47.6%)	19 (18.1%)	105

Sources: PANS, MG17, vol. 17, no. 90, 93, 97; PANB, RG2, RS8, group I, 1/4; PANB, RG4, RS24/861/re/1; *N.B. Assembly Journal*, 1861, appendix, p. 52; ibid., 1862, appendix, pp. 53–4; ibid., 1864, appendix, p. 51.

1 This table follows the categories used in the original reports submitted, and thus reflects their ambiguities. Although the definitions were never explained, it is likely that a student who had attained the age of 12, 15 or 18 during the first part of the year would be entered in a higher age category than one attaining such an age later in the year. The matter is complicated by the fact that the year reported upon was not the same in each case. However, with the one exception mentioned in note 2, it was a year ending in either October or November of the second calendar year specified.

2 For the female academy, the figures cited are for the year ending in 'December 1858.' PANS, MG17, vol. 17, no. 90.

3 The returns for the female academy in 1861–2 are questionable as to their accuracy. Other sources reveal that enrolment was seriously declining, and the sharply different figures given for 1861–2 from those of previous years suggest that some creativity may have been used in their compilation. This possibility is reinforced by the fact that slightly different figures were supplied to the Nova Scotia government for the same time period (PANS, MG17, vol. 17, no. 97) from the figures cited in the table, which were supplied to New Brunswick (PANB, RG2, RS8, group I, 1/4).

4 Figures for the male academy in this year included, without distinction, the few college students. *N.B. Assembly Journal*, 1864, appendix, p. 51.

TABLE 6
Later careers of Mount Allison graduates of 1863–9

	Source	Degree	Year	Profession	Location
Ayer, Nehemiah	1	BA	1864	doctor	Amherst, NS
Borden, Robert A.	1,2	BA	1866	lawyer/judge	Moncton, NB
Burbidge, D. Henry	3	BA	1867	teacher	Maritimes & Newfoundland
Burbidge, George W.	4	BA	1867	lawyer/judge	Saint John, NB, then Ottawa
Chesley, Samuel A.	1	BA	1866	lawyer/judge	Lunenburg, NS
Cogswell, William C.	1	BA	1869	?	rumoured that he 'went west'
Cowperthwaite, Humphrey P.	1,4,5	BA	1867	minister	Maritimes & Newfoundland
Flint, Thomas B.	1,4	BA	1867	lawyer/ politician	Yarmouth, NS
Fulton, Jotham McC.	4,5	BA	1865	minister	Maritimes & Bermuda, then USA
Hodgson, Thaddeus	1	BA	1866	mechanical engineer	River Philip, NS
Inch, James R.	6	BA	1864	professor/ educational administrator	New Brunswick
Mellish, John T.	7	BA	1869	teacher/ lawyer	Maritimes
Milner, William C.	8	BS	1864	lawyer/ journalist/ archivist	Maritimes, then Ottawa
Morris, Augustus	4,5	BA	1869	probationary minister	Maritimes. Died 1873
Morton, Arthur D.	5	BA	1864	minister	Maritimes
Rogers, Thomas	1,5	BA	1867	minister	Maritimes, then USA
Russell, Benjamin	4	BA	1868	lawyer/ professor/ judge	Dartmouth, NS
Seller, Joseph	5	BA	1868	minister	Maritimes
Smith, Alfred D.	4	BA	1867	professor	Sackville, NB
Sprague, Howard	5,9	BA	1863	minister/ professor	Maritimes
Stockton, Alfred A.	6	BA	1864	lawyer/ politician	Saint John, NB
Temple, William H.G.	1,4	BA	1868	merchant/ minister	Yarmouth, NS, then USA
Toddings, Seward S.	1	BA	1866	journalist	Bermuda
Weddall, Richard W.	5	BA	1868	minister	Maritimes
Weldon, Richard C.	6	BA	1866	lawyer/ professor/ politician	Maritimes

(TABLE 6 continued)

	Source	Degree	Year	Profession	Location
Wood, Charles H.	10	BA	1866	–	Various travels, on account of ill-health. Died 1871
Wood, Josiah	6	BA	1863	lawyer/ merchant/ politician/ lieutenant-governor of NB	Sackville, NB

Sources: 1. *Argosy*, May 1896. 2. *Busy East of Canada* (Sackville, NB), August 1915. 3. *Argosy*, November 1888. 4. MAA, R.C. Archibald papers, 5501/14. 5. G.H. Cornish, *Cyclopaedia of Methodism in Canada* (Toronto 1881). 6. W.S. Wallace, *The Macmillan Dictionary of Canadian Biography* (Toronto, 1963). 7. G.M. Rose, *A Cyclopaedia of Canadian Biography* (Toronto, 1888). 8. *Sackville Tribune*, 23 November 1939. 9. *Argosy*, March 1908. 10. *Argosy*, April 1902.

TABLE 7
Geographical origins of students at Mount Allison institutions, 1868

	Sackville	Westmorland Co., NB	Cumberland Co., NS	Halifax	Saint John	Charlottetown	Fredericton	NB	NS	PEI	Nfld.	Bermuda	Other	Total
College	3	3	2	1	1	3	–	7	8	4	1	–	1	21
	(14.2%)	(14.2%)	(9.5%)	(4.8%)	(4.8%)	(14.2%)		(33.3%)	(38.1%)	(19.0%)	(4.8%)		(4.8%)	
Male	25	34	3	4	3	2	–	49	26	6	1	1	1	84
academy	(29.8%)	(40.5%)	(3.6%)	(4.8%)	(3.6%)	(2.4%)		(58.3%)	(31.0%)	(7.1%)	(1.2%)	(1.2%)	(1.2%)	
Ladies'	31	40	1	7	10	1	1	57	25	1	1	–	3	87
academy	(35.6%)	(46.0%)	(1.1%)	(8.0%)	(11.5%)	(1.1%)	(1.1%)	(65.5%)	(28.7%)	(1.1%)	(1.1%)		(3.4%)	
Total	59	77	6	12	14	7	1	113	59	11	3	1	5	192
	(30.7%)	(40.1%)	(3.1%)	(6.3%)	(7.3%)	(3.6%)	(0.5%)	(58.9%)	(30.7%)	(5.7%)	(1.6%)	(0.5%)	(2.6%)	

Source: *Catalogue*, 1868–9, pp. 7, 22–4, 25–7. Nine college students were also taking classes in the academy, and were listed under both institutions. For purposes of this table, they have been counted as college students. Also included are the two theological students listed under the college.

TABLE 8
Locations in 1903 of Mount Allison Bachelor's degree graduates, 1863–1900

	Maritime provinces	Newfound-land	Bermuda	Ontario or Quebec	Western Canada	Eastern USA	Western or Midwestern USA	Other	Unknown	Total
1863–70	17 (63.0%)	1 (3.7%)	1 (3.7%)	2 (7.4%)	–	2 (7.4%)	2 (7.4%)	1 (3.7%)	1 (3.7%)	27
1871–80	29 (58.0%)	3 (6.0%)	–	2 (4.0%)	3 (6.0%)	3 (6.0%)	5 (10.0%)	5 (10.0%)	–	50
1881–90	42 (54.5%)	2 (2.6%)	–	6 (7.8%)	7 (9.1%)	11 (14.3%)	6 (7.8%)	3 (3.9%)	–	77
1891–1900	73 (48.0%)	7 (4.6%)	3 (2.0%)	13 (8.6%)	16 (10.5%)	19 (12.5%)	14 (9.2%)	7 (4.6%)	–	152

Sources: [Raymond C. Archibald], 'A list of the names of those persons on whom degrees have been conferred by the University of Mount Allison College,' 1 May 1903, MAA, Archibald papers, 5501/14. Where gaps exist in Archibald's listing, they have been filled as far as possible from the alumni columns in the following issues of the *Argosy*: April 1900; May 1901; November 1902; December 1903. Locations have been classified as far as possible as in the year 1903, but in some cases the location adopted is the last known location before 1903. In the case of those deceased by 1903 the place of death has been listed as the location.

TABLE 9
Occupations in 1903 of Mount Allison Bachelor's degree graduates, 1863–1900

	Clergy/ Missionary	Teaching/ Education	Law	Medicine	Civil service	Banking
1863–70	9 (33.3%)	3 (11.1%)	8 (29.6%)	1 (3.7%)	–	–
1871–80	19 (38.0%)	10 (20.0%)	8 (16.0%)	4 (8.0%)	–	1 (2.0%)
1881–90	23 (29.9%)	9 (11.7%)	19 (24.7%)	9 (11.7%)	3 (3.9%)	1 (1.3%)
1891–1900	42 (27.6%)	26 (17.1%)	16 (10.5%)	24 (15.8%)	–	2 (1.3%)

(TABLE 9 continued)

	Business	Journal- alism	Engi- neering	Farming	Other	No formal employ- ment	Un- known	Total
1863–70	3 (11.1%)	2 (7.4%)	–	–	–	–	1 (3.7%)	27
1871–80	3 (6.0%)	1 (2.0%)	–	2 (4.0%)	1 (2.0%)	1 (2.0%)	–	50
1881–90	4 (5.2%)	1 (1.3%)	2 (2.6%)	–	2 (2.6%)	4 (5.2%)	–	77
1891–1900	4 (2.6%)	6 (3.9%)	4 (2.6%)	2 (1.3%)	8 (5.3%)	16 (10.5%)	2 (1.3%)	152

Sources: [Raymond C. Archibald], 'A list of the names of those persons on whom degrees have been conferred by the University of Mount Allison College,' 1 May 1903, MAA, Archibald papers, 5501/14. Where gaps exist in Archibald's listing, they have been filled as far as possible from the alumni columns in the following issues of the *Argosy*: March, April, May, December 1896; March 1899; February, April, November 1900; March, April, November 1901; January, February, March, May 1902. Occupations have been classified as far as possible as in the year 1903, but in some cases the occupation adopted is the last known occupation before 1903.

TABLE 10
Occupations in 1903 of Mount Allison Bachelor's degree graduates (women), 1863–1900

	Missionary	Teaching	Medicine	Journalism	Stenographer	Governess	No formal employment	Unknown	Total
1863–70	–	–	–	–	–	–	–	–	–
1871–80	–	–	–	–	–	–	1	–	–
1881–90	–	–	–	–	–	–	4	–	4
1891–1900	1	11	1	1	1	1	15	–	31

Sources: [Raymond C. Archibald], 'A list of the names of those persons on whom degrees have been conferred by the University of Mount Allison College,' 1 May 1903, MAA, Archibald papers, 5501/14. Where gaps exist in Archibald's listing, they have been filled as far as possible from the alumni columns in the following issues of the *Argosy*: March 1899; April, November 1901; January, February, March, May 1902. Occupations have been classified as far as possible as in the year 1903, but in some cases the occupation adopted is the last known occupation before 1903.

Note: Two of the graduates of the period 1891–1900 listed as having no formal employment (L.J.M. Deinstadt and H.S. Olive) are known to have worked in journalism for a time after graduation, before returning to live at home. See the *Argosy*, March 1899, February 1902.

TABLE 11
Enrolment at Mount Allison institutions in selected years, 1870–1941

	1870–1	1880–1	1890–1	1900–1	1910–11	1920–1	1930–1	1940–1
College/University[1]	17	25	62	73	155	173	395	391
Theology	7	10	17	18	43	22	7	2
Post-graduate	–	2	2	3	2	1	5	13
Ladies' academy/college	78	76	174	168	303	299	269	not available[2]
Male academy and commercial college	78	66	73	103	154	206	159	152
Summer school	–	–	–	–	–	–	152	98
Special students and others	10	2	13	12	21	24	55	61
Total	190	181	341	377	678	729	1042	717

Sources: *Catalogues* and *Calendars* of Mount Allison institutions.

1 This category comprises only those enrolled in the regular undergraduate degree courses. 'Special students,' who would be enrolled to take only a few university-level courses, are not included; nor are theological students, unless also registered in arts.

2 No list of students was published by the school for girls (the successor of the ladies' college) for this year; but it is likely that many of these were also enrolled as special students at the university, and so would still appear in the total given for the overall student body. The principal's report for the year reveals that there were 41 students in attendance during the year, but this figure cannot be incorporated into the table in the absence of a list of names, since it would be impossible to check for students who were registered at more than one of the institutions.

TABLE 12
Geographical origins of students at Mount Allison institutions in selected years, 1870–1941

	1870–1		1880–1		1890–1		1900–1	
	College	Total	College	Total	University	Total	University	Total
New Brunswick	5 (29.4%)	127 (66.8%)	11 (44.0%)	88 (48.6%)	21 (33.9%)	172 (50.4%)	40 (54.8%)	200 (53.1%)
Nova Scotia	5 (29.4%)	42 (22.1%)	12 (48.0%)	73 (40.3%)	33 (53.2%)	118 (34.6%)	25 (34.2%)	114 (30.2%)
Prince Edward Island	5 (29.4%)	12 (6.3%)	1 (4.0%)	5 (2.8%)	4 (6.5%)	18 (5.3%)	2 (2.7%)	18 (4.8%)
Newfoundland	2 (11.8%)	2 (1.1%)	1 (4.0%)	1 (0.6%)	2 (3.2%)	9 (2.6%)	4 (5.5%)	14 (3.7%)
Bermuda	–	–	–	4 (2.2%)	1 (1.6%)	7 (2.1%)	2 (2.7%)	6 (1.6%)
Canada (outside Maritime region)	–	–	–	–	–	3 (0.9%)	–	2 (0.5%)
USA	–	3 (1.6%)	–	3 (1.7%)	–	3 (0.9%)	–	11 (2.9%)
British Isles	–	4 (2.1%)	–	–	–	–	–	2 (0.5%)
British West Indies	–	–	–	–	–	–	–	2 (0.5%)
Other	–	–	–	–	1 (1.6%)	2 (0.6%)	–	1 (0.3%)
Unknown	–	–	–	7 (3.9%)	–	9 (2.6%)	–	7 (1.9%)
Total	17	190	25	181	62	341	73	377

(TABLE 12 continued)

	1910–11		1920–1		1930–1		1940–1	
	University	Total	University	Total	University	Total	University	Total
New Brunswick	64 (41.3%)	361 (53.2%)	63 (36.4%)	346 (47.7%)	161 (40.7%)	556 (53.4%)	164 (41.9%)	329 (45.9%)
Nova Scotia	67 (43.2%)	190 (28.0%)	69 (39.9%)	246 (33.9%)	152 (38.5%)	310 (29.8%)	130 (33.2%)	216 (30.1%)
Prince Edward Island	5 (3.2%)	30 (4.4%)	5 (2.9%)	35 (4.8%)	24 (6.1%)	84 (8.1%)	17 (4.3%)	42 (5.9%)
Newfoundland	10 (6.5%)	25 (3.7%)	27 (15.6%)	57 (7.9%)	20 (5.1%)	28 (2.7%)	35 (9.0%)	46 (6.4%)
Bermuda	–	3 (0.4%)	–	–	3 (0.8%)	3 (0.3%)	2 (0.5%)	7 (1.0%)
Canada (outside Maritime region	2 (1.3%)	19 (2.8%)	8 (4.6%)	25 (3.4%)	17 (4.3%)	24 (2.3%)	32 (8.2%)	54 (7.5%)
USA	3 (1.9%)	13 (1.9%)	–	12 (1.7%)	8 (2.0%)	15 (1.4%)	9 (2.3%)	14 (2.0%)
British Isles	2 (1.3%)	20 (2.9%)	1 (0.6%)	2 (0.3%)	8 (2.0%)	11 (1,1%)	–	1 (0.1%)
British West Indies	–	1 (0.1%)	–	–	2 (0.5%)	4 (0.4%)	2 (0.5%)	5 (0.7%)
Other	2 (1.3%)	7 (1.0%)	–	1 (0.1%)	–	6 (0.6%)	–	3 (0.4%)
Unknown	–	9 (1.3%)	–	1 (0.1%)	–	1 (0.1%)	–	–
Total	155	678	173	725	395	1042	391	717

Sources: *Catalogues* and *Calendars* of Mount Allison Institutions.

TABLE 13
Home background of Maritime province students at Mount Allison in selected years, 1870–91

	1870–1		1880–1		1890–1	
	College	Total	College	Total	University	Total
Non-incorporated, population over 10,000	2 (13.3%)	34 (18.8%)	4 (16.7%)	20 (12.0%)	8 (13.8%)	29 (9.4%)
Incorporated, population 5001–10,000	4 (26.7%)	8 (4.4%)	–	8 (4.8%)	2 (3.4%)	17 (5.5%)
Incorporated, population 2501–5000	–	–	1 (4.2%)	11 (6.6%)	2 (3.4%)	15 (4.9%)
Incorporated, population 1001–2500	–	5 (2.8%)	4 (16.7%)	7 (4.2%)	3 (5.2%)	13 (4.2%)
Sackville	–	48 (26.5%)	2 (8.3%)	35 (21.1%)	2 (3.4%)	76 (24.7%)
Other non-incorporated, or incorporated population 1000 or less	9 (60.0%)	86 (47.5%)	13 (54.2%)	85 (51.2%)	41 (70.7%)	158 (51.3%)
Total	15	181	24	166	58	308
Non-Maritime or unknown	2	9	1	15	4	33

Sources: *Catalogues* and *Calendars* of Mount Allison institutions; Canada, *Census of Canada, 1931*, vol. 2, table 8, pp. 8–14.

TABLE 14
Home background of Maritime province students at Mount Allison in selected years, 1900–41

	1900–1			1910–11		
	University	Total	Maritime pop.	University	Total	Maritime pop.
Incorporated, population over 10,000	12 (17.9%)	30 (9.0%)	92,261 (10.3%)	27 (19.9%)	60 (10.3%)	134,760 (14.4%)
Incorporated, population 5001–10,000	6 (9.0%)	32 (9.6%)	45,420 (5.1%)	21 (15.4%)	70 (12.0%)	68,813 (7.3%)
Incorporated, population 2501–5000	4 (6.0%)	29 (8.7%)	61,175 (6.8%)	15 (11.0%)	52 (9.0%)	43,187 (4.6%)
Incorporated, population 1001–2500	15 (22.4%)	104 (31.3%)	22,359 (2.5%)	20 (14.7%)	178 (30.6%)	38,690 (4.1%)
Incorporated, population 1000 or less, or unincorporated	30 (44.8%)	137 (41.3%)	672,738 (75.3%)	53 (39.0%)	221 (38.0%)	652,505 (69.6%)
Total	67	332	893,953	136	581	937,955
Non-Maritime or unknown	6	45		19	97	

(TABLE 14 continued)

	1920–1			1930–1		
	University	Total	Maritime pop.	University	Total	Maritime pop
Incorporated, population over 10,000	32 (23.4%)	88 (14.0%)	173,392 (17.3%)	66 (19.6%)	157 (16.5%)	183,634 (18.2%)
Incorporated, population 5001–10,000	14 (10.2%)	97 (15.5%)	86,650 (8.7%)	62 (18.4%)	144 (15.2%)	95,139 (9.4%)
Incorporated, population 2501–5000	8 (5.8%)	50 (8.0%)	49,775 (5.0%)	46 (13.6%)	86 (9.1%)	55,309 (5.5%)
Incorporated, population 1001–2500	21 (15.3%)	143 (22.8%)	39,783 (4.0%)	41 (12.2%)	230 (24.2%)	33,461 (3.3%)
Incorporated, population 1000 or less, or unincorporated	62 (45.3%)	249 (39.7%)	650,728 (65.1%)	122 (36.2%)	333 (35.1%)	641,543 (63.6%)
Total	137	627	1,000,328	337	950	1,009,103
Non-Maritime or unknown	36	98		58	92	

(TABLE 14 continued)

	1940–1		
	University	Total	Maritime pop.
Incorporated, population over 10,000	94 (30.2%)	178 (30.3%)	244,446 (21.6%)
Incorporated, population 5001–10,000	49 (15.8%)	73 (12.4%)	81,355 (7.2%)
Incorporated, population 2501–5000	35 (11.3%)	58 (9.9%)	58,823 (5.2%)
Incorporated, population 1001–2500	42 (13.5%)	112 (19.1%)	40,105 (3.5%)
Incorporated, population 1000 or less, or unincorporated	91 (29.3%)	166 (28.3%)	705,681 (62.4%)
Total	311	587	1,130,410
Non-Maritime or unknown	80	130	

Sources: *Catalogues* and *Calendars* of Mount Allison institutions; Canada, *Census of Canada, 1901*. Vol. 1, table 1, pp. 2–5; ibid., 1911, vol. 1, table 1, pp. 2–172; ibid., 1921, vol. 1, table 1, p. 3; ibid., 1931, vol. 1, table 1a, pp. 348–50; ibid., vol. 2, table 8, pp. 8–14; ibid., 1941, vol. 1, table 1, pp. 563–5; ibid., vol. 2, table 16, pp. 188–210.

TABLE 15
Attendance of students, and ages, at Mount Allison ladies' academy, 1869–76

	Enrolment		Boarders		Ages		
	Total	Average at one time	Total	Average at one time	Under 15	15 and over	Average age
1869–70	76	59	40	29	10	66	18
1870–1	78	60	49	37	6	72	19
1871–2	82	64	54	40	8	74	19
1872–3	65	54	41	35	6	59	18
1873–4	90	75	71	63	9	81	17
1874–5	104	90	85	70	7	97	17
1875–6	87	76	63	50	12	75	17

Sources: *N.S. Assembly Journals*, 1871, appendix 21, p. 40; 1872, appendix 13, p.u.; 1873, appendix 14, p. 42; 1874, appendix 15, p. 46; 1875, appendix 14, p. 52; 1876, appendix 7, p. 56; 1877, appendix 5, p. s. These were the only years for which these statistics were reported for the two academies.

TABLE 16
Attendance of students, and ages, at Mount Allison male academy, 1869–76

	Enrolment		Boarders		Ages		
	Total	Average at one time	Total	Average at one time	Under 15	15 and over	Average age
1869–70	66	55	41	34	13	53	17
1870–1	86	65	56	42	19	67	17
1871–2	85	66	59	45	15	70	17
1872–3	68	60	57	49	14	54	17
1873–4	89	72	82	60	19	70	17
1874–5	109	80	90	70	15	94	18
1875–6	106	85	89	76	14	92	17

Source: *N.S. Assembly Journals*, 1871, appendix 21, p. 40; 1872, appendix 13, p.u.; 1873, appendix 14, p. 42; 1874, appendix 15, p. 46; 1875, appendix 14, p. 52; 1876, appendix 7, p. 56; 1877, appendix 5, p. s. These were the only years for which these statistics were reported for the two academies.

TABLE 17
Home backgrounds of Maritime provinces undergraduates at Mount Allison, 1900–31

Home Community	1900–1	1901–2	1902–3	1903–4	1904–5	1905–6	1906–7	1907–8
City or town, population over 10,000	12 (17.9%)	11 (14.3%)	11 (13.4%)	16 (18.4%)	26 (24.5%)	27 (24.5%)	17 (17.0%)	23 (19.5%)
City or town, population 5001–10,000	6 (9.0%)	2 (2.6%)	6 (7.3%)	3 (3.4%)	3 (2.8%)	10 (9.1%)	11 (11.0%)	12 (10.2%)
Town, population 2501–5000	4 (6.0%)	5 (6.5%)	9 (11.0%)	9 (10.3%)	10 (9.4%)	2 (1.8%)	2 (2.0%)	7 (5.9%)
Town, population 1001–2500	15 (22.4%)	18 (23.4%)	18 (22.0%)	19 (21.8%)	17 (16.0%)	15 (13.6%)	16 (16.0%)	22 (18.6%)
Other	30 (44.8%)	41 (53.2%)	38 (46.3%)	40 (46.0%)	50 (47.2%)	56 (50.9%)	54 (54.0%)	54 (45.8%)
Total Maritime	67	77	82	87	106	110	100	118
Non-Maritime	6	9	6	9	10	8	12	17
Total	73	86	88	96	116	118	112	135

(TABLE 17 continued)

Home Community	1908–9	1909–10	1910–11	1911–12	1912–13	1913–14	1914–15	1915–16
City or town, population over 10,000	20 (15.4%)	27 (20.8%)	27 (19.9%)	22 (18.8%)	18 (15.1%)	23 (17.7%)	21 (15.9%)	22 (18.3%)
City or town, population 5001–10,000	15 (11.5%)	20 (15.4%)	21 (15.4%)	20 (17.1%)	19 (16.0%)	15 (11.5%)	18 (13.6%)	11 (9.2%)
Town, population 2501–5000	10 (7.7%)	12 (9.2%)	15 (11.0%)	9 (7.7%)	9 (7.6%)	13 (10.0%)	14 (10.6%)	12 (10.0%)
Town, population 1001–2500	28 (21.5%)	22 (16.9%)	20 (14.7%)	15 (12.8%)	20 (16.8%)	20 (15.4%)	19 (14.4%)	21 (17.5%)
Other	57 (43.8%)	49 (37.7%)	53 (39.0%)	51 (43.6%)	53 (44.5%)	59 (45.4%)	60 (45.5%)	54 (45.0%)
Total Maritime	130	130	136	117	119	130	132	120
Non-Maritime	20	24	19	15	25	27	20	14
Total	150	154	155	132	144	157	152	134

(TABLE 17 continued)

Home Community	1916–17	1917–18	1918–19	1919–20	1920–1	1921–2	1922–3
City or town, population over 10,000	13 (14.1%)	15 (16.3%)	18 (17.3%)	29 (18.4%)	32 (23.4%)	36 (24.2%)	28 (20.7%)
City or town, population 5001–10,000	10 (10.9%)	10 (10.9%)	11 (10.6%)	22 (13.9%)	14 (10.2%)	20 (13.4%)	14 (10.4%)
Town, population 2501–5000	11 (12.0%)	11 (12.0%)	15 (14.4%)	15 (9.5%)	8 (5.8%)	11 (7.4%)	13 (9.6%)
Town, population 1001–2500	17 (18.5%)	13 (14.1%)	13 (12.5%)	28 (17.7%)	21 (15.3%)	18 (12.1%)	28 (20.7%)
Other	41 (44.6%)	43 (46.7%)	47 (45.2%)	64 (40.5%)	62 (45.3%)	64 (43.0%)	52 (38.5%)
Total Maritime	92	92	104	158	137	149	135
Non-Maritime	12	10	17	28	36	33	28
Total	104	102	121	186	173	182	163

(TABLE 17 continued)

Home Communtiy	1923–4	1924–5	1925–6	1926–7	1927–8	1928–9	1929–30	1930–1
City or town, population over 10,000	23 (19.2%)	36 (20.1%)	38 (19.1%)	44 (20.7%)	51 (22.7%)	67 (23.6%)	62 (19.7%)	66 (19.6%)
City or town, population 5001–10,000	14 (11.7%)	23 (12.8%)	39 (19.6%)	43 (20.2%)	42 (18.7%)	50 (17.6%)	55 (17.5%)	62 (18.4%)
Town, population 2501–5000	14 (11.7%)	21 (11.7%)	27 (13.6%)	30 (14.1%)	29 (12.9%)	38 (13.4%)	51 (16.2%)	46 (13.6%)
Town, population 1001–2500	26 (21.7%)	35 (19.6%)	31 (15.6%)	32 (15.0%)	37 (14.4%)	40 (14.1%)	38 (12.1%)	41 (12.2%)
Other	43 (35.8%)	64 (35.8%)	64 (32.2%)	64 (30.0%)	66 (29.3%)	89 (31.3%)	108 (34.4%)	122 (36.2%)
Total Maritime	120	179	199	213	225	284	314	337
Non-Maritime	26	28	28	27	22	40	42	58
Total	146	207	227	240	247	324	356	395

Sources: *Calendars* of Mount Allison University, 1901–31; Canada, *Census of Canada, 1931*, vol. 2, table 8, pp. 8–14.

1 This table includes neither special students nor summer school students; theology students are included only if also enrolled in the regular Arts programme.

2 Census data of 1901 are used for the years up to and including 1904–5; data of 1911 are used for the years from 1905–6 to 1914–15 inclusive; data of 1921 are used for the years 1915–16 to 1924–5; data of 1931 are used for the years from 1925–6 to 1930–1.

Index

Acadia Athenaeum (Wolfville, NS) 124
Acadia College: *see* Acadia University
Acadia Ladies' Seminary: *see* Acadia University
Acadia University 16, 74, 100, 131, 135–6, 141, 168, 182, 219–20, 249, 256, 263, 266, 267, 277, 282; and university consolidation 133, 150, 151, 166, 238; ladies' seminary 145, 171, 213; *see also* Horton Academy
Adams, Augusta 63
Adams, Mary Electa 59–60, 62–3, 69, 70, 119, 170
Adelaide Academy 59
Alberta 254–6
Albert College 164
Alberta College 254
Albion Seminary, Michigan 59
Albion Vale School 5
Alcorn, Bessie 210
Alder, Robert 6, 9, 17, 18, 20, 22, 24, 29, 34, 36–8 passim, 40, 42, 51, 52, 54, 64
Alline, Henry 9
Allison, Charles Frederick xi, 9, 13, 35, 36, 39, 48, 62, 66, 101, 134, 161, 196, 246; conversion to Methodism 11; merchant career 11–12; proposal of 1839 3–4, 15, 17–18; role in establishment and opening of academy 18–20, 22–5, 51; role at academy 41, 52, 53, 68; supports academy for female students 50, 55; death 78; establishment of Allison chair 79–80, 98
Allison, David 94, 100–1, 111, 144, 145, 147–8, 160, 166, 179, 195, 216, 223, 233, 246, 255, 315n114; teacher at academy 63, 69, 97; recollections of early academy 64, 68, 262; member of college faculty 90–1, 108, 197, 203, 237; appointed president (1869) 106; as president (1869–78) 115–6, 136, 140–1; views on women's education 118–9; and University of Halifax 132–3, 141; resignation as president (1878) 143; reappointment as president (1891) 199; as president (1891–1911) 203–5, 219,

229, 230, 234, 245, 248, 250, 251–2, 257, 258–9; and prohibition question 226–7; resignation as president (1911) 259; assessment 261–2
Allison, John 69, 70–3, 80, 81, 90–1, 96–7, 104, 170
Allison, Louisa DeWolf 69
Allison, Martha L. 69, 70, 96–7, 170
Alumnae Association 118, 175, 198, 211, 239, 240, 258–9, 274–5, 318n36
Alumni Society 117–18, 135, 162, 164, 166, 211, 258–9, 274–5, 283–4, 318n36
American Chemical Society 201
Amherst, NS 4, 59, 101, 123, 155, 189, 211, 218, 219, 236, 241, 243
Anderson, John H. 68
Anderson, T.R. 342n166
Andrews, Nellie Greenwood 188, 212
Andrews, Wilbur William 183, 190, 206, 212, 244, 247, 258, 268, 271, 273, 283; appointment to faculty 188–90; influence on science curriculum 188–9, 200–1; research 189, 201; and engineering school 197–8, 207–8, 235–7, 240, 243, 245–6, 252; advocates extension programme 201–2; and social gospel 225–6, 246; departure for Regina 254–6
Anglicans 9, 10, 11, 13–16 passim, 32, 37–42 passim, 75, 90, 130
Annapolis Royal, NS 5
Annand, William 38
applied science: *see* engineering
Archibald, Mary Mellish 174, 242, 260, 279; becomes teacher at ladies' academy 112; and Alumnae Association 118, 175, 211; as chief preceptress and vice-principal 170–1, 175, 176, 213, 214, 238–9; death 238–9; establishment of memorial library 239
Archibald, Raymond C. 239, 249, 257–8, 260, 281, 285
Argosy: *see* student life
Atkinson, Christopher 18
Avard, C.C. 241
Avonport, NS 170

Baie Verte, NB 72
Bailey, Loring Woort 138
Bain, Francis 202
Baker, Emma S. 239, 269
Baptists 4, 9, 13–16 passim, 19, 21, 42, 59, 74, 80, 90, 99, 134, 195, 213
Barry, James Miranda Stuart 319n52
Bear River, NS 172, 265
Beecham, John 5–9 passim, 65–6
Beer, Lemuel L. 163
Beethoven Hall 242, 278, 343n192
Bell, A.M. 257, 259
Bell, Andrew 13
Bell, Ralph Pickard 284
Bell, Winthrop Pickard 188, 257–8, 270–1, 273–5, 284, 287
Belleville, Ont. 164
Berkeley, George 137, 180
Bermuda 65, 96, 102, 110, 116, 117, 127, 163, 164, 170, 214, 231, 244
Bertram, James 246
Berwick, NS 173
Bigelow, H.E. 111, 190, 266–8, 270, 285
Bishop's University 276
Black, F.B. 259
Black, J.L. 163, 166, 259
Black, John 40
Black, William 6, 9, 10, 161
board of governors: *see* board of regents
board of regents (also board of trustees, board of governors): composition and membership 53, 67–8, 76, 117–8,

162–5, 211, 257–9, 274–5, 278, 318n37
board of trustees: *see* board of regents
Bond, G.J. 282
Borden, Byron Crane 216, 224; principal of ladies' college 170–1, 172–6, 208–14, 217, 238–43, 247, 248, 252, 279; member of university faculty 186, 190, 244, 258, 269; and social gospel 225–6, 262–3, 271; criticizes board of regents 257–8, 260–1; appointed president (1911) 259–61, 262–5; as president (1911–23) 265–6, 267, 270–1, 272–3, 280–6
Borderer and Westmorland and Cumberland Advertiser (Sackville, NB) 78
Boston, Mass. 70, 242, 248, 270
Botsford, A.E. 38–42 passim, 76
Botsford, William 13
Bowser, George T. 234
Boyce, W.B. 91, 96, 98, 102
Brecken, Ralph 138–9, 182–4, 190, 223, 224, 227, 340n125
Brewster, John 88
Bridgetown, NS 4
Bridgewater, NS 258, 259
British Association for the Advancement of Science 201
British Columbia 206, 256
British North American Wesleyan Methodist Magazine (Saint John and Fredericton, NB) 19, 23, 29, 49
Brookfield, S.M. 259
Brown, James 31, 36–7
Brown, W.C. 163
Brown University, Rhode Island 249, 285
Brunton, J. Noel 277–9
Bugbee, Charles 18
buildings: construction and design 18–19, 56, 61–2, 72–3, 87–8, 89–90, 102–3, 126, 146, 157, 160–1, 175–6, 192, 207, 210, 234, 235–6, 239–41, 247–9; *see also* Centennial Hall, Fawcett Hall, Hart Hall, Lingley Hall, Owens museum
Bunting, Jabez 7–8, 21
Burke, Edmund 210
Burwash, Annie 169
Burwash, John 109, 111, 134–7 passim, 148, 184, 185, 188
Burwash, Nathanael 109, 206, 255
Busby, Sampson 24, 51
Butler, Percy 219

Calgary, Alta. 255–6
Calvinism 7
Campbell, G.M. 260–1, 278–9
Campbellton, NB 216
Canada Temperance Act: *see* temperance movement
Canada West 35, 59–60
Canning, NS 351n143
Carman, Albert 203–6, 221–2
Carnegie, Andrew 246, 282
Carnegie Corporation of New York 138
Cassidy, R.A. 284
Centennial Hall 161, 192, 210
Central Academy, PEI 16
Chandler, E.B. 39, 76, 102
Charlottetown, PEI 16, 23, 55, 58, 68, 117, 145, 163, 202, 259
Chatham, NB 37, 216
Chicago, Ill. 211, 270
Chignecto Post and Borderer (Sackville, NB) 124, 146, 160, 166, 184, 212–19 passim, 231–2
Chignecto Ship Railway 192, 197
Chipman, J.D. 259
Chipman, Ward, Jr 14

Chipman, Zechariah 158, 162
Chisholm, C.L. 232, 341n145
Christian Visitor (Saint John, NB) 134
Church of England: *see* Anglicans
Church of Scotland: *see* Presbyterians
Churchill, Charles 83
Cobourg Ladies' Seminary 59
Cobourg, Ont. 17, 35, 50, 59; *see also* Victoria University
Colebrooke, Sir William 24, 42–3, 75, 133
College of New Brunswick: *see* University of New Brunswick
Collège St-Joseph 193, 220, 321n103
Collegiate School (Fredericton, NB) 216, 301n41; *see also* University of New Brunswick
Colonial Presbyterian (Saint John, NB) 81–3 passim, 88
commercial college, Mount Allison 146–7, 176, 215–17, 280
Common Schools Act, New Brunswick 114–16
Connexionalism 21, 205–6, 234, 264
Cornell University 120
Cornwallis, NS 11, 13
County Grammar Schools Act, New Brunswick 13
Cowperthwaite, H.D. 118
Crandal, Joseph 21
Crane, William 11–13, 17
Crawley, E.A. 16
Croscombe, William 5
Cumberland County, NS 20, 35, 58, 68, 194, 197; *see also* Amherst, NS
Cunard, Joseph 37
Cunard, Samuel 12
curriculum 3, 4–5; at academy, before 1862 31–4, 36–7, 43–4, 91, 300n23; at ladies' academy/college 60–1, 69, 70–2, 91, 112–13, 146, 173–6, 213, 240–2, 247, 249, 277–9; at college/university 85, 90–3, 111, 125, 135, 136–7, 141–3, 148, 149–50, 177–81, 184–90 passim, 197, 200–3, 236–8, 275–7, 323n123, 330n87; at academy, from 1862 91, 146–7, 215–17; of University of Halifax 141–2, 148, 323n123; at post-graduate level 143, 179–81, 203
Curtis, Levi 259
Curtis, P.V. 343n4

Daily Sun (Saint John, NB) 200, 204–5, 207, 284
Daily Telegraph (Saint John, NB) 142, 165, 219
Daily Times (Moncton, NB) 168, 174–5, 178, 201, 205, 267
Dalhousie College: *see* Dalhousie University
Dalhousie, Lord: *see* Ramsay
Dalhousie Gazette (Halifax, NS) 124, 134, 219
Dalhousie University 19, 134, 136, 141, 151, 161, 168, 182, 185, 245, 258, 277, 297n58; origins and early difficulties 15–16, 54, 99–100; provincial grants to 100, 131; law school 106, 111, 167, 203, 237; and university consolidation 130–2, 139, 150, 166–7, 238; sports 218–20
D'Anna, Saverio 113
Darwin, Charles 109, 127, 200
Davies, Emily 319n49
Davis, T.H. 68
Davis, T.T. 169–70
Davison, Frank 259
Dawson, James 35, 37
Dawson, S.E. 209

Dawson, Sir William 75, 109
Day, Frank Parker 244, 245, 338n90
debating: *see* student life
DesBarres, F.W.W. 254, 272
DesBrisay, Albert 23, 38–41, 56, 66
DeWolfe, Charles 49, 80, 87–8, 98, 101, 103, 106, 304n94
disciplinary regulations: *see* student life
Dixon, Charlotte 57
Dixon, Edward 13
Dorchester, NB 39, 47, 123, 160, 210, 219, 220
Douglas, George 204–5
Douglas, Sir Howard 14

Eclectic Society 124
Educational Review (Fredericton, NB) 201, 237, 249–50
Emerson College of Oratory 242
engineering 197–8, 201, 207–8, 235–7, 245, 276
Eurhetorian Society 94–5, 124, 125, 220–1, 224
Evans, Edwin 163
Evans, Ephraim 54, 56–7, 59, 63, 66, 68, 97
Evening Mail (Halifax, NS) 167, 168, 226
evidences of Christianity 32–3, 93, 142, 149, 179
examinations 49, 81, 142, 148, 151, 178, 229, 277
extension programmes 201–2

faculty: academy 31, 43, 62–4, 69–70, 111–12, 215, 280, 303n68; ladies' academy/college 59–60, 62–3, 69, 70, 96–7, 112–13, 170–1, 174–5, 214, 239, 279; college/university 86, 90–1, 106, 108–11, 135–9, 184–91, 223, 227, 236–7, 244, 254–6, 269–73
faculty salaries 87, 91, 98, 111, 135, 139, 198, 255–6, 257, 270, 313n84
Fairweather, G.E. 161
Falmouth, NS 9
Fawcett, Charles 247
Fawcett, Charles W. 247
Fawcett Hall 247–9, 251, 262
fees 30–1, 71, 115, 116, 141, 279–80, 281–2
finances: *see* Mount Allison institutions
fine and applied arts 60, 69, 70–1, 112–13, 173–4, 176, 208–10, 213, 247, 249, 279
fires 100–1, 159, 233, 249, 267, 315n114
Fisher, Charles 77
Fisk, Willbur 23, 30, 299n8
Fort Lawrence, NS 192
Fraser, John J. 210–11
Fredericton, NB 5, 10, 14, 15, 20, 23, 31, 37, 38, 42, 59, 70, 76–7, 79, 80, 87, 91, 103, 129, 158, 163, 165, 216, 218, 221; *see also* University of New Brunswick
Freud, Sigmund 228, 229
Fuller, A.J. 272
Fulton, Stephen 68
fund-raising 20, 30, 55, 78, 79, 80, 87, 99, 101, 102, 103, 116, 156–60, 162, 203–6, 234–5, 246, 261, 264–5, 280–5, 306n119, 326n9, 327n23, 351n143

Gagetown, NB 216
Gallagher, Alice 72
Gallagher, Mary 72
Gaumont Company 282
Gazette (Montreal, Que.) 209
Genesee College 69
Gibson, Alexander 158, 163, 183

Gilchrist, John Borthwick 181
Gilchrist scholarships 181–2, 184–6 passim
Given, P.L. 270
Goodwin, W.L. 181, 184–5, 186, 330n107
government grants 24–5, 30–1, 300n14; from province of New Brunswick 20, 21, 22, 31, 37–42 passim, 55, 72–3, 98–9, 102, 113–16, 300n14, 308n136; from province of Nova Scotia 20, 21, 22, 31, 38, 41, 54–5, 73, 99–100, 115–16, 131, 141, 150–2; withdrawal of 113–16, 151–2, 155–6, 285
graduate careers 34, 83–4, 95–6, 101, 128–9, 181–2, 211, 230–1, 254, *tables 6, 8, 9, 10*
Graham, J.W. 246–7, 271, 272
Grand Pré, NS 214
Grant, G.M. 131
Gray, John Hamilton 75
Gray, John Warren 112–13, 174, 209
Greenwood, Nellie C.: *see* Nellie Greenwood Andrews
Gush, William 66

Halifax, NS 4, 10, 14–17 passim, 20, 43, 55, 58, 59, 65, 68, 76, 77, 88, 100, 101, 105–7 passim, 111, 130, 131, 140, 142, 148, 157, 163, 165–8 passim, 170, 218, 220, 226, 229, 245, 246, 248, 253, 257–9 passim, 283, 284; *see also* Dalhousie University, St Mary's College, University of Halifax
Halifax, Harry 126
Halifax Conservatory 277
Hambourg, Boris 278
Hambourg, Jan 278
Hamilton, Bermuda 96
Hamilton Conservatory 276
Hamilton, Ont. 117
Hamilton, Sir William 137, 180
Hammond, John 209–10, 213, 233
Harrison, C.W. 198, 214–18
Hart, Jairus 246–7, 250
Hart Hall 247–9, 250, 344n14
Hart, Thomas 173
Harvard University 125, 182, 218, 239, 268
Hatheway, George 114
Hea, Joseph R. 25, 31, 43, 44, 45, 62, 81–3, 87, 302n66, 303n68, 309n8
Head, Sir Edmund Walker 75, 77
Heartz, Jane 211
Henderson, Andrew 5
higher criticism 221–4, 227–8, 271–4
Hill, George S. 42–3
Hill, G.W. 130, 132, 148–9
Hill, P.C. 130, 132, 149
Hockin, Arthur 351n143
Holmes, S.H. 149, 150
Horton, NS 4, 11, 13, 14, 16, 80, 163
Horton Academy 4, 13, 16, 80; *see also* Acadia University
household science 197–8, 240–1
Howe, Joseph 21, 38, 51, 54, 73, 130
Hoxton Theological Institue 80
Huestis, S.F. 163
Hunt, A.S. 143
Hunton, Sydney Walker 188, 190, 232, 236, 244, 250, 266, 267, 269; appointment to faculty 185–6; and honours course in mathematics 185, 237; support of sports teams 185, 219

Inch, Annie 185
Inch, James R. 132, 149, 161, 164, 166, 185, 242, 248, 257; teacher at academy 62, 69–70; member of college faculty 90–1, 108, 124, 136, 137,

190; vice-principal and principal of ladies' academy 96–7, 106, 111, 113, 118, 170; advocates university education for women 118–19, 121, 148, 169; appointed president (1878) 143–5; as president (1878–91) 150, 155, 162, 165, 167–8, 186, 191, 195; resignation as president (1891) 198–9; assessment 198; as New Brunswick superintendent of education 198, 241; death 262
India 13, 181
Inglis, Charles 9, 14
Intercolonial Railway 140, 155, 253

Jack, William Brydone 87, 91, 138, 313n84
Jackson, George 273
Jacob, E.F. 87
Jerusalem, NB 91, 144
Johnston, Hugh 34, 38–9, 41
Jost, Cranswick 105, 108–9

Kant, Immanuel 137, 180
Kennedy, David 136, 145, 170
Keswick, NB 144
Killam, Amasa 18
King, George E. 114–15
King's College, Fredericton, NB: *see* University of New Brunswick
King's College, Windsor, NS 13–14, 15, 16, 19, 100, 129, 131, 134, 136, 150, 168
Kingston, NS 172
Kingston, Ont. 35; *see also* Queen's University
Kingswood School 4, 5
Knight, Laura C. 69
Knight, Matthew Richey 248–9
Knight, Richard 18, 19, 34, 50, 52, 56–7, 66, 68, 69, 78

Laird, G.J. 185
Lathern, John 161, 168, 205–6, 208
Laurier, Sir Wilfrid 226
Lawrencetown, NS 276
Leipzig Conservatory 112, 113
Leggett, William 19
libraries, Mount Allison 134–5, 138, 182–3, 249, 321n100
Lingley, Bartlett 61, 66
Lingley Hall 61–2, 66, 71, 78, 90, 94, 102, 181, 195, 203, 210, 239, 247, 248–9, 267, 286–7
Liverpool, NS 10
Lockhart, Grace Annie 120–1, 169
London, England 9, 18, 21, 29, 42, 50, 51, 57, 71, 78, 102, 112, 116, 181, 183, 186, 194, 209, 277; *see also* University of London
Longley, Benjamin 145, 147, 324n148
Longley, George 324n148
Lower Horton, NS 5, 43, 309n8
Loyalist and Conservative Advocate (Fredericton, NB) 37–8
Lunenburg, NS 17

Macaulay, Thomas Babington 177, 180
McClelan, A.R. 87, 235
McClelan School of Applied Science 235–7, 240–1, 245, 254, 276
McClung, R.K. 254–5
McCulloch, Thomas 14, 16, 54
McCully, A.D. 159
Macdonald, John A. 155
McGill College: *see* McGill University
McGill University 75, 185, 218, 220, 235–7 passim, 245, 254, 276, 277, 319n49

MacGregor, J.G. 150
Machum, E.R. 284
Mack, Albert A. 174–5
McKeown, H.A. 148
McKinley, William 228
McLeod, Alexander 44, 54
McMurray, John 68, 86
McNutt, Alexander 20, 22
Madras schools 12–13
Manitoba 164, 254
Manners-Sutton, J.H.T. 77
Maritime provinces, economy of xi–xii, 50–1, 55, 62, 66, 79, 155–6, 157–8, 171, 194–5, 200, 231, 243, 252–4, 285–6, 292n7, 206n119, 307n128, 325n2; *see also* Sackville, NB, shipbuilding
Martens, Theodore 112, 113
Marysville, NB 158, 163, 259
Massey, Chester 282
Massey, Hart A. 233–4, 240, 241, 246, 250
Massey School of Household Science and Art, Toronto, Ont. 241
Massey-Treble, Lillian 240–1
Massey-Treble School of Household Science 240–1
Mechanics' Institute, Sackville, NB 48, 304n89
Mellish, Mary E.: *see* Mary Mellish Archibald
Memramcook, NB 193, 321n103
Methodism: in Great Britain 6–8, 21, 24, 64–5; in Maritime provinces 5–7, 9–11, 16–17, 19, 21, 24, 64–6, 74, 99, 116–17, 157, 193–4, 206, 221–6, 231, 263–4, 272–3; elsewhere in British North America/Canada 10, 16–17, 64, 116, 157, 193–4, 206, 221–2, 225–6, 263–4, 273
Methodist Church, governing bodies
– Bible Christian Church 163, 293n18
– British Conference 3, 6, 7–8, 64–5, 66, 67, 116
– Eastern British America Conference 64–6, 67, 73–4, 76–7, 79–80, 86–7, 88–9, 98, 99, 102, 103, 113, 116–17, 129, 136, 164
– Methodist Church (Canada) 137, 203, 205–6; union of 1874 116–17; union of 1884 163–5; general conferences 117, 136, 149, 162, 196–7, 217, 225, 258–9; educational society/board of education 117, 164, 205–6, 246–7, 255, 271, 282
– Methodist Episcopal Church 116, 163, 203
– Methodist Episcopal Church (United States) 6
– New Brunswick and Prince Edward Island Conference 117, 147, 155, 158, 162, 163–4, 198, 221–2, 225–6, 244, 260, 263, 272–3, 283
– New Brunswick District 3–6, 17, 18, 20, 22–3, 25, 40, 49–50, 52, 53, 64–6, 291n1
– New Connexion Methodist Church 116
– Newfoundland Conference 117, 163–4, 259
– Nova Scotia Conference 117, 133, 151, 158, 162, 163–4, 198, 222, 225–6, 272–3, 282
– Nova Scotia District 3–6, 17, 18, 21–2, 49–50, 52, 53, 54, 64–5, 291n1
– Primitive Methodist Church 163
– Wesleyan Methodist Missionary Society 5–7, 8–9, 11, 17, 18, 21–3, 24, 50, 51–2, 53, 64–5, 66, 74, 98, 101–2

Miller, A.D. 254, 255, 259
Millet, Jean François 209
Milligan, George S. 70, 86, 90–1,302n66
Milner, Christopher 13
Milner, W.C. 124
Miramichi River, NB 12, 23, 31
Monro, Alexander 72
Moncton, NB 155, 158, 168, 174, 178, 188, 201–2, 205, 218, 219, 236, 253, 267
Montreal, Que. 113, 117, 145, 164, 196, 204, 205, 209, 253, 277, 284; *see also* McGill University
Morning Chronicle (Halifax, NS) 142, 226
Morning Freeman (Saint John, NB) 115
Morning Herald (Halifax, NS) 120, 148, 150, 190
Morning News (Saint John, NB) 106, 159–60
Morton, A.D. 110, 234–5
Mount Allison Academic Gazette (Sackville, NB) 56, 57, 59, 60, 61, 68, 83, 97–8
Mount Allison institutions
- academy (also Sackville Academy, Wesleyan Academy): establishment proposed 3–4, 17–18; preparations for opening 18–25; opening 25; official opening 29; early years, to 1855 29–66; incorporation 51–3; institutional developments at, 1855–81 67–70, 100–4, 111–12, 145, 146–8; institutional developments at, 1881–1914 156, 159–60, 162, 169–70, 198, 214–18, 249, 250, 279–80; *see also* commercial college
- ladies' academy/college: establishment proposed 49–51; preparations for opening 55–7; opening 57; early characteristics 57–61, 62–3; institutional developments at, 1855–81 68–9, 70–3, 96–8, 104, 112–13, 145–6; institutional developments at, 1881–1914 156, 162, 169, 170–6, 198, 208–14, 238–43, 247–9, 250, 260–1, 276–9; *see also* women's education
- college/university: establishment proposed 74–5; charter of 1858 76–7; problems encountered 79–81; proposal renewed 81–7; preparations for opening 87–9; opening 89–90; early characteristics 90–6; institutional developments at, 1862–81 98–100, 105–7, 108–11, 118–21, 129–44, 148–52; institutional developments at, 1881–1914 156–62, 164–9, 177–91, 196–9, 200–3, 206–8, 227–8, 230–8, 245–7, 249–50, 250–60, 261–75, 275–7, 280–6
Mount Allison institutions, financial management 19–21, 24, 30–1, 55–6, 61, 63, 77, 78–9, 96–9, 101–2,113–17, 134, 145, 152, 156–60, 162, 170, 198, 206–8, 214, 216–18, 233–5, 250, 250–2, 261, 279–82, 284–5; *see also* faculty salaries, fees, fund-raising
Mount Royal College 256
Motyer, Arther J. 244
Munro, George 167
music 60, 69, 70–1, 112–13, 173, 174–6, 213, 247, 275, 276–9

Naples Conservatory 113
Nappan, NS 197
Narraway, Bessie 169
Narraway, J.R. 83, 161–2
national policy 155, 252

New Brunswick: *see* government grants, Methodist Church, student enrolment
New Brunswick Courier (Saint John, NB) 35, 37, 40, 41, 46
Newfoundland 35, 43, 65, 102, 110, 116, 117, 127, 128, 163, 164, 214, 231, 258, 259, 277, 285, 309n8, 343n4
newlights 9–11 passim
Newmarket, NH 4
Newport, NS 68, 69, 91
New York 69, 174, 209, 211, 238, 270
New Zealand 169, 209, 336n50
Nicolson, F.W. 138, 182
Nova Scotia: *see* government grants, Methodist Church, student enrolment
Nova Scotia and New Brunswick Wesleyan Methodist Magazine (Halifax, NS) 6
Nova Scotia Technical College 245

Oberlin College 40, 59
O'Brien, J.W. 190, 227
Odell, W.H. 76
Ogden, Ethel 210
Ontario Business College 215
Ottawa, Ont. 96, 196
Otty, Allen 44–5
Otty, Robert 45
Owens, John 208–9
Owen gallery: *see* Owens Museum of Fine Arts
Owens Museum of Fine Arts 208–10, 214, 233, 240, 249, 250

Paisley, C.H. 147, 223, 227, 228, 271, 340n125
Paley, Wiliam 32–3, 93, 274
Palfrey, G.F. 276
Palmer, James Marshall 216–18, 235, 257, 260, 267, 279–80, 281
Parish School Act, New Brunswick 72
Parish School Advocate and Family Instructor (Baie Verte, NB) 72
Parrsboro, NS 11
Paton, James 259
Patterson, Arthur McNutt 69, 303n68, 321n100
Peacock, Fletcher 262–3
Perkins, Simeon 10
Pettit, Maude 214, 351n150
Pickard, Hannah Maynard 25, 63
Pickard, Humphrey 9, 35, 56, 63, 68, 78, 84, 97, 98, 116, 118, 160, 170, 280; protests status as assistant missionary 6, 24; personal background 23–4; appointment as academy principal 23; arrival in Sackville 25; inaugural address 29–34, 115; as principal (1843–69) 38, 40–2, 45, 46–7, 50–1, 52, 55, 57, 59, 62, 63–4, 66, 69, 96, 104, 300n23; and preparations for college 77, 83, 86–8; appointed president (1862) 87; as president (1862–9) 90–1, 95, 98, 102, 313n84; resignation (1869) 105–6; as member of board of trustees 144, 157, 169; death 195–6
Pickard, Thomas 43, 62, 63–4, 69, 90–1, 109, 171, 203
Pickles, Michael 68
Pictou Academy 14, 16, 19, 295n34
Pictou, NS 14, 16, 19, 167
Pitblado, C.B. 137, 143
Pitts, J.S. 258, 259
Point de Bute, NB 19, 36, 110, 243
Portland, NB 23, 208
Potts, John 205–6
Powell, H.A. 110, 166, 202–3
Power, L.G. 148
Presbyterian Banner (Pictou, NS) 19

Presbyterians 10, 14, 16, 19, 34, 39, 90, 99, 130, 131, 137, 143
Presbyterian Witness (Halifax, NS) 100
Prince Edward Island 10, 16, 35, 117, 127, 163, 202, 258, 293n18, 307n128; *see also* Charlottetown, PEI
Prince of Wales College 16
prohibition: *see* temperance movement
Provincial Wesleyan: see *Wesleyan*
Purdy, Amos 44, 45–7, 94

Queen's University (Kingston, Ont.) 131, 180, 184–5, 189
Queen's University (Ireland) 85

Ramsay, George, 9th Earl of Dalhousie 15
Rand, Ivan C. 244
Ratchford, Mrs C.E. 59
Ratchford, Elias 11
Ray, Gilbert T. 68
Reed, Robert 208–9
Regina College 254, 255
Regina, Sask. 254–5
Reid, Alexander S. 43, 62, 69, 309n8
research 138–9, 188–90, 201, 270–1
Rhodes Scholarships 238, 244–5
Rice, E.E. 172–3
Rice, S.D. 20, 102–3
Richey, M.H. 161
Richey, Matthew 17, 21, 67–8, 161, 296n43
Robb, James 15
Robson, Thomas 47
Rockefeller, J.D. 282
Rockport, NB 12, 210
Roman Catholics 10, 16, 114–15, 204
Roosevelt, Theodore 221
Ross, James 19, 161, 297n58
Rowley, Alfred 259
Royal Canadian Academy 209
Ruggles, W.T. 265
Russell, Benjamin 63, 95, 106, 134, 166
Ryan, Mabel 247
Ryerson, Egerton 30, 75, 296n43

Sackville, NB xi, 36, 78, 110, 112, 126, 168, 202, 207; proposed as location for Wesleyan academy 3–4; local economy xii, 11–12, 34, 48–9, 140, 158, 195; early schools 12–13; students from 35, 57–8, 104, 127; town-Mount Allison relations 47–9, 50, 142, 170, 184, 191, 215, 217, 231–2, 248, 255, 267, 283; sports 123–4, 220
Sackville Academy: *see* Mount Allison institutions
Sackville Tribune (Sackville, NB) 241, 244, 248, 259, 262, 263, 269, 278, 282, 283
St Dunstan's College 16
St Francis Xavier University 100, 131, 134, 136, 150
Saint John, NB 3, 4, 18, 22–3, 34, 35, 41, 47, 51, 55, 57, 58, 61, 62, 63, 68, 77, 81, 83, 86, 101, 104, 112, 115, 120, 126, 134, 140, 144, 155, 161, 164, 200, 204–5, 208–9, 210, 218, 219, 233, 259, 260, 283, 284
Saint John Globe (Saint John, NB) 119, 144, 241
St John's, Nfld 43, 117, 277, 309n8
St Mary's College 16, 19, 100, 131, 134, 136, 150
St Stephen, NB 155, 158, 259, 261, 310n22
Saskatchewan 254–5
scholarships: at Mount Allison 55, 103, 113, 182–4, 230; *see also* Gilchrist Scholarships, Rhodes Scholarships

science: teaching of 32, 46, 85–6, 92–3, 109, 177, 188–90, 200–2, 276; apparatus 20, 93, 102, 134–5, 138, 182–3, 330n107; and religion 32–3, 109, 127, 190, 274, 304n94; research 138, 189, 201
Scott, Sawdon Dunn 142, 166, 168, 205
Sexton, F.H. 245
Shediac, NB 13, 137, 278
Sheffield, NB 23
Shelburne, NS 80
Shenstone, W.E. 17
Shenton, Sarah H.L. 169
shipbuilding 12, 49, 50, 68, 155, 158, 208, 252
Silliker, C.J. 241
Simcoe, Ont. 214
Smith, Sir Albert J. 76, 102
Smith, Alfred D. 136, 148, 150, 166, 181, 186, 190, 192, 197, 241, 249, 269; appointment to faculty 110–11; teaching style 110–11, 137, 237; salary 135, 198
Smith, F.M. 343n4
Smith, Gaius 182
Smith, Sarah E. 126
social gospel xii, 10–11, 66, 193–5, 224–7, 229, 243, 262–4, 271–2
Somerville, James 14–15
Spencer, Herbert 123, 127
sports: *see* student life
Sprague, Howard 89–90, 144, 163, 224–5, 258, 271–3
Springhill, NS 194
South Kensington School of Art 112
Stanley, Edward G.G.S., Earl of Derby, Baron Stanley 42
Stanstead College 170, 260, 279, 287
Starr, George H. 68, 157, 163, 340n25
Steel, George 278
Stern Conservatory, Berlin 277
Stewart, Charles 116, 118, 124, 148, 166, 190, 196, 198–9, 204, 221, 224, 273; appointment to faculty 109–10; as chaplain 110, 181; theological tenets 109–10, 222–3, 227–8; as dean of theology 136, 139, 227–8; death 262
Stewart, Harriet Starr 118, 121, 148, 168–9, 259
Stockton, A.A. 118, 129, 164–5, 166, 197
Stockton, Amelia Pickard 118
student enrolment: numbers attending 36, 43, 51, 57, 62, 71, 73, 89, 97–8, 103, 104, 117, 127–8, 135, 145, 146–7, 176, 190–1, 215, 217, 229–30, 238, 239–40, 244, 247, 257, 268, 276, 279, 286, *tables 1, 2, 3, 4, 5, 7, 11, 12, 13, 14, 15, 16, 17*; geographical origins 35, 51, 55, 58, 71, 104, 127–8, 140, 214, 285, *tables 1, 2, 3, 4, 7, 12, 13, 14, 17*; social origins 34, 35, 58, 98, 127–8, 140–1, 171–2, 214, 230–1, 300n26, *tables 13, 14, 17*; age structure 37, 74–5, 145, 146, 280, *tables 5, 15, 16*
student life
– general discussion 44–8, 93–5, 121–7, 172–3, 191–5, 218–21, 229–30, 265–9, 278–9
– debating 45, 94–5, 124, 220–1
– disciplinary regulations 4–5, 31, 32, 46–7, 63, 93–4, 147, 172–3, 181, 212–13, 216, 256–7, 265–9, 280, 324n148, 347n81
– initiation 191, 256–7, 267
– religious life 38–41, 81, 126–7, 193–4, 223–4, 266
– residences 46, 125–6, 192, 206–7, 234, 256–7, 266–9

- segregation of sexes 57–8, 122–3, 172, 192–3
- sports 45–6, 61, 94, 123–4, 176, 193, 218–20, 266, 338n90
- student publications: *Mount Allison Students Repository* 45, 68; *Allisonia* 240; *Argosy* 121–4 passim, 124–7, 134, 135, 138–9, 142–3, 144, 159, 169, 178, 181–4 passim, 186, 188, 189, 191–4, 195, 199, 202, 203, 208, 210, 211, 213, 218–21 passim, 223–4, 228, 229–30, 232–3, 234, 236, 238, 245–6, 255–6, 262–3, 265–7, 269, 271, 283, 334n12, 342n166; *Eclectic Journal* 124; *Eurhetorian Argosy*: see *Argosy*
- student self-government 191–2, 266–9

Stuttgart Conservatory 174
Sumichrast, F.C. 142, 149, 151–2
Sutherland, Alexander 199
Sweetser, W.J. 236
Syracuse University 69, 91

Tait, Mary Elsinore 277
Taylor, James 172
Teed, J.F. 160–1, 210
temperance movement 12, 45, 66, 126–7, 185, 194, 226–7
Temple, William 3, 6, 9, 10, 18, 19, 21–2, 24, 29–30, 38, 51, 68
theological education 73–4, 79, 80, 98, 106, 109–10, 125, 136–7, 221–3, 227–8, 271–2, 281–2
Thompson, Sir John S.D. 148, 204–5
Tidnish, NS 192
Tilley, Sir Leonard 72–3, 86, 102, 205
Toddings, Seward 96
Toronto, Ont. 21, 59, 117, 164, 167, 168, 188, 206, 210, 229, 241, 253, 278, 282, 284; *see also* University of Toronto
Toronto Conservatory 276
Toronto School of Music 276
town-Mount Allison relations: *see* Sackville, NB
Transcript (Sackville, NB) 160
Trueman, George Johnstone 185, 260, 279–80, 287
Trueman, Thompson 36
Truro, NS 256, 263
Tuck, William H. 47, 203–5
Tweedie, William Morley 189–91 passim, 224, 236, 244, 250, 256, 269, 273; as student at Mount Allison and University of Halifax 142, 148; Gilchrist scholar 181–2, 186; appointment to faculty 186; approach to teaching 186–8, 222, 237; dean of residence 233, 266

Unitarianism 225, 272
Uniacke, James Boyle 54
University of Berlin 188, 287
University of British Columbia 256
University of Calcutta 133
University of Edinburgh 43, 137, 181–2
University of Glasgow 14
University of Gottingen 270
University of Halifax 168–9, 177; origins 129–32; and Mount Allison 132–3, 141–3; problems encountered 132–3, 142, 148–50; end of active existence 150–2; efforts to revive or replace 166–7
University of Heidelberg 111, 129, 186
University of London 42, 85, 131–2, 133, 181–2, 185, 186
University of Manitoba 185, 254
University of Missouri 256

University of New Brunswick (including College of New Brunswick, King's College) 31, 70, 72, 74, 136, 138, 182, 201, 216, 219, 220, 221, 266; origins 14; reconstitution as King's College 14–15; debates concerning, 1840s and 1850s 37–8, 41–3, 75–8, 301n41; reconstitution as UNB 78, 79, 81–9 passim; faculty salaries 91, 135; curricula 178–9, 180; *see also* Collegiate School
University of Oxford 29, 129, 245
University of Strasburg 239
University of Toronto 85, 167, 179, 180, 196, 199, 201, 229, 239, 276, 277, 327n32
Upper Canada Academy: *see* Victoria University
Upper Sackville, NB 47

Van Horne, Sir William 210
Victoria College: *see* Victoria University
Victoria University, Cobourg and Toronto, Ont. (including Upper Canada Academy, Victoria College) 30, 109, 111, 145, 179, 185, 188, 214, 227, 254, 255; Upper Canada Academy 16–17, 21, 35; female students at academy 50, 59; reconstitution as Victoria College 50, 59; faculty of theology 137, 189, 223, 271, 273; becomes Victoria University 164–5; and connexionalism 164–5, 206; and University of Toronto 196–7, 199, 327n32
Vincent, W.C. 213–14

Wallace, NS 44, 45, 68
Watson, John 189
Watson, William G. 227–8, 229, 254, 259, 271–3
Webster, J.C. 137–8, 142, 148, 182, 237
Weldon, Richard C. 106, 111, 135, 137, 139, 148, 166–7, 181, 185
Wesley, John 4, 5, 7, 29, 40, 53, 275
Wesley College, Winnipeg 185, 206
Wesleyan (Halifax, NS, and Sackville, NB) 17, 34, 44, 46, 54–5, 57, 62, 63, 70, 73, 74, 77, 78, 81–6, 89, 90, 95, 100, 101, 103, 105–7 passim, 119–20, 129–30, 133, 134, 138, 139–40, 143, 144, 146, 159–60, 168, 171, 174, 175, 190–1, 195, 197, 202, 205–6, 207, 208, 212, 218, 221–2, 226, 230, 237, 240, 245, 247, 250, 278, 283, 287
Wesleyan Academy: *see* Mount Allison institutions
Wesleyan Methodism: *see* Methodism
Wesleyan Methodist Missionary Society: *see* Methodist Church
Wesleyan Theological College, Montreal 204, 206
Wesleyan University, Connecticut 6, 23, 40, 43, 69, 91, 94, 105, 120, 138, 144, 149, 299n8, 300n23
Westcock, NB 12, 47
Westmorland County, NB 10, 20, 35, 38, 58, 76, 101, 104, 177, 203; *see also* Sackville, NB
Westmorland Grammar School 13, 297n58
Wheelock, Frank E. 256, 270
Whistler, J.M. 209–10
Whiston, S.E. 146–7, 215
Wilbraham, Mass. 4, 23
Wilmot, Elizabeth 174
Wilmot, L.A. 10, 15, 42–3, 53, 106–7, 108, 114–15, 174
Windsor, NS 5, 13–16 passim, 19, 49, 129, 134, 136, 198; *see also* King's College, Windsor, NS

Winnipeg, Man. 117, 185, 206
Wolfville, NS 80, 145; *see also* Acadia University
women's education 49–51, 55–61, 62, 69, 91, 97, 118–21, 122, 145–6, 148, 168–9, 170–6, 210–14, 240–2, 260–1, 268–9, 279, 307n132, 319n49, 319n52, 328n47, 336n51, *table 10*
Wood, Enoch 4, 9, 10, 15, 17, 18, 20–2, 23, 24, 34, 36, 37–43 passim, 51, 52, 64, 75, 133
Wood, Josiah 89, 90, 103, 157, 158, 160, 165, 177, 190, 204, 240, 248, 251, 258, 259
Wood, Laura 160
Wood, Mariner 68, 134, 157
Wood, Thomas W. 31, 43, 62, 83, 97, 147, 302n66
Woodbury, Frank 258, 259
Woodbury, Jessie Troop 173
Wootton, John J. 213

Yale University 111, 181, 256
Yarmouth, NS 68, 95, 99, 110, 155, 161, 256, 257, 272, 283
YMCA 222, 224
Young, A.W. 215
Young, Charles 68

Zion Church, Saint John, NB 208–9

www.ingramcontent.com/pod-product-compliance
Lightning Source LLC
LaVergne TN
LVHW010447080826
844660LV00027B/1229